First Certificate in English Course for Foreign Students

(incorporating the 2nd edition of Lower Certificate English Course)

Ona Low

First published 1974
by Edward Arnold (Publishers) Ltd
25 Hill Street, London W1X 8LL

Reprinted 1975, 1976, 1977, 1978

ISBN 0 7131 1848 2

A *Key* containing answers to all the exercises in this book, along with notes for teachers, is published separately and should be available from booksellers. Further information may be obtained from the publishers.

By the same author:

FIRST CERTIFICATE IN ENGLISH COURSE: KEY

FIRST CERTIFICATE IN ENGLISH PRACTICE
FIRST CERTIFICATE IN ENGLISH PRACTICE: KEY

CERTIFICATE OF PROFICIENCY ENGLISH COURSE
CERTIFICATE OF PROFICIENCY ENGLISH COURSE: KEY

SPEAK ENGLISH FLUENTLY 1
SPEAK ENGLISH FLUENTLY 2

Printed in Great Britain at the Benham Press
by William Clowes & Sons Limited
Colchester and Beccles

Preface

The reading passages in *Lower Certificate English Course* were designed to introduce a large number of points associated with vocabulary, grammar and construction that often cause difficulties to students. These have been retained within the structure of this edition together with the practice exercises which formed part of most chapters.

With the introduction of a considerably modified examination however, a large part of the earlier book has been rewritten so as to ensure adequate preparation for all sections of the new syllabus. The notes to each chapter have been condensed to essentials to allow additional material to be included together with guidance in pronunciation, special grammatical points and use of prepositions, related in each of these cases to the foregoing comprehension passage.

New sections have been added to most chapters, consisting of multiple choice questions based on the comprehension passage, a number of questions of the type that will appear on the Use of English paper and finally considerable practice in spoken English, including conventional usage, conversations, situations to be dealt with orally and discussion topics.

The chapter on Spoken English has been adapted to the new 'Interview' and 'play extract' reading passage with advice and examples included. Other sections deal with the new type of summary and with composition writing, though each of the proposed types of composition is presented separately as part of a chapter.

The student undertaking this course should already have a good elementary knowledge of English. When classes have as many as ten weekly lessons most of the material can be dealt with in class, but students in groups which meet for not more than 4–5 hours weekly have to do a good deal of preparation at home with class guidance and checking. A Key is available separately and the material is presented clearly enough to enable a student working alone to derive considerable benefit from it.

The vocabulary utilised is more extensive than that of Michael West's *General Service List*, which is to be used as a general guide in setting papers. While the book is oriented towards the First Certificate, it is intended to be of value to all intermediate level students, whether they intend to take the examination or not, and so seeks to cover as many everyday situations and needs as possible. Moreover many successful candidates will wish to start preparation for a more advanced examination, such as the Certificate of Proficiency or the English Language paper of the General Certificate of Education. Both these examinations demand a very wide vocabulary, much of it based on abstract and intellectual concepts and a student who embarks on a preparatory course for these examinations should have a sure knowledge of a wide range of everyday, practical words and expressions.

Contents

1

Passage for comprehension

Never trust appearances

Rush hour in a provincial town is certainly not so busy as in London, but even so there are plenty of people moving about. Long, patient queues wait wearily for buses. Never-ending lines of cars are checked while red traffic lights change to green. Thousands of people are packed tightly in trains, the men's faces buried in their evening papers while women try 5 in vain to knit. In a slow train it may well be an hour's journey to their station.

James Saxon is in his usual comfortable corner, quietly smoking a cigarette. When he is travelling by train at this time, he always reaches the station at ten past five by the station clock, but he never catches the 5.14 train. Instead 10 he travels by the train which leaves at twenty-four minutes past five so as to be sure of getting his corner seat. There are no first-class compartments or reserved seats on this train. He appears to be absorbed in the sports news on the back page of his paper and ignores the hurrying crowds.

Facing him this evening there is a Finnish youth of eighteen, Matti Arpola. 15 This is his first visit to England, though he already knows Geoffrey, the eldest son of the Jackson family, with whom he is going to stay.

As there are several people standing, James Saxon is the only person he can see clearly. Matti decides that he is probably a typical Englishman, and he observes James carefully. 20

'Can he really be typical?' he thinks. 'He has an umbrella, neatly rolled, but no bowler hat; in fact, no hat at all. Of course, he is reading about cricket and he is reserved and not interested in other people. But he is only of average height and his hair is not fair, but as dark as that of an Italian, and curly, with almost no parting. He is not smoking a pipe, and although we foreigners 25 think that a real Englishman ought to have a moustache, he is clean-shaven. His nose is slightly crooked. What a serious face he has! He is frowning a little, but the eyes beneath his worried-looking forehead are sincere and honest. I don't think he is intelligent.

'His clothes are anything but smart. In fact, they are rather old, though 30 well-brushed. Even though he is not wearing a wedding ring, he is probably married, with perhaps three children. His gloves are fur-lined and his trousers well pressed. He keeps far too many things in his pockets, so his suit looks badly out of shape. What dull, old-fashioned leather shoes he is wearing! His briefcase is old too and bulging, so that the zip-fastener does not close 35 properly. There are the initials J.S. on it. Is his name John Smith?

'I think he is probably an office clerk or a shop assistant. Does he look like a teacher, though? Anyhow, he lives with a plain wife and five children in a small worker's house with a tiny garden, where he spends his leisure time
40 digging and weeding and mowing the lawn, or painting the tool-shed. But to-night, first he is helping his wife to put the children to bed and then he is taking her to the cinema as this is pay-day. Or is he visiting the local pub? Does he drink whisky (I believe most Englishmen do) or does he prefer beer? I am sure he very much likes a cup of tea. He seems quite energetic,
45 but his complexion is pale and he is very thin. Does he find it difficult to satisfy the needs of his miserable wife and seven unfortunate children? Poor fellow! I am sorry for him.'

At last, shortly after a quarter past six by Matti's watch, the train reaches Lakewell Junction, and Matti immediately sees Geoffrey waiting for him.
50 They greet each other. At first Matti cannot find his ticket, but it is discovered in his bulging coat pocket. He gives it up to the ticket-collector and the two boys go off to find Geoffrey's father's car. Near it there stands another car, a magnificent Rolls-Royce, and a handsome, uniformed chauffeur is holding the door open while James Saxon steps in.

55 'Who is that?' Matti asks. 'Why is he getting into that car? Where does he live? He looks like a poorly-paid clerk or a workman.'

Geoffrey laughs loudly as if this is a good joke.

'That is Sir James Saxon,' he replies. 'He has a fortune of around two million pounds, and controls forty-two factories in this area alone. He is a
60 bachelor who lives in a fourth-storey luxury flat, so, if he feels like it, he can go off to the Riviera for a month or two. Next week he is flying to Japan on business in his private aeroplane, though people say he very much prefers travelling by train. He is said to have twenty-one suits, but he is always seen in the same old one. By the way, I remember now. His father and mother
65 are both Finns: perhaps that is why he takes no interest in cricket. His real name is Jussi Saksalainen, but he is now a naturalised British subject with an English name. He doesn't look at all Finnish.

'Here's your other case. Put it down a minute while I unlock the car. Do you enjoy gardening? If so, you can help me: digging, weeding and
70 mowing the lawn. And I'm painting the tool-shed to-morrow. You don't know how to play cricket yet, but I'm taking you to a match on Saturday. Can you speak English any better now? You can soon lose that Finnish reserve. Come along! Let's get going! I'm hungry and hot.'

Matti remembers sadly all that his school-teachers say about his over-active
75 and unreliable imagination. Perhaps they are right after all.

Notes on the passage

Vocabulary

line

1 *provincial* The provinces are the part of the country away from London.

2 *plenty of* is used with singular and plural nouns. Here are some other expressions with a similar meaning:

Singular forms He has {a great deal of / a good deal of / very much / a lot of} work to do.

Plural forms He has {many / a lot of} hobbies.

WRONG: a good (great) deal of hobbies
'Lots of' is used normally only in conversation.

3 *queue* (*N* and *V*) SPELLINGS: queueing. *Notice also:* buses; gases.

3 *wearily* 'tired' has no adverb.

3 *check* (*V* and *N*) hold back; stop; possibly temporarily; *check a disease; a check to his plans.*
and also: make sure of correctness; *check figures, oil and batteries; a careful check of examination marks.*
(*Adj*) with coloured squares; *a check tablecloth.*
cheque (*N*) *a travellers cheque; a cheque book.*

5 *their* there. Which? (i) ...... are (ii) ...... shoes (iii) over ...... (iv) put it ....

6 *a slow train* a fast train; an express; a goods train; an excursion train. A through train travels all the way to a certain place so one need not change.

8 *quietly* SPELLING: a *quiet* holiday but *quite* finished.

10 a *clock* on the wall a wrist *watch.*

11 *leave* BE CAREFUL: *leave* home early; *live* at home.

13 *reserved seats* NOT: sitting places.

13 the *sports* news or page. NEVER: sporting.

14 *ignores* takes no notice of: *He ignores me when he is angry;* is ignorant of: does not know: *He is ignorant of his real name.*

15 *youth* (*Unc N*) the time when one is young: *Youth is not always the best part of life.*
a (the) youth: a boy (not a girl) between about fifteen and twenty-one.

17 *eldest elder* used only for members of a family: *his eldest son.*
'elder' cannot be followed by 'than': *He is older than his brother.*

17 *the Jackson family* NOT: the family Jackson.

22 *no hat at all* *I have none at all. He is doing nothing at all. at all* makes the negative stronger.

23 *interested* DO NOT MIX THESE:

interested spectators	interesting films
an absorbed reader	absorbing books
annoyed parents	annoying disturbances
excited children	exciting games

bored students	boring lessons
amused listeners	amusing jokes

NOTICE: Anybody *interested*, please ask for information. (NOT: interesting); I am very interested. (possibly also 'interesting' but not always!)

24 *fair hair* is more normally used than 'blonde hair'—possibly coloured or dyed.

25 *we foreigners* we students. NOT: we other students.

30 *clothes* (*A N*) cloth (*Unc* and *C N*) clothing (*Unc N*) clothes (*Pl N*) (see Pronunciation Page 5)
cloth either material or a piece of material for a special job: to buy cloth (*Unc*) tablecloth, floorcloth, dishcloth (all *C*).
clothing (*Sing*) } these mean the same, the second being the more
clothes (*Pl*) } commonly used.
A single *piece of clothing* is *a garment* (*C*).

31 *well-brushed* The adverb *well* can be used with several past participles to form adjectives. EXAMPLES: well-dressed; well-made; well-spoken (speaking correctly and pleasantly); well-educated; well-known; well-pressed (carefully ironed); well-preserved (still in good condition); well-mannered; well-paid. Opposites usually start with 'badly': badly-made etc. though 'little-known' is normal and 'poorly-paid' (l. 56) is possible.

NOTICE: 'So you passed your examination. Well done!'

32 *fur-lined.* An outdoor coat has a *lining* inside it. What is the meaning of this proverb: Every cloud has a silver lining?

34 *out of shape* The *shape* of a table, a room, a geometrical figure. What shape is it? NOT: What form?
That cardigan has been washed twenty times and yet it still keeps its shape. It has not gone out of shape.

38 a *plain* woman (not beautiful); a plain cake (not rich); a plain answer (with no unnecessary words); a plain explanation (clear); a plain (flat land).

41 *put the children to bed* go to bed NOT: to the bed.

42 *take* someone or something to another place: *take his wife to the cinema. lead* living things by walking in front: *Officers lead the soldiers when they march through a town. conduct* someone to a place, usually with ceremony: *The Bishop will conduct the Queen round the new church.*

46 a *miserable* person (OPPOSITE: cheerful); miserable weather.

51 *a ticket-collector collects* or *inspects* railway tickets. He is NOT a controller who controls them.
An official *examines* your passport, though his office may be known as Passport Control.
The normal meaning of *control* (l. 59) is 'have power over' or 'keep under discipline'.

52 *another* SPELLING!

53 *handsome* A man is *handsome*. A woman is *beautiful*. A child is *pretty*. *Good-looking*, with much the same meaning, is used to describe either a man or a woman.

61 *off* fall *off* the table—SPELLING!

62 *aeroplane* aerodrome but: *air*port airman Air Force SPELLING.

64 *his father and mother* NOT: his father and his mother.

71 *cricket* and football are *games*. We *play* games.
'Hamlet' is a play. We *act* in plays. But: He plays the part of Hamlet.

72 *Can you speak English?* NEVER: Can you English?

Pronunciation

SPECIAL DIFFICULTIES: Ítaly [itəlɪ] but Itálian [ɪtǽljən]; Japán [dʒəpǽn] but Jápanése [dʒǽpəniːz]; forehead [fɔ́rɪd] or [fɔ́rəd]; comfortable [kʌ́mf(ə)-təbl]; clerk [klaːk]; magnificent [mægnífɪsənt]; unreliable [ʌnrɪláɪəbl]; suit [sjuːt]; cloth (kləθ); clothing (klóuðiŋ); clothes (klouðz).

Day: today [tədéɪ] (STRESSED) but yesterday [jéstədɪ]; holiday [hɔ́lədɪ]; Monday [mʌ́ndɪ] and other names of days (ALL UNSTRESSED).

ə (as in *a*go): *a*bsorbed [əbzɔ́ːbd]; m*ou*stache [məstáːʃ]; leis*u*re [léʒə]; miser*a*ble [mizrəbl]; hands*o*me [hǽnsəm]; bach*e*l*o*r [bǽtʃələ]; initi*a*ls [iniʃəlz].

ɪ (as in c*i*ty): aver*a*ge [ǽv(ə)rɪdʒ]; crook*e*d [krúkɪd]; unfortun*a*te [ʌnfɔ́ː-tʃənɪt]; b*u*sin*e*ss [biznɪs].

SILENT LETTER: *k*nit [nɪt]; STRESS: ciga*rette* [sɪgərét]; energetic [enədʒétɪk].

OTHERS: worried [wʌ́rɪd]; gloves [glʌvz]; bulging [bʌ́ldʒɪŋ]; discovered [diskʌ́vəd]; uniformed [júːnifɔːmd]; queue [kjuː]; wearily [wiərɪlɪ]; instead [instéd]; buried [bérɪd]; height [haɪt]; chauffeur [ʃóufə]; area [ɛ́ərɪə]; Riviera [rɪvɪɛ́ərə]; naturalised [nǽtʃərəlaɪzd].

Special grammatical and structural points

(i) *When* *If* Do not confuse these.
Compare: When I get my pay, I spend it. If I get my pay, I spend it.

(ii) *so as to be sure of getting* *so as* followed by an infinitive can express *purpose*.

(iii) *there are several people standing* (l. 18) *standing*, the present participle, shortens and is more normal than 'who are standing'.

(iv) *anything but smart* (l. 30) means 'not at all smart'.

In these two cases *but* means *except*. *You can choose anyone but me. I want to live anywhere but London.*

(v) *look like* (l. 31) *feel like* (l. 60) *His garden looks like a park. I feel like something the cat has brought in.*
Second meaning: *I feel like having a bathe. I'll go if I feel like it.*
look as if *feel as if* +subject and verb. *He is so strongly built that he looks as if he can lift an elephant, but when he is a bit ill, he says he feels as if he is going to die.*

(vi) *greet each other* (l. 50) *greet* normally has an object. People do not just greet.

(vii) *am is are* hungry, thirsty, hot, cold, right, wrong, ten (years old).

(viii) *trousers; scissors; shears* ARE (plural) *A pair of* trousers, scissors, shears IS (singular).

(ix) laughs *as if* (though) this is good joke. You are walking *as if* you are (were) tired.

(x) *not no not* makes a verb negative. *no*, the opposite of 'yes', may also mean 'not any'.
Which? It is ...... cold. I have ...... money. There is ...... more left. I do ...... need any more. That is ...... business of yours.

(xi) *Notice: person people*—the plural form 'persons' is unusual. The word *people* is always followed by a *plural* verb form: People *are sitting* in cafés.

(xii) *Countable and Uncountable Nouns*
Most nouns are the names of things of which there can be one (Singular) or more than one (Plural). These are *Countable* nouns. Some nouns have only a Singular form. These are spoken of as *Uncountable.* They cannot be preceded by *a* and they normally have *no plural form.*
Examples: Countables: coin; table; loaf; box; kick.
Uncountables: money; furniture; bread; shopping; unkindness.
Notice however: (*a*) some Uncountables may be preceded by *a* when they are defined in some way: a *darkness that made him afraid to go on.*
(*b*) some may be Countable or Uncountable according to their meaning: a light/lights light and darkness.
Be careful: 1 *a hair/hairs* = separate ones. *hair of the head* (*Unc*).
Both his and his wife's hair is white now.
2 *journey* (Countable) *A journey from London to Bath.*
travel (Uncountable) *I enjoy travel. Travel broadens the mind.*
3 *news* is *singular only. The news is mainly bad. It is worrying.*

(xiii) *Verbal Constructions*
Deciding the form of the second verb in a sentence group is a difficulty for students as it may take any one of these forms:
1 an infinitive
2 a gerund—that is, a noun formed by adding -ing to a verb.
3 a clause, with subject and verb.
There are few rules to help so examples have to be learned as they occur. Here are some examples from the passage:
(*a*) *Infinitive* *try* to knit; *help* to put
he *is said to be* a millionaire
know how to play
(*b*) *Gerund* *enjoy* gardening
spend time painting but time *is spent* (in) painting.
(*c*) *Clause* he *decides* that he is an Englishman; he *thinks* he is a clerk.

Prepositions

(*a*) I enjoy travelling by / in a car/aeroplane by / on/in a train/bus go by boat be on/in a ship DO NOT USE *with*: I go to town with my dog (but not my car). (*b*) read, think, learn, talk *about* something but discuss something. (*c*) interested *in*/absorbed *in* a book. (*d*) stay *with* a friend. (*e*) sorry *for* a person (feel pity). sorry *about* a thing or event: *about your illness.* (*f*) *on* the back page. (*g*) a visit *to* England. (*h*) *of* average height. (*i*) *facing* him. (*j*) wait *for* a bus. (*k*) five o'clock *by* the hall clock. (*l*) live *in* a flat *on* the fourth storey. (*m*) sure *of* getting. (*n*) CAREFUL: *near* (prep.) *NOT* near of, near by, near from: *near London, near the fire station.*

Expressions to introduce into written work

When you write English, you of course never translate from your own language. One of the best ways of improving your style of writing is to make use of expressions you have found in your reading and which you really understand how to use. After each reading passage in this book, a list of expressions for you to learn and make use of is given.
(*a*) trains/buses/shops can be *packed with* people. (*b*) women try *in vain* to knit. (*c*) he *is said to be* a millionaire (*d*) *it may well be* an hour's journey/*there may well be* a thousand victims. (*e*) *absorbed in* the sports news/in doing a crossword puzzle. (*f*) *of average height.* (*g*) *even though* he is tired, he is still working. (*h*) he *spends his leisure time painting.* (*i*) he *gives up* his ticket to the ticket-collector. (*j*) he *looks like a* poorly-paid clerk. (*k*) *if he feels like it,* he can go to Majorca. (*l*) *by the way,* I remember now. (*m*) perhaps they are right *after all.*

Multiple choice questions

On the examination paper you will find after the comprehension passage or passages a number of questions or unfinished statements about the passage, each with four suggested ways of finishing it. You must choose the one which you think fits best. For the present exercise, write in each case the bracketed number of the question or statement followed by the letters **A, B, C, D,** and then cross through the letter of the answer you choose. Give one answer only to each question. Read the passage right through again before choosing your answers.

1 James Saxon does not catch the 5.14 train because
A he does not want to hurry **B** the later train is less crowded when he arrives **C** he has not reserved a seat in it **D** it is a slow train

2 Why is Matti uncertain whether James Saxon is really an Englishman?
A he looks very quiet **B** he is reading about cricket **C** he is not wearing a hat **D** he is not interested in other people

3 Which of the following details of his appearance show that James Saxon pays some attention to what he looks like?
A his shoes **B** his briefcase **C** his suit **D** his trousers

4 Matti thinks James may be a teacher. He clearly thinks that all but one of the following things is characteristic of a teacher. The exception is:
A he does not take any care of his clothes **B** he looks anxious **C** he carries too much about with him **D** he is probably not intelligent

5 Matti is sorry for James for all but one of these reasons. The exception is:
A his wife and children give him little happiness **B** he is thin and so may be underfed **C** he spends most of his spare time gardening **D** his life has little variety

6 What is the only one of these things that is clear from the passage that Matti and James have not got in common?
A their nationality **B** they both keep too much in their pockets **C** they have no enthusiasm for cricket **D** they both seem shy and reserved

7 How long does the journey to Lakewell Junction take?
A less than an hour **B** about half an hour **C** nearly an hour and a half **D** just a little more than an hour

8 Geoffrey laughs loudly because
A he thinks Matti has made a joke **B** he is amused by Matti's mistake **C** he considers James a funny person **D** he thinks it funny for a workman to have a chauffeur

9 What is the only right idea Matti has in this story?
A James Saxon is married **B** he cares little about his appearance **C** he has a dull badly-paid job **D** you can judge a person by his appearance

10 Why does Matti feel sad?
A he must help in the garden **B** his teachers think he is unreliable **C** he cannot trust his own ideas **D** he is disappointed in Geoffrey.

Reading comprehension

In this exercise you must choose the word or phrase which best completes each sentence. Write first the number of each sentence followed by the letters **A, B, C, D, E**, and then cross through the letter of the correct answer in each case. Give one answer only to each question.

1 The house was burgled while the family was ...... in a card game.
A entertained **B** buried **C** busy **D** absorbed **E** helping

2 No one is so ...... as the person who has no wish to learn.
A intelligent **B** ignorant **C** useless **D** simple **E** unwise

3 He wrote his name ...... and carefully at the top of the paper.
A seriously **B** largely **C** attentively **D** obviously **E** clearly

4 Normally he is rather ...... but sometimes he talks freely about himself.
A sociable B reserved C serious D peaceful
E ignorant

5 Although only of ...... intelligence, he speaks four languages fluently.
A average B middle C minor D high E slow

6 He sends his ...... wishes for your future happiness.
A honest B deepest C sincere D many
E hopeful

7 The guide is ...... a line of tourists through the narrow passage with the help of his torch.
A conducting B taking C leading D guiding
E bringing

8 He took a ...... with him to clean the windscreen of his car.
A garment B cloth C clothing D stuff E towel

9 In ...... the room resembles the letter L.
A form B pattern C figure D formation
E shape

10 Why are you always so ...... ? You never smile or look cheerful.
A angry B sorry C pitiful D unfortunate
E miserable

Use of English

1 Fill in each of the numbered blanks with *one* suitable word.
Christopher is not married yet: he is still a .... (1). He is interested .... (2) football, which is an exciting .... (3) and enjoys .... (4) to watch a football .... (5). So most winter Saturday afternoons he puts on his old raincoat, which is badly out of .... (6) and .... (7) the house at five past twelve so .... (8) to arrive early. He goes .... (9) bus and gets .... (10) the bus at the football ground. Even .... (11) it may be raining, he finds thousands of .... (12) already waiting in a long .... (13) outside the gates. Sometimes, if it is raining .... (14) hard for him to enjoy himself, he watches another match on television .... (15) of going out. He likes to spend Saturday evening .... (16) about football matches .... (17) the back page of the newspaper. Some people like to spend the evening .... (18) in noisy pubs but Christopher prefers his comfortable and .... (19) sitting-room. He feels as .... (20) he is a completely happy man until work starts again on Monday morning.

2 Finish each of the following sentences in such a way that it means exactly the same as the sentence printed before it.

Example: This is his first visit to England.
He is ....

Answer: He is visiting England for the first time.

1 I think it may rain.
It looks as ....

2 He will come because he wants to be sure of meeting you.
He will come so ....

3 Walking in the rain gives him pleasure.
He enjoys ....

4 Most of a child's life is spent in playing.
A child spends ....

5 The fox was unsuccessful in reaching the grapes.
The fox tried in ....

6 His briefcase is too full for the zip fastener to close properly.
His briefcase is so full ....

7 People say that he beats his wife.
It is ....

8 He appears to be running away from your fierce dog.
It looks ....

Composition and summarising

1 Write five or six short sentences on one of these subjects. Use very simple English. Some of the expressions in the reading passage may be useful.

(*a*) Describe what one of your relations or friends looks like.

(*b*) You are a very rich person with no family. How do you spend your time?

(*c*) What ideas have you about the typical Englishman—his appearance, clothes, manners, interests and ways of spending his time?

Example: Here is a possible beginning to subject (*a*):
My Uncle Jock is forty-four but he looks much younger. He is of average height and has a round face, red hair and green eyes. He likes to wear ....

2 Taking your information only from the reading passage, write a paragraph of not more than 120–180 words about all Matti's mistakes in his ideas about James Saxon.

Notice: This is an easy example of the summary-type question which forms part of the Use of English paper. Here are some suggestions about how to answer it.

(i) Read through the passage again. As you do so, make a list of the ideas which answer the question. You must remember that it is only the *mistakes* that you must write about, so many details about James Saxon's appearance will not be included. In addition, Matti has many ideas that are not proved wong: for example, James may like a cup of tea, enjoy gardening, be not very intelligent (not all millionaires are). So choose carefully. Secondly, you must remember that you must limit the number of words used, so only the main facts, with rather little detail, can be given.

Here are a few ideas you will find:

(*a*) He has not a wife and several children: he is a bachelor.
(*b*) He is not a poorly-paid employee but the millionaire owner of many factories.
(*c*) Matti thinks he should be pitied for his hard life but many people might envy him.

What other ideas ideas can you find?

(ii) When you have found all the ideas you want to use, start writing your paragraph. At present keep the sentences short and use simple words. Try to use your own words as far as possible: do not just copy from the passage. Here is a possible first sentence:

Matti thinks that James has a wife and several children but he is in fact a bachelor.

(iii) Remember that the summary must be written in not more than 120–180 words. If the number of words did not matter, this information would not be given. *You must not use more than the number of words stated.*

Here is a similar exercise:

What ideas about Matti himself can you find in the passage? Geoffrey's ideas about him can be included. Write these in the form of a paragraph of not more than 120–180 words.

Spoken English

Shortened verbal forms

Practise using these, so that you can use them automatically, without having to stop and think.

I'm he's she's it's we're you're they're Tom's the bread's here's there's that's I've he's we've you've they've I can't I mustn't I mayn't I'm not he's not (he isn't) we're not (we aren't) I haven't he hasn't I don't he doesn't we don't

Pronunciation

we're [wɪə]; you're [jɔː]; they're [ðɛə]; mustn't [ˈmʌsənt]; mayn't [ˈmeɪənt]; aren't [aːnt].

Exercise

(i) Give the short forms:

(*a*) he is out. (*b*) we have not time. (*c*) he does not smoke. (*d*) you may not come. (*e*) they cannot see. (*f*) I do not like it. (*g*) are you not coming? (*h*) it is cold. (*i*) has she not a car? (*j*) the dog is not barking. (*k*) I have not a ticket. (*l*) that is right. (*m*) here is your briefcase. (*n*) here is my glove.

(ii) Say something about each of the following, using a shortened verb form. Then repeat the statement, first about one of your friends and then about two (he or she/they)

(*a*) your age. (*b*) a language unknown to you. (*c*) the weather now. (*d*) how many great-grandparents you have. (*e*) the name of the smallest village in Australia. (*f*) driving a car when drunk. (*g*) how many elephants you have in your home. (*h*) your intelligence. (*i*) how often you are in prison.

(iii) Give a short answer (Yes/No, Subject and Verb) to each of these questions:

(*a*) Can you speak Ancient Egyptian? (*b*) May people smoke in non-smoking compartments? (*c*) Does James enjoy travelling by train? (*d*) Is it snowing now? (*e*) Are you ninety? (*f*) Have I any tigers in my house? (*g*) Are there any mice in your room? (*h*) May we drive past a red traffic light? (*i*) Must train passengers have tickets? (*j*) Are there people living on the moon?

Got

Got is often used with the verb *have* in Spoken English, and what is said seems more natural as a result. It is not necessary in Written English.

I've got a cold. Fred hasn't got a ticket. Have you got a car? Haven't the children got anything to eat? We've got to hurry = We have to (must) hurry.

Make sentences with *got* together with these expressions:

(*a*) (he) a headache? (*b*) (we not) any tea. (*c*) (the postman not) a bicycle. (*d*) (I) to telephone. (*e*) (you) give it back? (*f*) (I) to do it again?

Practise using these forms whenever possible when you speak.

Forms of address when speaking to people

Sir and *Madam* are used in hotels and some shops when the person's name is unknown. Public servants such as officials and policemen use these forms. A young man speaking to an older man or a boy speaking to his teacher may say 'sir'. A woman teacher should be called by her name: Mrs Lane/Miss Day. Strangers who do not know each other rarely have any special form of address. Somehow they avoid the necessity of using one.

People who are not worried about making a polite impression—assistants in small shops, newspaper sellers, bus conductors—may call a man 'mate' or 'Joe' (or any short Christian name) and a woman of any age 'love', 'duck' or 'dear'.

A boy may be called 'son' or 'lad' and a girl 'dear'. 'Miss' is normally only used when calling a shop assistant or waitress, though children sometimes use this form to a woman teacher or a woman unknown to them.

Useful expressions: Travelling by train

Booking Office: Two singles (returns) to Brighton, please. (The passenger says 'first class' if he wants this). A weekly season ticket to Victoria, please. May I reserve a seat on the Plymouth train leaving at 8.30 tomorrow morning? Second class, window seat, facing (back to) the engine, if possible, please.

Barrier or Information Office: When does the next train for Waterloo leave, please? Does it stop at Basingstoke? What platform does it leave from? Do I have to change anywhere?

In the Train: Is this seat free? Would you mind helping me to lift my case down, please? Can I help you with your luggage (case)? Thank you. That's very kind of you. It *is* rather heavy.

Giving your own opinions

Give your own ideas about any of these subjects. Think a moment before you speak so as to make as few mistakes as possible.

(*a*) Describe the kind of person you think is typical of your own fellow-countrymen.

(*b*) Give three reasons why many people think that smoking is a bad habit.

(*c*) For what reasons do some people take an interest in clothes and others not?

(*d*) How do you enjoy spending your leisure time?

(*e*) Why do some people very much enjoy gardening? What is your opinion?

(*f*) What are some of the things that may help you to guess a stranger's nationality?

General guidance and practice

Two present tenses

(*a*) THE PRESENT SIMPLE TENSE

I eat he, she, it eats we, you, they eat

Use

This tense is used for actions that are *habitual* (that is to say, actions that happen all the time, or regularly or several times).

Many Swiss people speak three languages: French, German and Italian.
A cat likes rabbit.
Students often make mistakes.
He occasionally works in the evening.

(*b*) THE PRESENT CONTINUOUS TENSE

I am sitting he, she, it is sitting we, you, they are sitting

Uses

(*a*) This tense is used for an action that is happening *now, at this moment*:

I am now learning about tenses.
The birds are singing. Can you hear them?

The action may last for some time continuously, but it extends through now even though nothing may actually be happening at the moment one is speaking.

Your work is improving.
We are all getting older.

The following examples show the difference between the Present Simple and Present Continuous tenses:

She knits beautiful jumpers; just now she is knitting a silk one.
They are drinking coffee, though normally they drink tea.

(*b*) The Present Continuous tense also expresses an ARRANGED FUTURE action:

He is making a speech at the meeting to-morrow.
The train is leaving in five minutes.

(The Present Continuous of the verb 'to go' with an infinitive may also express the future. This is explained in Chapter 11, Page 94.)

(*c*) In conversation the Present Continuous is sometimes used with the adverb 'always' to express a repeated action. Notice the position of 'always':

That student is always coming in late.
You are always causing trouble.

Certain verbs are rarely used in the Present Continuous tense (except in a few cases to express the arranged future).

A few of these verbs are:

can, may, must, ought
*see, hear, *smell
seem, *appear, matter, mean
*think, know, (understand), (remember), (forget), recognise
notice, (wonder), believe, suppose
(like), (love), dislike, (hate), (want)
own, possess, consist

The verbs given in brackets may under certain circumstances be found in the Present Continuous tense, but are best not used in this way by students.

**Notice:*

I *am seeing* him next Monday.
The flower *smells* sweet but She is *smelling* the flower.
He *appears* stupid but He *is appearing* in the new film.
What is he doing! I *think* he *is thinking* hard.

Notice that if either the Present Simple or the Present Continuous form can be used, the *first* is more often used unless the present moment is stressed:

The river flows into the sea.
The river is flowing more swiftly after yesterday's rain.

Use the correct form of either the Present Simple or the Present Continuous tense in each of the following sentences:

(*a*) Look! They (laugh) at his story.
(*b*) People (laugh) when they are amused.
(*c*) The baby (cry). Give him some food.

(*d*) Children (cry) when they are frightened.
(*e*) That naughty boy (throw) stones. Send him away.
(*f*) In winter she (throw) out crumbs for the birds.
(*g*) Peaches (ripen) in warm sunny places but not in the shade.
(*h*) He (seem) very thoughtful. I (think) he (write) a poem.
(*i*) We (buy) a new refrigerator next month.
(*j*) Soldiers (salute) their officers.
(*k*) He (play always) his trumpet when I (want) to sleep.
(*l*) The famous violinist (play) in to-night's concert. He (play) superbly.
(*m*) I (lose always) my umbrella! What (happen) to all the umbrellas people (lose)?
(*n*) Every day I (work) by the window, so I (see) everyone who (come) to the house. The postman (come) now. He (carry) two letters.
(*o*) She (work) as a nurse in a hospital but as she (have) her holiday now, she (stay) at the seaside.

Negative and interrogative verb forms

(*a*) *The Present Simple Tense*

NEGATIVE FORMS:

I do not understand
he, she, it does not understand
we, you, they do not understand

In conversation '*do not*' usually has the form '*don't*' and '*does not*' the form '*doesn't*'.

The *interrogative* form is:

do I look?
does he (she, it) look?
do we (you, they) look?

In the case of *the anomalous verbs*: '*have*', '*be*', '*can*', '*may*', '*must*', '*ought*', '*should*', '*need*' and '*dare*', a simpler form of negative and interrogative is used (though in the cases of the verbs 'have', 'need' and 'dare' there are exceptions, which are explained later).

I am not
he, she, it is not
we, you, they are not
I may not, he ought not, etc.

'Cannot' is the one case in which the 'not' in full is joined to the verb itself.

INTERROGATIVE FORMS:

am I? are we (you, they)?
is he (she, it)?

Notice the unusual first person singular form '*aren't I?*'

may I? ought he? must they? etc.

(*b*) *The Present Continuous Tense*

WRITTEN	SPOKEN (NEGATIVE FORMS)
I am not staying	he, she, it isn't staying
he, she, it is not staying	we, you, they aren't staying
we, you, they are not staying	*or:*
am I walking?	I'm not staying
is he (she, it) walking?	he's, she's, it's not staying
are we (you, they) walking?	we're, you're, they're not staying

Questions

When the question begins with an interrogative adjective, adverb or pronoun which is not the subject of the following verb, THE INTERROGATIVE FORM OF THE VERB MUST FOLLOW:

Where are you going?
What exercise are the students doing?
Whom do the people want as their President?
How many workers does that factory employ?

But: Who likes chocolate?

The following sentences are answers to questions. Give each of the questions. (In most cases the form of the answer is suggested by the word or words in the bracket.)

(*a*) I live in England. (Where?)
(*b*) Yes. A dog certainly eats meat.
(*c*) The train arrives at eight o'clock. (When?)
(*d*) There are two boys and three girls in my family. (How many?)
(*e*) No. The committee is not meeting until to-morrow evening.
(*f*) He is crying because he is hungry. (Why? the baby)
(*g*) The students travel by the 36 bus. (What bus?)
(*h*) Yes, the whole exercise must be completed.
(*i*) The journey takes an hour. (How long?)
(*j*) No one knows how birds can find their way. (How?)

Using the ideas given below construct *negative* sentences, giving both the full written form and the spoken form in each case. Only the infinitive of the verb is given; the right tense must be supplied:

(*k*) Kangaroos—live—in Europe.
(*l*) The sun—shine—to-day—and the birds—sing.
(*m*) Why—you—study? Your book—be—open.
(*n*) You—can—use the lift. It—work.
(*o*) Housewives—buy—bread—at the butcher's.
(*p*) Why—people—like—hard work?
(*q*) People—meet—polar bears—in the streets of Helsinki.
(*r*) It—be—always foggy in London.
(*s*) Even English people—can—always spell their language correctly.

(*t*) Cost—a horse—very much money?
(*u*) All Italians—sing—the whole day.

Exclamations

FORMATION

What (a) (ADJ.) NOUN (SUBJECT VERB)
What a surprise! What nonsense! What a silly thing to say!
What a donkey you are! What a cold day it is to-day!
How ADJECTIVE/ADVERB (SUBJECT VERB)
How strange! How kind of you! How cold it is to-day!

Write the exclamation you would make in each of the following circumstances:

(*a*) The weather is wonderful.
(*b*) I am very tired.
(*c*) Mary Lloyd is very pretty.
(*d*) That doctor writes badly.
(*e*) You spend a lot of money.

Passive forms

A tailor *makes* suits.
Suits *are made* by a tailor.

In the first of these sentences the tailor, the subject of the verb, does the action of the verb. The verb is in the ACTIVE VOICE.

In the second sentence the action of the verb is *done to the subject*, which does nothing. The verb is in the PASSIVE VOICE.

Only transitive verbs, those that take an object, can be used passively. It is the object of an Active form which is usually the subject of the Passive form, as in the example above.

Here is the passive form of the PRESENT SIMPLE TENSE:

I am carried
he, she, it is carried
we, you, they are carried

and here of the PRESENT CONTINUOUS TENSE:

I am being carried
he, she, it is being carried
we, you, they are being carried

To change an active to a passive form

(1) Decide the tense of the Active form.
(2) Form the same tense of the verb 'to be'.
(3) Add the past participle of the verb being used.

'He takes' is in the Present Simple tense. The Present Simple form of the verb 'to be' is 'he is'. The past participle of the verb 'to take' is 'taken'. The passive form therefore, is 'he is taken'.
The preposition 'by' is used before the agent.

Change the verbs in the following sentences into the Passive Voice:

(*a*) An announcer is reading the news.

(*b*) Horses pull carts.

(*c*) The Queen is opening that hospital next week.

(*d*) The Headmaster is making a speech.

(*e*) A policeman is using the telephone.

(*f*) A greengrocer sells potatoes.

(*g*) Teenagers greatly admire 'pop' singers.

(*h*) Architects design buildings.

(*i*) Father is cooking the dinner. Mother is cleaning up the kitchen afterwards.

(*j*) Several small boys are feeding the monkeys.

Word order in sentences

We have seen how the order of subject and verb depends on whether the sentence is a statement or a question.

In a simple statement containing a direct object, the words are usually in the following order:

Subject	*Verb*	*Direct Object*	*Adverb*
The man	is having	a meal	in a restaurant

It may sometimes happen that the adverb comes first, especially in the case of a *time* adverb:

Adverb	*Subject*	*Verb*	*Direct Object*
This morning	the housewife	is doing	her washing

But Spanish-speaking people must remember that it is far less common in English than in Spanish to put adverbs of place at the beginning of a sentence and the subject after the verb.

English people do not say: In the sky are stars.
but: There are stars in the sky.
They seldom say: In this office work two clerks.
but rather: Two clerks work in this office.

A VERY COMMON MISTAKE: Remember that 'very much' and other adverbs *must not* separate the verb from a short direct object unless these words qualify the direct object.

It is *quite wrong* to say: 'I enjoy very much the cinema.'
But we can say: 'I very much enjoy the cinema.'
or: 'I enjoy the cinema very much.'
(We can of course say: 'A small bird does not need very much food', because 'very much' qualifies the direct object 'food'.)
It is wrong to say: 'He is writing slowly his letter.'
'He is writing his letter slowly,' is correct here.

Arrange the following groups of words in correctly formed sentences:

(*a*) her shopping/in a paper bag/is carrying/the woman.

(*b*) beautifully/the/piano/she plays.

(*c*) very much/like/children/fairy stories.
(*d*) must/at the top of the paper/you/your name/write.
(*e*) writes/his homework/neatly/this student.
(*f*) porridge for breakfast/dislikes/he/very much.
(This can be arranged in two ways with two different meanings. What are they?)
(*g*) from the canal/boys/are fishing.
(*h*) are hanging/in the classroom/many children's drawings.

German and Scandinavian students must remember not to change the order of subject and verb after an adverb at the beginning of a sentence.

NOT Then eat we our supper. *But:* Then we eat our supper.
NOR To-day go I go the dentist's. *But:* To-day I am going to the dentist's.

Spanish and Italian students (and some other nationalities also) must be very careful not to leave out the subject of a verb, especially when they are speaking quickly.

You *cannot* possibly say in English:

Is a fine day *or:* Is not at home now.

The apostrophe

This has two different uses:

(*a*) To show that a letter (or letters) have been left out.

It appears mainly in conversational verb abbreviations: 'I've', 'he's', 'we're', 'you'll', 'isn't', 'they'd' and so on.

Notice the apostrophe in 'o'clock' (of the clock).

(*b*) It is used to show the possessive case of nouns.

Usually the apostrophe is *put before the -s* when the possessor is singular and after when the possessor is plural:

a lady's shoe ladies' shoes

But when the noun indicating the possessor does not add -s to form the plural, the apostrophe still comes before the -s even in the plural form.

This normally affects only a few words:

men's policemen's
women's children's
workmen's people's

The time expressions: second, minute, hour, day, week, fortnight, month, year, century, may all be used possessively, according to the rule:

a second's delay three weeks' pay
two months' holiday five years' imprisonment

Notice the following sentences:

They are now at the Saunders'.
I sometimes go into Woolworth's.

In the first case, one is referring to the Saunders' house, and in the second to Woolworth's shop.

Here is a conversational expression which indicates slight impatience: 'For goodness' sake hurry up!'

The possessive pronouns: hers, its, ours, yours, theirs, *have no apostrophe.*

Be careful not to mix 'it's' = 'it is' and 'its' = 'belonging to it'.

It is not impossible for nouns indicating things to be used possessively but it is safer for the intermediate student to use the longer form:

the handle of the door;
the price of the book;
the name of the street.

Show where apostrophes are needed in the following:

(*a*) He doesnt know where hes going
(*b*) the students memory
(*c*) the students minds
(*d*) policemens wives
(*e*) for goodness sake be quiet
(*f*) five hours sleep
(*g*) Its a long way
(*h*) Is this yours?
(*i*) Old Peoples Homes
(*j*) We spent the evening at Joans
(*k*) The book is losing its cover
(*l*) four oclock
(*m*) the dolls dress
(*n*) a brother of Henrys.

Word order related to phrasal and similar verb forms

Here is another rule which in a small way affects the order of words in a sentence:

A number of verbal forms are made up of more than one word: the verb itself together with one or more preposition or adverb. Examples of such forms are: put on (a hat); put off (an appointment); put back (a book).

Many such forms are known as PHRASAL VERBS and the adverbs or prepositions are then called PARTICLES.

When these verbs have a *noun* as their *direct object*, the noun in most cases can stand either between the verb and the particle or after the particle.

He is putting on his hat. *or:* He is putting his hat on.

When the *direct object* is a *pronoun* it usually stands between the verb and the adverbial particle:

He is putting it on.
not: He is putting on it.

Notice that the verb 'look' is often followed by a preposition which is not a particle. In this case the preposition must be *followed* by the noun or pronoun it is governing—neither can come before it.

I am looking at it
His mother is looking after him
You must look for them

'Look up' is, however, a phrasal verb. It is therefore impossible to say 'I must look up it'. This should be 'I must look it up'.

Copy the following sentences, putting in its correct place the noun or pronoun object in brackets at the end of each, and indicating in which cases this could stand in more than one position:

(*a*) Put down on the floor. (the basket)
(*b*) He is bringing back to-morrow. (them)

(*c*) You can hang up in the corner. (it)
(*d*) Write down in your notebook. (the words)
(*e*) They are putting off until next Friday. (it)
(*f*) Are you looking after carefully? (her)
(*g*) Look at carefully and then put away. (the picture) (it)
(*h*) Your shoelace is undone. You must do up. (it)
(*i*) They are looking up in the dictionary. (the spelling)
(*j*) You can either undo your coat or take off. (it)
(*k*) Give back. (it)
(*l*) Fill in. (the form)
(*m*) Give in. (your work)
(*n*) Please pick up. (the chalk)
(*o*) Be careful when you pick up. (it)
(*p*) I am ringing up. (him)
(*q*) Throw away. (it)

Numbers

(*a*) Notice the hyphen in all numbers from twenty-one to ninety-nine except the tens.

(*b*) 185 is written as words or spoken as one (or a) hundred and eighty-five. 364—three hundred and sixty-four.

(*c*) Dates, such as 1924, are usually written as figures and spoken as: nineteen twenty-four, though nineteen hundred and twenty-four is not wrong.
The number itself is spoken in the second way, or as one thousand nine hundred and twenty-four.

(*d*) 532,478 is spoken as five hundred and thirty-two thousand, four hundred and seventy-eight.

(*e*) *Notice:* four hundred and ten, three thousand and twenty, five million, six hundred thousand (no plurals).
But: hundreds of pounds, thousands of people, millions of insects.

(*f*) Notice the spellings: *four*, *four*teen, but f*o*rty.

(*g*) Ordinal numbers are used in dates.
Dates can be written: 1st January, 2nd February, 3rd March, 4th April, 21st May, 22nd June, 23rd July, 31st August.
Otherwise 4th, 5th (fifth), 8th (eighth), 9th (ninth), 11th, 12th etc.
At the head of a letter the date is written: 9th February, 1910.
In other written work 'the ninth of February' is usual.

(*h*) Kings are indicated by ordinal numbers written in Roman figures: George VI (George the Sixth).

(*i*) Fractions are written as one-half, two-thirds, three-quarters and so on. Decimals are read aloud as 15·36—fifteen point three six.

Write the following as words:

44, 175, 832, 2,407, 2,436,000, 500, the year 1425, the date 3.9.1930 (on a letter), Henry VIII, $\frac{4}{5}$, 27·82.

Times

Many students are unsure of the correct way of telling the time.

The British do not always use the twenty-four hour clock. 'a.m.' indicates 'before midday', 'p.m.' 'after midday'.

However one does not say 'I go out at twenty past eight a.m.', but: 'I go out at twenty past eight in the morning.'

8.00 eight o'clock
8.15 (a) quarter past eight
8.30 half past eight
8.45 (a) quarter to nine.

The figures in the first column are used mainly in timetables, in the second in everyday speech.

Notice the difference:

five past eight ten past eight
twenty-five to nine twenty to nine
BUT *one minute* past eight
seven minutes past eight
eighteen minutes to nine, etc.

B.C. is used with years to indicate the time before Christ. A.D. indicates the time after Christ (Latin—Anno Domini).

Write the following in words as they are used in everyday speech:

9.15 a.m., 10.30 p.m., 6.45, 4.25, 3.14 p.m., 7.43, 11.2, 8.52, 1.18 a.m.

First At first Last At last

FIRST is used when some kind of list of happenings is suggested or at least the idea that another action or other actions are following:

He first hangs up his hat and coat and then he is ready to start his morning's work.

AT FIRST always suggests that the action it is used with is followed by a completely different action or often the opposite:

He worked hard at first, but later he did nothing.

LAST suggests that no more actions should happen later:

It should be the teacher who arrives in the classroom last.

AT LAST suggests that there has been a long wait before the expected action:

At last the spring has come after a long winter.

Which of the four expressions should be used in each:

(*a*) This term is ending ......
(*b*) ...... put in a coin and then press the button.
(*c*) ...... he knew nobody but now he has many friends.
(*d*) The slowest runner usually comes ......
(*e*) ...... knock at the door and then go in.
(*f*) ...... the bus is coming.
(*g*) Tom, who is always sleepy, is the one who gets up ......

2

Passage for comprehension

Settling down in England

My husband and I are Danish. As a matter of fact, many of my ancestors were English: I was born in England and was originally of British nationality. My parents were killed in a car crash when I was a baby, so I was brought up in Denmark by my grandmother and educated in Danish schools so that Danish is really my native language. 5

We arrived in England last February at five o'clock on a Wednesday morning after an appallingly rough crossing. Waves which seemed as high as mountains rocked the boat from side to side. We were both sick on the journey and a fine drizzle met us as we disembarked. To make matters worse, Klaus, my husband, left his camera on the ship; I lost a gold bracelet, (which 10 has never been found to this day) and we nearly forgot to tip the taxi-driver, a surly individual, who grumbled about our luggage and seemed to be in a thoroughly bad temper. Few visitors can have experienced such an unfortunate beginning to their stay, and we certainly felt like going straight home again. 15

We stayed for a week in a hotel, and were then lucky enough to find a furnished bungalow in the suburbs of London. It is not so convenient as our flat in Copenhagen, but it is less expensive than some we saw advertised. Klaus is studying at the local Technical College and, in addition, he often attends public lectures at the University of London on as many subjects as 20 possible, chiefly to improve his English. He is a qualified engineer who has been employed for several years in a factory. Our two children have joined us, and they are being educated in an English private school. I am working as a part-time nurse in a hospital, and I have so much to do that I have almost no leisure time. 25

Most of the neighbours are kindly, but not so sociable as people at home. They tend to ask dull questions, such as: 'What is the weather like in Denmark?' or 'what kind of games do you play?' We are occasionally paid some odd compliments. I remember the time when a well-meaning old lady told us, 'You have such delightful manners. I always think of you both as 30 quite English.' I think she meant this as the height of flattery.

We have made a few close friends, who often invite us to their homes. One of them, who is a widower living on the other side of London, even fetches us in his car on Sunday mornings and brings us back in the evenings. Little Kristina, our small daughter, calls him Uncle Sunday. He speaks 35 Swedish and has an elderly Swedish housekeeper, who has been looking after him for more than twenty years, so we chat for hours in a language that is in some ways similar to our own.

Our children can already speak English more fluently than we can. They 40 obviously feel superior to us, and are always making fun of our mistakes, but spelling causes all of us many headaches.

Notes on the passage

Vocabulary

line

Title *settle down*—stay in one place *a settler*—someone who settles in a new country or place *settle* (*up*) a bill (pay it) *settle a matter*, *an argument* (decide it) *settled* weather (not changeable).

1 *ancestors*—great great grandparents etc. *descendants*—great grandchildren etc. the present *generation* (which you belong to).

2 *originally*—earlier, in the beginning the *origin* of the trouble (beginning or cause)—of a word (what language or idea it comes from) *original*—first, fresh or new: *the original manuscript the original plan an original writer or thinker who has original ideas* *originality* is the quality of being clever and fresh.

2 An Englishman/Englishwoman, a Scot/Scotswoman, a Welshman/Welshwoman and some Irishmen/Irishwomen are *of British nationality* (British by birth). Great Britain is the bigger of the two islands; the United Kingdom is Great Britain and Northern Ireland and the British Isles are the two islands.

3 *a car crash*—this could be a *collision* in which two cars *run into* each other.

3 *bring up* children in the home (upbringing) *educate* them in school (education).

7 *appallingly* should mean completely horrifying and shocking. In conversation it often has only the meaning 'very'. Similar words used with this meaning in conversation are *awfully*, *terribly*, *dreadfully*, *frightfully*.

7 a *rough* sea (OPP. calm) a rough surface (OPP. smooth) a rough boy (OPP. gentle) a rough answer (OPP. exact).

7 a sea *crossing* a level crossing (where a railway crosses a road) a pedestrian crossing for people to cross the road.

7 a mountain is *high* buildings are *high* or *tall* a man is *tall* (NEVER long).

8 *sick* as a result of over-eating or travel *ill*=not well.
Notice however: people who are ill visit this spa but: sick (NOT ill) people visit this spa. *ill* almost never precedes a noun.

9 a *drizzle*, a *shower*, a *downpour*, a *cloudburst* are all kinds of *rain* (*Unc*) to drizzle, to pour (with rain) are the only verbs.

9 *embark on* a boat, *disembark from* a boat (or: go ashore) One can also embark on a new scheme: *the company is embarking on a new production line.*

10 *gold* is the metal: *a gold ring* *golden* is the colour: *golden hair.*

10 a *bracelet* is worn round the arm; a *necklace* is worn round the neck; an *ear-ring* is worn in the ear; a *brooch* is used for fastening a dress.

11 *forget* NOT: I sometimes forget my book at home. This is quite wrong. You can say: I sometimes *forget to bring* my book. or: I sometimes *leave my book at home.*

12 *surly* means rough and bad-mannered *sullen* means silently angry and bitter: *after years of ill-treatment he became sullen and hard* *sulky* usually refers to a child who will not speak because he cannot get what he wants.

13 in a *bad temper* A person can be only in a good or a bad temper. He can however be in a good, bad, cheerful, friendly, contented, optimistic, pessimistic, depressed (etc.) *mood* (*Adj* moody = of changing moods, often miserable ones).

14 *go straight home*—go home immediately.

16 *lucky*—getting good things by chance: *lucky at cards. happy*—contented.

17 a *bungalow*, a house, a flat (a block of flats), a cottage, a farmhouse.

17 the town *centre*, the *suburbs* (*Adj* surburban), the *outskirts* of a town.

17 *convenient*—well-situated for work, buses and trains. *comfortable*—built and furnished to give ease and pleasure. *Is it convenient for me to come tomorrow?*

18 *expensive*—costing a lot. *dear*—costing more than it should: *an expensive fur coat; eggs are dear just now.*

18 *advertise* (*N* advertisement)—publicise something (make it known) so as to gain something. *announce* (*N* announcement) make something important known to people.

20 *attend* (*N* attendance) be present at a meeting, class, performance. *assist* (*N* assistance) help.
NOT: *I assisted in the lecture* but: *I attended the lecture.*
NOT: *I assisted in an accident* but: *I saw* (*or: was involved in*) *an accident.*

20 A *lecture* is given by a lecturer on a certain subject.
Reading (*Unc N*) is an enjoyable pastime. *Charles Dickens often gave readings* (*C N*) *from his novels.*
A conference of international eye specialists will take place in Vienna.
The teachers will have a staff meeting this afternoon.

21 *improve* (*N* improvement) improve one's English, writing, etc. (make it better) His behaviour/work/standard/manners has/have improved. (got better) *better as a verb* is rarely used: better oneself (get a better position or job). A teacher *corrects* or *marks* written work and pupils *do corrections.*

21 *qualified* (*N* qualification) *for* a job with the right knowledge to do it *experienced*—knowing the job from having done it for some time.

disqualified from—not allowed to take part (Example: in sport) usually because of bad conduct or unsuitability.

21 An *engineer* may design and construct. A *mechanic* repairs and maintains.

22 A *factory* is a place where things are made. A *fabric* is a material.

26 *sociable* (*Adj*) liking to mix with other people.
a *society* (*C*)—a club: a Dramatic Society.
society (*Unc*)—(*a*) people living in a community: *a danger to society.* (*b*) a group of rich people who entertain a lot: *he wanted to be accepted in society.*
a *social*—an informal party. (*Adj*) referring to community life: *the social history of England.*
an *associate*—(*a*) a friend (*b*) a title for a member of certain learned societies.
associate with (*V*)—be or mix with other people. an *association* a club or organised group.

27 a *dull* question or book (OPP. interesting) a dull boy (*Opp* bright or clever) a dull sky (*Opp* bright).

27 *tend to*—happening very often. *day temperatures tend to be high in this region.*

29 *compliments*—the word *flattery* in line 31 is the art of paying compliments.

29 *odd* strange. But also: *odd numbers:* 1, 3, 5 etc. *even numbers:* 2, 4, 6 etc.

30 *manners* (*Pl*)—have good or bad manners (politeness); *table manners.* *manner* (*Unc*)—way: *he is behaving in a strange manner.*

31 *height*—abstract noun from high.
Notice also: long—*length* wide—*width* broad—*breadth* deep—*depth.*

32 *close* friends (*Adj* see Pronunciation Page 27) but: close to (Preposition): *he lives close to the park.*

33 *elderly* young, middle-aged, elderly, old, aged.
Notice: the Middle Ages—*Adj* medieval.

34 *take* from here to there: *take your books home after class;* take away. *bring* from here to there: *bring your books to class again tomorrow. fetch*—go to something and bring it here: *Fetch a doctor quickly!* (But when writing a letter, think of yourself as the person you are writing to: *Shall I bring my skis with me when I visit you in Scotland?*)

36 a *housekeeper* is paid to look after a house for someone.
a *caretaker* is paid to look after a building—he may have *cleaners* to help.
a *housewife* is the lady of the house (without wages).

37 *chat* together about unimportant things. *chatter*—talk a great deal.

38 *similar/dissimilar to*=very like (*N* similarity)/unlike.
identical to=exactly the same as *different from.*

40 *superior to*=better than (*N* superiority) BUT: an *advanced* course/class.

40 *make fun of* someone's mistakes; *mock* in a cruel way; children *tease* one another (*N* mockery).

Pronunciation

APPARENTLY DIFFICULT: thoroughly [θʌ́rəlɪ].

STRESS CHANGES: áncestors [ǽnsɪstəz] or [ǽnsestəz]; ancéstral (*Adj*) [ǽnséstral]; órigin [ɔ́rɪdʒɪn]; oríginal [əríʤɪnl]; originate [əriʤɪneɪt]; originálity [ərɪʤɪnǽlɪtɪ]; súburbs [sʌ́bəːbz]; subúrban [səbə́ːbən]; ádvertise [ǽdvəːtaɪz]; advértisement [ədvə́ːtɪzmənt]; sócial [souʃl]; sóciable [sóuʃəbl]; society [səsáɪətɪ]; associate (*V*) [əsóuʃɪeɪt]; (*N*) [əsóuʃɪət].

ə (as in *a*go): husb*a*nd [hʌ́zbənd]; Febru*a*ry [fébruərɪ]; *a*ppallingly [əpɔ́ːlɪŋlɪ]; cert*a*inly [sə́ːtnlɪ]; c*o*nveni*e*nt [kənvíːnɪənt]; lect*u*res [léktʃəz]; hospit*a*l [hɔ́spɪtəl]; neighb*ou*rs [néɪbəz]; simil*a*r [símɪlə]; *o*ccas*io*n*a*lly [əkéɪʒənəlɪ]; obvi*ou*sly [ɔ́bvɪəslɪ].

ɪ (as in c*i*ty): mount*ai*ns [máuntɪnz]; brace*le*t [bréɪslɪt]; neckl*a*ce [néklɪs]; lugg*a*ge [lʌ́gɪʤ]; coll*e*ge [kɔ́lɪʤ]; *e*ng*i*neer [inʤɪníə] or: [enʤɪníə].

STRESS: mistéiks [mɪstéɪks].

OTHERS: mean [miːn] but meant [ment]; close (*V*) [klouz] (*Adj: Prep.* and *Adv.*) [klous]; rough [rʌf]; qualified [kwɔ́lɪfaid]; headaches [hédeiks]; brooch [broutʃ].

Special grammatical and structural points

(i) When two pronouns or a noun and a pronoun, one of them in the first person, are connected by a conjunction, the first person pronoun always has the second place: *You and I. The children and I. We* and *they* are seldom used in this way. The sentence: 'The children and we went out' would more probably be written: *We went out with the children.*
Notice: the pronoun as object: *Father met John and me at the station.* after a preposition: *The farmer was angry with John and me.*

(ii) *I was born* in London in 1960. NOT: 'I am born' which is always wrong.

(iii) *a* normally precedes a Countable Noun after the verb 'to be' (in many languages it does not). *I was a baby. He is a qualified engineer, who is a widower.*

(iv) *last February* *last week* *He arrived last February. It happened last week.*
the last week *the last day* *He arrived in the last week of the year. It happened on the last day he was here.*
next week *the following week* *He is coming next week. He came the following week.*

(v) *a few* visitors = *some* *A few visitors came to the hotel even in the winter.*
few visitors = a very small number indeed *Few visitors ever returned.*
a little work = some (with *Unc N*) *He has done a little homework, more than he did yesterday.*
little work = too little *Many of the newcomers had no jobs as there was little work for them in that area.*
Notice however: *only a little* *only a few* NOT: only little/only few.

(vi) *most of the neighbours* *both the brothers* NOT: the most/the both of them.

(vii) he *feels well, ill, tired, cold* etc. NO reflexive —self form with 'feel'.

(viii) I remember *the time when/the place where* something happened. (In most cases it is normal to say: I remember when/where.)

(ix) *I have so much/little to do that life seems rather dull He has so many/few troubles that he has little interest in life.*

(x) she works *as a nurse*—this is her job she works *like a slave* = very hard. *Which?—as or like?* he eats—a horse; —a lawyer, he can give legal advice; he practises—a doctor; she sings—a nightingale; he is serving —a soldier.

(xi) *Uncountable Nouns: luggage My luggage is in my car. It is heavy. weather We had beautiful weather. What cold weather! England has many different kinds of weather.*

(xii) VERBAL CONSTRUCTIONS

(*a*) *Infinitive: seem/appear* to be; *tend* to ask he attends lectures *to improve* his English (*Purpose*) lucky *enough to find* (construction with '*enough*'

(*b*) *Gerund: felt like* going

(*c*) *Infinitive or Gerund* (with meaning change)
remember/forget to do something that should be done *remember/forget doing* something that has been done.
Which? I have forgotten — my book. (bring). Do you remember— to read? (learn) Please remember—some bread (buy). I shall never forget—the mountain in midwinter (climb).

Prepositions

(*a*) arrive *in* a place (England, Canterbury) but *at* a point (London Airport, our hotel: *We arrived in Hull at four but did not reach our hotel before five.*

(*b*) be at home but go home leave home. invite someone home or to one's home.

(*c*) We arrived *last February/in* February *at* five o'clock *on* Wednesday (morning). but: in the morning, in the afternoon, in the evening, at night. early in the morning late at night.

(*d*) *in:* stay in a hotel; in the centre and in the suburbs (but: *on* the outskirts); employed in a factory; fetch us in his car; in a bad temper; killed/injured in a car crash; chat in a language that is similar.

(*e*) *on:* on the journey; lecture (*N* and *V*) on something; live on the other side of London; embark on a ship (but: disembark from); leave something on a ship (on/in a bus, train in a car).

(*f*) *to:* a beginning to our stay; superior/inferior to (but: better than).

(*g*) *at:* be educated at Cornchester School (but: in a Grammar School) study at University, at a Technical College.

(*h*) *of:* of British nationality; make fun of.

(*i*) *about:* grumble about.

Expressions to introduce written work

Learn and whenever possible make use of these:

(*a*) *thorough(ly)* in a thoroughly bad temper; make a thorough search; clean, wash, examine, check something thoroughly.

(*b*) *feel like* having a cup of tea, going for a walk, changing my job.

(*c*) we were *lucky enough to* find, make several friends, have good weather.

(*d*) the *local* school, people, firms, bus service, customs etc.

(*e*) work *as* a nurse think of her *as* a friend say something *as* a joke.

(*f*) they *tend to* ask; the summers tend to be hot; children tend to be noisy.

(*g*) a *native* language speak a language *fluently*.

(*h*) it is *in some ways* similar in some ways it is ideal

(*i*) *What is the weather like?* What was your holiday/the film/the journey like?

(*j*) a *well-meaning* person a person who means to be kind but is not always successful.

(*k*) *Adverbials: As a matter of fact* he happens to be my cousin the boat rocked *from side to side*. I have never found it *to this day*. *To make matters worse* we lost our way. He is interested *chiefly* in music. You are lazy, untidy and bad-mannered and, *in addition*, you can't even spell your own name properly. He saves as much money *as possible*.

Multiple choice questions

Here are a number of questions or unfinished statements about the passage, each with four suggested ways of answering or finishing it. You must choose the way you consider most suitable. Write in each case the bracketed number of the question or statement followed by the letters **A**, **B**, **C**, **D** and then cross through the letter of the answer you choose. Give one answer only to each question. Read the passage right through again before choosing your answers.

1 The writer speaks Danish as her native language because
A she is Danish by birth **B** her grandmother was Danish **C** Danish was the first language she learned **D** she went to school in Denmark

2 Which of these ideas is not suggested about their arrival in England?
A neither of them was really well **B** the weather was unpleasant **C** it was bitterly cold **D** it was still dark

3 All but one of these things which made matters worse are correct. The exception is
A they nearly forgot to pay the taxi-driver **B** some jewellery was lost **C** the driver was disagreeable **D** something was left behind

4 They were lucky in finding a flat but one of these statements is not true. Which is it?

A they found it fairly quickly **B** it was quite suitable **C** it was reasonably inexpensive **D** it was not too far from the centre

5 Klaus attends the Technical College
A to learn more English **B** to study to become an engineer **C** to give specialist advice **D** to gain additional knowledge of his subject

6 Which of these statements about the neighbours is apparently untrue?
A they spend too much time gossiping **B** they do not mix much with other people **C** they are not unpleasant **D** they have little real interest in the world

7 The neighbours' questions are described as 'dull' because
A sport and weather are very dull subjects **B** these are very obvious questions, showing little real interest **C** they are the only two questions they ask **D** the Danish couple have no interest in sport or the weather

8 Why did the well-meaning old lady think her remark was the height of flattery?
A she believed it was only English people who had good manners
B she was trying to be polite **C** she considered that good manners were very important **D** she thought it was the kindest thing she could say

9 What is the chief reason they enjoy their visits to their widower friend?
A they have the opportunity of seeing another part of London **B** he is their only friend **C** the children are fond of him **D** they can express themselves in their own language and so feel relaxed

10 The English of the father and mother is apparently
A very good **B** almost non-existent **C** not very good **D** excellent

Reading comprehension

(i) In this exercise you must choose the word or phrase which best completes each sentence. Write first the number of each sentence followed by the letters **A, B, C, D, E,** and then cross through the letter of the correct answer in each case. Give one answer only to each question.

1 The mechanic examined the car engine .... but could find nothing wrong with it.
A throughout **B** exactly **C** thoroughly **D** suitably **E** altogether

2 Angus Graham is the person who can advise you best. ...., he is coming here tomorrow.
A it is true **B** even so **C** in effect **D** originally **E** as a matter of fact

3 The flat we have rented is very .... for the Underground station.

A suitable **B** distant **C** comfortable **D** convenient **E** near

4 Are you going to attend Dr Barker's .... on 'Brain Electronics' tomorrow?
A conference **B** lecture **C** meeting **D** discussion **E** reading

5 I can't find my umbrella. I must have .... it on the bus.
A lost **B** left **C** forgotten **D** put **E** mislaid

6 The policeman looked me .... several times and obviously disliked what he saw.
A over and over again **B** up and down **C** from side to side **D** round and round **E** in and out

7 You must remember to .... all your belongings out of this classroom today.
A fetch **B** take away **C** bring **D** take **E** put

8 He always studies the .... in the paper as he wants to find a good second-hand car.
A reclamations **B** advertisements **C** publicity **D** announcements **E** publications

9 It was a horrible ride through pouring rain. .... he had a puncture and for the last hour had to push the bicycle.
A as a matter of fact **B** even so **C** to make matters worse **D** in fact **E** in some way

10 Spanish is the .... language of most Spaniards.
A mother **B** home **C** native **D** natural **E** birth

Use of English

(ii) The five sentences below are the answers to five questions that could be asked about the Reading Passage. Write suitable questions. The first one or two words of each question are given to assist you.

EXAMPLE: His father and mother are Danish. (What)

Question: What nationality are his father and mother?

(i) A fine drizzle met us when we arrived. (What was)
(ii) We felt like going straight home again. (What)
(iii) He attends public lectures to improve his English. (Why)
(iv) I have almost no leisure time. (How much)
(v) She has been looking after him for more than twenty years. (How long)

2 Write down the ten words in list A below, and against each the one word from list B which rhymes with it (that is, ends with the same sounds). Example: two words which rhyme are: come and sum: two others: Swede and read.

A	B
weary	breather
leather	hurry
leisure	theory

A	B
bury	work
height	whether
clerk	eight
worry	dairy
queue	cherry
greet	bite
great	sorry
	pleasure
	park
	few
	beat

3 The word in capitals at the end of each of the following sentences can be used to form a related word that fits suitably in the blank space. Fill each blank in this way.

Example: On our arrival we were greeted by an enormous dog. ARRIVE

1 Do you know the .... of St. Paul's Cathedral? HIGH

2 Switzerland is a .... country. MOUNTAIN

3 He is very anxious about the .... of his passport. LOSE

4 The nineteenth-century faith in the power of science is now very .... QUESTION

5 George made an unusually .... remark about his wife's new dress. COMPLIMENT

6 A person with an .... complex can be very disagreeable. INFERIOR

7 He has put on his .... as it is bitterly cold. COAT

8 There was loud .... as the clown fell off the ladder. LAUGH

9 We had an .... day sailing our new boat. ENJOY

10 Although he is now middle-aged, he still looks quite .... YOUTH

Composition and summarising

1 Write about eight simple sentences on one of these subjects. Use only words and expressions you already know, and even though this probably means you cannot write all the things you want to, write only the things you know how to express. Make use of the new words and expressions you have already learned in this book whenever you can.

(*a*) A very unpleasant journey by boat, train or car.

(*b*) Different ways in which you spend Sunday or some other day you have free every week.

2 The elder of the two Danish children, who now speaks English quite well, is writing a letter to an English friend in Denmark. In one paragraph he (she)

gives information about his (her) life in England: where he (she) lives, the neighbours, what his (her) parents are doing, school and how Sundays are sometimes spent. The whole paragraph is not more than 120–180 words long, so no unnecessary words are used.

Using only ideas that are in the reading passage, write this paragraph, in no more words than the number suggested. You could begin:

We are now living in a furnished flat in the suburbs of London. Use you own words as far as this is possible.

Spoken English

More shortened verbal forms

I/he wasn't we/you/they weren't I hadn't I couldn't I didn't

Notice: The form hadn't is normally used only as part of the Past Perfect tense. The usual Past Simple question is 'Did you have ....?' with the Short Answer form: 'Yes, I did' or 'No, I didn't.'

HAVE TO

Do you have to help? No, I don't.
Did you have to help? No, I didn't.

(*a*) Give short answers ('Yes' or 'No' followed by Subject and Verb) to these questions:

1 Did the couple enjoy their journey? 2 Were the children with their parents? 3 Was the sun shining when they arrived? 4 Could the Romans fly? 5 Have you ever written a book? 6 Did I write the first sentence in French? 7 Has the Queen asked you to Buckingham Palace yet? 8 Did you have a headache when you woke this morning? 9 Was the sun shining when the couple arrived in England? 10 Have you been learning English for more than ten years?

(*b*) Answer each of these questions or suggestions, using at least one shortened verbal form in each case.

1 Why couldn't the Romans fly? 2 Why don't you offer me a cigarette? 3 Why don't you learn Cornish? (an almost-forgotten language of Cornwall) 4 Suggest one reason why the family were pleased with their flat. ('family' can be thought of as either Singular or Plural) 5 Why do many people have difficulties in a foreign country? 6 What two European countries haven't you visited yet? 7 Why can't pigs fly? 8 Why don't the family see much of the neighbours? 9 Why didn't Julius Caesar sail to America? 10 What kind of weather don't you like?

(*c*) Say at least 15 words about each of these subjects, using a shortened verbal form.

(*a*) last winter (*b*) watching television (*c*) yesterday's weather (*d*) people's holidays two hundred years ago (*e*) children's education long ago (*f*) books and people in the Middle Ages

Expressing similarities

Here are two ways of agreeing, the first with affirmative, the second with negative statements.

(*a*) *Affirmative:* 'I'm afraid of large hairy spiders.' 'So am I.'
'We must hurry.' 'What's the time then? My goodness! So must I'
'You look really well.' 'So do you.'
'Factory-workers had to work very hard long ago.' .'So did farmers.'

(*b*) *Negative:* 'I haven't got any free time.' 'Neither (or: nor) have I.'
'Students don't always want to work.' 'Neither do teachers.'
'Primitive people didn't think much.' 'Nor do most modern people.'
'My husband wasn't very pleased with me when I came back from the sales.' 'Neither was mine.'

Add statements similar to those above to the following remarks. Where an unknown subject must be introduced, this is suggested in brackets.

(*a*) I enjoy freshly-fried fish. (*b*) You talk too much. (*c*) We don't like living in this town. (*d*) My teacher is angry with me and (Father). (*e*) I couldn't sleep last night. (*f*) My husband forgot my birthday. (*g*) I didn't pass the exam. (*h*) The porter grumbled about our luggage and (the taxi-driver). (*i*) Motorists have to be careful on the road and (cyclists). (*j*) I must go and visit Aunt Jane in hospital and you. (*k*) I can ride a bicycle. (*l*) Teachers didn't have to work to-day and (bank clerks) (*m*) My son had to write home for extra money and (Fred's).

Meeting people

(*a*) A formal greeting at a first meeting:

How do you do?
Answer: How do you do?

An informal greeting:

Glad to meet you. I'm Pete. What's your name?
or: Hallo, Margaret. I'm Joan. Can I fetch you some coffee?

A formal greeting to someone you have already met:

Good morning/afternoon/evening. How are you?

Answer: Very well, thank you. And how are you?
Oh, I'm fine, thank you.

'Good night' is used when seeing someone for the last time in the day if this is after about 5 p.m.

If you've been ill, you may be asked:

Are you feeling better now?

Answer: Much better, thank you.
or: Well, not too good yet. Better than I was though.

(*b*) After a journey:

Have you had a good journey?

Answer: Very pleasant, thank you.

After a sea crossing:

Did you have a good crossing?

Answer: No, I'm afraid not. It was really rough and I'm not a good sailor.

Useful expressions

(*a*) *A Telephone Enquiry about Something Lost.*

A Hallo. I want to make an enquiry about something I've lost. Could you put me through to the right department, please.

B Yes, sir. That'll be the Lost Property Department. Just a moment. I'll put you through. (Pause). You're through now, sir.

C Lost Property Department. Can I help you?

A I wonder if you have a camera of mine. I left it on the 'Margate Mermaid' when we crossed from Ostend yesterday morning.

C Have you any idea where you left it, sir?

A Probably in the restaurant, though I might have put it down when we were collecting our luggage from the storage space.

C Can you describe the camera?

A It's a Wonderview model in a brown leather case and there's an exposure meter in a case attached.

C Just a minute. (Pause) Yes. The camera was handed in to the purser.

A Oh, that's good. What a relief! But how can I get it? I live in Northampton. Look, could you send it to your London office and I'll call for it there at the end of next week?

C Yes, we could do that. There'll be a small charge, of course. Can I have your name and address please? Thank you. I'll see that it's sent off.

A Thank you very much. Goodbye.

(*b*) *Booking a Hotel Room*

GUEST: Have you a single/double room for to-night and to-morrow night with telephone and shower?

RECEPTIONIST: We haven't any rooms with a shower free just now, but there's a bathroom available on each floor.

G All right. That'll do. How much is the room for the night?

R Four pounds. That includes full English breakfast, of course.

G Yes, I'll take the room.

R Room 108. On the first floor. Here's your key and the lift's just round the corner. The porter will be back in a minute and he'll bring up your luggage.

G Thank you. And could I arrange to be called at seven to-morrow please?

R Certainly sir.

Giving your own opinions

Give your own ideas about any of these subjects. Think a moment before you speak so as to make as few mistakes as possible.

(*a*) Do you prefer to travel by aeroplane, train, boat or car? What are the advantages and disadvantages of each method?

(*b*) You have to spend a year in a foreign country. Do you think it better to have your own flat, to live in a hostel or to stay with a family? What are the advantages and disadvantages of each?

(*c*) Give some examples of good manners.

(*d*) What advantages have children in learning a new language compared with adults? What advantages have the adults?

(*e*) What difficulties in English cause you 'many headaches'?

General guidance and practice

The Past Simple, Present Perfect Simple and Present Perfect Continuous Tenses

The Past Simple

I took I did not take Did I take?

is used to express an action that happened in the past and is FINISHED.

Sometimes a definite time in the past is stated:

He *died* last year. He *arrived* a minute ago.

The action may have happened *only once*:

I *took* a chocolate from the box.

repeatedly:

The teacher who usually *took* us for Geography was Mr. Winter.

(If the suggestion that the action no longer takes place is very strong, the form 'used to take' would be used here—see Chapter IV.)

or *continuously:*

For several years he *worked* for the B.B.C.

(The Past Continuous could be used here if the *length* of the time were emphasised. 'He was working for the B.B.C. for a very long time.')

In many languages the Present Perfect is used in cases where only the Past Simple is correct in English. It is important to remember that in cases where a definite past time is stated or understood, the Present Perfect form is wrong in English.

The Present Perfect (Simple)

I have taken

(*a*) In very many cases *the Present Perfect tense is used for an action* WHICH STARTED IN THE PAST *but is* IN SOME WAY CONNECTED WITH THE PRESENT TIME:

Have you been here long?

I *have written* three letters this morning. (It is still morning.)

Compare: I *wrote* three letters this morning. (It is now afternoon.)

Henry Smith *has written* many novels. (He is still alive.)

Compare: John Brown *wrote* many novels. (He is dead and can write no more.)

He has not yet fully recovered from his illness.

(*b*) *The Present Perfect is also used for actions* WHICH HAVE ONLY JUST FINISHED, *provided that no past time is stated:*

He *has* just *come* in.

Compare: He came in a moment ago.

I *have* at last *decided* what to do.

(*c*) *The Present Perfect can suggest that while the action happened in the past, the* RESULT IS STILL EFFECTIVE:

I *have made* some coffee. Would you like some?
They *have made* many changes recently.
She *has moved* to a new flat.
I *have lost* my dictionary. *Have* you *found* it?

(*d*) *The Present Perfect is also used for actions which happened* AT SOME VAGUE INDEFINITE TIME IN THE PAST:

He has said that many times before.
(There is a strong suggestion that he is now saying it again.)

The Present Perfect Continuous Tense

I have been taking

This is a tense *which conveys the same meanings as the Simple Present Perfect*, but it is the *length of time* taken by the action which is emphasised. Verbs like 'live', 'stay', 'sleep', 'wait', 'work', 'travel', 'lie (flat)', 'rain', 'snow', 'shine' are often used in this tense, though other verbs may also be used when *a continuous action extending through the past until the present is expressed.*

Verbs which rarely appear in the Present Continuous tense appear equally rarely in this tense.

How long *have* you *been living* in England?
It *has been raining* all day.
I *have been waiting* for an hour and a half.
You *have been spending* far too much money.

Use the correct form of the Present Simple or Continuous, Past Simple or Present Perfect Simple or Continuous Tenses in the following sentences. The adverb in (*e*) and (*g*) comes after the auxiliary (or helping) verb.

(*a*) He (work) at present in an office.
(*b*) He (start) work last Christmas.
(*c*) It (be) now time for lunch. I (work) all the morning.
(*d*) He (open) the window and then I (shut) it. Now it is open again. Who (open) it?
(*e*) He is still a young man but he (already visit) many countries.
(*f*) When he was a diplomat, he (visit) many countries.
(*g*) The children (finish) their dinner an hour ago and their mother (now wash) up.
(*h*) I am sorry. I (forget) to bring my book to class.
(*i*) When I was at college I (speak) four languages but I (forget) all but a very few words.
(*j*) Where (hide you) since breakfast?
(*k*) He (comb) his hair and now he is ready.
(*l*) For the past hour I (try) to work but you (make) too much noise.

The Past Simple, Present Perfect Simple and Continuous Tenses: Passive Forms

PAST SIMPLE: I, he was taken
we, you, they were taken

PRESENT PERFECT (SIMPLE): I, we, you, they have been taken
he has been taken.

The Passive form of the Present Perfect Continuous is complicated and very seldom used.

The impersonal pronoun 'one' is less often used in English than in some other languages. Instead of making it the subject of a transitive verb, English usage often prefers to express the idea in the Passive Voice. 'French is spoken here' is the form of the shop-window notice,
NEVER 'One speaks French here'.

MAIN USES OF THE PASSIVE

1 To express an action that is *performed by a subject* that is *unknown or of so little importance* as to need no mention.

Other pronouns and generalised nouns such as 'people' can usually be omitted from the passive forms unless they are specially emphasised.

ACTIVE: They are counting the votes.
PASSIVE: The votes are being counted.
ACTIVE: We are making tea.
PASSIVE: Tea is being made.

2 In apparent contrast: to *emphasise the agent*
Penicillin was discovered *by Sir Alexander Fleming.*
The car was being driven *by a man of ninety.*

When the pronoun subject of the Active Voice is emphasised, therefore, it will still appear in the Passive form.

You caused the breakdown.
The breakdown was caused by you.

Notice: 'People say' becomes 'It is said.'

Rewrite the following sentences in the Passive Voice. Remember that it is the object of the active form which usually becomes the new subject. Use the same tense as the one given.

(*a*) They are making new arrangements.

(*b*) They keep lost property in a special office.

(*c*) People have praised the play highly.

(*d*) Our new friends have invited us home.

(*e*) Our Member of Parliament made a speech.

(*f*) People believe that they are soon introducing important changes. (There are two verbs here.)

Capital letters

The use of capital letters differs in English from their use in various other languages. It is important to learn carefully these differences.
The following have capital letters:

(*a*) Days of the week, months of the year and special holidays: Christmas, Easter, Whitsun, August Bank Holiday.

(*b*) Names denoting nationality and languages and adjectives referring to these: A Spaniard, Spanish.

(*c*) Names of places including rivers, seas and mountains.

Notice: a river *but* the River Thames
a station *but* Victoria Station
a street *but* Oxford Street

(*d*) Names of theatres, cinemas, hotels, restaurants, museums, ships, trains, aeroplanes: The Palace Theatre, The Grand Hotel, The Mayflower, The British Museum, The Blue Train.

(*e*) The more important words in the title of a book, play, film, chapter, composition: The Way of the World, The Uses of Steel.

Use capital letters where necessary in the following:

last saturday; in july; a dutch painter; the study of latin; the fortune theatre; the red lion hotel; the golden arrow (a train); the concorde (an aeroplane); guy fawkes day; a little guide to the english hills and mountains; a siamese cat.

Comparisons

(i) *Comparisons of Equality*

(*a*) His scientific discoveries have been *as important as* those of Sir Isaac Newton.
The doctor came *as soon as* he could.

(*b*) He is *not so clever* as I expected.

'as' may be used instead of 'so' in negative comparisons. It is rather more common in the negative comparison of adverbs:

He doesn't speak as fluently as he should.
He can't run as quickly as his brother.

(ii) *The Formation of Comparative and Superlative Forms*

(These rules are mainly for reference.)

'-er' and '-est' are added to the adjective (with certain spelling changes) when:

(*a*) The adjective consists of only one syllable, e.g. long, longer; big, biggest. *Notice:* far, farther, farthest (or further, furthest).

(*b*) A two-syllabled adjective ends in: -y (changed to -i), -le, -er (exceptions: eager, tender), and -ow, e.g. happier, humblest, cleverer, narrowest.

Remember the irregulars:

good	better	best	little	less	least
bad	worse	worst	much	more	most

'more' and 'most' precede the adjective when:

(*a*) The adjective consists of more than two syllables: more comfortable; most generous.

(*b*) The adjective is a participle: more tiring; most tired.

(*c*) The adjective ends in the suffix: -ful (harmful), -less (harmless), -ant (distant), -ent (silent), -est (honest), -al (central), -id (timid), -ish (foolish), -ive (active), -ous (jealous), -ward (awkward), -emn (solemn), -age (savage), -ed (sacred).

(*d*) The adjective has a negative prefix, e.g. kind, kinder; unkind, more unkind (though unkindest is found).

Both forms: commoner, commonest and more common, most common exist. Also: politer, politest and more polite, most polite.

A superlative adjective or adverb is preceded by 'the'

the last train   the most intelligent   the most fluently

'Most' is occasionally used with the meaning 'very' before a few adjectives. It is not then preceded by 'the'.

'a most interesting story'

ADVERBS *always have comparative and superlative forms with 'more' and 'most' respectively.*

Use the correct form of comparison in the following sentences. There may be some spelling changes:

(*a*) A bicycle is not (......fast......) a car.

(*b*) An elephant is (big......) a camel.

(*c*) To a European, Chinese is (......difficult......) French.

(*d*) A vegetable is not (......beautiful......) a flower, but it is (......useful).

(*e*) An apple tree is seldom (......tall......) an oak tree.

(*f*) She is much (pretty......) her sister, but is not (......attractive......) her charming mother.

(*g*) Try to write (......much......) possible.

(*h*) A boy usually runs (......quickly......) a girl.

(*i*) Do you agree that men are usually (......impatient......) women?

(*j*) Nothing is (bad......) than arriving late at a (......important) meeting in shoes that squeak as one walks to one's place.

(*k*) That is the (......extraordinary) idea I have ever heard.

Distinguishing between the Definite and Indefinite Articles

The name given to each of these forms suggests the general use, the one indefinite, possibly unknown, the other definite and known.

(*a*) *The indefinite article is used with a noun introduced for the first time and therefore unknown.* The next time the same noun appears, it is usually accompanied by the definite article:

A man I know lives in *an* old twelve-roomed house in *a* village. He has *a* son who occupies *a* modern three-roomed flat in *a* nearby town. *The* son pays more rent for *the* small flat in *the* town than *the* man pays for *the* large old house in *the* village.

(*b*) *The indefinite article suggests that the person or thing it accompanies is one of several; the definite article shows either that the person or thing is the only one of its kind or that a special known case is being referred to.*

He is studying at *a* college in Chingfield. (There are several there.)
He is studying at *the* college in Chingfield. (Either there is only one college in Chingfield or we already know which one is being spoken of.)
The house he has bought.
The Queen (of England), *The* National Gallery (of Great Britain), *The* Nile Delta, *The* Isle of Wight.

Notice: (i) *Doctor* used as a title has no definite article.
Dr. Green.

This also applies to such titles as Uncle and Aunt.

(ii) A proper noun qualified by an adjective has no definite article.
Little Susan.

Insert the definite or indefinite articles *where necessary* in the following sentences:

(*a*) He is......member of......City Council of Birmingham.

(*b*) He lives in......house at......seaside not far from......factory where he works.

(*c*) ......special announcement was made on......radio this morning. I don't know what it was.

(*d*) ......Prime Minister made......speech to......chief representatives of his party.

(*e*) Yesterday...... Queen opened...... hospital, received...... group of foreign delegates, and visited...... children's home, all in different places.

(*f*) ...... Doctor Smith works in...... hospital in London, near...... British Museum.

(*g*) During last night's fog, ... train was derailed and...... ship ran aground in...... Thames estuary.

(*h*) We have bought...... new refrigerator; now we must get rid of...... old one.

(*i*) Once upon a time, in...... far-distant country, there lived...... great king, who had...... lovely daughter.

(*j*) It was...... cold dark evening and...... warm fire and...... book seemed ...... best way of passing...... time.

Such a, such, so

(*a*) so is used with an *adjective* when no noun follows, or with an *adverb*.

I am *so tired.*
He speaks so quickly.

(*b*) SUCH A is used with a singular countable noun, with or without an adjective.

He is *such a liar.*
It is *such a long way.*

(*c*) SUCH is used with uncountable nouns and also plural nouns.

I have never before experienced *such cold weather.*
He told *such stupid lies.*

(*d*) so is used with nouns when these are preceded by 'much' 'little' 'many' or 'few'.

so little time *so many* people

The construction *so* (*adjective*) *a* (*noun*) is also used but less commonly.

It was so long a story that we nearly fell asleep.

Notice: 'noise' is not uncountable: such a noise.

Use one of the expressions in each of the following:

...... many friends; ...... courage; ...... wonderful garden; ...... dull journey; ...... few opportunities; ...... noise; ...... impossible events; ...... hard work; ...... little money; ...... unfriendly people.

Remember that these expressions serve to *emphasise* the quality of a noun, adjective or adverb. It sounds unnatural to say, 'In our school library are such dictionaries'. This should be: 'There are dictionaries of this kind (like this) in our school library.'

Prepositions

Complete the following sentences with suitable prepositions or particles. They are all based on examples from the first two passages for comprehension.

(*a*) At what time did you arrive...... Edinburgh?

(*b*) The bus which left the Market Place...... twenty-six minutes to nine ...... the Town Hall clock had only one passenger.

(*c*) He was absorbed...... the crossword puzzle...... the back page.

(*d*) The concert started...... eight o'clock...... Thursday.

(*e*) Before the hospital treatment he looked...... a skeleton, but a month later he said he felt...... an Olympic champion.

(*f*) Foreigners are always grumbling...... the English weather.

(*g*) He prefers to travel...... bus because he can wait...... it...... the terminus...... his home.

(*h*) We are sorry...... the misunderstanding.

(*i*) He moves...... the country very often...... business, but he has so many friends that he is usually able to stay...... a family he knows.

(*j*) His oil paintings are superior......his water-colours.

(*k*) People tend to be sorry...... him because he is lame, but he is interested ...... so many things and enjoys reading...... them so much that he is anything...... unhappy.

(*l*) He has been...... such a bad temper all day.

(*m*) Remember not to give...... the return half of your railway ticket.

(*n*) He was only...... average height but he had unusually broad shoulders.

3

Writing a composition

General suggestions about composition writing

BEFORE WRITING

1 *Understanding the Question*

READ the question you intend to answer VERY CAREFULLY. Make sure you understand exactly what you are being asked to write about. It is only too easy to read quickly and get the wrong idea. Many marks can be lost in an examination if you write on the wrong subject.

2 *Obeying the Instructions*

You may be asked to use a certain number of words or to write one, two or three paragraphs or perhaps to give a conversation between two or possibly three people. Other such instructions may be given. Read the question and *understand and obey the instructions.*

3 *Preparation and Planning*

(*a*) Before starting, spend several minutes thinking about what you are going to write and how to arrange it. This time is not wasted: in fact it may be time saved. You can write with far less hesitation and delay if you know already what you are going to say.

(*b*) Plan your work carefully. Your ideas must be in the right order, following each other logically. Even in a short composition, some paragraph arrangement may well be necessary. It is a very good idea to decide on the subjects of your paragraphs before you begin writing, to make some kind of PLAN.

WHEN WRITING

1 *Simple Ideas*

You are a student whose knowledge of English is growing but is still not wide and you have to put ideas on paper in this language. Possibly you have read, thought and studied a great deal in your own language and can use that language to express interesting ideas or a good technical or commercial knowledge, but you still have not enough English to deal with these ideas as you would like to.

As a result you must either write only about the easier facts and less complicated ideas or simplify what you have to say so that it can be written correctly.

2 *Simplicity of Vocabulary, Sentence Construction and Expression*

In all kinds of written work it is very important indeed to think in English and not to translate from your own language. Translation from your own language encourages mistakes and also unnatural English.

MISTAKES. Every language is different in many ways from all other languages. When you translate, it is very easy to forget these differences. A French student translating into English may easily forget the differences in the use of the present perfect tense and a German may introduce examples of German word order. If either is actually working on a translation, this has all his attention and he is prepared for these differences. But if he is trying to express his own ideas, he easily forgets these differences and may make many bad mistakes. And the ideas which come to him in his own language may be too difficult for him to express in the English he knows.

NATURALNESS. Each language has its own atmosphere which it is difficult to express in another language. So ideas and expressions which seem natural and right in one language may seem unnatural and unsuitable in another, even when they are not grammatically wrong. By using the English he is already familiar with and avoiding translation, the student is far more likely to write in a natural English way.

Remember to write at first very simply indeed. Keep sentences short and use word groups you have learned already, forms which you know are natural everyday English expressions.

Here is an example of the very simple English you will start with.

In about 80 words describe your journey to school or work each day.

My office is in a suburb of Paris, about five kilometres from the centre. I leave home just before half-past seven in the morning. I walk to the nearest bus stop. Usually I wait there for two or three minutes. When I get off the bus, I have to walk for about five minutes. I go into the building and go by lift to the fourth floor where my office is. I arrive just before eight o'clock.

(77 words)

As you have more practice in writing, and learn more constructions and expressions, your way of writing will improve and you will be able to express many more ideas correctly and clearly. But you are still thinking only in English.

3 *Remember to write in paragraphs, each about one subject—as you have already planned*

AFTER WRITING

1 *Reading Through*

Read very carefully through what you have written, sentence by sentence. Look for mistakes of all kinds, especially those connected with the following:

(*a*) AGREEMENT OF SUBJECT AND VERB

(*b*) VERB TENSES

(*c*) THE ARTICLES 'THE' AND 'A'

(*d*) GRAMMATICAL AND SENTENCE CONSTRUCTIONS

(*e*) WORD ORDER

(*f*) COMPLETE SENTENCES

(*g*) PUNCTUATION—ESPECIALLY THE CORRECT DIVISION OF SENTENCES

When you have to make changes, cross out and write again rather than cause confusion by altering on the word itself.

2 *Learning from Corrections*

Studying the corrections written on a piece of work by your teacher is one of the most useful parts of language learning. After all, the things corrected are either those you still have to learn or those you are still so unsure of that you can be careless when using them. Copy out correctly each group of words where there is a mistake and try not to make the same mistake again.

USING A DICTIONARY

There is nothing against the occasional use of a dictionary giving meanings in your own language. The word that has to be discovered is often remembered best. But a dictionary should be used only under certain conditions.

(*a*) Use a dictionary only to find the *single word* you are not sure of. The whole phrase should already be clear in your mind in the English you already know but there may be just one word you have to look up.

As he ran towards the bus, he (put his foot down badly=stumbled) and nearly fell.

(*b*) When using a dictionary for this purpose, make sure that it is one large enough to contain all the possible meanings of the word, if possible together with some examples of how to use the word with each of these meanings. Check that you have chosen the right word by looking up its meaning at the other end in your own language—or in an English dictionary.

In nearly all examinations the use of a dictionary is forbidden.

A POCKET DICTIONARY is useful out of doors in England itself. As you walk or travel around, you can see many new words. Look them up and write them down in a small notebook.

THE MOST USEFUL DICTIONARY you can have is an ENGLISH ONE INTENDED FOR FOREIGN STUDENTS. This should show not only the meanings of a word but also examples of how to use it and constructions of which it forms part.

THE CONVENTIONS OF WRITTEN ENGLISH

These mainly concern the differences between the spoken and the written forms of the language. Here are a few to remember. They do not apply when you are writing actual conversation or when you want to give the impression of speaking to the reader.

(*a*) *The various verbal abbreviations such* as: 'n't' for 'not', ''s' for 'is' or 'has', ''ve' for 'have', ''ll' for 'will' or 'shall', ''d' for would' or 'should' *are not used in formal written English.*

(*b*) Numbers except in dates are usually written as words.

(*c*) *Avoid colloquial English and slang.* Avoid also the over-used words 'nice' and 'lovely'—try to find a more exact adjective. The colloquial 'awfully', 'terribly' and similar forms should be used only in conversation.

(*d*) *Abbreviations* like 'etc.' and 'e.g.' *are not used* in formal written English.

> The main industries in my town are light engineering, furniture-making, sugar-refining, etc.

can be written:

> The main industries in my town include light engineering, furniture-making and sugar-refining.

Suggestions for practice

(*a*) Write an account of a morning when everything went wrong. Use between 120 and 180 words.

SUGGESTIONS: Decide first how the morning was spent. Perhaps you were working somewhere.
So the story divides itself into these three parts, each of them a paragraph:

(1) Before leaving home
(2) Travelling to work
(3) At work.

Before you begin to write, make a list of some misfortunes you can describe in the English you know. Perhaps you woke up with a headache, had to wash in icy cold water and broke a plate while having breakfast.

Each paragraph will have an average length of 50 words, about three or four sentences. Remember not to write too much—or too little.

(*b*) Someone stops you one day and says he/she is an old school friend whom you have not seen for ten years. After a time you remember him/her, but your old friend has changed very much. Describe how and when you met and how your friend has changed. Use between 120 and 180 words.

The paragraph division is obvious here:

(1) The meeting
(2) A description of your friend in earlier days
(3) Your friend now

The description will probably include appearance, manner of dressing, personality and behaviour. You may want to suggest what has caused these changes apart from the passing of time.

4

Passage for comprehension

An Irish wedding

Have you ever been to an Irish wedding? I have just returned from one. It is a quarter to five in the morning; the sun has already climbed above the horizon; the birds are busy celebrating the new day and have eagerly been in search of food. But some of the guests have not yet left. They are still 5 prolonging the night: dancing, singing, gossiping, postponing the unfortunate necessity of undertaking a day's work in the fields after a sleepless night.

Throughout most of her life, Bridget Mary, the bride, has been living in the small whitewashed thatched cottage I have just left. Twelve children have been brought up there but only two are still living at home. The eldest 10 son, heir to the small farm, is helping his father with the farm work, (they employ no farm labourers); the youngest daughter is still at school. Two years ago, Bridget Mary went to England to take up domestic work in a hospital and it was while she was living there that she met her future husband, Terry. He himself is an Irishman who used to live in Dublin and now has a 15 well-paid job in a light engineering works in England. They got engaged and started saving. Now they are thinking of buying a small semi-detached house near Terry's factory.

The wedding ceremony was performed in the church in the nearest town at half-past eight yesterday morning. Another couple were being married 20 at the same time. Nobody worried about the cost of the celebrations: four luxurious cars brought bride, bridegroom, family and friends home, and forty people were crowded into the tiled kitchen and the tiny living-room, hung with framed school certificates and religious pictures. An enormous meal was eaten; the wedding cake was cut and toasts were drunk in whisky 25 or sherry. And while the remains of the feast were being cleared away and the rooms swept, the four cars set out again, taking the married couple and relations for a drive round the countryside.

The evening party was to have started at ten o'clock, but by nine o'clock many of the guests were already arriving. A few of the nearer male relatives 30 were looking rather awkward in evening suits with smart bow ties, and the pleasant, unsophisticated countrywomen appeared a little self-conscious in their Sunday best. By the time I arrived at eleven o'clock, the party was in full swing. Two men squeezing accordions provided the music: the old Irish tunes that have been played at weddings for many years. Half the people in 35 the room were dancing the square dances and reels which have been enjoyed even longer. Drinks were being handed round. A score of men stood in the narrow dark hall, leaning against the wall, drinking beer from bottles and speculating about crops, cattle and the current political situation. And whenever the dancing stopped, somebody would start singing one of the sentimental, treasured Irish songs: the exile longing for his home, the grief- 40 stricken lover mourning his fate. Sometimes we all joined in the chorus, sadly and solemnly, before getting up to dance again.

Irish weddings are almost certain to have been celebrated in this way for generations. The very old and the teen-agers, the middle-aged couples who take time off from their families, all meet together to keep up the old tradi- 45 tions and enjoy themselves as their ancestors did. I have been to wedding receptions where champagne has been served to the accompaniment of soft unnoticed orchestral music; I have listened to carefully-prepared speeches and eyed a little enviously the model gowns of women far more elegant than I could ever hope to be. I have been impressed, and a little bored. I have just 50 been sitting up all night in a small, uncomfortable Irish cottage and I have been enjoying every moment of it.

Notes on the passage

Vocabulary

lines

Title a *wedding* is the ceremony a *marriage* is the life partnership.

3 *horizon* (*N*) *horizontal* (*Adj*)—OPP. *vertical*
a *precipice*—a very steep slope—is almost *perpendicular.*

3 *eagerly* OPP. *reluctantly* He was eager / anxious to help. He got up reluctantly.

4 a person, a car or a place can be *searched* by the police to find stolen goods. The police are *looking for, searching for, seeking* the stolen thing. *At ten o'clock they were still in search of somewhere to spend the night.*

5 *prolong* time (one's visit or stay) (*N* prolongation). *extend* a road or building (*N* extension. A passport or working permit is also extended. *lengthen* a dress.

5 *gossip* (*V*) chat about unimportant things. gossip (*Unc N*) talk about other people's affairs. a gossip (*C N*) a person who does this.

5 *postpone* or put off (more colloquial) an arrangement till a later date. *N* postponement
delay (*N* and *V*) = cause to happen later or be late: *fog delayed the train. cancel* (*N* cancellation) = not allow something to happen. *cancel a meeting because nobody is interested.*

6 *undertake* (*N* undertaking) (*a*) take on a job: *a firm undertakes the production of a new type of lorry* (*b*) promise: *I undertake to return all the books I borrow from the library.*
An undertaker makes all the arrangements for funerals.

7 The *bride, bridegroom, best man* (who assists the bridegroom) and the *bridesmaids* all take part in a formal wedding.

10 An *heir* or *heiress* will *inherit* his/her parents' property. This will be his/her *inheritance*.
An *heirloom* is something valuable handed down from one generation to the next.

10 *work* (*Unc N*) *a job* (*C N*) *do* housework, homework (normally NO PLURAL) What is your job? What work do you enjoy doing? This is *a difficult job*.
works with special meanings
(*a*) gasworks, waterworks, the works (the factory)
(*b*) the works of a clock, watch or machine: 'something wrong with the works'
(*c*) public works (State building operations), road works
(*d*) good works, works of charity
(*e*) the works of Shakespeare, of Beethoven. 'Hamlet' is a work of Shakespeare.
labour—hard, heavy work (a labourer working on the roads).
toil—hard work.
drudgery (a drudge)—hard work that is unpleasant and earns little money.

12 *domestic work*—cleaning and cooking. *cooks*, *maids* and *butlers* are in domestic service. a *daily woman* comes in for a few hours daily or weekly to help the housewife.

15 *be/get engaged* (*to*); *be married* (*to*)/get married (to)/marry someone; *get a divorce* they are now divorced but NOT: they divorced.

16 *save* money/someone's life/time *savings* are money saved.
spare (*V*)—have enough to give away some: *I have no bread. Can you spare me some?* spare (*Adj*) extra: spare time, a spare room, tyre.

18 a *ceremony* (*C N*)—wedding, opening of a new building—is *performed*. ceremony (*Unc*) *The President was greeted with great ceremony.* (ceremonial).
A performance of a play. Also: *the actor* (*sportsman*) *gave a fine performance.*

18 *nearest next* Which? my—relatives; the—lesson; the—house after the Post Office; the—seaside place to London; we must stop at the—filling station along this road; where is the—filling station to this house? he ran to the—telephone to call the fire brigade.

19 yesterday morning/afternoon/evening last night; this morning/afternoon/evening to-night; to-morrow morning/afternoon/evening/night. NOT: to-day in the afternoon.

23 *enormous* immense huge gigantic, tremendous have almost the same meaning. *mighty* suggests powerful.

24 a *toast* (*C N*) to someone's good health or fortune toast (*Unc N*) grilled bread.

24 *drunk* he was drunk but: a *drunken* man; a *drunkard* is habitually drunk.
He has aged/learned a lot (*V*). (*Adj*) agèd, learnèd, blessèd, nakèd, sacrèd.

25 The *remains* of the meal were thrown away. The *rest* of the meal was now served.
Three quarters of the material was used to make a dress, the *remainder* an apron.
We visited the castle *ruins*.

25 a *feast*—a very fine meal a *banquet*—a ceremonial meal.
a *festival*—a special celebration, possibly with the performance of plays and music e.g. the Edinburgh Festival, a harvest festival.

26 *sweep* with a broom. *dust* with a duster. a sweep—a man who cleans chimneys

26 go/take someone for a walk, drive, picnic.
drive a car, lorry/bus. ride a horse, bicycle, motor-cycle—with one's legs over it.

30 *awkward* and *clumsy:* A clumsy person tends to knock things down and bump into things.
An awkward person cannot fit easily into his social surroundings. Boys and girls in their early teens can be awkward in company because they are unsure of themselves.
Awkward can also be used in these ways: A bicycle is an awkward thing to carry up steps. Getting rid of a talkative neighbour when one is in a hurry can be awkward.

30 a *bow* [bou] is (*a*) a weapon used with an arrow (*b*) a special knot in a ribbon used in the hair or for a tie.
A man [bauz] or leans forward to show respect. A woman curtseys [kə́ːtsiz].

31 The term *peasant* may refer to some Irish *country people* but not to modern English ones who are spoken of as 'farmers', 'small farmers' or, when only a little land for vegetables, chickens and possibly other livestock is owned, 'smallholders'.

31 *self-conscious* uncomfortably aware of oneself in company;
self-assured or *self-confident*—sure of oneself; *self-centred*—interested only in oneself; *selfish*—wanting everything for oneself; *self-controlled*—keeping one's emotions in check.

33 *squeeze* press in from either side.
squash—force the liquid out of something or damage by pressure. Lemon or orange squash are names of soft drinks.

36 a *score* = 20 a *dozen* = 12 a *gross* = 144

38 *speculate* (*N* speculation) (*a*) try to decide what the future will be like (*b*) invest money in a risky way in an attempt to make a big profit.

38 *crops* the produce of the farmer's work in his fields or orchards.
crop up—A subject which comes into a discussion by chance 'crops up'.

38 *cattle* bulls, cows, oxen (working animals), bullocks (raised for meat) and calves.
poultry—chickens, ducks, geese and turkeys.

40 *exile* (*N* and *V*): an exile has been turned out of his home country. an *emigrant* (*V* emigrate) goes of his own accord.
an *immigrant* (*V* immigrate) comes into a country to live.
a *migrant* (*N* and *Adj*) (*V* migrate) moves about: *migrant birds.*

40 a *grief-stricken* mother; a *panic-stricken* crowd; a *conscience-stricken* murderer.

41 *mourning* can be the feeling of sorrow for loss by death or the clothes worn to show grief.

41 *fate=destiny.* BUT: a fatal accident. *He at last reached his destination.*

41 The *choir* sang the verses of the hymn and the congregation joined in the *choruses.*

42 Do not mix *get up* (especially from bed) and *stand up.*

45 get *time off* from work; have time off or take time off.

47 *reception:* the President's reception at the airport; a reception committee; a wedding reception; the play had a hostile reception. A *receptionist* may work for a doctor, dentist or in a hotel.

47 *accompaniment* There can also be a piano accompaniment played by an accompanist.

49 *envy* of someone who has something you want but cannot have.
jealousy of someone who seems to be taking someone's affection from you.

49 a *model* gown—only one dress of this type exists.
a model of a ship—a small replica. a model student—a perfect one.

50 *bored* having lost interest. *annoyed*—a little angry.

51 *sit up* not go to bed. *wait up* for someone—not go to bed before he comes.

Phrasal verbs

TAKE *take up* a new hobby, interest, type of work; *take in* (*a*) make a garment smaller; (*b*) deceive; *take away* (*a*) remove, (*b*) subtract; *take off* (*a*) remove a garment (*b*) (for an aeroplane) leave the ground; (*c*) imitate; *take to* like (usually a person); *take down* (*a*) write, often from dictation; (*b*) remove from a wall; *take over* start doing another person's job for him. Which? (i).........your shoes; (ii) my dog has.........you; (iii) she has.........singing; (iv).........one's teacher to make people laugh; (v).........these old newspapers; (vi) can you.........my job for the next hour?; (vii).........this letter in shorthand please; (viii) ....three.........from ten; (ix) don't be.........on the 1st April.

CLEAR *clear away* dishes after a meal (clear the table); the weather *clears up*; *clear up* a mystery; *clear up* an untidy room.

KEEP *keep up* old traditions; *keep away* from a person with a cold; *keep back* crowds; *keep in* a lazy child who must stay longer at school; *keep* (and *keep on*) continue; *keep* bad news *from* someone; *keep down* prices; *keep up* efforts (continue to try); *keep out* not allow to go in.

Pronunciation

SPECIAL DIFFICULTIES: certificate [sətífikɪt]; chorus [kɔ́ːrəs]; choir [kwáɪə]; champagne [ʃæmpéɪn] (English pronunciation); awkward [ɔ́ːkwəd].

STRESS CHANGES: horízon [həráɪzn]; horizóntal [hɔrɪzɔ́ntl]; céremony [sérəmənɪ]; ceremónial [serəmóunɪəl]; lúxury [lʌ́kʃərɪ]; luxúrious [lʌksjúəriəs]; sophísticated [səfístɪkeɪtɪd]; sophisticátion [səfɪstɪkéɪʃn]; órchestra [ɔ́ːkɪstrə]; orchéstral [ɔ́ːkéstrəl]; pólitics [pɔ́lɪtɪks]; polítical [pəlitɪkəl].

ə (as in *ə*go): labourers [léɪbərəz]; treasured [tréʒəd]; traditions [trədíʃənz]; accompaniment [əkʌ́mpənɪmənt]; enviously [énvɪəslɪ].

ɪ (as in c*ɪ*t*y*): kitchen [kítʃɪn]; religious [rɪlíʤəs].

ju (as in m*u*sic): situation [sitjuéɪʃən].

SILENT LETTERS: heir [ɛə]; heiress [ɛ́ərəs] or [ɛ́ərɪs].

ŋg (as in fi*ng*er): younger [jʌ́ŋgə]; youngest [jʌ́ngɪst].

OTHERS: search [səːtʃ]; throughout [θruːáut]; thatched [θætʃt]; couple [kʌpl]; mourning [mɔ́ːnɪŋ]; discreet [dískriːt]; eyed [aɪd]; quarter [kwɔ́ːtə]; eagerly [iːgəlɪ]; necessity [nɪsésɪtɪ]; spared [spɛəd].

Special grammatical and structural points

(i) he *went* to Scotland last week (and is probably still there) he *has been* to Scotland (he has visited Scotland at some time).

(ii) *one ones*

These Pronouns can replace a Countable Noun and so avoid repetition.

He has a large car and I have *a small one.*

Whose is this umbrella? Oh, it's *the one* I lost.

He likes the chocolates with hard centres but she prefers *the ones* with the soft centres.

The ones I like are of course the expensive *ones.*

When an adjective of colour, a comparative or a superlative is used, 'one' 'ones' can often be omitted.

He has a red car and I have a green. He has the larger and I the smaller.

(iii) An auxiliary (helping) verb can sometimes avoid the repetition of a verb.

She speaks with a French accent in the same way as her mother does.

People still celebrate Christmas as their grandparents did.

(iv) Notice this construction:

It was while she was living there *that* she met Terry.

Is it where you are born *that* decides your nationality?

It is how you behave in difficulties *that* shows what you are really like.

(v) He was born twenty years *ago.* NOT: for twenty years. BE CAREFUL!

(vi) *Positions of the body* are indicated by the *present participle* NOT the past participle, as in some languages: standing on a chair; sitting in a deck chair; leaning against a wall; kneeling in church; crouching, ready to spring.

(vii) 'he enjoyed the party' but NOT: he enjoyed at the party. *enjoy* must have an object: he *enjoyed himself* at the party.

(viii) VERBAL CONSTRUCTIONS

(*a*) *Infinitive:* hope to be
went to England to take up (Purpose)

(*b*) *Gerund:* used as *nouns*—names of actions: dancing, singing, gossiping.
after a preposition: before getting, the necessity of undertaking
two adjectives are followed by a gerund: *busy, worth* busy celebrating; is it worth going to town now?
start saving 'start to save' is also possible

(*c*) *Meaning Change:* they *are thinking of buying:* they have this idea in mind and may well carry it out.
they *think there will* soon *be* a water shortage: they think this will happen.

Prepositions

(*a*) *at* school (learning), at church (worshipping), in prison (as a prisoner), at the theatre (seeing a play), at the cinema (seeing a film), in hospital (as a patient).
BUT: in the school, in the church, in the prison, in the theatre, in the cinema, in the hospital: visiting the building for some purpose.

(*b*) *over* suggests movement—birds fly over the town
above suggests position: the sun is now above the horizon.
'over' is however often also used for position: the light over the table.
'above' usually suggests a contrast: above and not below, higher than.

(*c*) *in* the fields (remember: *in* the country); work in a factory; in search of; join in the dancing (BUT: join a club); toasts were drunk in whisky.

(*d*) *at* the same time.

(*e*) take people *for* a drive/a walk; long for his home

(*f*) return *from* school; drink beer from (out of) a bottle

(*g*) the necessity *of* undertaking (*h*) hung *with* pictures (*i*) heir *to*

(*j*) *throughout* her life (*k*) lean *against* a wall.

Expressions to learn and introduce into written work

(*a*) *throughout* (all through) most of her life/the night/his speech.........

(*b*) *it was* while she was living there *that*......... (see B3(iv) page 53)

(*c*) *perform* a ceremony (*d*) forty people *were crowded into* the kitchen

(*e*) the cars *set out* again (for.........) (*f*) appeared a little self-conscious

(*g*) in their Sunday best (*h*) by the time I arrived......

(*i*) drinks were being *handed round* (*j*) we all joined *in* the chorus
(*k*) *take time off* from (*l*) to the accompaniment of
(*m*) carefully-prepared speeches (*n*) *sit up* all night.

Multiple choice questions

Here are a number of questions or unfinished statements about the passage, each with four suggested ways of answering or finishing it. You must choose the way you consider the most suitable. Write in each case the bracketed number of the question or statement followed by the letters **A, B, C, D**, and then cross through the letter of the answer you choose. Give one answer only to each question. Read the passage right through again before choosing your answers.

1 What makes it clear that this is a country wedding?
A people are up so early **B** birds are singing **C** the people's occupations **D** the bride is one of a large family

2 No farm labourers are employed because
A they are not needed **B** the family is too poor **C** there are none available **D** the children can help

3 The young couple will not live at the farm after their marriage because
A there is no room for them **B** they have a house in England **C** they are both employed elsewhere **D** it is the bride's brother who will inherit the farm

4 Why were the guests taken for a ride round the countryside?
A to give them an opportunity of seeing the surroundings **B** to get them out of the way **C** to enable the neighbours to see the married couple **D** as a way of passing the time

5 The most likely reason for the men's awkwardness was
A they were unaccustomed to wearing clothes of this kind **B** the suits did not fit well **C** they were the only ones who were dressed up **D** they had obviously turned up too early

6 The women appeared slightly
A unsure of themselves **B** secretly pleased with themselves **C** uncomfortably aware of the impression they were making **D** aware of their own unusual importance

7 Which word best describes the atmosphere at the party?
A mournful **B** old-fashioned **C** formal **D** cheerful

8 What form did the conversation in the hall mainly take?
A a discussion of possibilities **B** an argument **C** advice being exchanged **D** a review of the situation

9 Which of these groups of people is not often seen at an Irish wedding?
A fathers and mothers **B** grandparents **C** youngsters **D** young working people

10 In which of these ways are the two types of wedding party described the same?
A the music B the drinks C the women guests D the idea of celebrating something

11 Why is the writer bored at some wedding receptions?
A the women look more elegant than she could B the music is not lively enough C the atmosphere lacks warmth D there are carefully-prepared speeches.

Reading comprehension

In this exercise you must choose the word or phrase which best completes each sentence. Write first the number of each sentence followed by the letters **A, B, C, D, E**, and then cross through the letter of the correct answer in each case.

1 The police must now .... the escaped convict in the surrounding counties.
A search **B** look after **C** look for **D** investigate
E be in search of

2 Your grandfather is rather tired so do not .... your visit.
A put on **B** prolong **C** lengthen **D** delay
E shorten

3 As we can wait no longer for the delivery of your order, we have to .... it.
A postpone **B** refuse **C** delay **D** cancel
E return

4 He has recently got an interesting .... in a textile factory.
A job **B** employment **C** work **D** occupation
E opportunity

5 With its expensive furniture and carefully-chosen colour scheme the room looked quite ....
A luxurious **B** luxury **C** convenient **D** homely
E luxuriant

6 Only thoroughly unpleasant people leave the .... of their picnics to spoil the appearance of the countryside.
A remains **B** remainder **C** rest **D** remnants
E waste

7 She studies many magazines and books about fashion, entertaining and correct social behaviour as she wants to appear ....
A fashionable **B** sophisticated **C** elegant **D** artificial
E polished

8 Many of the earliest .... into the United States established large plantations.
A exiles **B** immigrants **C** migrants **D** emigrants
E entrants

9 The judge said that he was .... by the high standards of performance by the riders.
A excited B impressed C interested D imposed
E touched

10 The sky looks lighter. I think the weather is ....
A clearing away B clearing C becoming clearer
D bettering E clearing up

11 If I had more time, I should .... golf as a hobby.
A take to B take on C take over D take up
E take in

12 You can .... your shorthand ability by taking notes in shorthand during lectures.
A keep on B keep in C keep up D keep back
E keep down

Use of English

(ii) 1 The five sentences below are the answers to five questions that could be asked about the Reading Passage. The first one or two words of each question are given to assist you.

(i) She went to England two years ago. (How)
(ii) No. Another couple were being married at the same time. (Were they)
(iii) Four luxurious cars brought them home. (How)
(iv) They were in their Sunday best. (What)
(v) Two men squeezing accordions provided it. (How)

2 Fill each of the numbered blanks in the passage with a suitable word.
When I at last .... (1) the town, I felt .... (2) tired to go in .... (3) of a room at once so I went into the .... (4) restaurant to where I had parked my car and sat down .... (5) a table. A waitress was clearing .... (6) the .... (7) of a meal which must have .... (8) eaten by at .... (9) forty people. She gave me a menu which I examined for a minute and I then .... (10) from her fried chicken and salad and a glass of wine. The waitress .... (11) the wine at once but I had to wait a long time .... (12) the .... (13) of the meal. When it came, there was so much on the plate .... (14) it must have .... (15) a whole bird. I .... (16) a little first and it was .... (17) delicious that I ate all of it. I was now neither hungry .... (18) thirsty and as a .... (19) of fact, I was no .... (20) tired .... (21).

3 Finish each of the following sentences in such a way that it means exactly the same as the sentence printed before it.

Example: The mountain roads are impassable because of heavy snow.
Heavy...

Answer: Heavy snow has made the mountain roads impassable.

He is back from York after three days there.
(i) He has been ....

He wrote that book during his holiday in Wales.
(ii) It was while ....

Christopher and his father can walk equally long distances.
(iii) Christopher can ....

It started raining last Friday and has not yet stopped.
(iv) It has ....

The market is less crowded than usual today.
(v) The market is not ....

He cannot speak because he is so angry.
(vi) He is too ....

He came home in a taxi.
(vii) A taxi ....

Jane was standing outside a shop when I saw her.
(viii) I saw ....

Composition and summarising

Narrative

A narrative composition can be one of two kinds.

The first is an exact account of what happened: a report of some national or local event appearing in a newspaper, the facts of a crime given in a police court, the details of an accident or some similar record. In this kind of account it is important to state all the facts quite correctly and in the most suitable order—usually the order in which they happened. But only these facts are given and unnecessary description and imaginative impressions have no place.

The second is a story. The intention is to interest the reader, to make him want to go on reading. The writer chooses the details which help to create the impression he wants to give, builds up interest to an important moment and includes some description to make the story more vivid.

Here is an example of this second kind of narrative: While you were waiting for a train on a station platform, something very unusual happened. Relate what it was in 120–180 words.

PLAN

1 The background—miserable people on the platform.
2 The performance.
3 The effect.

It was just after five and the platform was already half filled with people on their way home from work. Most of them looked miserable or perhaps they were just tired. Some were reading newspapers. A few were standing in groups but nobody seemed to be talking. The train was due in five minutes.

Suddenly there was a movement. Two men took off their overcoats and handed them to two women standing near. Then they asked people to move back, and spread newspapers on the ground. 'Watch, everybody,' shouted one, and he jumped straight on to the other's shoulders. A wonderful acrobatic display followed: jumping, balancing, swinging, tumbling. People crowded round watching them: others who could not see properly started talking to strangers, asking what was happening and wondering why.

Immediately they heard the train approaching, the men picked up the newspapers and put on their overcoats. 'Well,' said one, 'I hope you all feel a bit more cheerful now. Life isn't all that bad, you know.' And the people got into the train actually smiling. 176 *words*

SUBJECTS FOR PRACTICE

A *Exact Accounts*—in 120–180 words

1 You have had some kind of accident in your home. Relate what you were doing at the time, what happened and the results.

2 You have to prepare an account of any one of the following incidents for a radio news bulletin. Choose one of the subjects and write the account.

(*a*) A famous person has made an official visit to your town
(*b*) An important local building has been damaged by fire.
(*c*) A crowd of people have marched to the Town Hall to protest about some unsatisfactory thing in the town.

3 As he passes a shop, Police Constable Wright sees a light moving inside. He goes to investigate. Write the constable's report of the whole incident.

4 There is a statue of a well-known person in a town market-place. Write a passage for the town guide-book explaining who he is and how he became famous.

B *Stories*—in 120–180 words

5 How I missed the train.

6 You were taking a neighbour's dog for a walk on a lead. Suddenly he saw another dog and pulled so sharply that he escaped. Tell the story of what happened until you caught him.

7 You were walking down an empty street very late at night when you met an elephant. Relate what happened.

8 A dream in which you found yourself doing something impossible.

A report of Bridget Mary's wedding appears in the local paper, which is published in Clonlarny, where she was married (in St. Patrick's Church). The bridegroom's surname is O'Brendan and hers is Mulvany. The report includes references to the ceremony, the wedding breakfast, the drive and the evening party, but will clearly not mention the smallness of the cottage, the awkwardness or self-consciousness of the guests or the writer's feelings or impressions. Here is part of the report about the evening party:

> The evening party, which was held in the bride's home, was attended by relatives and many local people. Music was provided by two accordionists; there were many songs from the guests themselves and plenty of traditional dancing. (37 *words*)

Complete the report in not more than 130 words, *including only material which is in the passage or mentioned above* and using only those details which a quiet local paper, read by most of the guests, would publish.

Spoken English

Other short answers

Most of the verbs in the following answers would be followed by a verb in the infinitive, but this verb is already clear from the question, so is not repeated.

Study carefully these examples:

(*a*) Are you taking your exam next year?

- I'd like to.
- I want to.
- I hope to. If I can manage to. (it)
- I intend to. If I'm able to.
- I ought to. If I'm allowed to.

(*b*) May I use this dictionary of yours?

Yes, I've already {recommended / advised / told} you to.

(*c*) Does he actually work twelve hours a day?

- He seems to.
- He appears to. He has to.
- He tries to. He needs to.
- He likes to. He pretends to.
- No, he refuses to.

(*d*) Is he being helpful to you? He's trying to be.

(*e*) So you're buying a car after all. Oh, well, my wife persuaded me to.

Other possibilities

(*f*) Is it going to be warm tomorrow?

- I hope so. I think (believe) so.
- I hope not. I don't think (believe) so.

(*g*) Must we pay to go in? {I suppose so. / I don't suppose so.}

(*h*) He often ignores what you say because he is slightly deaf. Oh, I see.

(*i*) You really must try to control your temper. Yes, I know.

Exercise:

Answer these remarks and questions, *each in a different way*, using the forms suggested above.

1 Are you going skiing next winter?

2 Is Douglas buying a sports car?
3 Can you come to lunch next Saturday?
4 May I come to your lectures?
5 Is the sea warm enough for swimming?
6 Does she really clean her husband's shoes?
7 There are no trains because there's a strike.
8 Is your young sister going alone to England next year?
9 Must we give them a wedding present?
10 Will we have to pay duty on our new watches?
11 Does he really understand Anglo-Saxon poetry?
12 Could you help me with this suitcase, please?

(*a*) **Giving, accepting and refusing invitations**

(i) On the telephone: Is it Judy, there? Oh, hallo Judy. How are you? I do hope you're free next Saturday. We're giving a party to celebrate our second wedding anniversary. Cheese and wine and maybe some dancing to records. All quite informal, so wear what you like. You will be able to come, won't you. (We should be so pleased if you can come. We should so like you to come.)

(ii) I'd love to come. What time would you like me to turn up?

(iii) Oh, what a pity! I'd love to have come, but it's my father's birthday on Saturday and he'd be terribly disappointed if I didn't spend the week-end at home. I *am* sorry.

(*b*) **Saying Goodbye**

A Oh, I hadn't realised how late it was. I'm afraid I'll have to be going.

B Oh, not yet. I'm just going to make some coffee.

A I'm sorry, but I must, though I'd really love to stay. I've got to be up by six tomorrow morning, unfortunately. Thank you for a wonderful party.

Conversation at a party

A and **B**, who are strangers to one another, get into conversation.

B Hallo. I'm Brian Chester. Let me get you some more wine.

A Not at the moment, thank you. I'm André Laporte. Is London your home?

B No, I come from Wells, in the West Country. You speak English extremely well. Are you French?

A No, Belgian. My mother's English, though. Have you ever been to Belgium?

B Many times. I have to travel to Brussels for my firm. I'm a sales representative. How long have you been in England?

A Since September. I'm working in a hotel as part of my hotel management training. I've been a waiter, assistant cook, receptionist, secretary:

what else? I can hardly remember. Later I'll be taking a course in hotel management.

B So you haven't had time to see much outside London.

A Oh, I've spent two or three holidays in England with my mother's relations who live in the Midlands so I've got to know Oxford and Cambridge, Stratford and various other places fairly well.

B Where's your home in Belgium?

A Originally in Liège, though we recently moved to Antwerp. My father has taken over a hotel there not far from the town centre. I hardly know anything about the town yet as I was helping a lot in the hotel before I came to England.

B I'm in Antwerp occasionally for my firm. Maybe I'll try your hotel next time I'm there, if you can give me the name.

A Here's a card. And do tell my father you've met me. Tell him also that I'm behaving myself. No time not to, really.

Giving your own opinions and ideas

Give your own ideas about any of these subjects. Remember to think a little before you speak so as to avoid any unnecessary mistakes. Continue to express yourself in quite simple English.

(*a*) What kinds of rings do engaged and married women in your country have, and where do they wear them?

(*b*) What do you think is the ideal length of time for an engagement?

(*c*) Which is better: an expensive wedding with many guests or a quiet one?

(*d*) Do you consider it a good idea for poor people to spend a lot of money on a wedding?

(*e*) Do you prefer the old dances of your country or modern dancing? Why?

(*f*) If a young couple had very little money and no home of their own but very much wanted to get married, would you advise them to do so or not?

(*g*) Do you think a girl should have a dowry (money and household goods) provided by her parents as a condition of getting married? Why or why not?

(*h*) Do you prefer conventional well-organised parties or unconventional ones in which everyone takes an active part? Why?

General guidance and practice

The Past Continuous Tense

Examples from the reading piece:

Active Voice: She was living.
They were arriving.

Passive Voice: Another couple were being married.
Things were being cleared.

The name of this tense describes its general uses which are:

(i) *to indicate the longer of two actions, the action during which something else occurred:*

I was crossing the road, when the traffic lights changed.
The ghost appeared as the clock was striking twelve.

(ii) *to indicate two actions occurring at the same time and covering a period of time:*

I was trying to do some translation while he was watching television.

(iii) *to emphasise that an action covered a period of time:*

All day yesterday I was working in the garden.

(iv) Just as the Present Continuous can express an action extending through the point 'now', 'at this time', so *the Past Continuous can express an action extending through a definite point 'then', 'at that time'.*

This time last week, I was still enjoying my holiday.

The following uses are less common and can be studied later if this is preferred.

(v) The Past Continuous can express an intended action which never happened; principally with the verbs *go, come, intend, expect, look forward to, plan,* and *arrange.*

She was coming to lunch yesterday, but unfortunately she was ill.

(vi) The Past Continuous may be used for an action which has not yet started, but was already arranged and sure to happen:

At the airport, I met some friends who were flying to New York.

Verbs that are rarely used in the Present Continuous tense are equally rarely used in the Past Continuous form.

In the following sentences, use a suitable form of the Present Simple, Present Continuous, Present Perfect Simple, Present Perfect Continuous, Past Simple or Past Continuous tenses:

(*a*) At eight o'clock this morning I (wait) for you at the station.

(*b*) I (meet) him while I (travel) in Italy last year.

(*c*) It is my birthday to-day, and I (receive) at least ten presents.

(*d*) We must have looked very peaceful. My husband (read) and I (knit).

(*e*) I (speak just) to Mrs. White for an hour. Poor woman! The whole time she (tell) me about her many troubles.

(*f*) When the policeman (see) the stolen car, he (raise) his hand to stop it.

(*g*) Throughout yesterday's lecture, he (make) detailed notes.

(*h*) All the time he (explain) that point, I (think) about something else.

(*i*) He (plan) to spend last night in Manchester, but his car (break) down.

(*j*) (Understand) you what I (say) when we (discuss) our arrangements for yesterday evening?

(*k*) As the first drops of rain (start) to fall, everybody who (watch) the procession (put) up an umbrella.

(*l*) An hour ago, while the guests (put) on their hats and coats, they (chat) about their next meeting.

(*m*) My husband is lazy. Yesterday, when I (think) he (work) in the garden, he (sit) in a deck chair asleep.

Used to, would

He used to live	They used to sing
He used not to live	They used not to sing

The interrogative form is not common: usually the past simple 'Did he live?' or more rarely the expression 'Was he in the habit of singing?' is preferred.

This form suggests:

(*a*) *that the action was repeated or continuous over a fairly long period,*

(*b*) *that it no longer takes place,*

(*c*) *that it happened some time ago.*

Don't you want any chocolates? You used to like them.
When he had more time than now, he used to write long letters to the newspapers.

The auxiliary '*would*' may be used to give a similar meaning. But this *usually suggests that the action was deliberate or intended, and the time when it happened is generally mentioned or suggested in some way:*

When I was abroad, I would read as many newspapers as possible.

Notice the difference between:

When he was a child he used to (not 'would') live in the country.
When he was travelling in other countries, he would always live with local families.

Use the form 'used to' or 'would' (or both where suitable) in the following sentences:

(*a*) The days (seem) much longer than they do now.

(*b*) Our postman (knock) loudly on our door; now he merely slips the letters through the letter-box.

(*c*) When I had more money, I (often travel) by taxi in London.

(*d*) When I was a child and asked my father questions, he (answer) them in great detail.

(*e*) These old houses (be) very fashionable.

(*f*) In the eighteenth century writers (spend) hours in coffee houses, discussing the news of the day.

Am to, was to

PRESENT *forms*	PAST *forms*
I am to attend.	I said he was to listen.
He is not to go.	It was decided they were to learn.
They are to obey.	The results were to have been announced yesterday, but we have heard nothing.
Are we to give it back?	

This use of the verb 'to be' with the infinitive expresses a very firm arrangement and may be a form of command that will accept no refusal.

I am to see the director this afternoon.
You are to keep quiet.
No expense is to be spared.

The past form often appears in reported speech:

The teacher told the students that they were to stop talking.

The fact that the arrangement was not observed may be suggested by the use of a following perfect infinitive:

He was to have finished it by yesterday. (but he did not)

Exercise:

Rewrite each of these sentences so as to use one of the forms explained above.

(*a*) I have ordered anyone who disobeys to be punished.
(*b*) Be home early without fail.
(*c*) He told me to report at the Police Station.
(*d*) The doctor says that relaxation is important for me.
(*e*) We thought we would get our passports last week but they were not ready.
(*f*) Do not tell him anything.
(*g*) Must my essay be finished by to-morrow?
(*h*) The new regulations will be introduced by next week.
(*i*) The examination will be held in June.

Passives

The Passive form of the Past Continuous Tense

ACTIVE: She was cleaning.
PASSIVE: It was being cleaned
They were being cleaned.

Notice these uses of the *passive infinitive:*

I want this *to be repaired* at once.
He left his suit *to be cleaned.*

The verbs in the following sentences are in various tenses of the Active Voice. Rewrite the sentences using, in each case, the same tense of the Passive Voice. Do not include the agent unless it is clear who or what it is.

(*a*) Bees make honey.
(*b*) They have arrested the thief.
(*c*) An unemployed labourer was repairing my roof.
(*d*) Floods swept away the wooden bridge.
(*e*) They were drinking toasts.
(*f*) They closed the shop at one o'clock.
(*g*) Prisoners are building the new road.
(*h*) The Mayor is judging the fancy dress parade.
(*i*) They ought to finish this job by to-morrow. (Infinitive)
(*j*) A young student was driving the car.
(*k*) An unknown artist is to paint the King's portrait. (Infinitive)
(*l*) Mice must have eaten the cheese that the maid left out on the table. (Two verbs. Change the order of the two parts of the sentence.)

Yet, still

(i) *The adverb 'still' is used in connection with something which started in the past and is continuing now:*
They are still repairing damage resulting from the last war.

(ii) *'Yet' refers to the future, and is used in connection with things that may happen, but are not in existence at the present time:*
They have not started to build the new skyscraper yet.

(iii) *'Yet' may also be used with the meaning 'however', 'in spite of that'.*
He is very independent and yet he is popular.

Use either *yet* or *still* in each of the following sentences:

(*a*) He came for breakfast and is...... here.
(*b*) Good gracious! Hasn't he left...... ?
(*c*) Old traditions are...... observed in isolated places.
(*d*) It is after midnight. Are the Underground trains...... running?
(*e*) I don't believe the baby has gone to sleep.......
(*f*) How cold you must have been! You are...... shivering.
(*g*) Aren't you ready...... ?
(*h*) The young birds are...... in their nest. They have not flown away.......
(*i*) She speaks English fluently and ...... she prefers to chatter in French.

Yet referring to something that may happen in the future often comes at the end of its clause. It is rarely found in an affirmative statement.

While, as, when

While, When

The two following examples illustrate the difference in meaning between these conjunctions:

While she was doing the washing-up, she was planning her holiday.
When she did the washing-up, she used soap-powder.

WHILE suggests that *the action took enough time to complete to allow something else to happen* while it was going on. It really means '*during the time that*'.

When, As

> *As* I was approaching the house, the door opened.
> *When* I got to the door I knocked three times.

AS

This usually indicates '*at the exact moment that*'. The two things happen simultaneously.

WHEN

(i) *This may mean* '*whenever*' as in the first example given.

(ii) If often indicates *an action which is followed* immediately or quite soon after *by another action* as in the second example.

Here are some other examples:

> While the queue was moving into the theatre, the old man still went on singing.
> As the queue passed through the door, the attendant counted the number of people in it.
> When there was a queue outside the theatre, a man selling peanuts always appeared.
> When he had taken his place in the queue, he started eating his sandwiches.

In everyday use the three conjunctions are often used interchangeably.

Notice: WHILE can also have the meaning 'although'.

AS can also have the meaning 'because'.

Use *while, as* or *when* in the following sentences. In some cases more than one form may be used, with different meanings.

(*a*) ......he comes to-morrow, I shall ask him where he has been.
(*b*) ......he was speaking, everybody listened silently.
(*c*) ......he spoke to people, he seemed nervous.
(*d*) ......the National Anthem was being played, the audience all stood to attention.
(*e*) ......the door slowly opened, there was a hysterical scream of terror.
(*f*) ......the car passed I recognised the driver.
(*g*) I cannot allow you to whistle......you are doing an examination.
(*h*) Enjoy yourself......you are young.
(*i*) Come to me......you have finished.
(*j*) Have a good look at that man......you pass him.
(*k*) Peter is a wrestler......his twin brother Paul is an artist.
(*l*) ......he wants to pass his test, he is taking driving lessons.

Interrogative Pronouns and Adjectives—'what?', 'which?'

WHAT is used when the choice is unlimited.
WHICH suggests a known or limited number.

Use *what* or *which* in the following sentences:

(*a*) ......shoes did you take to be repaired?

(*b*) ......of your three sisters are you most like?

(*c*) '......can I get for you, Mrs. Adams?' said the grocer.

(*d*) He is so worried that he doesn't know......to do.

(*e*) ......is the correct way to address a duke?

(*f*) ......London park do you consider the most beautiful?

(*g*) I really don't know......his name is.

(*h*) ......side of the street do you live on?

Use a suitable preposition or adverb in each of the following sentences:

(*a*) People started coming at six o'clock and......half past six the hall was full.

(*b*) I am so tired. I am longing......some sleep.

(*c*) The driver was leaning......the side of the bus.

(*d*) All the guests joined......the dancing.

(*e*) The letter should be addressed......this way.

(*f*) May I have a day......to visit my mother?

(*g*) Do you still keep......your birthday?

(*h*) The snow remained......the winter.

(*i*) He is the heir......his father's estate.

(*j*) Can you write with both hands......the same time?

(*k*) When English coach tourists arrive......an interesting town, most of them go off in search......a cup of tea.

(*l*) I am not sure whether Dr. Wright has returned......his holiday yet.

5

Passage for comprehension

A gentle nightmare

The dream changed. For hours, it seemed, I had been wandering aimlessly through a silent forest of pine trees; now I was alone in a small boat which was drifting along lazily, past tree-covered islands, whose bare rocky edges rose abruptly from the transparent water. I was being carried between grassy banks where meadows sprinkled with buttercups sloped to the river. Soft 5
fluffy clouds were reflected in the velvet surface of the water. The current must have been steady and strong, for the boat kept moving forward smoothly, without meeting any obstacle, as though it were being steered by some invisible hand.

Soothed by the peace of my journey, I had lost all count of time but even- 10
tually I became aware that the boat was gliding slowly towards the bank. At this point, where a narrow stretch of silver sand was bounded on either side by heaped granite boulders, an old man was standing, his hand shading his eyes. As the boat ran aground, he came up to me, held out his hand, and greeted me courteously. 15

'You have reached us at last. We have been expecting you for so long. Would you follow me, please.'

I hesitated there for a moment. I had suddenly felt a chill conviction of danger, a shiver that suggested overwhelming evil. Yet this old man with the sensitive delicate features seemed kindly and gracious. He had noticed my 20
suspicion and he smiled at me reassuringly.

'You need not be afraid,' he murmured. 'You are deeply respected, indeed reverenced, by us all. Everything has been prepared for you. We have done everything in our power to honour you. Now please come with me to the place chosen for you.' 25

I dared not risk offending him. But for reasons I cannot explain, I avoided touching his hand outstretched to assist me as I stepped out of the boat, and I followed him reluctantly.

Our feet sank into the yielding sand as we made our way towards a low flight of marble steps which led up from the beach. The steps had been poli- 30
shed so skilfully that they seemed to glow in soft shades of rose, lilac and ivory. At the top my guide paused and looked back at me. I gasped in amazement at the incredible beauty of the scene which lay before me at that moment. And again I shivered involuntarily with an inexplicable dread.

Notes on the passage

Vocabulary

line

Title a *nightmare*—a bad dream (*N* and *V*) a *nightmarish* journey.
have a dream (NOT: see) a *daydream* (a fantasy).

1 *wander* wherever one feels like it, also: wander from the point when speaking about something; *stray:* leave a group and get lost: *a sheep strays from the flock* *stray* (*Adj*) without a home: *a stray cat. go astray* go off the right path with the result of getting into trouble: *the student was soon led astray by his new friends; ramble* (*N* and *V*) a walk (*walk*) in the countryside, often in an organised group; old people sometimes ramble when speaking.
a *rambling* house—one without careful planning that spreads anywhere.

2 *a pine tree* is a coniferous tree (a conifer), so-called because its fruit is a *cone.* Other conifers, which have needles, not leaves, are fir or spruce (Christmas) trees. Oaks, beeches, birches and elms have leaves.

2 *alone alive asleep afraid awake* } are used only predicatively, that is to say, they never precede the noun.
Dare you stay in this solitary house? (*lonely* refers to a feeling—a person who lives alone need not feel (or be) lonely) (*N* loneliness); solitude. *His grandfather is still alive. He is one of the greatest living novelists. The cat is now asleep. The sleeping cat sprawled across the rug. Some people are afraid of snakes. The frightened child dared not touch the dog. He is still awake.* (No other adjective has the same meaning. One would say: *The old lady, who was still awake, heard quiet footsteps outside.*)
The same is true of *ajar*=a little open: *We could hear voices through the door which was ajar* *Opp* wide open.
aloud (*Adv*) *Read this aloud* (so as to be heard). *audible* (*Adj*) *You must read in a more audible voice.*
Notice: I fell asleep at half past nine. NOT: I slept at half past nine.

2 *boat* and *ship* can both be larger vessels. BUT: travel *by boat* (not by ship) Smaller vessels are usually boats: *a rowing boat, a motor boat, a speedboat, a fishing boat. Cargo boats* can be quite large. *A ferry* is also a boat.

3 SPELLING: *past* (*N*) the past; (*Adj*) the past week; *Adv* he walked past (*Prep*) he walked past the school. *passed* (*V*) he passed the examination (*Past Simple*); he has passed the finishing-line. (*Past Participle*).

3 *tree-covered* grass/fur/paper-covered. *A paperback*—a book usually sold more cheaply because it has a *limp* and not a *stiff* cover.

3 *bare bareheaded barefooted barelegged.* The bare branches of trees. An unclothed person is *naked. barely, scarcely, hardly* are all adverbs with almost the same meaning: I earn barely (scarcely, hardly) enough to live on.

4 *transparent* glass; a *translucent* or *frosted* bathroom window; an *opaque* wall.

4 he spoke *abruptly* (without politeness); he spoke *sharply* (angrily); he spoke *bluntly* (without trying to soften his words). He stopped *abruptly* (suddenly).

5 *sprinkle* very small pieces or drops of liquid: a sugar-sprinkler, a water-sprinkler for the lawn in dry weather. *scatter* things in all directions: scatter crumbs for the birds, a scatter-brained person = one who very often forgets things; scattered villages; *spray* (*V* and *N*) force tiny drops out of something: spray roses, (*N*) sea spray, hair spray.

5 Common wild flowers: buttercup, daisy, dandelion, primrose, violet.

5 *sloped* a steep slope, a gradual slope.

6 Some materials: *velvet* (*Adj* velvety), *wool* (*Adj* woollen), *cotton*, *linen*, *silk* (*Adj* silky). Apart from woollen it is the Nouns that refer to the material: *velvet* curtains, a *silk* scarf.

7 *steady*—uninterrupted, regular, reliable: a steady worker/job. A ladder must be steady before a person can climb it.

8 An *obstacle obstructs* (gets in the way of) progress. A *hindrance hinders* or delays progress.

8 *steer* a boat or a car (*steering-wheel*).

10 SPELLING: peace (peaceful) and piece.

11 be/become *aware* that (of) *be unaware of* danger *unawares* (*Adj*): *The photographer caught him unawares* (not expecting this).

11 *glide*—move smoothly: *the gulls glided above the ship*; *glider* (*N*) a kind of aeroplane without an engine; *slip*—lose one's footing and possibly fall: *he slipped and fell down on the frozen snow; slide*—move forward quickly over a *slippery* surface: *slide on an ice-covered lake* (also *N*); *skid* (*N* and *V*)—a car skids when it unexpectedly changes direction.

11 *bank* of a river; *shore* of a lake or the sea; *beach*—where people can sit by a lake or the sea, often sandy; *coast*—where the land meets the sea. *fish from a bank; swim to the shore; lie on the beach; the coast of Wales.*

12 *narrow* has two opposites: *wide* and *broad.*

12 *bounded*—with a limit to it. a *boundary* of property/a village/a county; a *border* between two states: the Scottish border; a *frontier*—the official dividing line between two countries.

13 *heaped* a *heap* is a collection of things without arrangement; a *pile* of things, one on top of the other: *a heap of cut grass; a pile of books.*

13 an enormous *boulder;* a grey *stone;* many small *pebbles.*
gravel is a collection of tiny pebbles and sand.

13 *shading* A *shadow* is normally of one object and has a shape. *shade* (*Unc N*) is an area where there is protection from the sun a *sunshade*, a *lampshade*, *eye-shadow*. One shades a drawing (shading), one shadows (follows secretly) a person.

14 *run aground run ashore be adrift.*

15 *courteous* discourteous; polite impolite.

16 I *waited* half an hour *for* him as I had *expected* him to arrive earlier.

18 *a chill* can also be a kind of cold—to have a chill.
cool—pleasantly cold; *chilly*—unpleasantly cool: *the cool shade of trees; a chilly Autumn day. Keep cool! Don't panic. A cool distant manner.*

18 *conviction* has two meanings: (*a*) *convince* (*V*) make a person sure that something is true: *he convinced me he was right; he has strong religious convictions* (*Adj* convinced) (*b*) *convict* (*V* and *N*) (see Pronunciation)—prove guilty of a crime: *he was convicted of blackmail;* A *convict* has usually been in prison several times: he has several previous *convictions.* (For construction, see Special Grammatical and Structural Points Page 76.)

19 *shiver* with cold or fear; *shudder* with horror.

19 *overwhelming* One can be overwhelmed by work, sorrow, worry, relief. Here the meaning is 'very strong indeed'.

20 *sensitive* to cold, a sensitive artist; *sensible*—a sensible person does not usually do *senseless* things as he uses his *common sense.* The car driver lay *insensible* in the road after the accident. He had been driving so dangerously that he must have been *out of his senses.* What you have written *makes no sense.* The mouse *sensed* danger as the cat silently approached.

20 *delicate:* pale blue is *a delicate colour; delicate lace* is made with fine thread; *a delicate child* is often ill; avoid mentioning his dismissal: it's *a delicate subject.*

20 *features* (*a*) a part of the face; (*b*) a characteristic part: *overcrowding may be a feature of town life;* (*c*) a feature (main) film.

20 *kindly* may be part of a request, possibly with some impatience: Would you kindly be quiet.

20 a *gracious* and charming elderly lady; a *graceful* ballerina.

20 *notice* (*V*) something unusual; *remark* that the weather is fine (*say* something unimportant). *a notice* for people to read; *a remark* about the weather. He *observed* that his friend was ill. (said or noticed)

21 *suspicion:* if one has *suspicions* about someone's honesty, one is *suspicious of* him and *suspects* that he is not to be trusted.

22 A gentle wind, people in church, distant bees *murmur*. Very distant thunder *mutters:* the old woman muttered a curse. The boy who had not learned his lesson *mumbled* indistinctly.
The doctor and nurse *whispered* so as not to wake the patient (spoke without using their voices).

22 *respected*—Victorian parents were highly respected by their children.
respectful—Their children were usually respectful and obedient.
respectable—Can he really be a criminal? He seems such a *respectable* man.
respective—The candidates were interviewed in turn, according to their respective qualifications.

26 (*a*) *offend* someone, possibly by hurting his feelings so that he behaves coldly; take *offence* at something said—be offended by it: (*b*) *parking*

illegally is a motoring offence and anyone who does it is an offender against the law. (*c*) *After being on the defensive, the army suddenly took the offensive.* (*d*) *He was arrested for using offensive language to the Mayor, who is a very quiet, inoffensive little man.*

28 *follow*—walk behind, NOT: accompany. May I take you (or: go with you) to the station?

28 *reluctantly* *Opp.* here: *willingly.*

30 the *flight of birds.* a flight by aeroplane. Verb: fly, flew, flown *a flight from danger.* Verb: flee, fled, fled. *a flight of stairs.*

30 a *marble*, stone, brick wall NOT: in marble or of marble.

33 *incredible*—unbelievable. *incredulous*—unbelieving

34 *voluntarily*—of one's own free will. *involuntarily*—without intending to. a *volunteer*—someone who says he is ready to do some job willingly.

KINDS OF FEAR

uneasiness, anxiety, worry, nervousness

apprehension and *dread* are both felt when anticipating something one knows will be unpleasant—a visit to the dentist, an examination. 'Dread' is the stronger of the two.

Alarm is usually a sudden fear:

> The news of the approach of the enemy caused *alarm* among the population of the town.
> *alarming* reports
> Do not *alarm* the children.

Fright has a similar meaning, but refers more to a single experience:

> The boy jumped out on his sister and gave her a *fright.*

Panic is a desperate fear often affecting large groups, and causing uncontrolled behaviour.

Terror is very strong fear.

Horror is a mixture of fear, disgust and surprise.

Verbs include 'to fear', 'to be afraid of', 'to worry', 'to dread', 'to alarm', 'to frighten', 'to terrify', 'to horrify'.

Phrasal verb

14 COME *come across* something when one is not looking for it; flowers *come out* (from buds); a newspaper *comes out* (is published); *come by* (obtain); *come round* after losing consciousness for a while (=recover consciousness); an arrangement or event *comes off* (happens); *come into* (inherit) money; *come up to* (go up to) someone to sneak quietly up to him; *come on, come along*=hurry. Which? How did you come...... that snuff-box? I came...... it in an antique shop. Give him some brandy when he comes....... He has come...... his uncle's fortune. Snowdrops usually come ......in February. He came......me and asked my name.

Come......; your father's waiting. Do you think their wedding will ever come......? The magazine comes......once a week.

Notice: also: the play *came to an end;* a bus *came into sight;* his dream *came true.*

Pronunciation

OFTEN MISPRONOUNCED: surface [sɔ́:fɪs]; granite [grǽnɪt]; courteously [kɔ́:tiəsli]; suggested [sədʒéstɪd]; delicate [délɪkɪt]; suspiciously [səspíʃəslɪ].

ə (as in *a*go): sil*e*nt [sáɪlənt]; mirr*ore*d [mirəd]; obst*a*cle [ɔ́bstəkl]; feat*u*res [fí:tʃəz]; graci*ou*s [gréɪʃəs]; murm*ure*d [mɔ́:məd]; *o*ffending [əféndɪŋ]; lil*a*c [láɪlək]; iv*o*ry [áɪvərɪ]; inexplic*a*ble [ɪnekspli̋kəbl]; t*o*wards [təwɔ́:dz].

ɪ (as in cit*y*): for*e*st [fɔ́rɪst]; velv*e*t [vélvɪt].

SILENT LETTERS: i*s*lands [áɪləndz]; *h*onour [ɔ́nə]; s*c*ene [sɪ:n].

OTHERS: wandering [wɔ́ndərɪŋ]; covered [kʌ́vəd]; transparent [tra:nz-pǽrənt]; meadows [médouz]; steady [stédɪ]; dread [dred]; boulders [bóuldəz]; yielding [jí:ldiŋ]; involuntarily [ɪnvɔ́ləntərɪlɪ];

Special grammatical and structural points

(i) *Verbs used intransitively and transitively:*

(*a*) *rise rose risen; raise raised*

Most verbs can be used both *intransitively* (with no direct object) and also *transitively* (with a direct object)—*he was reading* and *he was reading a letter*. Some however are always intransitive: *stand*, *fly*, *sleep* and others always transitive, that is, they must have some kind of object: *enjoy*, *buy*, *throw*.

Intransitive verbs can have no passive form. *rise* is always intransitive, with no object or passive form: *raise* must have an object.

Which (with a suitable tense form)? My host......to greet me; the people have......in rebellion; a lock......the level of water; has the cake......? the Government has......the standard of living; the sun ......yesterday at seven; prices are......; the bus companies are...... their fares.

arise arose arisen (intransitive): *troubles*, *problems*, *difficulties arise*. *arise* is seldom used nowadays to mean *get up*.

Notice: rise (*N*) a rise in prices in the cost of living; ask one's boss for a rise.

(*b*) *lie lay*

These two verbs cause enormous confusion among English people as well as foreigners.

Lie, Lay, Lain—Intransitive with the meaning of 'place oneself (or be) in a flat position'.

INFINITIVE:	I want to *lie* down and sleep.
PRESENT SIMPLE:	Italy *lies* to the south of Switzerland.
PRESENT CONTINUOUS:	The handbag is *lying* on the table.
FUTURE SIMPLE:	The snow will *lie* for three or four weeks.
PAST SIMPLE:	The dog *lay* stretched out before the fire.
PRESENT PERFECT:	My hat *has lain* on the grass all night.

Lay, Laid, Laid—Transitive 'to put', 'to place' (and special meanings).

INFINITIVE:	The man decided to *lay* down his burden.
PRESENT SIMPLE:	He always *lays* his books on the floor.
PRESENT CONTINUOUS:	The waiter is *laying* the table.
FUTURE SIMPLE:	The Mayor will *lay* the foundation stone.
PAST SIMPLE:	The mother *laid* her baby in the cradle.
PRESENT PERFECT:	The hen *has laid* an egg.

(Which are the objects of the verbs in the second group?)

It is very easy to confuse these two verbs, as the form 'LAY' *is the Past Simple of the intransitive 'lie'* and *the Present and Infinitive of the transitive 'lay'*.

A completely different verb is '*to lie*' meaning '*to tell an untruth*': He lies, he is lying; he will lie; he lied; he has lied.

Which (with a suitable tense form)? a bricklayer......... bricks; the cat is......... on my slippers; I......... thinking all last night; he......... down his glasses and then could not find them; the baby will now...... quietly in her pram; your ball-point is......... on the sideboard; our hens have......... twelve eggs; he has often......... there for hours, watching the clouds; the Shetland Isles......... to the North of Scotland; .... the table in the kitchen for breakfast; why are you......... on the floor? many wreaths have been......... on the War Memorial.

(ii) *need* and *dare* may have *two* possible *negative* and *interrogative* forms when they are *followed by an infinitive*.

NEED

I need not *go*	Do I need *to go?*
Need we *help?*	Do we need *to help?*
No alternative	They did not need *to come*
	Did they need *to come?*

DARE

he dare not *stay*	does he dare *to stay?*
dare you *jump?*	Do you dare *to jump?*
Many dared not *speak*	Many did not dare *to speak*
No alternative	Did you dare *to refuse?*

BUT: I do not need anything more. Do you need help?

NOTICE: Fred dared his brother to steal the apples. (A challenge)

and: My shoes need cleaning. The house does not need redecorating yet.

(iii) *all everything everybody* (*everyone*)

Pronoun *all*, with its meaning of 'the undivided total', is less commonly found than *everything* = all the things, *everybody* = all the people. *Everything is perfect.* (All the things, not the undivided total.) *He ate everything. Everybody was surprised. He made everyone pay.* *all* is used when a relative pronoun follows or is understood: *All* (*that*) *I can say is* (*that*) *he has always been good to me.* (I personally know this.) Even in this case however everything (everybody) can often be used: *He destroyed all* (*the letters, or the insects, or the papers*) *he found. He destroyed everything* (*all the things*) *he found.*

The expressions 'all people' is rarely used: 'everybody' is far more common. *Everybody has his troubles.*

Which is the more common form? I saw...... that happened; ...... you need is a good rest; ...... is (or are(?)) talking about the mystery; ...... is now finished; ...... I know is that he has been arrested; he never tells me......; he knows...... in the district.

(iv) *so skilfully that: she mended the dress so carefully that it looked new; he had to wait so long that he became impatient.*

(v) *as though it were being steered*—this rare use of the subjunctive is explained in Chapter 12 Pages 215–16. *He looked at me as if* (*as though*) *I were not there.*

(vi) *urge* someone *to do* something (try to make him do it): *the doctor urged the overworked businessman to rest.*

persuade someone *to do* something (be successful in making him do it): *he finally persuaded the man to have a holiday.*

convince someone *that something is* true or right: *he convinced the man that a rest was essential. Galileo was convinced that his theories were correct.*

(vii) VERBAL CONSTRUCTIONS

Infinitive: we have done everything to honour you

Gerund: (i) after a preposition: without encountering

(ii) after other verbs: keep moving; risk offending; avoid touching.

Clause: I became aware that the boat was gliding.

(Compare: I became aware of singing.)

Prepositions

(*a*) drift *along* the stream; move/walk along the street. (*b*) *between* two things *among* more than two (*c*) sprinkled/decorated/patterned *with* flowers (BUT: *painted blue*) (*d*) mirrored/reflected *in* water. (*e*) bounded/marked *by* a large board (*f*) *on* either side (*g*) prepare/get ready *for* someone or something; choose something for someone; for various reasons (*h*) a man *with* delicate features/blue eyes/white hair/a long beard etc. (*i*) (un)aware/(un)conscious *of* danger; a feeling/conviction of danger (*j*) smiled *at* me BUT: laughed at me = made fun of me. (*k*) step *out of* a car. (*l*) *Notice:* walk/run/drift *past* something NOT: pass in walking.

Expressions to learn and introduce into written work

(*a*) I lost all count of time (*b*) eventually (*c*) I was/became aware that (*d*) at this point (*e*) on either side (*f*) he came up to me (*g*) everything in our power (*h*) for reasons I cannot explain (*i*) we made our way towards (*j*) I gasped in amazement at (*k*) I shivered involuntarily.

Multiple choice questions

Here are a number of questions or unfinished statements about the passage, each with four suggested ways of answering or finishing it. You must choose the way you consider the most suitable. Write in each case the bracketed number of the question or statement followed by the letters **A, B, C, D,** and then cross through the letter of the answer you choose. Give one answer only to each question. Read the passage right through again before choosing your answers.

1 The sides of the islands
A had trees on them **B** were covered only with grass **C** were covered with grass and flowers **D** had no covering

2 How did the boat move forward?
A rapidly **B** uninterruptedly **C** jerkily **D** feebly

3 While in the boat the writer felt
A relaxed **B** apprehensive **C** only half-conscious **D** helpless

4 The boat journey seemed to him to
A last a long time **B** be timeless **C** be shorter than his previous experience **D** be rather difficult to judge the length of

5 The passage suggests that
A the sun was shining in a clear sky **B** clouds hid the sun **C** the sun was shining but there were clouds **D** we cannot tell from the passage

6 Which of the following statements applies to the writer's arrival?
A his coming caused surprise to the people waiting **B** the old man held out his hand and bowed to the writer **C** the writer's arrival was long overdue **D** he could clearly go no farther

7 Why did the writer hesitate to leave the boat?
A he was suddenly afraid of the people waiting **B** he knew that horrible dangers lay ahead **C** he had a sense of something bad, powerful and horrible overhanging him **D** the old man had noticed his distrust and might be angry

8 Which of these attitudes was not shown in the old man's behaviour towards him?
A veiled hostility **B** deference **C** firmness **D** reassurance

9 Why did the writer eventually decide to leave the boat?
A he decided his fears were imaginary **B** he did not wish to

rouse the man's hostility **C** he felt safe so long as he did not actually touch the man **D** he could not have given any reason for doing so

10 Which of the following feelings did he not experience when he reached the top of the steps?
A wonder **B** disbelief **C** apprehension **D** admiration

Reading comprehension

(i) In this exercise you must choose the word or phrase which best completes each sentence. Write first the number of each sentence followed by the letters **A, B, C, D, E**, and then cross through the letter of the correct answer in each case.

1 Many difficulties have .... as a result of the changeover to a new type of fuel.
A raised **B** been raised **C** risen **D** experienced **E** arisen

2 The deep pool was so brown and weed-covered that it was almost.......
A transparent **B** solid **C** translucent **D** opaque **E** invisible

3 You must remember not to..............from the point when you write an essay.
A go astray **B** wander **C** diverge **D** ramble **E** go off

4 The..............of the lake is covered with reeds and rushes.
A beach **B** strand **C** coast **D** shore **E** bank

5 Paper clips, drawing pins and safety-pins were..............all over the floor
A scattered **B** sprinkled **C** sprayed **D** dispersed **E** separated

6 She..............her hand over the material, enjoying the smooth silky feeling of its surface.
A slid **B** glided **C** slipped **D** skidded **E** stroked

7 I wandered through the cool..............of the forest trees.
A shadow **B** dark **C** shade **D** obscurity **E** freshness

8 The neighbours do not consider him quite..............as most evenings he awakens them with his drunken singing.
A respectful **B** respected **C** respectable **D** worthy of respect **E** respective

9 The autumn air felt..............so she went to fetch a coat.
A cool **B** chilly **C** chill **D** shivery **E** tepid

10 The murderer proved to be an apparently well-behaved.............. middle-aged man.
A offensive **B** unoffending **C** inoffensive **D** innocent **E** unsuspicious

11 The crowd stared at the giant and the dwarf as if they were .... monsters.
A credulous **B** incredible **C** incredulous **D** creditable
E unbelieving

12 I was suspicious of his sincerity and remained .... by his many arguments.
A unconvicted **B** reassured **C** unconvinced **D** unconcerned
E undisturbed

Use of English

1 (ii) The five words or word groups below are the answers to five questions that could be asked about the Reading Passage. The first word of each question is given to assist you.

(i) grassy banks. (What) ....?

(ii) there were buttercups. (What)

(iii) it was quite narrow. (How)

(iv) for reasons I cannot explain. (Why)

(v) marble. (What)

2 Write down the twelve words in list A below, and against each the one word from list B which rhymes with it (that is, ends with the same sounds).

A	B
search	purse
busy	though
heir	spear
male	stuff
bow (*N*)	church
score	break
eyed	bough
bored	prayer
rough	warred
worse	dizzy
ache	stayed
lose	snail
	roar
	streak
	shoes
	bride
	horse

3 The word in capitals at the end of each of the following sentences can be used to form a word that fits suitably in the blank space. Fill each blank space in this way.

1 The judge was caught ...., admiring himself in the mirror in his new wig. AWARE

2 His examination results were so unsatisfactory that it seemed............... for him to continue studying. POINT

3 The ambulance-men carried the injured man into the hospital on a .... STRETCH

4 He bowed to the small girl with elaborate .... COURTEOUS

5 The new au pair girl proved to be quite different from the family's .... EXPECT

6 The scientific explanation was too difficult for me. I was quite out of my .... DEEP

7 He was bound hand and foot and so was quite .... to escape. POWER

8 It is thoroughly dishonest and .... to cheat in an examination. HONOUR

4 For one of the ideas in each of the following six phrases, five suggested explanations are given, from which you must choose the correct one. Write down the numbers (i) to (vi) and against each the letter **A**, **B**, **C**, **D** or **E** of the explanation you choose.

(i) Tom is late home today. He has probably been kept in.
A he has been asked to do extra work in the office
B he has to stay longer at school because of misbehaviour
C he has attended a works conference that has lasted longer than expected
D somebody has asked his advice just as he is leaving
E he has had a slow bus journey because of heavy traffic

(ii) Some people can easily be taken in.
A tricked **B** they are pleasant guests **C** it is easy to like them **D** it is easy to teach them **E** found accommodation for

(iii) I hope the house-warming party will come off.
A will not happen **B** will happen **C** will be successful **D** will be arranged **E** will be short

(iv) The hotel was to have been ready by next April.
A so it will be opened then **B** this was what I was told **C** but I think it will not be **D** that was a possibility **E** but this is absolutely impossible now.

(v) I must have told you about our meeting with the Joneses.
A I am almost certain I did **B** I had to tell you about it **C** I was ordered to tell you **D** I am absolutely sure I did **E** this is very likely

(vi) You sit there reading as though there were nothing to do.
A there is nothing to do **B** you think there is nothing to do **C** you are absorbed in your reading **D** there is a great deal to do **E** you ought to be helping.

Composition and summarising

Descriptions

There are two main kinds of description. In the first only facts are given. A police description of a wanted man, a house agent's description of a house, the details of interesting buildings mentioned in a town guidebook are all examples.

The second kind gives impressions as well as facts, so that the reader sees through his imagination as well as his mind. The writer provides atmosphere and feeling: of a half-ruined castle, a lake shore in early morning, a town square in carnival time. He chooses details, words and impressions to awaken the reader's imagination.

Such descriptions usually include carefully-observed facts as well as impressions. So, when describing an Underground station platform, he gives some exact information about the tunnels at either end, the rails, the platform and waiting passengers, the lights, seats, station names, advertisements and so on, besides impressions and atmosphere (of an enclosed space completely isolated from daylight, growing things and fresh air, clean, efficient, cold and inhuman, symbol of a technical age).

However, if only a short time is available for writing, the more factual type of description is more likely to be asked for. Here is an example. NOTICE THAT A DESCRIPTION NEEDS CAREFUL PLANNING. Describe an open-air café. Use between 120 and 180 words.

Plan

1 The weather. The café itself.
2 The waitresses. Other people.
3 The surroundings.

A few lazy clouds were passing slowly over a sunlit blue sky. Scattered over the smooth green grass there were about twenty tables with green and white plastic tablecloths fastened on them, and brightly-coloured sunshades above. Plastic and metal chairs of various colours stood round them and in the centre of the lawn, water from a fountain splashed into a pool in which goldfish were swimming.

The waitresses, pretty girls in light summer frocks, were bringing ice-creams, cool drinks and cream cakes from the kitchen of the house at one side. Half the tables were occupied: several women were sitting talking and a few men were enjoying the sunshine.

On two sides roses bloomed against an old wall with beds of June flowers in front. On the others, tall trees sheltered lawns white with daisies. Bees were buzzing and birds were singing. Work, cold, reality perhaps, no longer existed. (149 words)

Subjects for practice

These should be completed in between 120 and 180 words.

1 An English friend wants to buy three useful things in your country to take home with him or her. Describe three things you would recommend and the special qualities each has that make you choose it.

2 An English friend is coming to live in your home town. Give him some idea of what it will be like living there.

3 Turning out a cupboard you come across something you have not seen since your childhood and it brings back memories. Describe the object and some of your memories.

4 Two dogs are waiting with their owners in the waiting-room in a veterinary surgeon's (animal doctor) house. Describe each dog and its owner.

5 Compare your journey to school on a delightful summer day and on a cold unpleasant winter day.

6 Describe an ideal bed-sitting-room for yourself as a single person.

Write two paragraphs using not more than 125 words, the first mentioning all the pleasant sights and experiences that formed part of the writer's dream, the second the unpleasant ones. Use your own words as far as possible.

Spoken English

Making requests: Asking another person to do something

This is an aspect of English that needs particularly careful study as it might be possible to offend someone by apparently speaking abruptly. Practise these expressions whenever you have the opportunity.

FORMAL	INFORMAL	FRIENDLY	HELPFUL
May I have your name and address, please. (an official is speaking)	May I have another piece of cake? (in a family)		May (Can) I help you? May I take your case?
I'd like my bill, please. (in a restaurant)		I'd so (very much) like you to come and see us again.	Would you like me to help you?
Would you like to close the window, please. (teacher to a student)			
Would you like to sit down?			
	You don't mind if I hurry off, do you?	Do sit down (voice rising at the end) Won't you sit down.	Why don't you let me help?

Asking another person to do something for oneself

Would you serve my salad without oil, please?

Would you be able to help me in the house for one morning a week, please?

You won't forget to post that letter for me, will you?

Could you (possibly) move your car forward a bit, please?

You wouldn't be able to spare me some butter, would you?
Would you mind changing this ten-pound note for me, please? (to a shopkeeper)
I wonder if you'd mind if I used (my using) your telephone?
Would you be so kind as to lend me your pen for a moment, please?

A note on Please and Thank you

Please is used only when asking for something. *Yes, please* shows acceptance. Refusal is expressed by *No, thank you.* (NOT: thank you)
If there is a reply to thank you—usually none is in fact given—it is 'That's all right' or 'not at all. I was glad to help'. There is no need to say anything when handing something to a person, though Mother might say to the children 'Here you are.'

Excuse me and Sorry

Excuse me is a form of politeness, often used when speaking to an unknown person: Excuse me, can you tell me the way to .... It is also said when passing in front of someone or when trying to attract someone's attention.
I'm sorry is an apology for something that has caused pain, trouble or disturbance to another person.

EXAMPLES: (*a*) on treading on someone's foot: Oh, I'm so sorry. I hope I haven't hurt you. (*b*) on being late: I'm so sorry I'm late. I was delayed by the traffic. (*c*) disturbing someone: I'm sorry to disturb you but you're wanted on the telephone.

EXERCISES Express each of the following in a politer way. Wherever possible, show how the request could be expressed in more than one way. (You may need to make use of more than one section.)
(*a*) Give me my key (in a hotel). (*b*) Show me those photographs you have. (*c*) Tell me how to use this telephone. (*d*) I want a glass of water. (*e*) Weigh this parcel for me (in the post office). (*f*) Do you want another cup of coffee? (*g*) Come nearer the fire. (*h*) Tell me the time (to a stranger). (*i*) Drive more slowly. (*j*) Get these photographs printed by the week-end. (*k*) Have lunch with me tomorrow. (*l*) Turn down your radio. It's very disturbing.

Useful expressions: Holidaymaking

A How did you enjoy your holiday? Did you have a good time?

B I had a wonderful time but my wife was disappointed with it.

A Did the two of you go alone or as part of a group?

B We went on a coach tour organised by Faraway tours. (Alternatives: on a cruise, on a package holiday in Spain.) We booked through a local travel office. As in the case of a package holiday, everything—accommodation, fares, luggage transport, meals during the day, guides and tips—was included in the price.

A We went camping in the Lake District. We packed our tent, cooking utensils, some tinned food, camp beds and bedding besides the usual luggage in the boot of our small car. We stayed at two different camping sites and explored from there. Next year we'll do the same but we want to take a motor boat up the river and camp wherever we can.

Situations

Say what you would do in each of the following situations.

(*a*) You are alone in your car when it breaks down on a very lonely country road. It is some time since you have seen another car. You know nothing about a car engine. What do you do?

(*b*) You have run into a friend whom you have not seen for some years and have been invited to the friend's house for coffee. Two days after the arranged date you realise to your horror you have forgotten all about the arrangement. You telephone your friend at once. What do you and your friend say?

Giving your own opinions

Give your own ideas about any of these subjects. Try to introduce some of the new expressions you have learned.

(*a*) What do you think are some of the causes of different types of dreams?

(*b*) What are the attractions of a holiday spent paddling, canoeing, sailing or travelling by motorboat along a river?

(*c*) A sudden inexplicable feeling that danger lies ahead is called a premonition. Do you think people really have premonitions and if so, can they be explained in some way?

(*d*) To what extent do you think you can judge a person's character at a first meeting?

(*e*) How far does a person's face reveal his character?

(*f*) What things might offend you?

General guidance and practice

The Past Perfect Simple and Continuous Tenses

Simple form

ACTIVE: I had experienced.
He had spoken.

PASSIVE: The steps had been polished.

Continuous form

ACTIVE: I had been wandering.
PASSIVE: very seldom used.

The Past Perfect forms indicate an action which had happened before something else happened—in other words they express a time farther back than a certain point in the past.

(*a*) *This tense is often found in an adverbial time clause or accompanying main clause.* The conjunction 'before' may sometimes be followed by the Past Simple in such cases, but 'when', 'after', 'as soon as', 'immediately', and other conjunctions are often followed by this tense when the meaning suggests it, that is, when there is *emphasis* on the fact that one action came before the other.

He joined the class a fortnight after it had started.

(*b*) It is far less commonly used when the sentence consists of two main clauses:

He finished his breakfast and then went to school.

(*c*) It often replaces the Present Perfect or Past Simple tenses when one changes from Direct to Reported Speech:

I have lost my ticket.
He said he had lost his ticket.

The Past Perfect Continuous shows that the earlier action had covered a period.

He had been staying in Paris before he came to London.
The old man told me he had been living in the same house all his life.

The following passage is a well-known problem story. Copy it out, using the correct form of the verbs shown. The verb forms may include gerunds, participles, infinitives and passive forms. When you have finished, answer the question below, using the correct tense in your answer:

A certain man, who was the manager of a firm which (undertake) road repairs, (intend) to travel by train to Manchester. Before (set) out, he (look) up the times of the trains, and (discover) that there (be) three: one at seven, one at eight and one at nine o'clock. He (know) he (miss) the seven o'clock train, so after (pack) a small suitcase, he (start) out (catch) the eight o'clock train.

As he (walk) to the station, he (notice) one of his night-watchmen, who (sit) by his fire at the side of the road. (Know) that the man (work) for the railways previously, the manager (ask) him whether the eight or nine o'clock (be) the faster train.

The man (shake) his head solemnly. 'Usually the eight o'clock (be) very good,' he (say). 'But last night as I (sit) here, I (have) a terrible dream. In my dream I (see) a wrecked train. I (know) it (be) tonight's eight o'clock train I (can) see. There (be) a dreadful accident and everyone in the train (kill). (Go) not on that train to-night.'

The manager, who (be) superstitious, (decide) (wait) for the next train, which (travel) by a different route. It (be) a long journey, and after he (travel) all night, he (reach) Manchester. There, to his horror, he (learn) that the night-watchman (be) right. The eight o'clock train (have) an accident, and all the passengers (be) killed.

So he (put) a five pound note in an envelope and (send) it to the man, together with a note (dismiss) him from his job.

Passive forms

Revise the rule for forming the Passive from the Active Voice as shown in Chapter 1.

Write the following sentences in the Passive Voice (the Past Perfect form of which is shown at the top of the previous exercise). Be careful to give the correct tense.

(*a*) People had seen him behaving in a very suspicious manner.
(*b*) A wasp has stung me.
(*c*) My landlady does my washing.
(*d*) The cat laid the half-eaten mouse on the doorstep.
(*e*) They had decorated the room beautifully.
(*f*) Someone had obviously offended her.
(*g*) A young boy was steering the car.
(*h*) A hat shades his eyes.
(*i*) The mother soothed the frightened child.
(*j*) He is sprinkling pepper all over your meal.

Ought to, must, have to

Examples:

We must always try to be unselfish.
We have to eat in order to live.
We ought never to tell lies.

(i) MUST and HAVE TO are often used in the present and future tenses interchangeably. If any difference in meaning is conveyed, MUST *suggests a personal feeling of duty,* HAVE TO, *necessity*—from outside circumstances.

OUGHT TO *indicates duty and necessity in a much weaker way and there is often some suggestion of failure:*

You ought to be here at nine o'clock every day. (But you are not.)

When OUGHT *is followed by the perfect infinitive, failure is almost certainly suggested:*

They ought to have arrived by now. (But they haven't.)

(ii) MUST *has no past tenses. These are supplied by* HAVE TO.

I had to be home before dark.
I have had to open a window; the room is so stuffy.
She had had to write it out ten times before he was satisfied.

The future can be expressed by MUST *or emphasized by* SHALL HAVE TO, WILL HAVE TO. These two latter forms may express necessity.

You must be home by midnight.
You will have to be home by midnight as there are no trains after that.

(The future tense of other verbs is dealt with in Chapter 8.)

(iii) MUST *has two* NEGATIVES, *so far as meaning is concerned.*

You must not shout. (It is forbidden.)
You need not go away. } (It is not necessary.)
You do not have to go away. }

Notice the negative and interrogative forms:

I must not.	I ought not.	I do not have to.
Must I?	Ought I?	Do I have to?

Use a form of OUGHT TO, MUST or HAVE TO in each of the following sentences:

(*a*) I......go and visit my sister-in-law but I am too busy.

(*b*) Every weekday most people......get up early in order to get to work in time.

(*c*) You......do your homework more regularly. I insist.

(*d*) He......pay duty on his new camera on his return home last year.

(*e*) As it was raining hard, I ......catch a bus.

(*f*) The pupils......have been quiet while the teacher was away, but there was pandemonium in the room.

(*g*) A specialist......keep up to date with the latest medical developments in his field, but if he is busy, this is difficult.

(*h*) Do come and have tea with me. I......tell you about my holiday.

(*i*) He......have a tooth out yesterday.

(*j*) I......write three letters already to-day.

Express the following sentences in the negative and also in the interrogative. In the case of MUST give both forms of the negative, explaining the difference in meaning:

(*a*) You must always speak English.

(*b*) Wild animals ought to be kept in cages.

(*c*) The gardener will have to mow the lawn.

(*d*) The explorer had to face many dangers.

(*e*) Farm labourers have to work longer hours than factory workers.

(*f*) They have had to widen the lane.

(*g*) That stove ought to have been cleaned out yesterday.

(*h*) The examination must be written in pencil.

(*i*) The Prime Minister has to appoint a new Foreign Secretary.

The last sentence is a clear example of the possible difference between the present forms of MUST and HAVE TO.

If he MUST appoint a new Foreign Secretary, someone is saying that this is his duty.

But the previous one has retired, and it is *necessary* for him to appoint a new one; he has to do it.

Notice the difference between:

We didn't need to take a taxi. (so we didn't).
We need not have taken a taxi. (but we did).

MUST *is also used to express something that is almost certain to be true:*

It must be quite late now. It is already dark.
He must be our new neighbour. He has gone into the house.

The snow must have fallen during the night. Everything is white.
It must have been falling throughout the night.

The negative form of 'it must be' is 'it cannot be'.

The following sentences can be written in a slightly different way, using 'must' with the above meaning. Rewrite them accordingly.

(*a*) He is so fair that he almost certainly comes from Scandinavia or Germany.

(*b*) It is a long journey. You have certainly been travelling for two days.

(*c*) The sound of approaching footsteps almost certainly frightened the rabbit.

(*d*) You almost certainly noticed the new swimming-pool on your way here.

(*e*) I probably appear rather stupid, but I am a little deaf to-day.

(*f*) That cathedral was almost certainly built in the fourteenth century.

The order of adverbs and adverbial phrases in a sentence

Notice the order of adverbs and adverbial phrases in these examples:

	Manner	*Place*
The boat was gliding	(slowly)	(towards the shore).

	Place	*Time*
I hesitated	(there)	(for a moment).
	Place	*Time*
which lay	(before me)	(at that moment).

When more than one adverb or adverbial phrase follows the verb, the usual order is: Manner Place Time

Often, when there are two or three adverbial expressions, *one of them, usually a time adverb, is placed at the beginning of the sentence*:

I was living in Paris at that time.
At that time I was living in Paris.
You will be speaking quite fluently before long.
Before long you will be speaking quite fluently.
The birds were singing sweetly in the trees.
In the trees the birds were singing sweetly (adverb of place).

The order of words may change the emphasis in the sentence. If one of the adverbial expressions is especially important, the normal order may be changed. The one that is most emphasised comes last.

The cat went out reluctantly *into the freezing night.*
The cat went out into the freezing night *reluctantly.*

Copy the following sentences so that the words are in a suitable order. There may be more than one alternative.

(*a*) She waited (impatiently) (in the bus queue).

(*b*) I get up (during the winter) (reluctantly) (in my cold room).

(*c*) He walks (to the station) (slowly) (at the end of a long day).

(*d*) Wild animals go seeking their prey (after dark) (in the jungle).

(*e*) The snow fell (for thirty-six hours) (over a wide area) (continuously).

(*f*) The ship will dock (at Tilbury) (at eight o'clock).

(*g*) The water continued to pour (steadily) (into the tunnel).

(*h*) The discontented inhabitants start rioting (dangerously) (now and again) (in the streets).

The semi-colon and the colon

The semi-colon is used to separate two parts of a sentence, each of which is complete in itself:

I had been in a silent forest; now I was alone in a small boat.

A colon may be used for the same purpose, but in this case, each part of the sentence expresses essentially the same idea:

Christmas is becoming increasingly commercialized: shops and business interests see it merely as a way of making money.

A colon may introduce a list:

All cycles sold at this price have the following equipment: three-speed gearing, a carrier, a dynamo-operated lamp and a pump.

Insert semi-colons or colons in the following sentences:

(*a*) The gale inflicted terrible damage roofs were torn off and crops were flattened.

(*b*) The fugitive scrambled over the wall beyond he caught sight of the river.

(*c*) To-morrow is a bank holiday all shops and businesses will be closed throughout the day.

(*d*) I should like these special items delivered to-day a tin of coffee, a bar of household soap and a jar of marmalade.

(*e*) Far into the night he worked as day dawned he sank back into the chair, exhausted.

6

The summary

1 A and B, who are both Canadians, are discussing the attractions and drawbacks of Britain, in particular the country itself and not London, as a holiday place. Taking your information only from the conversation, write two paragraphs, in 175–200 words altogether, on this subject. In the first paragraph explain the drawbacks referred to and in the second the attractions, in both cases as these exist for the people speaking.

A So you're spending your holiday in London this year?

B No, anywhere but London. We want to see the country itself, not a cosmopolitan capital.

A But there's nothing whatever to see outside London. Stratford maybe, but that's swarming with tourists, and Brighton, where there isn't space for another transistor on the beach.

B You've been in England then?

A I was there for a year studying. In London of course.

B Did you do much touring?

A As I say, there's nothing to see. A lot of industry, especially in the North, a lot of large towns, all alike, and dreary weather. Winters are damp and cold and summers are damp and chilly. It's not just the rain but the grey skies and heavy feel of the air.

B I was in the tourist office today and got a completely different impression. Summers can be depressing but are sometimes wonderful and anyhow the rain makes everything very green. And unlike this country, where you travel hundreds of kilometres over the same kind of landscape, there's immense variety of scenery in a comparatively small area. There are mountains, hills and plains, newly-planned and built towns and almost medieval ones, Gothic and also twentieth-century cathedrals and practically every kind of seaside place. And away from the big towns and industrial areas, vast stretches of green natural countryside with small friendly market towns and lovely villages.

A Did you say mountains? There aren't any. Almost nothing over a thousand metres.

B All right. But those that are called mountains are very impressive—wild and rugged and lonely. They don't have crowds of people going up them by funicular and huge noisy restaurants on top.

A And isn't that typical? Catering for tourists is well below standard. Most hotels are old-fashioned and although there are rooms in private houses, you've usually got to go round and find them yourself, in England anyhow. Local tourist offices hardly exist.

B And that's just the point. Apart from the main tourist centres like London and Stratford, Britain isn't overrun by tourists and spoilt by them. I was told that there are many beautiful old cathedral cities and picturesque villages where people live their ordinary lives undisturbed by crowds of visitors who expect smart expensive restaurants and souvenir shops stocked with ugly rubbish.

A Anyhow there's nothing really old as there is in Greece and Italy.

B Really old things in those countries are mainly ruins. There are many inhabited buildings from the Middle Ages, thousands of old churches and still one or two walled towns. And very many beautiful homes from the fifteenth century onwards: palaces, mansions and country houses elegantly furnished that one can visit even though they're owned privately. And especially gardens. The Wrights have never stopped talking about the parks and gardens.

A If you like that sort of thing. I preferred the London night life. It hardly exists outside London. Most restaurants close early and may not open at all on Sundays.

B That may be a nuisance. However I suppose I'll manage. I'm spending a month there and I'm going to see as much as possible, including some of the seaside resorts, sand, blue sea, caves, cliffs and rocks. And I'm not even going to set foot in London.

A Well, I only hope you enjoy yourself.

Advice about dealing with this type of question

(*a*) Read through the passage twice, once to get a general idea of what it is about, the second time to notice especially the points you will be using. It is advisable to read the instructions above again before beginning the second reading.

Write down the words DRAWBACKS and ATTRACTIONS. Underneath each make a list of these as they appear in the passage.

Try to separate the *facts* from the less important details. For example, the variety of the landscape is important: details of towns and cathedrals can be included if you have words to spare but are less essential.

Here are some of the items to be listed. Those bracketed are less important details.

DRAWBACKS	ATTRACTIONS
Industry and large uninteresting towns	The variety of scenery (mountains, old and new towns and cathedrals, kinds of seaside places)
The frequently depressing weather	
No high mountains	The mountains, though not high, wild and lonely, unspoilt by noisy tourists

Little attention given to the needs of tourists (old-fashioned hotels, few tourist offices in England)	The few tourists mean that many places remain naturally beautiful.

(*b*) When your lists have been completed, it is a good idea to count the number of words you have already used. This will give some indication of the number you will need to write the paragraphs in full: allow for possibly 25% more words when your ideas are expressed in complete sentences. (This is only a very rough idea.) You may find you have included too many details and have to decide which you can leave out or, alternatively, that you can include more than you had thought. Do not begin writing the final paragraphs until you are fairly sure that your ideas can be expressed in the number of words suggested.

(*c*) Having decided on the ideas you can include, you now have to express them in sentences and connected paragraphs. The art of doing this lies in choosing words and making sentences that express your ideas *exactly* and *shortly* (without thinking in your own language), *thinking clearly and logically* and avoiding all unnecessary details.

Prepare your paragraphs in rough first. Keep checking the number of words you have already used in relation to the total number you are allowed.

Here is a possible opening of the first paragraph.

> The British weather may be cold, damp and depressing. Britain has large industrial areas and big uninteresting towns and no really high mountains. Little attention is given in England to tourists' needs.

(*d*) When you have finished the two paragraphs, have *checked the number of words* used and *read through* what you have written *carefully to find any language mistakes* you have probably made, make a final neat copy of the completed work.

2 A sixth-form teacher is having a discussion with her class of eighteen-year-old boys and girls. They are talking about advertising techniques. You are asked to write two paragraphs, together between 175 and 200 words in length in which you explain the various methods used to persuade people to buy a certain make of soap. The first paragraph should deal with the methods of the soap producers themselves to make the soap seem attractive and the second with the ways in which advertisers try to persuade the public to buy it.

Teacher	Let's discuss an everyday thing we all use: toilet soap. Which soap do you use, Jill?
Jill	Oh, Dewfresh usually.
Teacher	Why?
Jill	Well, it's good for my complexion. It softens my skin and makes it feel fresh.
Roger	The advertisers' wonder girl! She believes all they tell her.
Jill	But I'm sure it does. When I used Coolcrema, it didn't have nearly the same effect.

Roger	I've never heard of Coolcrema. It isn't advertised on T.V.
Teacher	So, Jill, what you want of a soap is something to improve your skin and complexion?
Jill	Yes, of course. Why else do we use soap?
Graham	I thought it was to make ourselves clean.
Catherine	So do you use household soap when you wash?
Graham	No. But neither do I use that rose-pink scented stuff that you girls like so much.
Teacher	Remember that all soap should make you clean. Everybody accepts that. So advertisers try to add some special quality to the soap they deal with. Most women want to be beautiful. And they can only too easily be made to believe that soaps can produce beautiful complexions and soft skins and that these qualities of themselves can create beauty. Dennis, what soap do you use?
Dennis	Whatever my mother provides. I'm not fussy. She buys it cheap in the supermarket.
Jill	Then it's probably no good. It's cheap because they make it with any old thing.
Teacher	So a soap has to be expensive to be good?
Jill	Well, you've always got to pay for value.
Teacher	Have you ever thought that that might be just another idea suggested by the advertiser? 'Our soap costs more and so must be better. Cheap soaps do you harm.' Or the snob appeal of a more expensive soap: 'This is what the best people use'. And yet you know most toilet soaps are basically the same. Anyhow what other things about a certain soap may attract you?
Catherine	The name, I suppose. Dewfresh, Honey Cream, Rose Petal Silk. They sound fresh and smooth and young.
Jill	And the wrappings too. Exciting pop-design wrappings or pretty colours and spring-flower designs. And the shape of the soap itself and some kind of picture or design on it. And its colour: fresh, pretty clean-looking colours, or for men, healthy white or gold or brown.
Dennis	How about the slogans: 'Give your face that radiant loveliness that will linger throughout the day and make you lovable'. Or perhaps not throughout the day, as they would want you to use the soap more than once or twice a day.
Teacher	Let's consider the slogans. What do they try to appeal to? Women first. Veronica, a suggestion from you.
Veronica	Oh, beauty, I suppose, that will attract dozens of boy friends. And for older people, smoothing away lines and wrinkles and all that. But how about men? They buy soap too.
Graham	They make less effort to make us buy because it's usually mother or the wife who buys the soap. But I suppose for us it's cleanliness, removing dirt and perspiration and making us nice to be near.
Teacher	Have you ever thought what can be done by connecting the soap with people or ideas that the general public admire?
Jill	You mean famous film stars who claim that this is how they

	preserve their beauty. And people believe that if the film star uses the soap, it must be fashionable and the right thing to use.
Graham	I suppose it's sportsmen, especially those very much in the news, that appeal to men. But I still think it's the idea of cleanliness and freshness and a neat smart wrapping that sell soap to those men who do buy it.
Catherine	This isn't advertising, but have you noticed that a lot of women smell soap before they buy it. They are more interested in the perfume than the soap itself.
Veronica	But a scented soap isn't pure. I always use Martins' Pure Oatmeal because it can't possibly harm my skin. And Martins have such a good name: they've been making soap for over a hundred years.
Jill	Perfume doesn't make any difference to the quality. And just because the company's old, it doesn't make the soap good. It's all part of sales technique. We're all deceived by it really. Glamour, that's what it is: an impression that an ordinary everyday thing like soap, just because it has a perfume or a pretty wrapping can work magic and change our skins and make our lives romantic.
Teacher	So you've discovered one of the secrets of modern sales methods. But you and I will still buy an X car, Y cigarettes or Z petrol because we've read the advertisements, even though we think we don't. We imagine we're more attractive, successful, daring when we use them, and can persuade ourselves that each has some special extra quality. All because of clever preparation by the producers and clever publicity by the advertisers.

Advice about dealing with this passage

This is a more difficult exercise as it is necessary to decide which of the methods referred to are used by the producers and which by the advertisers.

Here are some useful points for each paragraph:

PRODUCERS	ADVERTISERS
Providing attractive wrappings Perfume or no perfume (better for skin) A higher price suggesting better quality Colours and shapes	Presenting the idea that soap can create new beauty for young women and preserve the beauty of older women Names and slogans.

These points would have to be expanded considerably more than those listed for the previous passage so a good many more words will be needed to develop the complete answer. Bear in mind the number asked for.

Read again the other advice given for dealing with the first passage.

7

Passage for comprehension

Shelter for the night

The rain started as dusk was falling. He had been walking since ten o'clock and he was beginning to feel extremely tired. Overhead, heavy grey clouds were gathering ominously; a few streaks of what had been a fiery sunset gleamed for a while on the dark bog puddles ahead, but these soon faded, leaving a uniform greyness of earth and sky. 5

The narrow muddy path twisted to avoid boulders covered with spongy moss and the few scattered bushes. As the rain had now obviously set in and was falling with increasing determination, he wearily unfolded his raincoat and put it on. He fumbled in his pocket for his small torch, which he would probably need before long. He was getting hungry so he greedily 10 munched some of his stock of ginger biscuits and chocolate. He had no idea of how far he had still to walk; so far as he was concerned he was the sole inhabitant of a deserted world of gigantic, cloud continents, damp gloomy wastes of moorland, minute tinkling streams and driving soaking rain.

Suddenly he felt the path descending steeply. Peering through the dark- 15 ness, he could discern lights. Switching on his torch, he doubled his pace, and within a quarter of an hour was striding briskly along a paved street between rows of houses. At the crossroads he noticed a small public house with a board outside announcing that there was accommodation available on the premises. He hopefully pushed open the door, went through a dimly- 20 lit passage and entered a smoke-filled bar. Men were leaning against the counter, arguing stubbornly about business and betting, cricket and crime; a group of three in the far corner, who looked like commercial travellers, were very nearly quarrelling over politics, while a third group, quietly playing dominoes, seemed completely absorbed in their game. 25

The cheerful-looking woman serving behind the bar said good-evening to him in a friendly way but shook her head discouragingly when he asked about a room.

'I'm sorry,' she said, 'the local race week is starting to-morrow and every room has been taken. But it's bad weather to go hunting for rooms in. I 30 suggest you go and see Mrs. Parkins next door. Since her son has been called up, she usually has a spare room, and she never minds helping anyone who has nowhere to sleep, provided he's respectable.'

Notes on the passage

Vocabulary

line

Title *shelter* (*V*)*:* trees *sheltered* the house; he *sheltered* from the rain.
a shelter (*N*)*:* the cave provided *shelter*, a bus *shelter*; a *sheltered* spot.
a refuge (*N*)*:* a safe place; seek (take) refuge from an advancing army.
a refugee: someone who takes refuge in another country for political reasons.

1 *dawn* (*daybreak*), *sunrise*, *daylight*, *sunset*, *dusk* (*twilight*), *darkness* (*the dark*).
twilight ('two lights') can refer both to morning and evening.
day dawns; dusk falls; night falls; a mist thickens.
Notice: Gradually *it dawned on me* that I had taken the wrong road.

2 fairly, quite, very, extremely, exceedingly, excessively (too much).

2 *overhead*, underfoot, ahead.

3 *an omen* a sign suggesting what the future will be (often unpleasant).
an *ominous* silence (awaiting something unpleasant); an ominous speech (which suggests unpleasant things to come); an ominous sky (dark and threatening).

3 *a streak:* a narrow irregular strip: a streak of paint, a streak of cruelty in someone's nature; a *striped* dress, a tabby cat has *stripes*; a gold *band* round the cuff of a uniform; a *strip* of paper or material = a fairly long but narrow piece; *a comic strip* in the newspaper.
strip (*V*) = take off a covering: strip the bark from a tree-trunk; the doctor told the patient to strip.

4 *gleam* (*N* and *V*)—polished metal and a lake surface in moonlight gleam.
There was a gleam of interest (of excitement) in his eyes.
dazzle (*V*) shine so brightly as to make it impossible to see *blinding* is even stronger than *dazzling.*
sparkle (*N* and *V*)—a stream in sunlight sparkles.
glitter (*N* and *V*)—diamonds glitter in bright light (a hard bright light).
glow (*N* and *V*)—a dying fire glows.

4 *for a while*—for a time. *a little while. meanwhile.*—while this was happening.

4 *bog*—wet, muddy earth that can be dug out and burned as *peat* a *marsh* and a *swamp* are dangerously wet and muddy the swamps of the Amazon; the Essex marshes; an Irish bog.

4 a *puddle* in the street; a duck *pond*; a swimming *pool*; a *lake.*

6 a *muddy* path; *sandy* soil; a *rocky* valley; *stony* ground; a *pebbly* beach; a *grassy* slope; a *mossy* bank.

6 *twist*—twist a corkscrew into a cork before pulling; twist one's ankle. *wind* wool into a ball; wind up a clock; a *winding* road (wind wound wound DO NOT MIX: wound wounded wounded).
revolve: the earth revolves; a revolving door; a revolver.
a revolution in in effect a complete turning round or change *roll:* a ball rolls *a roll* and butter.

6 *spongy:* one can wash with a *sponge* and also eat a sponge (a soft cake). Both have small holes in them. Do not confuse *biscuits* and *sponge cake*. *a Swiss roll* is a layer of sponge cake covered with jam and then rolled.

6 Notice the proverb: 'A rolling stone gathers no moss' which can have two meanings. Suggest these.

8 *increase*—general expression for 'get or make more': increase one's income.
grow—plants, animals, profits grow. (*N* growth). *extend* 'get or make longer': *extend* a road, a large building—the *extension* of the motorway; *expand*—'get or make bigger': metals expand when heated; (*N* expansion). *swell*—'get bigger' (especially parts of the body): a painful *swollen* wrist (*N* swelling).

8 *fall*—rain falls; *fall down*—a child falls down; (Something already standing on the ground falls down). *drop*—let fall.
He dropped his stick NOT: let fall.

8 *unfold/fold up* *undo/do up.*

10 *munch* an apple; *crunch*—the dog crunched a small bone; *chew* food for some time (chewing gum); *lick* with the tongue—the dog licked my hand; *lap*—a cat laps milk; *snap*—the parrot snapped at my finger; *suck* a sweet.

11 *stock*—the shopkeeper has no atlases in stock: they are out of stock.
store (*V*)—goods are stored in a warehouse; (*N*) a store of food for the winter; a *department store*=a large shop selling many different things.

11 *ginger* is a *spice*. Other spices are cinnamon, nutmeg and pepper and they are added to food to give extra *flavour*.

13 *desert* (*N*)*:* the Sahara Desert; (*V*)*:* he *deserted* (abandoned) his friends when they were in danger; *a deserter*—someone who runs away from the army; a *deserted* house. *dessert*—the sweet course at the end of a meal (for pronunciation see Page 99).

13 *gigantic* (*Adj*) *giant* (*N*). OPP *tiny, minute* (*Adj*) *dwarf* (*N*) BUT: a dwarf tree or plant. (*V*)*:* the bus dwarfed the tiny car.

13 Asia is a *continent*. Europe, apart from the British Isles, is *the Continent.*

13 *damp* (dampness)*:* a damp climate, damp clothes (slightly wet in an unpleasant way).
moist (moisture)*:* bread should be kept moist (not quite dry).

13 *gloomy:* a gloomy dark room, a gloomy outlook, face, mood (gloom); a *dismal* expression on someone's face, weather; a *dreary* life, day, lesson.
gloomy suggests darkness; *dismal* sadness and depression; *dreary* monotony.

13 *waste* (*V*): waste time/money (*N*): a waste of time; desert wastes; (*Adj*): waste land; a waste-paper-basket. *Spelling: waist*—part of the body.

14 *stream* *Notice:* a stream is *a small river*, a *brook*. In a school, *streaming* is a division of children into classes according to their ability.

15 *descend*/descent *ascend*/ascent. Ascension Day is a religious festival.

15 *peer*—look with difficulty; *discern*—see with difficulty.

16 *double* (*V* and *Adj*) *treble* *quadruple.* A person's double is almost identical with him. Two children born at the same time are *twins*; three are *triplets*; four are *quadruplets. singles* (two players): *doubles* (four).

17 *stride* (*N* and *V*)—walking with long steps. sit *astride* a horse.

18 *crossroads* or *road junction;* a road can also *fork*; a *bend* in the road. *Turn to the left* at the crossroads: *bear to the left* where the road forks.

18 In a *public house* people can drink beer, wine and spirits. An *inn* is a country pub, sometimes offering *accommodation* for travellers. A *hostel* (youth hostel) provides accommodation for groups. A *boarding-house* is a kind of family hotel. *full board*—accommodation and all meals.

19 *available:* can be obtained or used. *accessible:* within reach. Cooking facilities are available. Venice is accessible by one road only.

20 He was *eager*/*anxious* to help. BUT: He was anxious (not 'eager') about his examination results.

22 *argument*—in which people take sides. In a *quarrel* they get angry. A *discussion* is an exchange of opinions.

22 *stubborn*/*obstinate* (obstinacy)—of similar meaning.

22 *betting* on horses. *gambling* with cards or in a Casino. *Football pools.* 'Let's have a bet on it.'

26 A *shop assistant* stands behind a *counter*. He *serves* the *customers.*

27 *shook her head* to say no. *shook her fist* to show anger (*at* someone). *shook hands with* someone. She *nodded* to say yes. She nodded because she was almost asleep.

31 *next door*—in the next house. *our next-door neighbour.*

31 *called-up* for compulsory military service. This is known as *national service* and the boy is a *conscript.* He does not *volunteer for* the army, though both he and the conscript are at first only *recruits.* Older experienced soldiers are *veterans.* Industry has *recruitment programmes,* schemes to get new workers.

Phrasal verbs

line

SET

7 bad weather *sets in. set out* for the place one is going to. *set up* a business: *the father set up his son in business.* to be *set upon* by criminals and robbed of one's money.

Other uses of set

Noun:	a set of glasses/artificial teeth; a tea/coffee set (or service); a radio/television set; a set in tennis. *setting:* music composed for certain words; frame in which a jewel is set; surroundings or background for a play, book etc.: *the story is set in Mexico, with exotic and dramatic settings.*
Verb:	the sun sets; a liquid (e.g. jelly) sets or becomes firm and solid; hair is set or arranged in waves; a surgeon sets a broken bone; a teacher sets homework; set a good example; set or lay a table; set food before someone; set fire to; set sail; set a trap; set to work (start working); set prisoners free; set the fashion; set seeds; set words to music.
Adjective:	a set expression on one's face = a fixed, determined expression; a set time (arranged); a set wage.

line

LOOK

23 *look like* another person/being a fine day; *look down on* someone considered inferior; *look at* a picture; *look for* something lost; *look into* a matter that needs explanation or investigation; *look forward to* something pleasant; *look after* children; *look out of* a window; *look out!*—a sudden warning of approaching danger; *look up* the meaning of a word in a dictionary; *look up to* someone very much respected; *look away from* an unpleasant sight; *look over* someone else's book; *overlook* (not notice) a mistake or something one should have done and has forgotten to do or something that deserves punishment but will be passed over on this occasion; *overlook* or *look out on* a park; *look upon* or *regard* someone *as* an expert; *look on* (an *onlooker*) without taking any active part; *look round* in a shop; *look through* something written, possibly to find any mistakes; *look through* a window.

Pronunciation

BE CAREFUL: fiery [fáɪərɪ]; spongy [spʌ́n(d)ʒɪ]; ginger [ʤíndʒə]; biscuits [bískɪts]; chocolate [tʃɔ́klət]; giant [ʤáɪənt]; gigantic [ʤaɪgǽntɪk].

SOUND CHANGES: omen [óumən]; ominously [ɔ́mɪnəslɪ]; minute (*N*) [mínɪt]; minute (*Adj*) [máɪnjúːt]; desert (*N*) [dézət]; desert (*V*) [dɪzɔ́ːt]; dessert (*N*) [dɪzəːt].

STRESS: overhead [óuvəhéd]; idea [aɪdíə].

ə (as in *a*go): moorland [múələnd or mɔːlənd]; stubborn [stʌ́bən]; accommodation [əkɔmədeíʃən]; commercial [kəmɔ́ːʃəl].
i (as in cit*y*): premises [prémɪsɪz]; discouraging [dɪskʌ́rɪdʒɪŋ].

OTHERS: streaks [strɪːks]; gleamed [glɪːmd]; puddles [pʌdlz]; uniform [júːnɪfɔːm]; torch [tɔːtʃ]; peering [píərɪŋ]; discern [dɪsɔ́ːn]; doubled [dʌ́bəld]; quarrelling [kwɔ́rəlɪŋ]; cheerful [tʃíəful].

Special grammatical and structural points

(i) *Present Participles*

These are all examples of the present participle taken from the passage. In the first group it is used adjectivally:

(*a*)......a board announcing.....(a board which announced)
......a group playing dominoes (who were playing)

and here the effect is that of an adverb:

(*b*) peering through the darkness, he saw......(when he peered ....)
these faded, leaving a uniform greyness......(when these faded, they *left*..............).

NOTICE:

(i) The present participle is found in written English, but rarely adverbially in spoken. 'Walking along the High Street, I met an old friend' would sound odd in conversation. It would be expressed as: 'I met an old friend as I was walking along the High Street.'

(ii) In any case, do not overdo the use of the present participle, as even in written English it often sounds strange. One would be unlikely even to write, for example: 'Going into his room he turned on the light' but: 'He went into his room and turned on the light.'
Use participles only in cases where you have already met and learned them in English.

(ii) *Uncountable and Countable Nouns in the Passage*

Uncountables: determination, darkness (abstract); accommodation (general); rain, mud, ginger; cricket (a game); betting (a gerund).
With Meaning Change: crime (in general)/a crime; business/a business; light/a light; chocolate/a chocolate.
Plural: premises.
Plural form but Singular meaning: politics/the news/mathematics/physics is worth studying. It is interesting.

(iii) *provided (that)/providing*—these two terms are interchangeable.
They can often replace *if* when the idea of fulfilling a certain condition is especially strong. They can begin a sentence but more often follow a main clause.

I'll come if I can. I'll come provided you pay my fare.

Take these tablets if you feel ill. ('provided' would be impossible)
Provided you continue taking these tablets, you will not be ill.

(iv) *Adverbial Phrases*

(*a*) Several adjectives end in *-ly*. These include: *friendly, chilly, leisurely, lovely, kindly, silly, jolly*. A very few writers use the adjectives as adverbs, but a far pleasanter effect is produced (a) by using an adverbial phrase such as: *in a friendly way*; or (b) by avoiding the adverb in some way: *he went for a leisurely walk through the town*; or (c) by using another adverb: *she sang beautifully*.

(*b*) Some adjectives, including most participles, have no adverbial form: *difficult*, *determined* and *interested* are examples. Where there is a corresponding noun, a 'with' phrase can sometimes be used adverbially.

EXAMPLES: He spoke with difficulty. He listened to the speech with interest. Even when an adverb exists, the 'with' phrase can sometimes be used when the adjective is modified by another adverb.

EXAMPLES: The rain was falling with increasing determination (No Adverb). He greeted me enthusiastically: with little enthusiasm. He awaited the results pessimistically: with increasing pessimism.

(v) *Verbal Constructions*

ALTERNATIVE CONSTRUCTIONS

		begin/start to write/writing
		(with little meaning change)
		but: *finish/stop writing.*
suggest	*Gerund*	He *suggested hiring* a car.
	also	He *suggested our hiring* a car.
	Clause	He *suggested (that) we (should) hire a car.*
mind	*Gerund*	Would you *mind waiting* a few minutes?
	Clause	Would you *mind if I use* your telephone?
		Mind how you go.

Prepositions

(*a*) *put on/take off* a garment; *put/turn/switch on/off* a light; *switch on/off* a torch; *turn on/off* a tap (NOT: open and close)/the gas. (*b*) *covered with/by* moss (*c*) before long (*d*) *within* a quarter of an hour (*e*) *on* the premises (*f*) enter a room (NO: in) (*g*) hunt animals BUT: hunt *for* a room (*h*) ask/argue *about* (Remember: discuss something) (*i*) no idea *of* how far ....

Expressions to learn and introduce into written work

(*a*) overhead, underfoot, ahead (*A short way ahead, I could see ....*) (*b*) for a (long) (short) (little) while; meanwhile (*c*) the rain had set in (*d*) this will need repairing before long (*e*) he had no idea of (the way etc.) but: he had no idea what to do next. (*f*) be/get/feel hungry, thirsty, tired, angry, bored etc. (*g*) So far as I am concerned, a sandwich would be enough, but Dick wants a cooked meal (*h*) he will telephone within a quarter of an hour (*i*) she never minds helping (*j*) accommodation available on the premises.

Multiple choice questions

Here are a number of questions or unfinished statements about the passage, each with four suggested ways of answering or finishing it. You must choose the way you consider the most suitable. Write in each case the bracketed number of the question or statement followed by the letters **A**, **B**, **C**, **D**, and then cross through the letter of the answer you choose. Give one answer only to each question. Read the passage right through again before choosing your answers.

1 When did the rain start?
A as the sun was just setting **B** when it was already quite dark **C** at ten o'clock **D** when the sun had set and it was beginning to get dark

2 The walker was moving towards
A the north **B** the south **C** the east **D** the west

3 It is clear from the passage that when the rain set in the walker
A did not know where he was going **B** was lost **C** did not know exactly where he was **D** was in danger of being caught in the bog

4 When did he put on his mackintosh?
A when it began getting dark **B** when dark clouds gathered **C** when it started to rain **D** after it had been raining for some time

5 Which of these possibilities had the walker made no preparations for?
A bad weather **B** being still on the moors after dark **C** getting hungry **D** not knowing where he was

6 Which of these feelings does the passage make clear that the walker experienced during his solitary journey in the rain?
A tiredness **B** fear of his desolate surroundings **C** keen hunger **D** intense loneliness

7 Why did he switch on his torch?
A because he was walking downhill **B** so as to be able to walk more quickly **C** because it was getting even darker **C** to see the lights ahead more clearly

8 What were some of the men in the public house doing?
A betting **B** fighting **C** gambling **D** talking about sport

9 Which of these words does not describe the woman serving behind the bar?
A pessimistic **B** welcoming **C** well-meaning **D** good-humoured

10 Why has Mrs. Parkins got a spare room?
A she keeps it for people with nowhere to go **B** her son is in the army **C** she is used to letting rooms to people **D** she lives alone

Reading comprehension

In this exercise you must choose the word or phrase which best completes each sentence. Write first the number of each sentence followed by the letters **A**, **B**, **C**, **D**, **E**, and then cross through the letter of the correct answer in each case.

1 Some of the older villagers prefer to .... tobacco rather than to smoke it.
A munch **B** crunch **C** chew **D** bite **E** gnaw

2 Many strands were .... together to make the rope really strong.
A twisted **B** woven **C** revolved **D** rolled **E** wounded

3 The melting of the snow has caused flooding by .... rivers.
A extended **B** expanded **C** overgrown **D** prolonged **E** swollen

4 The headlights of the approaching car were so .... that the cyclist had to stop riding.
A gleaming **B** dazzling **C** blazing **D** glittering **E** glowing

5 A blinding .... of lightning flashed across the sky.
A strip **B** streak **C** stripe **D** band **E** patch

6 Some useful ideas were suggested while the social committee was .... the club's programme for the coming season.
A arguing about **B** discussing **C** quarrelling about **D** disputing about **E** having a debate on

7 With an eighty-hour week and little change or enjoyment, life must have been very .... for the nineteenth-century factory worker.
A weary **B** anxious **C** dark **D** pessimistic **E** dreary

8 He is paving the garden .... with flat stones of various shapes.
A way **B** track **C** path **D** lane **E** alley

9 Weeks later he had still not found a job and he began to feel ....
A disappointed **B** disengaged **C** displaced **D** discouraged **E** displeased

10 A long line of traffic had to wait at the .... until the train had passed.
A crossroads **B** drawbridge **C** junction **D** level crossing **E** subway

Use of English

1 (ii) Fill each of the numbered blanks in the passage with *one* suitable word.

Thoroughly tired he .... (1) down on the bed and .... (2) asleep almost immediately. He was .... (3) by the sound of heavy footsteps in the attic .... (4). He took his torch and crept up the steep .... (5) of stairs, ... (6) the attic door silently. There were some cupboards inside but otherwise the room was .... (7) empty. He .... (8) on his torch now and started to examine .... (9) carefully, but found .... (10) to explain the sounds.

He leaned .... (11) a large wardrobe and .... (12) his head disbelievingly. He had no .... (13) .... (14) to do next. Then he noticed that the .... (15) of the floor was completely covered with dust apart from .... (16) own footprints. He made his .... (17) downstairs again but he .... (18) little that night. He kept .... (19) to every sound and wondering .... (20) the house might be haunted.

2 The five phrases below are the answers to five questions that could be asked about the reading passage. Write out the questions.

(i) since ten o'clock
(ii) rain had set in
(iii) he unfolded it
(iv) good evening
(v) next door

3 Write down the twelve words in list A below and against each the one word from list B which rhymes with it.

A	B
streaks	scored
fiery	bubble
leather	fear
sole	breather
peer	curled
rows	theory
board	Greeks
double	cows
weary	toes
sponge	diary
earth	bakes
world	whether
	birth
	goal
	ward
	plunge
	merge

4 Rewrite the following series of words to form complete sentences.

(i) writing there sits he long without never something.
(ii) so abroad do people why holidays many always their spend?
(iii) with students enough something have money to the them eat buy to.
(iv) very new learning down he much words them enjoys and writing them.

Composition and summarising

Explanations

The most important qualities of a good explanation are CLEARNESS, ACCURACY (CORRECTNESS) and CAREFUL ARRANGEMENT.

Here is an example of a more detailed explanation. In this, certain facts must be made clear first in the opening paragraph and then the other details are arranged so that the ideas follow one another logically.

Write a short report of the climate of the area you live in. This should include general information about temperatures, rainfall and wind directions, but it is not necessary to give any figures. Use between 120 and 180 words.

(The word 'explanation' can cover many things. Here the writer has to explain what the climate is like and why.)

PLAN (Southern England)

1 Position of Great Britain.
2 Winter climate.
3 Summer climate.
4 General tendencies.

Great Britain lies to the west of the Continent of Europe and has the Atlantic Ocean to the west. Winds most often come from that direction and are therefore damp and not too cold. The Gulf Stream, which flows around all coasts, helps to raise temperatures.

Winters are chilly and often damp but seldom really cold. There is some frost and occasional snowfalls, but normally the snow soon disappears. In some years there are longer periods of frost and snow.

Summers are fairly warm but never very hot though there may be occasional heat waves. It is often cloudy. Rain may fall at any time.

This is an island climate, with very changeable and moderate heat, cold and rainfall. It is impossible to give exact information about any period of the year. (132 words)

SUBJECTS FOR PRACTICE

Answer these in between 120 and 180 words.

1 Give an account of the main ways in which the people in your town or village earn their living.

Here is a possible plan:

(*a*) The most important industries (or kinds of farming)
(*b*) Trade and business
(*c*) Professional and general

2 Explain briefly how you celebrate any one of the following in your country:

a wedding
a twenty-first or other special birthday
Christmas Eve (or Christmas Day)
any national festival

3 Explain why you are learning English.

4 Explain the main difficulties you have had in learning English.

5 What are the advantages and drawbacks of living in a flat?

6 Explain why you enjoy or dislike living in the town or village where your home is.

7 As Secretary of a Youth Club you have to prepare an account of the aims, activities and meeting-times of the club. Write this account.

8 As a prospective Town Councillor you are preparing a letter to be sent to all the town residents. This mentions three things in the town which you think need improvement and how you think these improvements could be carried out. Write the information given in the letter—there is no need to put an address. You can write about an imaginary town if you wish.

9 The writer records his experiences and impressions in his diary that evening. Write what he records, using only material from the passage and not more than 130 words. Here is a suggestion for the first sentence:

'I set out at ten o'clock and was still on the moor at dusk.'

Spoken English

Words commonly used when speaking

The following words appear quite frequently with various meanings in spoken English.

mind — *Would you mind* waiting a few minutes? No, *I don't mind* in the least.
Mind how you go. (Advice to someone driving or cycling)
Mind that step! *Mind* the doors! (on the London Underground).
She *minds* the children while I'm at work. *Mind your own business* (Impolite).

manage — Can you *manage* that suitcase? Can you *manage* to be there at seven?
No, I'm afraid *I can't manage it*. He can't *manage* his own affairs, let alone a shop.

wonder — I *wonder* where he is. I *wonder if* I could do something to help you?
I wonder if you could let me have a stamp for this letter?

afraid — *I'm afraid* I can't tell you. *I'm afraid* he's ill.
Will it be cooler to-morrow? *I'm afraid so*/*I'm afraid not.*

trouble
bother — Sorry to {*trouble* / *bother*} you but I think I left my gloves here.
May I trouble you to move your chair a little? {*It's* / *That's*} *no trouble* at all.
Don't {*trouble* / *bother*} to knock. I hope I'm not *giving you too much trouble.*
What's the trouble? Oh, the engine's *giving trouble.*
If you say that to them, you'll *cause trouble.*
He's always been *a trouble to* his mother.

The trouble is that you're downright lazy. *Bother*, I've dropped it!

chance Is there *any chance of* getting a ticket? Are you *by any chance* Barbara's sister? Have you *by any chance* got a key like mine?
It was quite *by chance* that we stayed in that hotel.
So you think all accommodation will be taken? Well, we'll have *to chance* that. (Well, let's *chance it*.) I'll go if I *get the chance*.

good harm *It's no good* complaining. You'll have to put up with it.
A holiday will *do you good*. It'll *do you good* to have a rest.
A little hard work would *do you no harm*.
It might *be a good idea* (mightn't be a bad idea) to take some food.
I don't think I can but *there's no harm in asking*.
How about taking a camera? Yes, *that's a good idea. That's not a bad idea*.

doubt *I've not the least doubt* he can do it. *There's no doubt* he's a great actor.
There's no doubt about it. *I doubt whether* we've got time.
Will he ever finish writing his book? *I doubt it*.

VARIOUS

I just *can't help* making mistakes. *What on earth* are you doing?
I dare say you'll manage to pass the exam. though it's a bit doubtful.
Thank goodness I've found my purse!
It's a job to manage to live on £15 a week.
Oh, it's just starting to rain. *Never mind*, we're nearly there.

Emphasising an action

The auxiliaries DO and DID can be used to express strong emphasis:
I do wish you'd hurry! I tell you he did say that!
Other auxiliaries can be emphasised only by the voice, though WILL and WOULD can sometimes give similar emphasis: She will shout when she gets excited. He would keep thanking me for my help.

Express these ideas emphatically. The new subject is given. In some cases the new sentence will be much shorter:

(*a*) make a lot of mistakes (you).

(*b*) contradicting the statement that I had not telephoned (I).

(*c*) complimenting someone on a new hair style (it).

(*d*) missing you while you were away. (your dog).

(*e*) on expressing dissatisfaction with some new shoes you had insisted on buying (you).

(*f*) expressing irritation with a cat who always lies on your flower beds (she).

(*g*) expressing liking for a good detective story (I).

Asking the way

(*a*) *in the country:*

Excuse me, could you tell me the way to Sheepcote, please?
I'm afraid you're going in the wrong direction (going the wrong way). Follow this path back for about a mile. You'll pass a farmhouse on your right and just after that, you'll see a path branching off to the left. Follow that, and you should reach the village in about half an hour.

(*b*) *in a town:*

Excuse me, could you direct me to the General Post Office?
Go straight along this street to the traffic lights. Turn left there, and a short way along on the left, you'll see a cinema. Take the next turning on the right and you'll see the Post Office. It's a small building facing a big supermarket. It'll take you about ten minutes to get there. You could go by bus but it's hardly worth it.
(Greychapel Avenue? I'm afraid I've never heard of it. Are you sure you've got the name right?)

EXERCISES: Ask someone the way to and then give directions for finding:

(*a*) the nearest post office from your place of work or school.
(*b*) a cottage about two miles from a village you know of.
(*c*) the nearest hospital from your own home.
(*d*) the nearest large car park to the Town Hall where space will certainly be available.

Situations

What would you say in these situations: (*a*) you have been asked for advice about interesting places to see in your locality. (*b*) you have been asked to recommend a local restaurant. Give your reasons.

Expressing your own opinions

Give your own ideas about any of these subjects.

(*a*) When you are on holiday, do you prefer to stay in a large hotel, a small hotel, a country inn, a youth hostel, a holiday camp, a caravan, a boarding house or with a family? Why?
(*b*) What things can make a pub, café or restaurant attractive besides the food and drink served there?
(*c*) Do you enjoy walking in the countryside? Why or why not?
(*d*) If you could choose the weather throughout the year, what kind of weather or varieties of weather would you prefer? Explain why.

General guidance and practice

Notice the following INFINITIVE forms:

	Active	*Passive*
SIMPLE	To take	To be taken
CONTINUOUS	To be taking	—
PERFECT	To have taken	To have been taken
PERFECT CONTINUOUS	To have been taking	—

He likes *to lie* in the sun. (habitual action)
He wants *to take* a photograph. (in the immediate or distant future)
He seems *to be taking* a photograph. (at this moment)
He seems *to have taken* a photograph. (he has just finished)
He is said *to have taken* up politics. (action in the past)
He must *have been taking* photographs all day. (emphasis on a period of time)

The sentry told us we ought not *to have taken* (*been taking*) photographs of the aerodrome. (the perfect infinitive used with 'should' or 'ought to' in fact the photographs were taken.)
We should have asked him about it. (perfect infinitive—in fact we did not ask him)

Replace the words in brackets in the following passage with any suitable verbal form, active or passive, you have learned in this or a previous chapter:

Mrs. Parkins proved to be a motherly woman of about fifty. An apron (tie) round her neat blue skirt and she (seem) (smile) even before she (open) the door.

'I (just come) from next door,' he (explain). 'I (tell) that you sometimes (let) your spare room.'

Her face (cloud) over. '(Be) not that a pity!' she (exclaim). 'I (just promise) it to one of my husband's friends. He (send) here by his firm to-day to survey a new housing site.'

He (just turn) away, when she (stop) him. 'I (must) (think),' she (say). '(Come) in and (sit) down.'

He (lead) into a cosy sitting-room where a fire (burn). She (watch) television when he (knock), but after she (put) a kettle on in the kitchen, she (come) and (switch) the television off.

'I (think) of an idea,' she (inform) him. '(Mind) you sleeping on a camp bed in the attic? The mattress (air) two days ago, and the sheets (can) (air) now while you (have) some supper. What (think) you of that?'

He (say) this (be) a very good idea, and in less than half an hour an enormous supper of eggs, bacon and tomatoes (set) in front of him. As soon as he (eat) it, he (go) thankfully to bed. He (seem) (discover) a very comfortable lodging.

Word order in sentences (single word adverbs)

I. *Here are a few more rules:*

A. Single word adverbs of frequency: *always*, *usually*, *often*, *frequently*, *sometimes*, *occasionally*, *seldom*, *rarely*, *and never* may precede the verb when this is in the Present or Past Simple Tense (for exceptions see Note II). *Very often*, *very frequently*, *very seldom*, *very rarely*, *hardly ever*, *scarcely ever*, may do the same.

Among the other adverbs to which this may apply are:

(*a*) *soon*, *still*, *now*, *then*, *recently*, *possibly*, *obviously*, *evidently*.

(*b*) *many adverbs of manner when they are not stressed in any way:*
He entered the room and quietly sat down.
He entered the room noisily but sat down quietly.

(*c*) Most other unstressed adverbs.

B. A few adverbs indicating DEFINITE TIME like *yesterday*, *to-day*, *to-morrow*, *nowadays*, NEVER STAND BETWEEN SUBJECT AND VERB. The same applies to *early* and *late*.

He arrived here yesterday.

C. When single adverbs modify other words than main verbs they should normally stand as near the word modified as possible.

That dog is very *badly* trained.
You promised *never* to stay out late.
The day was *almost* over.

Most English people make mistakes when using '*only*'. They tend to put it between the subject and verb even when it does not modify the verb. Each of the following sentences has an entirely different meaning:

Only the solicitor showed the farmer the paper he had to sign.

The solicitor *only* showed the farmer the paper he had to sign.

The solicitor showed *only* the farmer the paper he had to sign.

The solicitor showed the farmer *only* the paper he had to sign.

The solicitor showed the farmer the paper *only* he had to sign.

The solicitor showed the farmer the paper he had *only* to sign.

D. In a *few phrases* where the adjective is used adverbially it never comes between the subject and verb.

Two examples are *to work hard*, *to stay long* (a long time).

II. *The exact position of the adverb depends on the form of the verb:*

(i) Except in the case of the verb 'to be' and also when there are two verbs together, *when the verb is a single word* (Present and Past Simple tenses) *a suitable adverb can be placed between the subject and the verb.*

He never answers my questions.
The maid quietly left the kitchen.

But: She is never late.
Such adverbs usually follow the verb 'to be' immediately.

(ii) *When the verb is made up of two or more words, a suitable adverb can be placed between the first two of these words.*

He must always salute his superior officers.
I have sometimes been annoyed with him.
She is now making a speech.
He can soon come out of hospital.

All these adverbs may come at the end of the sentence when they are specially emphasised:

This is not his first time in prison: he has been there often.

Notice: The whole subject of the order of adverbs is a difficult one as word order depends very much on traditional usage rather than rules. However, the above rules should help a little.

In the following sentences, indicate the different places where the adverb may be placed in the sentence, making it clear where the position would be an expected one and where the position indicates special emphasis.

(*a*) He goes to the cinema. (often)
(*b*) He is selfish. (sometimes)
(*c*) He has completed his novel. (now)
(*d*) They are opening a new school here. (soon)
(*e*) The rain has set in. (probably)
(*f*) The audience went home. (then)
(*g*) The old man went up to the window. (slowly)
(*h*) He was tired out. (obviously)
(*i*) Are you sitting there doing nothing? (still)
(*j*) The motor coach tourists have been allowed time to write letters (occasionally)
(*k*) The small boy was feeding the monkey with peanuts. (busily)
(*l*) The waiter spilt the soup on her new dress. (clumsily)
(*m*) He likes to get his newspaper. (early)
(*n*) Go and wash your hands. (now)
(*o*) Have you seen a pink elephant? (ever)
(*p*) The milkman forgot to call. (yesterday)
(*q*) I am afraid he is not working. (hard)
(*r*) Owls can see in darkness. (only)
(*s*) He has been spoilt. (completely)
(*t*) The stepfather treated the child. (cruelly)

EVER

Notice that the word 'ever' is normally found only in interrogative and negative sentences, or in what are in effect reported questions:

I wonder if he will ever come.

It is however found with 'hardly' or 'scarcely' in affirmative statements:

He is hardly ever away.

Direct and indirect objects

There are *three* groups of verbs in which the construction involving direct and indirect objects differs.

(i) I *sent* / I *wrote* / I *gave* } him a letter. I told him a story. I bought him a present.

The forms ME, HIM, HER, IT, US, YOU and THEM are all used to express the indirect object. This normally has no preposition and precedes any direct object, but for purposes of emphasis, it may follow the direct object, and, in this case, be accompanied by an appropriate preposition, usually TO or FOR.

I sent } a letter to him. / I wrote / I gave — I told a story to him. (uncommon)
I bought a present for her.

I sent
I wrote } a letter to him.
I gave

I told a story to him. (uncommon)
I bought a present for her.

The same rule applies in the case of nouns:

He gave his son a pound
He gave a pound to his son.

Other verbs in this group include *take, bring, show, make* and *sell.*

(ii) In the case of the verb ASK the indirect object is never accompanied by the preposition TO

I asked him a question.
Never I asked a question to him.

(iii) In the case of SAY, EXPLAIN and DESCRIBE the indirect object is always accompanied by TO, and must therefore always *follow* the direct object:

I said good-bye to him.
The teacher explained the rule to the students.
The guide described the historic battle to the tourists.

All verbs indicating WAYS OF SPEAKING (e.g. *shout, whisper, mutter*) belong to this group.

Arrange the direct and indirect objects correctly in the following sentences, adding any necessary prepositions. Indicate where there is a possible alternative and suggest any difference in meaning this may result in:

(*a*)	The postman gave	+a registered letter	+me
(*b*)	The man gave	+a bone	+his dog.
(*c*)	Why have you sent	+this	+me?
(*d*)	The scientist explained	+the experiment	+me.
(*e*)	One of the audience asked	+a question	+him.
(*f*)	Have you told	+everything	+them?
(*g*)	Why did you say	+that	+him?
(*h*)	The retired colonel wrote	+a letter	+the editor.
(*i*)	Why didn't you send	+a postcard	+her?
(*j*)	The witness described	+the accident	+us.

Inverted commas

(i) These are *usually in pairs*, though occasionally they are used singly.

(ii) *Where the direct speech begins*, the *inverted commas are usually upside down* [“]; *where it closes they are the right way up* [”].

(iii) They are *always above* the line:

'Good morning,' he said.

(iv) If the inverted commas open in the middle of the sentence for the first time in that sentence, *they are usually preceded by a comma and followed by a capital letter:*

Mrs. Bates glared at her husband and said, 'You need a haircut.'

(v) Direct speech ending in the middle of a sentence is followed by a comma.

(vi) If the same person starts to speak a second time in the same sentence, it is usual to open with a small letter:

The ticket collector said: 'You've just missed the train,' and added unsympathetically, 'and that was the last one to-night.'

(vii) Question and exclamation marks come inside the inverted commas:

'Where have you been?' he asked. (no comma in this case)

(viii) *Start a new paragraph with each fresh speaker:*

She turned on him indignantly. 'It isn't true,' she said. 'They will never believe that.'

He shrugged his shoulders. 'Whether it is true or not,' he assured her, 'they can be persuaded to believe it.'

Punctuate the following passage, inserting inverted commas, commas, question and exclamation marks and capital letters and also starting new paragraphs where necessary:

The shop assistant eyed me sulkily as I went up to the counter. Have you any of those reversible mackintoshes you had last week I asked. No madam she answered they are sold out. What a pity I exclaimed but perhaps I can take a nylon one. Have you one in blue? No madam said the assistant only yellow. I felt I was making no progress. Well I said I must have something. It's pouring now. Perhaps I can manage for the present with a cheap plastic one. You'll need outsize madam the assistant replied and they are in our stock room. Could you fetch me one I asked. No madam, it's my lunchtime now. Sorry. She examined herself in the shop mirror for a moment and then walked off, leaving me unattended. Unusually annoyed I asked to see the manager. He was very apologetic. I'm sorry he said we are always having complaints about that assistant. And yet you keep her I remarked. Yes but she's leaving to-morrow he replied. She says she has found a much better job as receptionist in a luxury hotel. I am wondering about two things, I meditated aloud, how she got such a job, and how long she will keep it.

(Do you need a question mark at the end?)

Uncountable and countable nouns

The passage includes:

A some nouns that are always uncountable,

B some that are uncountable or countable according to their meaning and;

C some that are always plural. Others are included in the following lists. Use each of these nouns in sentences so that its meaning and use are made clear. Those in B, have at least two meanings.

A	B	C
information	rubber	clothes
machinery	tea	police
furniture	wit	goods
advice	hair	surroundings
shopping	cold	premises
money	work	scissors
gambling	iron	
luggage	sense	
news	manner	
knowledge	force	
magic	pastry	
applause	tin	
elastic	wood	
dust	glass	
progress	ice	
water		

D What are:
(i) a compass
(ii) a pair of compasses

E 'dice' is strictly speaking plural but is used as though singular: a dice two dice

F one can speak of 'a table water' and also poetically of the waters of a river.

Spelling Rules—Doubling of final consonants

(i) Single syllables containing one vowel and ending in a single consonant (with the exception of -w and -y) double the final consonant before a suffix beginning with a vowel:

stir	stirred	stirring	big	bigger	biggest
hat	hatter		rot	rotten	

(but notice: bus, buses; gas, gases).

(ii) *Words of more than one syllable* with a single vowel in the last syllable and a single final consonant *double the final consonant when the stress is on the last syllable, provided that the suffix begins with a vowel.* There is no doubling when the final consonant is -w or -y.

When the stress is elsewhere there is no doubling, except when the final consonant is -l, which is always doubled so long as there is a single vowel in the last syllable, and the suffix begins with a vowel.

Three exceptions to this rule are: worshipped, gossipped and kidnapped, although in each case the second -p may be omitted.

be'gin	be'ginning	be'ginner
'tatter	'tattered	
re'fer	re'ferring	re'ferred *but* 'reference
'cancel	'cancellation	'cancelling
in'stal	in'stalling	in'stalled *but* in'stalment

Complete the following words by adding the suffixes indicated:

stop	-ed	-ing	-er
rub	-er	-ed	-ing
heat	-ed	-er	-ing
gallop	-ing	-ed	

quarrel	-ing	-ed	-some
confer	-ed	-ing	-ence
conquer	-or	-ing	-ed (qu are together a consonant)
offer	-ed	-ing	
shut	-er	-ing	
signal	-ed	-ing	-er
regret	-ed	-ing	-able
open	-ed	-ing	
admit	-ed	-ing	-ance
happen	-ed	-ing	
appear	-ed	-ing	-ance
matter	-ed		
compel	-ed	-ing	
transfer	-ed	-ing (transferable is an exception)	
benefit	-ed	-ing	

Remember: write wrote written
a dining-room a dinner table

8

Passage for comprehension

Fear for company

By the time she had finished tidying up, Bill was almost ready to go. He was looking for his gloves, which turned up eventually under a cushion.

'You need not worry about me, Mum,' he declared. 'If the fog thickens, Harold will put me up for the night. In that case, I promise I'll give you a
5 ring as soon as we decide. But even if I didn't get into touch with you, you'd know I was all right. I give you my word I'll take no risks.'

'I hope not,' she said bluntly. 'I shall be waiting up till you call. You'll be better off staying the night anyhow, if they don't mind.'

He grinned affectionately. 'I'll see,' he said. 'How about your dropping
10 in to see Aunt Maggie when I've gone? She'd be only too pleased.'

He kissed her goodbye, strode out to his motor cycle and swung one leg over the saddle. The engine roared into life and she watched him move off noisily down the road. He turned, waved, swerved to avoid a wandering dog and disappeared into the mist which was blotting out all but the nearer houses.

15 She had always enjoyed being alone. Bill had had the wireless repaired and if she felt like it, she could listen to whatever play was being broadcast that evening. She had the chance of trying out the new gramophone record she had been given for Christmas. And inevitably there was a pile of washing that needed ironing; there were clothes to be mended and patched, socks to
20 be darned. Had she wanted company, she would have taken Bill's advice and called at her sister's, who would have been delighted to have someone to share her solitude. But she was reluctant to go; she could not get rid of the persistent feeling that if she were to leave the house, she would have cause to regret it bitterly.

25 'It's absurd to be having such fancies,' she said to herself. 'I've obviously been overworking and am tired out. I could do with a sleep. I shall feel better when I wake up.'

She made up the fire with a few logs of wood and lay back in the rocking-chair. The clock ticked rhythmically; the logs crackled and flared. Her eye-
30 lids drooped and she dozed peacefully.

She awoke with a sick feeling of dread. The room was in darkness, with a heap of dying embers in the grate. Before turning on the light, she groped her way to the window. Fog, yellow and opaque, was pressing against the panes, muffling all sounds of the few pedestrians whom circumstances com-
35 pelled to be out of doors. She drew the curtains to shut out its grimy, dreary ugliness.

Her uneasy feeling of imminent catastrophe was increasing; she pulled herself together firmly and went to stoke the fire, this time with lumps of coal. Heavy steps were approaching the house; there was a single commanding knock. With the shovel still clutched in one hand, her fingers 40 automatically loosening her apron ribbons, she went to open the door. Blocking the open-sided porch, framed by the enveloping fog, stood a tall grave-faced policeman.

Notes on the passage

Vocabulary

line

Title *company* (*Unc*) having people with one: *he likes company.*
a company (*C*) a group of people associated for business: a limited company: a theatrical company.
Notice: an acquaintance; a friend (a school-friend); a companion = somebody with one; a fellow-student. 'comrade' is rare in English.

1 *tidy* (up) a room, tidy up; wash clothes, (do the washing); wash up (do the washing up) also: do the ironing. *She always looks neat and tidy.*

5 *touch:* get into touch with; be in touch with; keep in touch with; be out of touch with; lose touch with: *some people keep in touch with old friends by sending Christmas cards*; *doctors must keep in touch with new developments in medicine.*

6 SPELLING: all right.

9 *grin* (*N* and *V*)—smile broadly like a schoolboy; *sneer* (*N* and *V*)—smile cruelly and contemptuously (can also be used for a remark); *beam* (*N* and *V*)—smile with great enjoyment; *giggle* (*N* and *V*)—laugh in a silly way; ('*snigger*' has a similar meaning but includes furtive mockery); *chuckle* (*N* and *V*)—laugh quietly with great enjoyment.

11 *swing*—move like a pendulum; *sway*—with the upper part moving from side to side, as trees do in a wind; *swerve*—change direction suddenly to avoid something. A person sitting on a *swing* moves *backwards and forwards.* (At fairs there are *swings* and *roundabouts.*)

12 ANIMAL NOISES: a lion or tiger *roars*; a dog *barks*, and when angry, *growls* or *snarls*; a cat *meows*, and when pleased, *purrs*; a cow *moos*; a pig *grunts*; a sheep *bleats*; a hen *clucks*; a cock *crows*; a duck *quacks*; some birds only *twitter*; bees *buzz*; crickets *chirp*; snakes *hiss.*

12 *look at* something still (a picture); *watch* something moving (a game).

14 an ink stain on paper is a *blot*, and it can be partly removed by the use of *blotting-paper*. 'to *blot out*' is to make disappear.

16 a play is *broadcast* on the radio but *shown* on television.

17 *try out* some new thing to see whether it is satisfactory. *try on* a new dress (or shoes) to see whether it *fits* and *suits* the person wearing it.

17 This is a new *recording* of the concerto. A *record-player*. Also: sports records; a record of what has happened.

19 *patch* (*N* and *V*)—cover with material a worn place in a garment; Also: a patch of blue sky, of woodland.

22 *get rid of* something by *throwing it away* or *giving it away*; of unwelcome people by *sending them away*.

25 *a fancy*—something vaguely imagined. fancy (*V*): What do you fancy for dinner? (what would you like to have?); Fancy that! (an exclamation of surprise); (*Adj*): a fancy cake (not plain but decorated); a fancy handkerchief; a fancy-dress party (when unusual costumes are worn)

26 *overwork* (*N* and *V*)—do more work than is good for one's health; *overdo* things—do more than is good for one; also: this meat is overdone/underdone; *overrated*—thought too highly of; *overpraised*; *overcharge*; *overeat*; *overflow*; *overload*; *oversleep*; *overstrain*; *overweight*. *Notice:* *do overtime*—do extra work: overtime pay.

26 *tired out*—completely tired. A *worn* coat may be repaired. A coat that is *worn out* cannot. *eat up/finish up/use up*—completely.

28 *make up a fire* with extra *fuel*: coal, coke, logs of wood.

29 dry sticks burning may *crackle*; badly-fitting windows *rattle* in a strong wind; leaves *rustle*; old wooden stairs may *creak*; coins in a bag or glasses may *clink*; heavy iron chains *clank*; a heavy noisy bell *clangs*; a heavy silk skirt may *swish*.

29 *eyelids*; *eyebrows* are sometimes plucked; *eyelashes* are sometimes false.

30 *droop:* sink slowly: unwatered plants may droop.

30 *doze:* sleep lightly; ALSO: have a nap (a short sleep). BUT: a *dose* of medicine.

32 *embers*—the glowing remains of a fire; *cinders:* pieces of burnt-out coal; *ashes:* the cold remains of something burnt: an *ash tray* for cigarette ash.

34 *muffling:* a muffler is a thick scarf worn to protect the throat and neck—a person is then *muffled up*. When noise is muffled, the sound appears to have a thick muffler over it. *Notice:* a *muff* (to keep the hands warm); a *scarf*. A *shawl* is considerably larger than a scarf.

37 a *catástrophe* (catastróphic) is a *disáster* (disástrous).

37 *pull yourself together:* take control of yourself. *I have relaxed for an hour but now I must pull myself together and do some work. I know this has been a shock to you but you must pull yourself together and face it.*

40 coal is carried in a *shovel*; lumps of coal (and sugar) can be picked up in *tongs*; a fire is poked (pushed into) with a *poker*; a garden is dug with a *spade* and dead leaves are brought together with a *rake* and carried away in a *wheelbarrow*.

40 *clutch* something—seize it wildly; *grasp* something—seize it firmly; *cling* (to)—with the fear of losing; *grip*—hold very tightly; *clasp*—have one's arms or hand round. a *clasp*—a fastener not unlike a *buckle* on a belt. Which?—an opportunity;—the banisters when falling down-

stairs: a child—a puppy; some people—their lost youth; he could not escape from the policeman's—.

41 *lose* keys; *loose* (set free) a guard dog; *loose* (*Adj*) OPP. tight; *loosen*—make less tight. BE CAREFUL WITH SPELLINGS.

41 an *apron* hangs from the waist. a *pinafore* covers the front of the dress; (a pinafore frock); an *overall* should cover the clothes completely. A comprehensive insurance policy provides overall protection.

43 *grave* (*Adj*) = serious.
grave (*N*) = a hole in the ground where a dead person is buried.

Phrasal verb

line

2 TURN

turn against someone—take a dislike to someone known; *turn away* from an unpleasant sight; *turn away* people for whom there is no room; *turn back* and go home again; *turn down* an offer or suggestion (refuse it); *turn in* (go to bed); he *turned* the garage *into* a workroom;
turn on/off the light/the radio/the T.V./the gas/a tap;
turn out an unwelcome dog; the weather *turned out* fine; the boy *turned out* better than his parents had expected; *turn over* a page; the small boat *overturned* in the sea; he *turned round* to write on the blackboard;
turn up at a meeting (be there)
Which of the above? (with a suitable tense) ...... and see who is behind you; be sure you ...... for our party; ...... to the next page; ambulancemen cannot ...... from horrible sights; it's getting a bit late: I'll soon have to ......; he used to like you: why has he ...... you? the barman ...... the drunken man; she ...... his invitation to dinner; the ugly duckling eventually ...... a swan; the film ...... to be utterly boring; very cold water eventually ...... ice.

Other uses of TURN

(*a*) He turned pale. His hair turned grey.

(*b*) The weather turned cool (became). ('turned out' suggests there had been some doubt.)

(*c*) It has turned eight (is a little after eight).

Pronunciation

THESE NEED CARE:	*u* (as in g*oo*d)	*ʌ* (as in s*u*n)	*eɪ* (as in d*ay*)	
	bush	brush	apron	[éɪprən]
	cushion	crush	apricot	[éɪprɪkɔt]
	push	rush	acorn	[éɪkɔːn]
	puss	Russian	alien	[éɪlɪən]
			Asia	[éɪʃə]
	bull	gull	Avon	[éɪvən]
	full	hull	aviation	[éɪvɪéɪʃən]
	pull	lull(aby)	aviary	[éɪvɪərɪ]
		hush		
		blush		

STRESS CHANGES: récord (*N*) [rékɔːd]; recórd (*V*) [rɪkɔ́ːd]; Similar cases of noun and verb stress changes: permit; ally; conduct; contract; envelope; convict.

SOUND CHANGES: cycle [saikl] / bicycle [báɪsɪkl]; dropped [dropt] / drooped [druːpt]; dosed [doust] / dozed [douzd] / lose [luːz]; loose [luːs] / loosen [lúːsən].

SILENT LETTERS: ironing [áɪənɪŋ]; rhythmically [rɪ'ðmɪkəlɪ].

ə (as in *a*go): affectionate [əfékʃənɪt]; inevitable [ɪnévɪtəbl]; persistent [pəsístənt]; absurd [əbzɔ́ːd]; pedestrians [pədéstrɪənz]; circumstances [sɔ́ːkəmstənsɪz]; curtains [kɔ́ːtənz]; automatic [ɔːtəmǽtɪk]; policeman [pəlíːsmən] or [plíːsmən]; Christmas [krísməs]; obviously [ɔ́bvɪəslɪ]; gramophone [grǽməfoun].

OTHERS: shovel [ʃʌvl]; tidying [táɪdɪɪŋ]; ready [rédɪ]; flared [flɛəd]; opaque [oupéɪk]; grimy [gráɪmɪ]; catastrophe [kətǽstrəfɪ]; porch [pɔːtʃ]; muffled [mʌ́fəld]; ugliness [ʌ́glɪnɪs]; broadcast [brɔ́ːdkaːst]; solitude [sɔ́lɪtjuːd]; clutched [klʌtʃt].

Special grammatical and structural points

(i) whatever: anything that; it doesn't matter what; of any kind
You can do whatever you like. He has no sense whatever.
whichever: it doesn't matter which
Choose whichever you like
whoever: anybody that
Whoever said that must be mad.
whenever: any time that
Come whenever you feel like it.
wherever: any (every) place that.
Sit wherever there is room. Wherever he goes, he causes trouble.
however: in any way, it doesn't matter how.
However much he tries, he still makes mistakes.

Each of these can be a stronger form of the corresponding interrogative pronoun or adverb:

Whatever are you doing? Wherever have you been?

however may also have the meaning of *yet*.

(ii) *reflexive pronouns* are much less common in English than in many other languages. Be careful with these verbs:

he hid; he feels tired; he remembers; he escaped; he ran away; the flower opened; the museum opens on Sundays; the door opened/closed; he hurried.

Here are one or two English uses: he enjoyed himself (enjoyed the party); he washed himself (he got washed); he cut/hurt/injured/killed himself. Remember: he combed his hair; he broke his leg; he washed his face.
Notice these reflexives with prepositions:

talk to himself; look after himself; take care of yourself; pull yourself together; do it for myself; look at himself; he did/made it for himself.

There is a difference between: he did it by himself (without help)
he lived by himself (alone)

(iii) *Participles: Active and Passive*
The *Present Participle* is *active* in meaning:
an interesting book: the book provides the interest
The *Past Participle* is *passive* in meaning:
an interested reader: the reader is interested in or by something
Examples from the passage: fog, ... muffling all sounds ....
the shovel still clutched in one hand

(iv) *all but*; nothing but; everything but; anything but; nobody but; anybody but *but* is often (though not necessarily) used in these cases instead of *except*.

(v) *Infinitives: Active and Passive*
In these cases, when the infinitive is adjectival, either can be used: clothes to be mended/clothes to mend; socks to be darned/socks to darn.
Usually: a house to let; a book to read; time to waste.
Notice: a house for sale.

(vi) *Verbal Constructions*
Alternative Constructions: like/love/hate to do/doing
(with little meaning change)
but: should like to do
enjoy/dislike/detest/loathe doing
stop doing something to do something different
He stopped climbing to admire the view.

Infinitive:

Subject	*to be*	*adjective*	*infinitive*
he	is	ready	to go
they	will be	sure/pleased/ in a hurry	to leave

Exception: He is busy painting. Is it worth repairing?
Purpose: He swerved to avoid a dog

Gerund: How about your dropping in to see her?
She had the chance of trying it out.
You will (would) be better off staying the night.

Prepositions

(*a*) *for:* a tie for Christmas; go to Wales for a holiday (but: he is now on holiday); go to a concert for a change; do something for a bet.

(*b*) called *at* her sister's but: called *on* her sister

(*c*) in/out of touch *with* (*d*) worry *about* (*e*) get rid *of*

Expressions to learn and introduce into written work

(*a*) *By the time* you get there, it will be dark.

(*b*) It may rain. *In that case,* we shall have to cancel the picnic.

(*c*) *Even if* you leave at once, you will still be late.
(*d*) *I give you my word* (I promise).
(*e*) He *had the chance of* appearing on television.
(*f*) She would *have cause to regret it*/be thankful.
(*g*) She *pulled herself together*.
(*h*) You will *inevitably* fail because you are so lazy.

Multiple choice questions

Here are a number of questions or unfinished statements about the passage, each with four suggested ways of answering or finishing it. You must choose the way you consider the most suitable. Write in each case the bracketed number of the question or statement followed by the letters **A**, **B**, **C**, **D**, and then cross through the letter of the answer you choose. Give one answer only to each question. Read the passage right through again before choosing your answers.

1 Which of the following does Bill tell his mother she can be sure of?
A Harold will ask Bill to stay the night **B** Bill will not be in danger **C** If there is no message, Bill will be all right **D** Bill will ride slowly

2 Bill's mother makes it clear that she expects her son to do one of the following. Which is it?
A telephone her **B** stay the night **C** drive with extra care **D** return in the evening if it is possible

3 Bill promised to telephone his mother if he stayed overnight because
A the weather might cause her special anxiety on his account **B** she was nervous of being alone **C** she knew he enjoyed riding fast **D** she always worried about him when he was away for some time

4 She could spend some of her time alone in all but one of these ways, the exception being
A visiting someone **B** doing some household jobs **C** watching a play **D** playing a new gramophone record

5 Her 'absurd fancies' (line 25) were
A it might be dangerous to go out **B** she might later wish she had stayed at home **C** there was some risk to her son in riding in the thickening mist **D** she might be sorry she had not gone out

6 She realised that she must have been sleeping for a long time because
A the fog was much thicker **B** of the time by the clock **C** of the condition of the fire **D** she felt sick, as though she had slept soundly

7 She found her way to the window by
A switching on the light **B** feeling intervening objects **C** the light of the dying fire **D** the yellowish light of the fog

8 Why did she take the shovel with her to the door?
A she was so worried that she was unaware she was holding it **B** she had nowhere to put it down **C** she could use it as a weapon if necessary **D** she happened to be using it just then

Reading comprehension

In this exercise you must choose the word or phrase which best completes each sentence. Write first the number of each sentence followed by the letters **A, B, C, D, E**, and then cross through the letter of the correct answer in each case.

1 One of the tigers has got .... Warn everyone of the danger!
A lose **B** loose **C** loosened **D** lost **E** escaped

2 There was a .... of parchment as the solicitor unrolled the will written on it.
A rattle **B** swish **C** creak **D** crackle **E** clink

3 You must .... that book before you sit down at table.
A give away **B** get rid of **C** put away **D** do away with **E** leave

4 The man standing on the edge of the roof .... slightly and nearly fell
A swerved **B** swung **C** swayed **D** glided **E** skidded

5 The gangster .... at his helpless victim and put a cigarette just out of reach.
A giggled **B** beamed **C** grinned **D** chuckled **E** sneered

6 The terrified hunter, ... in the arms of a huge bear, fought desperately to loosen its grip.
A clutched **B** clasped **C** grasped **D** clinging **E** nestled

7 The dressmaker .... the half-finished blouse but it was obviously too small.
A tried on **B** tested **C** tried out **D** tried **E** put on

8 The Andersons have not turned .... yet and I doubt if they will now.
A up **B** out **C** in **D** away **E** over

9 I should like to .... touch with old friends but I have so little time
A get into **B** be in **C** keep in **D** lose **E** be out of

10 Wolves were .... mournfully in the nearby forest.
A roaring **B** barking **C** snarling **D** howling **E** growling

Use of English

1 The five phrases below are answers to five question that could be asked about the reading passage. Write out the questions.

(i) she should drop in to see Aunt Maggie

(ii) noisily

(iii) to avoid a wandering dog

(iv) trying out a new gramophone record

(v) in the rocking-chair

2 Write out the following words, and in each case show which part of the word is stressed when it is spoken by underlining the part clearly.

Example: photograph photographer
photograph photographer

(i) EVENTUALLY (ii) DISAPPEARED (iii) CATASTROPHE
(iv) ENVELOPING (v) DETERMINATION (vi) AUTOMATIC
(vii) MUSEUM (viii) PREFERABLE (ix) CERTIFICATE
(x) HOTEL

3 The meaning of the sentence: 'She is too lazy to make much progress' can be expressed by a negative sentence using 'hard-working' and 'enough' instead of 'lazy' and 'too'. Change each of sentences (i) to (v) below in the same way. Write out the sentences in full.

(i) The light is too dim to read by properly.

(ii) He is too miserable to be popular.

(iii) She is too rough to take care of her baby brother.

(iv) The book was too boring for me to enjoy reading it.

(v) The actor was too ugly to take the part of Orlando.

4 Finish each of the following sentences in such a way that the new sentence means exactly the same as the one printed before it.

It is unnecessary for you to change your dress.

1 You need ....

You'll be better off staying the night.

2 It will ....

Bill had had the wireless repaired.

3 Bill had arranged ....

I could do with a sleep

4 A sleep ....

She awoke with a feeling of terror.

5 When she ....

With a lot of luck, you may get your novel published.

6 If you ....

Composition and summarising

Dialogues

There are two ways of writing a dialogue:

1 In the form of a conversation:

> 'Good morning,' said the waitress. 'What would you like?'
> 'Just a cup of coffee, please,' said Anne.
> 'Black or white?' asked the waitress.
> 'Black, please,' Anne replied, and then added, 'and I'd like a biscuit with it.'

2 As dialogue in a play is written:

A Excuse me. Can you tell me the way to St. Peter's Church?
B I'm sorry. I'm afraid I can't. I'm a stranger here. Oh, but wait a moment. It's about five minutes down this road.
A Thank you very much.
B No, it isn't St. Peter's. I remember now it's St. John's. Have you any idea what it looks like?
A No, I've never seen it. I'm really looking for the house just opposite it.
B Then it isn't the church I passed before that. That was opposite a hospital. Let's ask that man coming along.

The question itself should suggest which of these forms is wanted. IF NOTHING IS SUGGESTED, the SECOND form may be accepted as a DIALOGUE, the FIRST one as a CONVERSATION.

Points to remember

(*a*) Read the question carefully. Make sure that all the necessary ideas are included in the dialogue and that this is a suitable length.

(*b*) Try to write really natural conversation. Remember the following points:

(i) VERBAL AND NEGATIVE ABBREVIATIONS ARE NORMAL IN DIALOGUE AND CONVERSATION—in contrast to their use in formal written English.
These include: I'm; don't; can't; there's; How's?

(ii) Short simple constructions. People often answer in only one or two words or perhaps an incomplete sentence. 'And' and 'but' join parts of sentences: the more complicated constructions are far less common.

(iii) Simple colloquial forms. Have you noticed how often people say 'Well', 'Oh', 'I'm afraid—', 'I wonder if—', and many similar forms with no very definite meaning?

(iv) Short answers.

(v) The many other expressions and constructions which make conversation sound more natural.

(vi) In the case of a conversation, be careful to punctuate according to English convention (see Pages 112–113).

Here is an example of a dialogue which includes several of the things mentioned above:

A car has been stolen. The owner is telephoning the local Police Station to report the theft. Write the dialogue that takes place in 120–180 words.

A Updown Police Station. Can I help you?
B John Driver of 1 Highlands Road, Updown, speaking. I've just discovered my car's been stolen.
A Can you give me details of the car, sir? What make is it?
B It's a red Lightning sports car.
A What's the registration number?
B 65432 ABC.
A When did you lose it?
B I've just come out of Updown General Post Office. I left it outside but it has now gone.
A I see. You didn't lock it, I suppose?
B Well, no, I'm afraid I didn't. And what's worse, I'd left the keys inside. I was in a bit of a hurry.
A Well, that's asking for trouble, isn't it. Anything special inside?
B Yes, there was. My golf clubs and two bottles of brandy.
A Well, we'll see what we can do. Have you a telephone number?
B Updown 6420.
A Thank you. By the way, you realise it's a no parking area outside the Post Office, don't you?
B Er . . . yes. I believe so. I'm in trouble, aren't I?
A It does seem so. We'll be getting in touch with you as soon as possible.
B Thank you. Goodbye.

Subjects for practice

Each answer should consist of between 120 and 180 words.

1 A conversation between a door-to-door salesman and a lady whom he is trying to persuade to buy an encyclopedia.

2 You are in a hurry to catch a train. On the way to the station you run into an old acquaintance whom you have not seen since you both left school some eight years before. You have only one minute to spare. Write the conversation that takes place.

3 While you are exploring an unknown town, you see an interesting-looking building, so you stop a passer-by and ask about it. Write the conversation in the form of a dialogue.

4 You are walking along the street when you are stopped by a radio interviewer and asked your opinion about whether space travel is a waste of money. Write what is said in the form of a dialogue.

5 Later the woman in the story wrote to her husband, who was a ship's officer, about the events of that day. Write the two paragraphs of her letter in which she dealt with the material in the passage that would interest him. Use between 175 and 200 words. Here is a suggested opening:

'The mist was thickening when Bill left yesterday. He realised I was slightly worried about his journey so he promised to telephone after deciding whether to spend the night at Harold's, and also to go carefully . . .'

Spoken English

Making suggestions

Each of the following opening statements can introduce some kind of recommendation or idea of something that might be done.

What do you think of (*about*) seeing the football match to-morrow?
Wouldn't it be a good (*better*) *idea* to reserve seats in advance?
It might be a good idea to wait and see what the weather's like.
Would you like to go on a river-trip up the Thames?
Shall we have lunch at the 'Good Cheer' restaurant?
How about having some wine with our lunch?
Let's have a party.
Why not put off your visit till next week?
We'd (*we had*) *better* leave now.
We might as well sit down while we're waiting.

EXERCISES: (*a*) Express each of the above as it would follow the words 'he has suggested'.
The first will be: He has suggested our seeing the football match to-morrow.

(*b*) Express each of the following ideas as a suggestion, using as many ways of doing so as are suitable in each case.
let our friends know we're coming; have the car serviced before our holiday; consult a doctor; throw all these old newspapers away; have the house redecorated; take an umbrella.

Expressions from the passage

I'll give you a ring. I'll ring you up. (I'll (tele)phone you)
(I'll drop you a line = I'll write to you.)
He's well off: (*a*) he has a lot of money. (*b*) he's always grumbling: he doesn't know when he's well off.
He's better off/than I am/without your useless advice/living at home.
It's better for you to live at home. You'll be better off living at home.
He'd be only too pleased to see you. I could do with a fortnight's holiday.
I see = I understand. *Do you see? I'll see* = I'll think about it.
I'll see about it = I'll think or do something about it. *I'll see to* that splinter in your finger = I'll do whatever is necessary to put things right.

Which of these forms with SEE?

Can we go to the circus next week? ......
This tap needs a new washer. All right, ...
You see, he's so terrified of water because years ago he nearly drowned. Oh, ...
Could you knit me a pair of warm gloves? Well, ...
It's already one o'clock. ...... lunch.

(*a*) **On the telephone**

R Admass Publicity. Good afternoon.

P Good afternoon. This is Miss Pelham speaking. May I speak to Mr. Tavistock, please?

R I didn't quite catch your name. Would you spell it, please? . . . Thank you. Would you wait a minute, please. I'll see if he's in. . . . I'm sorry. I'm afraid he isn't in just now. Can I put you through to his secretary?

P If you would, please.

S Miss Somerset speaking. Mr. Tavistock isn't in now but perhaps I can help you.

P This is a personal matter which is rather urgent. If Mr. Tavistock will be in soon, perhaps he can ring me back.

S I'm afraid he's in Bristol to-day.

P Is it possible to get into touch with him there?

S No. You see, he'll be making calls all day and then going on to Cardiff.

P This is really an emergency. Are you his private secretary? Can I tell you something in confidence?

S Most certainly you can.

P I'm the Nockling probation officer. His son has been arrested for robbery with violence and as his mother's in hospital, I've been asked to get hold of his father, needless to say, as soon as possible. Is there any way at all of getting a message to him?

S I could ring one or two of our clients in Bristol to ask about his whereabouts. I'll do my very best to make contact. What number should I give him?

P I'd be so pleased if you would. It's 67890/54321. Miss Pelham. Thank you.

(*b*) *A Conversation about Health*

He I'm sorry. I feel a bit faint and giddy (dizzy). My head's swimming. Do you mind if I sit down?

She Of course not. Here, sit in this armchair. Now relax. It might be a good idea to put your head down. I'll get you some water. Would smelling-salts or brandy help?

He No, it's all right. I feel a bit better now. It's a touch of the sun, I think.

She Lie back quite still for a few minutes. I should take it easy for the rest of the day and stay in the shade.

Situations

(*a*) A sixteen-year-old boy is going on a cycling holiday with a friend, but for the first time without his parents. He may be camping or staying in youth hostels. What various pieces of advice do his parents give him before he leaves?

(*b*) The four-year-old child that an au-pair girl is in charge of has run away and she cannot find him. What does she do and say in these circumstances?

General guidance and practice

1 The Future Simple: Active and Passive

Active		Passive	
I shall take	we shall take	I shall be taken	we shall be taken
you will take	you will take	you will be taken	you will be taken
he will take	they will take	he will be taken	they will be taken

The auxiliaries are reversed: I, we will take; You, he, they shall take:

(i) chiefly to express *determination:*

I will go whatever happens.
(in the second and third persons, it is the speaker, not the subject, who is determined.)
He shall apologise to you. (the speaker has decided.)

(ii) to express a *promise* (first person):

I will do it to-morrow without fail.

(iii) to express *willingness* (first person):

We will do it if you like.

In conversation the forms *I'll, we'll, you'll, he'll, she'll, it'll, they'll* are common

In the negative the spoken forms are: I, we shan't (won't), you won't (shan't), he, she, it, they won't (shan't).

(I'll not etc. is also possible.)

Will and won't are commonly heard in spoken English as first person auxiliaries indicating the Simple Future. Their use in this way is better avoided in writing.

Use a suitable auxiliary in each of the following sentences:

(*a*) The football match ...... take place to-morrow afternoon.

(*b*) ...... you be going out this evening?

(*c*) I ...... not be back for lunch.

(*d*) I ...... speak to my son very seriously and he ...... pay for the broken window.

(*e*) We ...... bring it for you if it ...... help you.

(*f*) ...... I take my raincoat?

(*g*) You ...... now sit quietly for ten minutes.

(*h*) I ...... not obey you.

(*i*) Your shoes ...... be ready in two days.

(*j*) We ...... bring you back an exciting present.

2 Forms of the Future Simple

	Active	*Passive*
SIMPLE	I shall take	I shall be taken
CONTINUOUS	I shall be taking	—
PERFECT	I shall have taken	I shall have been taken
PERFECT CONTINUOUS	I shall have been taking	—

Uses

(*a*) FUTURE SIMPLE

This expresses a future action, often with a suggestion of INTENTION or that this is a NEW IDEA.

Compare: I am / shall be telephoning her to-morrow, so I can tell her the news then.

Hasn't she heard the news? I shall telephone and tell her as soon as possible.

(*b*) FUTURE CONTINUOUS: This expresses:

(i) an arranged future action.

He will be attending a conference in Milan next week.

(ii) an action that will be happening at a certain future time.

This time to-morrow I shall be swimming in the Mediterranean.

(iii) a future action whose duration is stressed.

The miners will be working all through the holiday.

(*c*) FUTURE PERFECT

This expresses an action which will have been completed by a certain future time.

Active: By Saturday they will have repaired the television.
Passive: By Saturday the television will have been repaired.

(*d*) FUTURE PERFECT CONTINUOUS

This expresses a continuous action which comes up to (though is not necessarily completed by) a certain future time.

When he takes his driving test, he will have been learning for six months.

An arranged future action can be expressed both by the Present Continuous and Future Continuous tenses. In the latter the speaker may be imagining himself already at the future time referred to but any real differences between these tenses is extremely slight.

Use the correct future form of the verb in the following sentences:

(*a*) I (make) a cup of tea in a few minutes; would you like one?

(*b*) I intended to write him a letter this afternoon. I (do) it to-morrow.

(*c*) By this time next week the new scheme (introduced). (Passive)

(*d*) Who (win) the hundred metres in the next Olympic Games?

(*e*) Many more tourists (arrive) by the time the week is over.

(*f*) By next June you (live not) here long enough to become naturalised.

(*g*) If the publishers agree about the need for additional copies, more editions of that book (produce) than any other he has written. (Passive)

(*h*) The retired statesman (spend) next winter in Southern Spain.

(*i*) If my money continues to disappear like this I (beg soon) in the streets all day.

(*j*) By the time he sits for the examination, he (learn) English for ten years.
(*k*) Next September all bus fares (increase). (Passive)
(*l*) (Go) you to the library this afternoon?

3 Verb tenses in adverbial time clauses

In adverbial clauses of time beginning with such conjunctions as WHEN, BEFORE, UNTIL, AS SOON AS, etc., the PRESENT SIMPLE, CONTINUOUS OF PRESENT PERFECT are used in English where logically the Future might be expected.

As soon as the ship *docks*, the passengers will be allowed to land.
I shall be pleased to see the photograph, *when* it *has been printed.*

This does not apply to a noun clause object of a verb.

Do you know *when he will return*?

Use the correct form of the verbs bracketed in the following sentences:

(*a*) He will expect dinner to be ready when he (come) home.
(*b*) Immediately the sun (rise), the priests will offer a sacrifice.
(*c*) As soon as the referee (appear), the game will begin.
(*d*) You will not begin eating until after everybody (sit) down.
(*e*) It will be raining before they (be) ready.
(*f*) Will you have completed the course when you (sit) for the examination?
(*g*) While he (enjoy) a holiday in Italy, I shall be doing night work in Birmingham. (continuous)
(*h*) When you (read) the newspaper, please let me have it.
(*i*) He has not told me when he (write).
(*j*) After the bus company (introduce) the new timetable, there should be a better bus service.

4 The Future in the Past and Conditional forms. These forms are very similar, and have these four forms in the Active and Passive:

	Active	*Passive*
SIMPLE	I would/should tell	I would/should be told
CONTINUOUS	I would/should be telling	—
PERFECT	I would/should have told	I would/should have been told
PERFECT CONTINUOUS	I would/should have been telling	—

The first person forms of the *Conditional* usually have the auxiliary SHOULD, the second and third person forms WOULD.

WOULD is normally used in all persons of the *Future in the Past* tense, which is used in Reported Speech.

Notice the spoken forms which replace both SHOULD and WOULD:

I'd, you'd, he'd, she'd, we'd, they'd.

The Three Types of Condition

I POSSIBLE

Condition	*Result*
if he *works*	he *will succeed.*
If he *is working*	*come* in as quietly as possible.
(Any Present form)	(Any Future form or the Imperative)

II UNLIKELY

Condition	*Result*
If he *worked,*	he *would succeed.*
If he *were to work*	he *would succeed.*

The meaning of the two above sentences is approximately the same. Notice the use of the subjunctive of the verb 'to be'.

(Past Simple, Past Continuous, or the Past Subjunctive of the verb 'to be' with the infinitive)	(Conditional Simple or Continuous)

III IMPOSSIBLE

Condition	*Result*
If he *had worked* Had he worked }	he *would have succeeded.*
If *he had been working* Had he been working }	he *would have sent* us away.
If you *had eaten* those berries Had you eaten }	you *would have been* feeling ill now.
(Past Perfect Simple or Continuous)	(Conditional Perfect Simple or Conditional Perfect Continuous)

The second type of condition can range from the vaguely possible to the almost impossible, or unreal

If pigs had wings, they would fly.

Notice that COULD may be a past simple or a conditional form.

I could understand everything he said.
If you gave him a lift, he could be here earlier.

Note: It is a good idea to learn by heart a simple example of each of the three conditions:

If he works, he will succeed.
If he worked, he would succeed.
If he had worked, he would have succeeded.

(i) Pick out examples of conditions from the reading piece and say which type each of them is.

(ii) Finish the following sentences:

(*a*) If the train is late, ...

(*b*) If it rained, ...

(*c*) If she had had more money, ...

(*d*) If I had some eggs, ...

(*e*) If there had been an accident, ...

Finish these sentences with an 'if' clause:

(*f*) He will go on a cruise ....

(*g*) My solicitor would advise you ....

(*h*) The harvest would have been good ....

(*i*) The riots would not have started ....

(*j*) I should probably recognise him ....

(*k*) He will certainly earn more ....

IF = WHEN Constructions

If may also be a near alternative to *when* and the action or state referred to is then habitual. Notice the tense change in the RESULT clause.

If
When I feel cold, I *turn* on the electric fire

Compare: If I feel cold this evening, I *shall turn* on the electric fire.

The meanings of *if* and *when* as used in these cases are not quite identical as *if* still suggests a *condition*, *when* (whenever) a *time*.

Who, whom, which

Each of these may be used interrogatively:

Who is there?
Whom have they chosen?
Which of us is right?

or as a relative form:

There is the actress *who* has just had a nervous breakdown.

Mary is the sister (*whom*) you have met.

She is the one (*whom*) you were speaking about.

The coat (*which*) you bought is very smart.

} 'whom' and 'which' can be omitted in these sentences (see Chapter X).

WHO is used for the *nominative* (subject) form.

WHOM is used for the *accusative* form (*object of the verb or governed by a preposition*).

WHO is often used for WHOM in conversation but the correct form should be used in written English.

Insert the correct form of the interrogative or relative pronoun in these sentences. In these examples use it in each case, even where it may be omitted.

(*a*) ...... will they elect as President of the Sports Club?

(*b*) Nobody knows ...... is the most likely candidate.

(*c*) Mr. Smith is the one ...... most people seem enthusiastic about.

(*d*) I don't know ...... I shall vote for.

(*e*) ...... suggested Mr. Brown?

(*f*) ...... of them is the most popular?

(*g*) The election, ... will take place on Friday, will be quite exciting.

(*h*) The results, ... the local newspaper will publish the next day, may cause some ill-feeling.

(*i*) ...... are you working for now?

(*j*) ...... of these newspapers have you finished with?

Have something done

EXAMPLES:

I *am having* a dress *made.*
He *had* his shoes *repaired.*
He *has had* his photograph *taken.*
They *will have* their house *redecorated.*
She should *have* her eyes *tested.*
We want *to have* the money we paid for our tickets *refunded.*
Nobody enjoys *having* a tooth *drilled* and *filled.*

In spoken English *get* often replaces *have.*

I am getting a dress made.

Construction and Word Order

have (in a suitable tense and form)	*something*	*Past Participle*
have	a dress	made

Meaning
The *past participle* shows the real *action* being carried out.
The subject of the sentence is not doing this action, but is *causing someone else to do it for him.*

In the first example, *I* am not making the dress but arranging for someone else to do this for me.

EXERCISE: Rewrite the following sentences with the italicised form serving as or suggesting the new subject of the sentence. The main verb *have* will have the same tense or form as the verb in **heavy type** where this is shown. Otherwise some kind of infinitive is needed.

EXAMPLES:

They **are building** a new house for *us.*

We are having a new house built.

They must check *your* brakes as soon as possible.

You must have your brakes checked as soon as possible.

(*a*) They **are cleaning** *William's* suit.

(*b*) They **are installing** a refrigerator for *our neighbour.*

(*c*) They **are shortening** *his* overcoat.

(*d*) They **were copying** the documents for *the lawyer.*

(*e*) They **fitted** a new lock for *my landlady.*

(*f*) They **will wash** *Giles*'s car to-morrow.

(*g*) They are going to train *Elizabeth*'s voice.

(*h*) They **have set** *your* hair.

(*i*) *He* wants them to publish his eight-hundred-page novel.

(*j*) I think that they can develop and print *your* films at Mitchell's.

9

The interview

These three subjects are dealt with in the ten-minute interview which forms part of the examination.

A (about five minutes) The examiner will ask the candidate to look at a photograph for a few moments. He will then ask questions designed to provide the candidate with opportunities of demonstrating his ability to communicate in spoken English, the main basis of assessment in this part of the test. Some preparatory questions will be specifically on the scene or event shown in the photograph, and some will lead to related general topics. Candidates will be expected to answer questions as fully and variously as they can, and to develop the conversation freely.

B (2–3 minutes) The candidate will be given an extract from a play to prepare ten minutes before the interview, and a further opportunity to look through it before the joint reading with the examiner. The main emphasis in the assessment will be on pronunciation factors, including stress, intonation and rhythm, the appropriate handling of these being a test also of comprehension of the passage.

C (2–3 minutes) The candidate will be given a booklet containing brief descriptions of a number of situations and asked to turn to a particular passage, which the examiner will read aloud. The candidate should then make the appropriate response, paying due attention to tone and manner and the use of socially acceptable and appropriate forms; these are the basis of assessment in this part of the test. Each candidate will be given five of these exercises.

Advice about Part A: Questions related to a photograph

1 Look carefully at the picture.

2 Listen equally carefully to anything the examiner tells you and to the questions. If you don't understand it, ask the examiner to repeat it.

> 'Would you mind asking the question again, please.'

If there is one word you don't understand, you can say:

> 'I'm sorry, but there was one word in the middle of the question that I didn't understand. Would you mind repeating the question please.'

Never just look at the examiner without speaking if you haven't understood the question. Ask for the question to be repeated.

3 Look at the picture again and find the answer. Ask for an explanation if this is necessary:

> 'You spoke of a man on the left but there seem to be two men there. Which one do you mean?'

(This might be an example of a question of this kind.)

Answering

4 (*a*) You can take a few seconds to think so don't rush into words.

(*b*) You are being judged on how well you can express yourself, so if you answer in only four or five words, the examiner will be unable to give you a good mark. If it is possible to give several ideas, do so.
If for example you are asked to describe somebody, give as many details as you can: possible age, size, expression on the face, details of hair and clothes, how the person is sitting or standing and what he is doing.
Never just answer yes or no and at least for the time taken by the oral, forget any natural shyness. Remember that the examiner knows just how you are feeling, having had the same experience earlier himself. On the other hand, don't just chatter without any attention to the mistakes you are making.

(*c*) Marks will depend partly on your knowledge of the meaning and correct use of words and common constructions, so show that you can use a number of varying constructions and that you have a wide vocabulary.

(*d*) Use abbreviated colloquial verb forms. It is not really advisable to use slang as this may be old-fashioned or used in the wrong place but the many colloquial expressions that are very commonly used by English-speaking people should be introduced where possible. These include expressions such as 'Oh,' 'Well' 'I'm afraid that' 'I wonder whether' and 'By the way'. Practise using expressions of this kind naturally and easily.

(*e*) Speak clearly and slowly. Correct pronunciation is easier to remember when you are reading aloud but it is also necessary in conversation if you want to get a high mark. In any case, there must be no bad faults in your pronunciation and everything you say must be clearly understood.

Practising beforehand

5 You will probably get some speaking practice in school, but when classes are large, you may not have much opportunity of speaking yourself, though you can listen carefully to (and either learn from or silently criticise) the class member who is speaking. You can also practise when you are alone. Ask yourself questions: about what you have done that day, your surroundings, a story you have read, a picture. Answer aloud, with careful attention to pronunciation so that a good pronunciation becomes almost automatic. You can also practise with a friend. Correcting a friend's English or pronunciation may well benefit your own.

Questions and answers: Two examples

1 *The Café*

1 What's the subject of this picture?

It's a picture of a café or small restaurant in a department store, with some people sitting at the tables. The café's on a balcony from which they can look down into the shop.

2 Are there many people in the shop?

There are a few people walking about in the shop though I can't see anybody actually buying anything. There are several women and children in the café however; in fact most of the seats that I can see in the picture have been taken.

3 Describe the three people nearest the camera.

A lady and two girls are sitting at a table. The two girls are sitting side by side with the lady facing them. I'd guess that the lady's about thirty-five though she might be older. She's got fair hair that's very neatly waved and arranged and a black and white patterned dress with a wide white collar. One girl's hair seems to be fair and the other one's is light brown and they may have either blouses and skirts or dresses on. I don't think the lady's with the girls because she's eating a meal but they've got only long drinks.

4 What noises can probably be heard?

There'd be the sound of people's voices and there's probably a nearby counter with plates and dishes and cutlery being moved about on it. There may be some quiet music from loudspeakers.

5 What do you think the lady at the second table is saying to the small child?

'Now eat that up nicely and be careful not to drop anything on the floor. Are you sure you can manage or shall I help you?'

6 Describe a much smaller café in your country.

As in the picture there are usually tables with plastic tops but almost everything else is different. A small town café is more like the front room of a house with shop windows. There are usually between six and ten tables with four chairs at each and a cruet and an ash tray on each table. At one end there's a counter with perhaps a coffee-making machine on it and cakes and sandwiches under glass covers. A doorway leads to the kitchen and on the wall there's a list of meals and prices and perhaps a list of matches played by the local football team. It's clean but not beautiful.

7 Suggest why some department stores have cafés like this.

Well I suppose they can make some profit from the café itself. But what's more important is that people are likely to spend more time in the shop if they can get some refreshment there. A housewife may meet her friend there and they can spend the whole afternoon wandering round, with a cup of tea as a break. If the café's really good, people may come there just to get something to eat, but, especially in the type shown in the picture, they may see things in the shop itself that interest them and they may also buy something.

CLIVEDEN
ENGLISH AND
PHILLIPS

2 *The Auction Sale*

This is a picture of an auction sale. The things are being sold to the person who offers to pay most for them.

1 Where is the sale taking place?
It's in an extremely large round tent.

2 What's the elderly man doing?
He's standing on a platform holding a large vase in front of him so that people can see it. He may be describing it to them and drawing their attention to its qualities.

3 Tell me something about the other people.
A fair number of them are sitting but I should say the majority are standing. Most of them are holding papers, perhaps lists, and they're examining the vase. Some men will probably soon be taking photographs and a woman at the side is writing things down in a book.

4 Where are the photographers?
They're at the back near the side of the tent.

5 Suggest some other things that might be sold in an auction.
Valuable pictures probably get most publicity, because of their high prices. Other expensive things are jewellery, antique furniture, first editions of famous books and beautiful old clocks. But quite ordinary things can be bought at auctions like kitchen equipment and radios. And houses too can be sold in this way.

6 Why do some people enjoy going to auctions?
A lot of people go because they hope to get something much more cheaply than in the shops and they're delighted when they manage this. Others have seen that something that they'd very much like to own themselves is being sold and they're overjoyed if they can get it. I could imagine going myself to an auction of beautiful and valuable things just to admire them and learn something about them from the auctioneer's description, though I wouldn't specially want to buy them myself.

7 Suggest three ways in which a street market would be different from this kind of auction.
People are moving round all the time, only stopping to buy something. There are very many stalls loaded with a variety of things for sale. Most of the things on sale are food or clothing and very few of them cost a lot of money.

SHEPHERDS BUSH

Other examples for practice

1 *Street Scene*

1. The old lady walking along has probably already done most of her shopping. How can you see this from the picture?
2. What time of year do you think it is? Why do you think so?
3. What are some of the things that the people are doing?
4. How long have the ladies in white been sitting there? Why do you think so?
5. Describe the lady on the far right.
6. What will the two ladies have to do before they can leave?
7. Describe what you can see of the houses on the far side of the street.
8. What noises can be heard in the street?
9. Give a general idea of what this picture is about.
10. Would you enjoy living in or near this street? Explain why or why not.
11. Explain why you enjoy going shopping or why you don't. Do you prefer some kinds of shopping to others? In this case which do you prefer?
12. Suggest why many people enjoy sitting in a street café of this kind.
13. Are there any street cafés of this type in your country? If so, how are they different from this one? If there aren't any, is there any reason for it?

FIRST FOR QUALITY
AND FAMOUS GIFTS
FRANKLAND
CONFECTIONER
SENIOR
SERVICE
satisfy
Coca-Cola
CONFECTIONER
EEL & PIE SHOP
& SON
SHELLEY AVE
HIGH St Nth E12

2 *The Queue*

This photograph was taken at the time of a forty-eight-hour bakery strike in Britain when housewives hurried to buy what bread there was. These are waiting for the next lot of bread to be brought to the shop.

1. What do you think the weather was like that morning? Why do you think so?
2. In what ways were the people prepared for the weather?
3. Whose is the only unhappy face in the picture? Suggest why.
4. Describe the man standing in the queue.
5. Queueing for bread isn't enjoyable. Suggest why the people might have been laughing.
6. What do you think happened when the bread at last arrived? How did the people behave?
7. One of the women described this part of the morning to her husband the same evening. What did she say?
8. Describe two or three of the ladies you'd like to have as your neighbours and say why you'd choose them.
9. Can you think of some other situation where a joke has made things less unpleasant?
10. Do you consider the ordinary housewife's day an interesting or a boring one? Explain why.
11. You have to spend an hour in a doctor's waiting-room. You don't feel very ill. In what ways can you make the time fairly interesting?

FIRST FLOOR FOR FASHIONS
FIRST FLOOR FOR MENSWEAR
FIRST FLOOR FOR HARDWAR
We give
GREEN
SHIELD
stamps
SCHWARTZ
23
6
9
10½
DUNDEE CAKES
3/-
KEILLERS SHORTBREAD
7/6
REGAL MILK

3 *The Supermarket*

1. In what ways is it clear that the man in the light coat is an assistant and not a customer?
2. Why are the cashiers working very hard here?
3. What things does a supermarket cashier have to do?
4. What are some of the jobs that other assistants in a supermarket have to do?
5. What expressions have the customers got on their faces? Why?
6. What things that you can see in the photograph make shopping in this supermarket easier?
7. How long ago did you last go into a supermarket and what did you buy then?
8. Say what you do from the time you go into a supermarket until you come out.
9. This photograph was taken when the British prices were in pounds, shillings and pence. For what reasons do you think that the decimal system with a hundred pence in a pound was introduced?
10. Why do most shopkeepers prefer the help-yourself service of a supermarket? Suggest several reasons if you can.

Section B The reading passage

In the second part of the interview the candidate has to read an extract from a play that he has already prepared for ten minutes and has had a further opportunity to look at while he is with the examiner.

The following points in his reading are considered important:

(*a*) stress (*b*) intonation (*c*) rhythm

The ability to deal with these correctly may show whether the candidate has understood the full meaning of the passage.

A good pronunciation of individual vowels and consonants is also important.

In reading the extract the examiner takes the part of one speaker and the candidate reads that of the other.

Preparing the passage

1 Read straight through the passage to get a general idea of the meaning.

2 You probably already know which English sounds you have to be most careful with, so pick out and practise quietly any words that have these sounds in them. A wrong pronunciation of the indefinite article (*a*) and failure to distinguish between the pronunciation of 'the' before a consonant and a vowel are bad mistakes.

3 Practise any words that might give trouble.

4 Practise any spoken abbreviations that you are not sure of (an example might be the expression 'that'll').

5 Decide how questions should be read, whether with an upward (Yes/No answer) or downward ending.

6 Decide about question tags, if there are any, whether upward (surprise or a real question) or downward (confirmation) ending.

7 Notice the stressed words and where to make pauses.

8 Read silently through the passage as you think it should be read aloud.

9 Remember it is much better to read too SLOWLY than too quickly. Read calmly and never rush in and hope for the best. Fast reading is NOT good reading.

None of the following practice passages would be likely to appear in a stage play but each might be possible as part of a radio or television play. Prepare each as if you intended to read it aloud with an examiner.

I In this extract the examiner would read the part of Peter.

Dennis: I say, aren't you Peter Partridge? We were at school together, I think.

Peter: I'm Peter Partridge all right. But who are you?

Dennis: Don't you remember me? I'm Dennis Nightingale. I'm the fellow who sat at the back and always gave the wrong answers.

Peter: Now I remember you. You were captain of the school football team.

Dennis: But this really is a surprise. It must be five years since we last met, in London, wasn't it? And now to run into each other in Paris! Do you often come here?

Peter: It's my first visit. I'm on my honeymoon. Meet my wife, Rosita.

Dennis: So you're actually married! How very nice to meet you, Rosita! Is this your first visit to Paris too?

Peter: Rosita speaks almost no English. She comes from a small Italian village.

Dennis: Don't say you went wandering round small Italian villages before you made the acquaintance of Paris.

Peter: We met in London. Rosita was at a language school there.

Dennis: And how much Italian do you speak? So far as I remember, you weren't particularly good at languages at school.

Peter: Not a word.

Dennis: So you don't speak Italian and Rosita doesn't speak English. How on earth did you manage to get married?

Peter: Looking back, I've no idea. But at least we haven't quarrelled yet.

II In this extract the examiner would read the part of Gray.

Greene: Oh, he's bringing the soup now. We must have been waiting a quarter of an hour.

Gray: He isn't bringing it here. That's not our waiter.

Greene: Isn't he? I've no idea what he looked like. You're right. It's for the table over there. Just how much longer have we got to wait?

Gray: Is it always as crowded as it is now?

Greene: It used not to be. It must be getting more popular. I think I preferred it when it was quieter.

Gray: That's our waiter coming now.

Greene: At last! I only hope the food's worth waiting for. The soup smells good, doesn't it.

Gray: Yes, it certainly does.

Greene: Oh no, this won't do at all. It's almost cold. What's yours like?

Gray: Well, it's not as warm as it might be.

Greene: This is too bad. And there's far too much salt in it, anyhow. Horrible! I'll send it back.

Gray: Don't for goodness' sake. We'll be here till five o'clock if we have to wait again.

Greene: All right. I suppose you're right. Look, I'm awfully sorry about this. After all the wonderful things I said about this place! One thing's quite certain. I'll never come here again. I do hope you're not too disappointed.

III In this extract the examiner would read the part of Joyce, who is travelling in Jane's car.

Joyce: How much farther is it?

Jane: Oh, we're nearly there. Two minutes more at the most.

Joyce: Thank goodness! We should just about be in time then.

Jane: What time does it close?

Joyce: Five o'clock. Only ten minutes.

Jane: Don't worry. We'll make it. Oh, traffic lights! These ones are always a nuisance. They take ages to change. Ah, that's it. Oh, you stupid man! Why on earth do you have to step into the road just as they change? You dare turn right in front of me, sir! Oh well. One day you'll be too clever. First on the left past the museum and we're practically there.

Joyce: You can't turn here. There's a diversion sign behind that lorry. The road's up.

Jane: Oh no! And it's only a few yards down with space for parking just opposite. Now what do we do?

Joyce: Can we park anywhere and walk?

Jane: Not here we can't, that's quite certain. There's a space . . . no it's a bus stop . . . look at that enormous queue. Now if he moves out . . . no, I daren't wait. And I'm sure I mayn't park in front of the police station. I know. We'll turn left here, leave the car in the cinema car park and hope that nobody notices and cut through a small passage that'll bring us out at the side entrance to the shop.

Conversation passages from the Spoken English sections which form part of most other chapters may provide additional practice material.

10

Passage for comprehension

Originality is not everything

There were once three sons of a wealthy businessman. Whenever they met, the two eldest, who were twins, used to quarrel about which of them should be his father's heir. The youngest, who was not in the least ambitious, took no part in their arguments. As soon as they left home, the father arranged for an adequate income to be provided for each of them, but insisted that apart 5 from this they were to be financially self-supporting.

The elder twin, who had the advantage of good looks and a striking personality, decided that he would take up the stage as a career. He joined a small repertory company, acted in minor parts, was invariably unpunctual at rehearsals and was accordingly unpopular with his fellow-actors. He earned 10 little and so had to live mainly on his allowance. He occasionally thought of changing his profession, but always put off making a decision, and he became increasingly bored and disillusioned.

His twin brother considered himself unconventional and original, so he set up as an artist. He rented a large dirty attic, which he converted into a 15 studio, grew a beard and haunted the cafés patronised by similar young men who would sit for hours condemning contemporary standards and declaring themselves the pioneers of the school of 'Neo-Revelationism'. He earned nothing, spent all his allowance, ran up a very large number of bills and was accordingly always in debt. 20

The youngest son, who had no special artistic talent, worked hard and was awarded a University scholarship. After taking his degree, he decided he would like to be a teacher, and having completed the necessary training, he obtained his professional diploma. He was appointed to a teaching post in a Grammar School, where he earned enough money to live on and was able to 25 save his allowance.

After years of failing health, the father eventually died. The will, which had been drawn up some years previously, was read to the family. The elder twin had inherited his father's business, the younger was to receive all the money that was not invested in the business, while the youngest boy was left 30 his father's house and estate as his share of the property.

Unfortunately an actor who cannot even be punctual should not be expected to manage a business, and it was not long before the firm went bankrupt. The artist had no doubt that within a short time he would be making a fortune by speculation. He believed in taking risks, the more 35 spectacular the better, and he invested in schemes which should have provided an unusually large profit. They failed completely in their purpose, and in less than a year he was penniless. Nobody knows now what became of either of the brothers who were always hoping for too much.

40 But the youngest brother was able to fulfil his own modest ambition. With the capital he had saved, he converted the house into an orphanage. He gained the approval of the Local Authority, who made a grant large enough to provide for its upkeep. Influential people contributed donations, and with the help of a few assistants he was able to care for homeless and 45 backward children. He achieved contentment.

This is a story that has the old-fashioned moral that thrift may bring more rewards than material ones. No genuine neo-revelationist would accept so outworn a philosophy, which, nevertheless, resulted in a surprising amount of happiness for a considerable number of people.

Notes on the passage

Vocabulary

line

1 The word *merchant* is not often used nowadays except for a coal merchant (who sells coal) and the Merchant Navy as distinct from the Royal Navy. The following words, each with a more exact meaning, have replaced it: *a businessman*, *a shipping agent*, *an exporter and importer*, *a shipowner*, *a shopkeeper*, *a wholesaler* (selling in large quantities), *a retailer* (selling in small quantities), *a dealer* (a general term for one who buys and sells things).

3 The expression 'in the youngest time' does NOT EXIST in English. *recently* is the most likely word.

3 DO NOT MIX: please *take a seat;* the meeting will *take place* next Monday; he is *taking part* in the play/in the meeting; *take your place* in the procession; he will *take the place of* the absent performer; nothing can *take the place of* a good home.

5 A *salary* and *wages* are *earnings:* a salary is usually an annual amount, paid in twelve equal monthly parts; wages are paid for the hours worked or the amount achieved—usually weekly. *Income* is all the money received, from earnings, investments, rents, pension etc. *Income tax* is paid on it to the Government. *Rates* are paid to the Local Authority. *Duty* is paid on imported goods and *value added tax* on other goods and services. *Interest* is paid on some *bank accounts* and *dividends* on *shares*.

7 *striking* catching the eye. *struck by lightning*. Workmen *strike* (*go on strike*) for better conditions. People *strike matches*. *It struck me that* he had changed a lot recently.

8 *a career* is an occupation, often extending throughout life. It is not, as in some languages, merely an occupation offering prospects of promotion.

9 *a repertory company* is a group of actors who present plays which are

changed frequently, often once a week. Such companies are more often found in provincial towns. *A West End company* is one that usually gives performances in well-known London theatres. *A repertoire* is a collection of plays, songs or other forms of entertainment that a performer or group of performers knows well enough to present to an audience.

10 *a rehearsal* of a play; *a dress rehearsal* is the final practice with the conditions those of an actual performance, ready for the *first night.*
repetition is merely repeating: *repetition aids memorising.* (*Adj* repetitive).
recite a poem (speak it formally) (*N recitation.*)

11 *mainly* = principally, chiefly. A main road; a main line (railway); the main imports. *mostly* is more common in speech than in writing.

11 *an allowance: His father allows him a certain sum each month: he gives him an allowance. permission: He allows his daughter to use his car: she has his* permission to use it. *He has permission to stay away from school.*
A soldier's holiday is *leave.* 'leave' may sometimes mean permission: *he gave me leave to remain seated.*

13 *increasingly bored* sounds rather better in written English than *more and more* bored (important, unpleasant); increasingly cold = colder and colder.

13 *disillusioned* (disillusionment)—having lost one's illusions (there is no corresponding adjective for 'illusion'). An *illusion* of something that does not exist (an optical illusion); a *delusion* (deluded) is similar, but with a strong idea of deception, a definite falsifying of things. A sick person may have delusions. 'delusions of grandeur'.

15 *rent* (*V*) for a period: *rent a house, a television*; (*N*) pay/charge rent.
hire (*V*) for short time only: *hire a bicycle, car, boat.*
The *owner* of a house may become a *landlord* or *landlady* by *letting* his house to a *tenant.*

15 an *attic* may be a room that is lived in; things are stored in a *loft* (*Adj* lofty = high). Both are at the top of a building.
Below a building, a *basement* may be lived in or be part of a shop; a *cellar* however is used for storage.
A *garret* is a poor unpleasant room under the roof.

15 *convert* (*V*) = to change, often used for religion: to convert someone *to* another faith; *a convert:* someone who has been converted.
Missionaries are people who try to convert people of other religions or *heathens* (without any religion) to their own faith (which may be Christianity). *Atheists* do not believe in a God.
Other meanings of *convert:* He *converted* some of his investments *into* ready cash. He has *converted* his house *into* separate flats. *N conversion.*

16 SPELLINGS: *Plurals of words ending in -o: studio,* soprano, concerto, piano, solo and similar words that are still clearly Italian in origin add -s: studios, pianos. Other words, more completely absorbed into the language, add -es: potatoes, tomatoes, heroes, echoes, mottoes.

16 A *patron* is an important person who takes an interest in a society or a charity or (especially in eighteenth-century Europe) a person's creative

work, and provides money and other help; *to patronise* can mean to treat someone considered an inferior with obvious kindness: *He examined my work in a patronising way and said that it was not bad for a beginner,* St. George is the *patron saint* of England, St. Andrew of Scotland, St. David of Wales and St. Patrick of Ireland.
In the passage, *patronise* means visit and make use of (a café, club, shop).

17 *condemn* (*V*) = say something is thoroughly bad: *condemn cruelty to animals; condemn someone to death.* (*condemnation*)
blame (*V* and *N*) = say someone is the cause of a bad thing: *he was blamed for the accident; he took the blame* (but: it was his *fault*).
criticise—give an opinion about the value of something (often concentrating on faults): *criticise a film. N criticism* a *critic Adj critical* (also from 'crisis'): *a critical moment in his life*). Newspapers publish *reviews* of books, plays, films and concerts.

17 *contemporary* (*Adj*)—of the same period. *Shakespeare and Bacon were contemporaries* (*N*) Often the adjective means 'of the present time': *contemporary or present-day furniture. modern* is a wider term: *the modern age. up-to-date* is emphatically modern (OPP. *old-fashioned*). *fashionable* suggests a short period only, as fashions soon change. Avoid 'to-day's' as an adjective: '*present-day* English styles/opinions' is more usual.

20 When a person *owes* money he is *in debt.* If a firm or person cannot find enough money to pay their or his debts when these must be paid, they or he are (or go) *bankrupt.* The *bankruptcy court* settles the amount to be paid. A person would be *a bankrupt.*

22 Prizes are *awarded* when the decision is made about who shall receive them. They are *presented* when they are actually *given.*
Money and marks are also awarded.

22 A *scholarship* is a payment of money to enable a clever student to undertake a certain course of study, as for example, in a university, a Grammar School, or in a school or college abroad.

22 A *degree* is a title given by a university to a student who has reached a satisfactory standard in certain subjects at the university. He is then a *graduate*; before he gets his first degree and while he is studying at University, he is an *undergraduate.* Notice that a graduate must have a University degree, with which he graduates.

24 A *diploma* is a title which may be awarded by a university, by a school or college or by a professional society. Diploma subjects are in some cases practical ones such as Domestic Science, Architecture, Social Studies—though diplomas and degrees may sometimes be awarded in the same subjects.

24 One *applies for* a post or job, and, if successful, one is *appointed.* On leaving the job, one *resigns* (sends in or hands in one's resignation), or *is dismissed.* When one reaches a certain age one *retires* from work. One may then receive a *pension.*
NOUNS: *application, appointment, resignation, dismissal, retirement.* An *old age pensioner.*

25 *British state secondary school education*, for children over the age of eleven,

may be obtained in three types of schools: *the Grammar School*, for the more academically-minded children, who may go on to University, *the Technical School*, which may train for industry or commerce, and *the Modern School*, with a general education. The *Comprehensive School* caters for all three types of children. Nowadays various other types of school are being introduced in different areas.

25 *live on* the money one earns; he *makes his living by* giving private lessons. What do you *do for a living?*

27 One *fails* (failure) or *passes* (a pass) an examination. First one *enters for* it and later one *takes* or *sits for* it. One *enrols* for a study course. *Notice* however: *fail to* do something but: *succeed in* doing it.

27 *Do not mix:* he *died* and he *is dead.* ALSO: *disease and decease* (death)

27 *a will* states money and property arrangements to be carried out after a person's death. This is sometimes entitled 'Last Will and Testament' but a *testament* is one of the two divisions of the Bible: the Old and the New Testament.

31 An *estate agent* arranges the buying, selling, letting and managing of property.

32 *punctual*—coming at the right time. *exact*=precise: *the exact number.* The train arrived *on time.* Jane had arrived *in time for* it.

35 *a fortune*=a lot of money. *fortune* (*Unc*) =luck: good or bad fortune. (*Adj fortunate*) (*Adv fortunately*) a *fortune-teller* tells *fortunes.*

35 I *believed* his story. He *believes in* enjoying life, in science, in God.

37 *on purpose=intentionally, deliberately:* OPP *accidentally, unintentionally. You broke that cup on purpose. No, it was accidental (an accident).*

38 *What has become of your silver brooch? I haven't seen you wearing it lately. I don't know what has become of it.* This expression is used only in questions. *What will become of Colin if his parents get a divorce?*

39 She *wants* a new dress. She *wishes* she could travel. She *hopes* to visit London next Easter. (make a wish; have hopes: *He has hopes of studying in London.*)

40 *modest*=in the passage the opposite of this word would be 'excessive' or 'exaggerated'.
A different opposite is *conceited: he is modest/conceited about his achievement. N modesty/conceit. proud* and *humble* are opposites. *N pride/humility. He bowed humbly before the proud king. They manage on a modest income.*

41 *interest* is earned on *capital* invested. Vienna is *the capital of* Austria. *Adj* a *capital letter. capital punishment* is punishment by death (the death penalty).

41 An *orphanage* is a home for *orphans*, children without parents. A child is *adopted* by another couple or family. A parent's remarriage may give a child a *stepfather* or *stepmother* (a *stepchild*). A *foster child* is temporarily part of another family. A *guardian* may take the place of dead parents and the child is then a *ward.*

42 A *local authority* = the local Town Council or County Council. Some people *have authority* over others, who must obey. He is *an authority on* Roman coins.

42 *A grant* is a sum of money awarded for some special purpose, often by a local authority: *a grant to maintain a student at University. to grant* a request = permit it to be realised: *Parliament granted the king the right to tax the people.* A *loan* (*V* lend) must be given back: *the loan of money, of a book.*

43 *provide* help, money, goods. *provide for* a family: work to let them have what they need. A *provident* person saves for the future. *Providence* is the supernatural power providing the necessities or good fortune of human beings. *The arrival of the police at the moment of the kidnapping was providential. He has been given the post provisionally for one year* (*to be extended if he is suitable*). *provisions* are food, especially that taken on a journey.

43 A *donation* is usually money *contributed* (*N contribution*) to some useful cause. *a blood donor. alms* were once given to the poor. (an *almshouse* for old and poor people). *charity* (*Unc*) is giving to those in need and *a charity* organises this. A *fund* is all the money collected for use.

44 *care* (*V*) (*a*) I don't care (it is nothing to me) (*b*) he only *cares* about football (*c*) I don't *care for* that colour (*d*) a mother *cares for* her children. *N* (*a*) she has had a lot of care and looks *careworn* (*b*) *take care of* your handbag/the children (*c*) Her address is: *care of* (*c/o*) Mrs. Smith.

45 *achieve* success, happiness, an ambition, fame (all abstract and needing effort to obtain) His discovery/invention/election was a great *achievement.*

46 *thrifty* OPP. *extravagant thrift/extravagance meanness/generosity.*

47 *reward* (*N* and *V*) = (give) a kind of prize for a special service: *Lost: a three-month-old tortoiseshell kitten: reward offered. recompense* (*V* and *N*) = repay (repayment for) effort or trouble: *have money repaid in recompense for an agency's unsatisfactory holiday arrangements. compensation* paid in the case of injury suffered as a result of work or an accident. *In compensation for your missing the party, we are sending you a bottle of brandy.*

47 *material* (*Adj*) OPP. *spiritual.*

47 *genuine* = true: a genuine antique, picture. OPP. *false.* A genuine person is sincere.

47 *accept* a present, an idea. OPP. *refuse. agree to* a suggestion. *agree with* an opinion. *acceptance. agreement. sign an agreement.*

Phrasal verbs

12 PUT *put off* (postpone) an arrangement till a later date; *put up* friends for the night; *put* a pen *down* on the table; *put* food *away* in the larder; *put forward* a suggestion at a meeting; *put back* a book on the bookshelf; *put by* money for one's old age; *put on* a coat; *put on/off/out* a light; be *put out* (either: offended or: given trouble) by someone's annoying behaviour; *put up with* small inconveni-

ences without doing anything about them; *output*—the amount produced.

Which of the above? he is putting .... as much money as possible in case he loses his job; the firm has doubled its ....; he has put .... some excellent ideas; put .... that carving-knife at once; put .... the light; don't put .... your visit too long; he was quite put .... by your criticism; poor woman, she has a lot to put ....; put the bread .... in the cupboard when you have finished with it; she is putting .... the dog's collar before he goes out; as the last bus had gone they put me .... in their spare room.

19 RUN *run up* bills by not paying for the items which one buys; the car *ran into* a tree; he returned from his holiday early because his money *ran out;* a car may *run out of* petrol and stop; *run away from* an angry bull; the dog *ran after* the cat; he was *run over* by a car; he is always *running down* his boss.

Which of the above? the unhappy child ran......from his home; I wish he didn't run......his friends; he is careful never to run......bills; four cars ran......one another on the motorway; he nearly ran...... three chickens in the country lane; owing to the strike, the factory has run......essential supplies; the small brave explorer was running ......a large terrified tiger.

Other meanings of *run*

Colours can *run into* one another.
A manager *runs* a business or a hotel.
A boy of sixteen can *outrun* a younger brother. (run faster than)

Pronunciation

BE CAREFUL: adequate [ǽdɪkwɪt]; career [kəríə]; repertory [répətərɪ]; contemporary [kəntémpərərɪ] pioneers [páɪəníəz]; considerable [kənsídərəbl].

STRESS CHANGES: varíety [vəráɪətɪ]; inváriably [ɪnvɛ́ərɪəblɪ]; várious [vɛ́ərɪəs]; contríbute [kəntríbjuːt]; contribútion [kɔ́ntrɪbjúːʃən]; móral [mɔ́rəl]; moréle [mərάːl]; patron [péɪtrən]; patronise [pǽtrənáɪz].

DO NOT MIX: dingy [dínʤɪ]; dinghy (small boat) [díŋgɪ].

ə (as in *a*go): standards [stǽndədz]; talent [tǽlənt]; scholarship [skɔ́ləʃɪp]; diploma [dɪplóumə]; previously [príːvɪəslɪ]; purpose [pə́ːpəs]; backward [bǽkwəd]; philosophy [fɪlɔ́səfɪ]; surprising [səpráɪzɪŋ].

ɪ (as in cit*y*): rehearsals [rɪhə́ːsəlz]; modest [mɔ́dɪst]; orphanage [ɔ́ːfənɪʤ]; rewards [rɪwɔ́ːdz].

ʃ (as in *sh*ip): ambitious [ǽmbíʃəs]; financially [faɪnǽnʃəlɪ] or [fɪnǽnʃəlɪ]; influential [ínfluénʃəl]; profession [prəféʃən].

ʒ (as in plea*s*ure): occasionally [əkéɪʒənəlɪ]; decision [dɪsíʒən]; disillusioned [dɪsɪlúːʒənd].

ju (as in *u*se): unpopular [ʌnpɔ́pjulə]; spectacular [spektǽkjulə]; genuine [ʤénjuɪn].

OTHERS: wealthy [wélθɪ]; beard [bɪəd]; condemn [kəndém]; debt [det]; awarded [əwɔ́ːdɪd]; schemes [skiːmz]; accept [əksépt] or [ǽksépt].

Special Grammatical and structural points

(*a*) *Missing Tense Forms of Defective Verbs*

	Infinitive	Pres. Simple	Past S.	Pres. Perf.	Future S.
can	to be able	can is able	could was able	has been able	can will be able

He would like to be able to walk.
He can/will be able to come to-morrow.
He has been able to eat a little to-day.

	Infinitive	Pres. Simple	Past S.	Pres. Perf.	Future S.
must	to have to	must have to	had to	has had to	must will have to

He is said to have to work fifteen hours a day.
All her life she has had to work hard.

	Infinitive	Pres. Simple	Past S.	Pres. Perf.	Future S.
may	to be allowed	may/might is allowed	might (reported speech) was allowed	has been allowed	may will be allowed

You ought to be allowed to stay out later.
My boss said I might have the day off.
I was allowed to have the day off.

(*b*) *the more.........the better*
Notice these constructions: *the more spectacular, the better; the smaller, the better; the more he had, the more he wanted; the older he grew, the worse he looked; the less he spoke, the more he heard.*

(*c*) *having completed his training* OR *after completing* his training. It is clumsy to write: *after having completed.* Rewrite each of these in two different ways: after having completed his novel; after having written his letter, he went to post it.

(*d*) There is a considerable difference between: *he worked hard* and *he hardly worked.*

(*e*) Two uses of the *reflexive pronoun* in the passage: he considered himself intelligent (compare: he considered buying a flat); they declared themselves pioneers of a new school (compare: they declared (that) they were pioneers).

(*f*) *he earned nothing* is more emphatic than 'he did not earn anything'. Rewrite each of these statements to emphasise the negative meaning: I did not touch anything; he has not anywhere to live; he does not ever complain; we do not know anybody in the town.

(*g*) VERBAL CONSTRUCTIONS
Infinitive: he arranged for an income to be provided
he expects (is expected) to manage
enough money to live on
too poor to be happy

Gerund: believe in taking risks; put off making
Alternatives: he insisted on their being; he insisted (that) they must be.

Prepositions

(*a*) *in* debt; invest in a business; result in happiness for. (*b*) the approval *of*; the (dis)advantage of good looks; with the help of. (*c*) unpunctual *for* (at) rehearsals. (*d*) live *on* his allowance. (*e*) appoint *to* a post. (*f*) (un)popular *with*.

Contrasting Forms: he is *acting in a play;* the group are *acting a play. convert* someone *to* one's own ideas; convert a house *into* flats. *provide* someone *with* a meal. *provide* a meal *for* someone. *fail* an examination; fail *in* one's purpose. *believe* a story; *believe in* taking risks. *similar to; different from; in contrast to. as:* take up the stage as a career; set up as an artist; he got the house as his share.

Useful expressions to learn and introduce into written work

(*a*) *not in the least* ambitious/interested/important (*b*) *take* (*no*) *part in* a discussion (*c*) *apart from* his occasional forgetfulness, he is very reliable (*d*) *had the* (*dis*)*advantage of* good looks/a wealthy family/a good education (*e*) he was *appointed to* a post (*f*) *draw up* a will (*g*) parents *should not be expected to* pay for expensive schoolbooks (*h*) Jane paid ten pounds *as her share of* the expenses (*i*) he *believed in* enjoying life (*j*) he succeeded *in his purpose* of becoming a doctor (*k*) I wonder what *has become of* all that money I drew out of the bank (*l*) his suggestion *gained the approval of* the committee (*m*) he climbed the tree *with the help of* a ladder (*n*) *a considerable amount of* money/*a considerable number of* expressions to learn (*o*) he became *increasingly annoyed* (*p*) he is *invariably* polite (*q*) he is a bad driver and *accordingly* has had several accidents (*r*) *unfortunately* he is a bad sailor (*s*) but *nevertheless* he usually travels by sea.

Multiple choice questions

Here are a number of questions or unfinished statements about the passage, each with four suggested ways of answering or finishing it. You must choose the way you consider the most suitable. Write in each case the bracketed number of the question or statement followed by the letters **A**, **B**, **C**, **D**, and then cross through the letter of the answer you choose. Give one answer only to each question. Read the passage right through again before choosing your answers.

1 The youngest brother did not quarrel with the others because
A he disliked arguments **B** he was much younger than they were **C** he was not interested in the subject of their quarrels **D** he was quiet and shy

2 When the brothers went out into the world, the father
A expected them to be independent **B** gave them the money

they wanted **C** gave them money to be independent and then no more **D** saw to it that they had just enough for food and accommodation.

3 Which of the following statements does not apply to the eldest son's theatrical career?
A he was never particularly successful **B** he was not well-liked **C** he was a type of person who attracted attention **D** he was always too late for rehearsals

4 Which of these adjectives does not describe the eldest brother?
A weak-willed **B** lacking in purpose **C** inconsiderate **D** misunderstood

5 The second brother became an artist because he believed that
A he had talent **B** his ideas were new and different **C** he should help to reform society **D** this was a worthwhile career

6 The second brother was all these things except one, which is
A contemptuous of wealth **B** extravagant **C** idle **D** impractical

7 Which of the following is not necessary for a fully-qualified graduate teacher in a Grammar School?
A suitable training for teaching **B** a scholarship **C** a degree **D** some kind of certificate of proficiency awarded after training

8 What was the main reason for the second son's losing his father's money?
A his undue optimism **B** his senseless extravagance **C** his incurable laziness **D** his undeserved misfortunes

9 In which of these ways was the money for the orphanage not obtained?
A the youngest brother's inheritance **B** with the help of town and county funds **C** the youngest brother's savings **D** assistance from important people

10 The moral of the story is
A that carefulness with money may bring genuine happiness **B** that money saved may prove a worthwhile investment **C** the proverb 'Waste not, want not.' **D** the proverb 'A little saved is a little gained'.

11 Which of the following would a genuine neo-revelationist not disbelieve?
A that money can bring real happiness **B** that thrift can be a virtue **C** that happiness resulting from hard work and thrift can be genuine **D** that people may benefit from saving money

Reading comprehension

In this exercise you must choose the word or phrase which best completes the sentence. Write first the number of each sentence followed by the letters

A, B, C, D, E, and then cross through the letter of the correct answer in each case.

1 Now that he has retired, he lives partly on his pension and partly on the .... on his post office savings account.
A income **B** wages **C** dividend **D** interest
E salary

2 Every day thousands of .... fly the Atlantic for negotiations with American firms.
A merchants **B** dealers **C** businessmen **D** tradesmen
E negotiators

3 He .... spends his holidays in the mountains though occasionally he goes to the seaside instead.
A usually **B** invariably **C** constantly **D** rarely
E always

4 She worships the sun and .... she always spends her holidays in Greece.
A nevertheless **B** accordingly **C** yet **D** however
E at all events

5 .... to leave early is rarely granted.
A allowance **B** permission **C** leave **D** the privilege
E a permit

6 She is leaving her husband because she cannot .... his bad temper any longer.
A put up **B** put away **C** put by **D** put off
E put up with

7 The weather was .... the exceptionally poor harvest.
A blamed for **B** condemned for **C** accused of
D found fault with for **E** criticised for

8 Before you run .... other people, it is as well to consider your own faults.
A over **B** up **C** down **D** after **E** into

9 You must have .... the examination before Friday, so bring your money to the office as soon as possible.
A passed **B** taken **C** sat for **D** enrolled for **E** entered for

10 His .... for his loyal support of the party was a seat in the Cabinet.
A recompense **B** repayment **C** reward **D** compensation
E prize

Use of English

1 (ii) The five word groups below are the answers to five questions that could be asked about the Reading Passage. Write out the questions.

(i) the stage (ii) minor ones (iii) a studio (iv) enough to live on (v) thrift may bring more rewards than material ones.

2 Notice these two expressions: the more spectacular the better; the less noise you make, the less possibility of your discovery.
Copy the following sentences, adding similar comparative forms to produce the same kind of sentence.

(*a*) The .... I teach him, the .... he seems to understand. It is hopeless.

(*b*) The .... you work, the .... you will earn. So work harder.

(*c*) The .... south one travels, the .... the temperature becomes.

(*d*) The .... the price, the .... the quality.

(*e*) I want to buy a good watchdog, the .... the ....

(*f*) The Government must do something to control rising prices, the .... the ....

3 In each of the word groups below, a sentence is followed by the beginning of a different way of writing the same sentence without change of meaning. Complete each new sentence.

According to his arrangement, a pension will be provided for everyone over sixty.

(i) He has arranged ....

Our teacher insists that we write all our essays on alternate lines.

(ii) Our teacher insists on ....

After many years of hard work, he retired.

(iii) After he ....

With the money he has saved, he can buy a house.

(iv) His savings can ....

It was not long before he had an accident.

(v) His ....

It would be better for you if you worked in a bank.

(vi) You would ....

He thinks it is a good idea to eat a lot of fruit.

(vii) He believes ....

4 Complete each of the following sentences suitably, using not more than five words.

(*a*) He would eat something if he ....

(*b*) I shall not be able to carry this unless ....

(*c*) We shall have dinner as soon as it ....

(*d*) He would have lit the fire if it ....

(*e*) I cannot do the washing-up until ....

(*f*) There will be an open-air performance of 'Twelfth Night' this evening provided ....

5 The following passage contains eleven impossibilities. State clearly what each of these is, using not more than 15 words in each case. Your answers should be affirmative, not negative.

Example: it was eight o'clock in the evening and the sun was just rising.
Either: The sun rises in the morning. *or:* The sun sets in the evening.
Not: The sun does not rise in the evening.

He walked towards the sun which had now risen high above the horizon. The road continued to wind steeply upwards towards the mountain pass. He could see the country people already at work haymaking in the hillside meadows and he felt happy in his freedom. Only a fortnight before he had celebrated Christmas in the crowded English city fifty miles away and now his shadow, which moved ahead of him as he moved, was the only sign of a living person. He stopped to drink from a stream, which was flowing in the same direction as he was walking. The banks of the stream were covered with white buttercups and the leaves of the fir trees rustled in the breeze. Refreshed but hungry, he turned back to return to the inn where he was staying. Supper would be served in half an hour, so he must hurry. He started the long straight ascent back to the village.

Composition and summarising

Letter writing

Each country has its own conventional system of setting out a letter and addressing an envelope. The English system differs in several details from those of other countries. Here is a summary of the most important requirements:

The Envelope

(*a*) It is not usual for the sender's address to be written on the back of the envelope (though this is a good idea, provided the address is also on the letter itself. Many people keep letters and throw away envelopes).

(*b*) The name and address are usually written on the lower half of the envelope.

(*c*) A man is usually addressed either as:
Mr. J. A. Brown or J. A. Brown, Esq., (the full Christian name is sometimes used).
His wife is Mrs. Brown, his daughter Miss Brown, and his young schoolboy son Master Brown.
The full stop after Mr. and Mrs. is optional and may be omitted.
There is no stop after Master or Miss.
Letters signifying military, civil or academic honours may follow the name, if the addressee prefers this or the contents of the letter make these appropriate.

(*d*) The name of the house occupies the next line if the house has no number.

(*e*) On the next line the number followed by the street is written. According to correct business convention, 'Road', 'Street', etc., are not abbreviated. The comma after the number is optional.

(*f*) The town and county (the latter in the accepted abbreviated form) follow. If the town shares the county name as in the case of York, Warwick, Hertford and several more, the county is usually omitted.

(*g*) Each line can begin immediately below the beginning of the one above, or a short equal space may be left each time.

(*h*) For maximum clearness block capitals can be used

(*i*) A comma follows the surname and ends each line except the last. After the number it is optional.

J. A. Brown, Esq.,
12, Green Street,
DANBY,
Hants DY9 9XZ

(Hants stands for the county, Hampshire.)

The Letter Superscription

(*a*) This is written at the top of the letter at the right-hand side.

(*b*) It consists of the address of the sender (but *not* his name), followed by the date.

(*c*) It is arranged in a similar way to the address on the envelope.

(*d*) The date is normally written: day, month (in full), year (in full): 8th February, 19—. (Remember the abbreviations: 1st, 2nd, 3rd, 4th, 21st, 22nd, 23rd, 31st.)

The full stop after the year is optional but there is usually a comma after the month.

(*e*) In a business letter the name and address of the receiver of the letter usually follows, but on the left-hand side. (It may be written at the end of the letter.)

(*f*) The letter opens: Dear Sir, Dear Madam, Dear Mr. Brown, Dear Mary—according to how well the person is known by the writer. (Notice there is no exclamation mark.)

(*g*) The letter itself begins a short way below at some distance from the side.

The Ending

This may be:

Yours faithfully, (Yours truly,) for business correspondence. (The opening phrase will have been 'Dear Sir or Dear Madam.')

Yours sincerely—indicating some degree of friendship or acquaintance, though occasionally used in semi-business correspondence to avoid an impression of coldness.

Any other ending which seems appropriate in letters to close friends or relations.

Here is a possible example of the superscription and ending of a letter to an acquaintance.

1, West Avenue,
Bolchester,
Lancs.
BM1 1VQ
22nd November, 19—.

Dear Patrick,

It . . .

Yours sincerely,
Leslie Smith.

The Letter

(*a*) PARAGRAPHING is important. Plan out what you intend to say before you begin writing. A short letter may introduce two, three or four subjects. Each should be dealt with in a separate paragraph.

Remember to start each fresh paragraph at a short distance from the side.

(*b*) CLEARNESS and CONCISENESS (shortness) are important, especially in business letters. A friendly letter may of course spread indefinitely (unless you are limited in an examination to a certain number of words).

(*c*) SIMPLICITY is equally important. Do not try to be ambitious.

(*d*) It is possible to introduce conversational abbreviations in a letter to a friend to give the effect of conversation, but *never* in a business letter. Even in a letter to a friend these should not be used too much, and are perhaps best avoided in an examination.

(*e*) If an examiner asks you to write a letter, he wants to see whether you know how to set it out correctly, paragraph and punctuate it and write clear, simple English in well-constructed sentences on the subject set. He also wants to see whether you understand instructions. Accordingly *if limits to the number of words are mentioned, you must keep within these limits.*

Here is an example of a simple letter to an acquaintance.

An English correspondent has written to say that his/her middle-aged parents would like to spend a holiday in your country. They wish to stay in a place that is beautiful, reasonably quiet and with plenty of opportunities for excursions in the surroundings. You have also been asked to recommend a small hotel or pleasant boarding-house for them. Write your reply in between 120 and 180 words. You should make the beginning and ending like those of an ordinary letter but the address is not to be counted in the number of words. Here is a suggested paragraph plan for your letter.

1 Reference to the letter received.
2 The place recommended and its surroundings.
3 The inn suggested.
4 Offer to call on them and give further help.

14 Parnassus Avenue,
Lindenbaum,
Ruritania.
22nd February, 19—.

Dear Shirley,

I am very pleased to hear that your parents intend to spend their holiday in Ruritania. There are so many delightful places here that it is difficult to choose the most ideal.

My own choice would be Montamare, a medieval walled city by the sea with a castle and small cathedral. There are long sandy beaches and a harbour with red-sailed fishing-boats. Forest-covered hills rise behind with vineyards and orchards on their slopes. There are castles, deep blue lakes dotted with islands, caves and several picturesque old towns in the surrounding area.

Near the harbour stands a three-hundred-year-old smugglers' inn, with low beamed ceilings, wooden balconies lined with flower-boxes and lovely old polished furniture. It is comfortable and spotlessly clean. The food is excellent and the price reasonable. I can certainly recommend it and I enclose the address.

Please let me know when your parents are coming. I should be delighted to call on them and show them some interesting places. Can't you possibly manage to come with them?

Yours sincerely,
Helena.

(174 words)

(Notice that the word 'nice' is not used at all.)

EXERCISES

Each of the following subjects should be dealt with in a similar way and the letters should be *between 120 and 180 words* in length, apart from the address heading. You are recommended to work out a *plan* for your letter first and this will probably include *three* or *four paragraphs*.

1 You have recently changed your address and wish to inform a friend of this change. Write a short letter in which you say why you have changed and what your new home is like.

2 Write to a friend inviting him or her to spend a few days in your home and suggesting some of the things you can do during the visit.

3 You have just arrived in a foreign country where you are spending a holiday. On the first night write a letter to your parents reporting your safe arrival and your early impressions and promising to write at greater length in a day or two.

4 You are returning by post a friend's book you have kept far too long. Write a letter apologising for and explaining the delay and expressing your good opinion of the book.

6 You have been successful in an examination. Write to the teacher who prepared you for it, thanking him or her for helping you to achieve this result. Include some news about what you are now doing.

8 You have taken an 'au pair' job with an English family. The English lady has written to you in your own country, giving details of your duties which will allow no regular time for classes. Write a reply suggesting politely that as your main purpose in coming to England is to study, you will need a definite period each day free for attending classes. Ask for one or two pieces of additional information.

7 A holiday cottage you have rented has proved quite unsatisfactory. Write to the owner, explaining the reasons for your dissatisfaction and asking for some kind of compensation.

Explain the part played by money in the lives of the three brothers. Deal with each brother in a separate paragraph and use between 170 and 190 words altogether. Here is a suggested beginning.

> The eldest brother used to quarrel with his twin about their later inheritance. Like his brothers, on leaving home he received from his father enough to live on . . . .

Spoken English

Question tags

These short forms, added at the end of a sentence, are common in spoken English.

Formation

Question tags consist of two words: a verb or suitable auxiliary followed by a pronoun.

In many cases, a negative question tag follows an affirmative main verb in the preceding statement and vice versa.

NOTICE: I am right, aren't I. (Notice the first person interrogative form.)
Your father isn't ill, is he?
You can't understand this, can you.
The children take after their father, don't they.
Your friend had a shock, didn't he.
You won't be there before Tuesday, will you.
You did ask him, didn't you.

An extra auxiliary is sometimes used in the opening statement.

Uses

1 Seeking confirmation of what is being said.

No question mark, and a falling intonation at the end.

The answer is expected to agree with the suggestion in the statement.

You were dismissed from that job, weren't you.
He wouldn't give a definite answer, would he.

2 As a surprised question. A question mark and a rising intonation at the end.

The school children aren't going on strike now, are they?
You won't give up your job, will you?

3 As a special request: You will help me, won't you. (no question mark)

4 As a challenge: You stole that money, didn't you. (no question mark)

EXERCISE: Complete the following to make statements followed by question tags. The verb tense and subject are suggested.
Seeking confirmation: make some tea (you—Past Simple); need more petrol (we—Present); your birthday to-morrow (it—Future); come from Norway (Kurt—Present Simple with extra auxiliary); like porridge (the children—Conditional); may still come (he—Present); stop here (train—Present with extra auxiliary). 2 A surprised question: not speak Portuguese (Robert—Present Simple); not do the journey in one day (they—Future); have your breakfast before you left (you—Past Perfect); not buy a sports car (your sister—Present Continuous); not a storm last night (there—Past Simple); write to you (I—Past Simple with extra auxiliary); not get loose again (the dog—Present Perfect); not exceed the speed limit (Aunt Matilda—Past Continuous). 3 A request: write to me (you—Future Simple); not lose your keys (you—Future). 4 Challenge: break that window (you—Past Simple).

Talking about the weather

Sunshine: It's a lovely day to-day, isn't it. What a glorious day! Scorching hot. Sultry/Close (*Adj*). It's a bit cloudy but it won't rain.

Rain: It looks like rain. It's just starting to rain. It's pouring with rain. It's only a shower. It'll soon pass over. Dull, Wet.

Wind: It's very windy to-day. A strong wind. A gale.

Storm: I think there'll be a thunderstorm. What a vivid flash of lightning! That was a loud clap of thunder. He was struck by lightning.

Cold: It's bitterly cold. There's a hard frost. It's freezing hard.

Talking about one's job

A What's your job? (What do you do for a living?)

B Oh, I'm (the) secretary to the sales manager of a food processing factory.

A Do you get good pay? (a good salary?) (is the job well paid?)

B Pretty good, though I have to work hard for what I get. And there's quite a lot of overtime.

A What qualifications have you got? (What are the qualifications needed?)

B I got a degree in Economics and then took an intensive course in Shorthand, Typewriting and various forms of Office Training. There aren't many opportunities for women in Management: secretarial work seems to be the only thing available.

B How about holidays?

A Only a fortnight a year. But I have to travel sometimes with my boss and I enjoy that.

B Do you think I'd make a good secretary?

A No, I'm sure you wouldn't. You're not methodical enough and you're far too forgetful and untidy.

B Thank you. Well, you wouldn't make a good artist and that's what I'm going to be. You've got no imagination.

Talk about your job: pay, duties, hours, holidays, conditions of work, sickness and pension benefits, why you like or dislike it, the type of person best suited for it.

Situations

Explain what you would do or say in each of these cases.

(*a*) You have won £5000 in a lottery. (*b*) You are late for work or an appointment. (*c*) You want to borrow some money (i) from your bank (a request to the manager) (ii) from a friend. (*d*) You have to ask someone to repay a loan. (*e*) You are annoyed with a friend who has kept you waiting a long time and has not apologised.

You are being interviewed for a teaching post by a head teacher. With the help of another student, show what you think is said in this interview.

Giving your opinions

Give your own ideas about one or more of the following subjects.

(*a*) What are some of the attractions and drawbacks of a stage career?
(*b*) How about teaching as a career?
(*c*) Would you prefer a career involving plenty of adventure and possibly some risks or one which guarantees security?
(*d*) What conventions do you regard as really useful ones?
(*e*) What are some of the things that have been done by pioneers.
(*f*) What would constitute happiness in life for you?

General guidance and practice

Table of tenses—Active voice

	Past	*Present*	*Future*	*Future in the past*
SIMPLE:	I told	I tell	I shall tell	I would tell
CONTINUOUS:	I was telling	I am telling	I shall be telling	I would be telling
PERFECT:	I had told	I have told	I shall have told	I would have told
PERFECT CONTINUOUS:	I had been telling	I have been telling	I shall have been telling	I would have been telling
SIMPLE INFINITIVE:	to tell			
CONTINUOUS INFINITIVE:	to be telling			
PERFECT INFINITIVE:	to have told			
PERFECT CONTINUOUS: INFINITIVE.	to have been telling			
PRESENT PARTICIPLE:	told			
PAST PRINCIPLE:	told			

Use the correct form of each of the verbs shown in brackets.

(*a*) I know how I (spend) the money you (give) me last Christmas. I (keep) it till now in my Post Office Savings Account. I (just see) a beautiful cameo brooch in a jeweller's shop. I (go) to the Post Office to-morrow, and when I (draw) out the money, I (buy) the brooch.

(*b*) If the milkman (call) before I (come) back, (ask) him if he (bring) me some cream to-morrow. I (already use) up what I (buy) yesterday.

(*c*) Milton (write) much of his greatest poetry after he (become) blind and while he (live) in lonely and unhappy retirement. We (owe) the poem 'Samson Agonistes' to the fact that he (suffer) so intensely.

(*d*) By this time to-morrow I (buy) my ticket and at this very moment I (sit) in the train before it (leave).

(*e*) The experts (say) that people (use) far more electricity during the last few cold days, and there (be) further power cuts if the public (not economise) more. Last winter the electricity authorities (say) that more power (be) available this year, but recently they (not be able) to keep up with the extra demand.

(*f*) My family (do) all the packing for the holidays this morning while I (still sleep). They (open) drawers and cupboards all the time, but I (hear) nothing.

(*g*) I have never seen such a long queue before. By the time we (reach) the box office they (sell) all the tickets. We (queue then) for five hours and I (be) sure we (get) nothing.

Table of tenses—Passive Voice

	Past	*Present*	*Future*	*Future in the past*
SIMPLE:	I was told	I am told	I shall be told	I would be told
CONTINUOUS:	I was being told	I am being told	—	—
PERFECT:	I had been told	I have been told	I shall have been told	I would have been told
PERFECT CONTINUOUS:	—	—	—	—

INFINITIVES

SIMPLE:	to be told
CONTINUOUS:	—
PERFECT:	to have been told
PERFECT CONTINUOUS:	—

PARTICIPLES

PRESENT:	being told
PAST:	having been told

Convert these sentences from the Active to the Passive Voice. In sentences (*g*), (*h*), (*i*) and (*j*), there are two verbs to change. Be careful to use the same tense:

(*a*) They have made mistakes before.

(*b*) An old man was sweeping up the dead leaves.

(*c*) We are preparing a room for you.

(*d*) They recorded the broadcast speech.

(*e*) Some of the workers have organised an unofficial strike.

(*f*) A panel of distinguished authors will judge the literary competition.

(*g*) Experts will have examined the newly-discovered prehistoric wall-paintings, before they give an opinion.

(*h*) They estimate that the new oil-wells will yield millions of gallons annually.

(*i*) They would have completed the investigations into the causes of the air disaster by to-morrow, but the injured pilot has now revealed new facts.

(*j*) They had checked the cargo carefully before they unloaded it.

Convert the following into the Active Voice. In some cases the new subject will have to be suggested in accordance with the meaning of the sentence:

(*k*) The men were being paid much better by the new boss.

(*l*) The job was done by a skilled workman.

(*m*) The corn was being harvested early this year.

(*n*) The garden has at last been weeded by my husband.

(*o*) The bridge had been washed away by floods and the fields were covered by water.

(*p*) Their new premises will be designed by an architect and constructed by a well-known firm of builders.

(*q*) All the sheep will have been sheared by the end of this week.

(*r*) The logs are floated down the river to the sawmills in summer and autumn.

(*s*) Beautiful articles of porcelain have been produced by that firm for nearly two centuries.

(*t*) The railway line was being electrified and it was hoped that a faster train service could be introduced.

(*u*) The letter would have been registered if the envelope had been properly sealed.

(*v*) That tap ought to have been turned off properly.

Should Ought to

SHOULD is often used instead of OUGHT TO. In this case the following infinitive is not preceded by 'to'. SHOULD is the form used with all persons.

He ought to report the incident.
He should report the incident.

Notice that, as in the case of OUGHT TO:

(1) SHOULD *indicates duty* that is not necessarily fulfilled. The use of the perfect infinitive often suggests that this duty has not been fulfilled:

You should have given in your homework last Wednesday.

Neither SHOULD nor OUGHT TO is as strong as MUST.

(2) SHOULD and OUGHT TO may convey the idea, not of duty, but of probability:

The house should be ready in September

Rewrite the following sentences using SHOULD instead of OUGHT TO.

(*a*) The train ought to be leaving soon.
(*b*) You ought to chew your food before you swallow it.
(*c*) People ought not to shelter under trees in thunderstorms.
(*d*) Ought you to have locked the safe before you left the room?
(*e*) They ought to be having beautiful weather in the Mediterranean.
(*f*) You ought to have been enjoying a good rest while I was out.

Compose two sentences containing SHOULD which might be used by someone in answer to each of the following statements. One sentence should blame the speaker in some way, the other suggest what should be done:

(*a*) I have caught a bad cold.
(*b*) I have lost my passport.
(*c*) I am very cold.
(*d*) I am badly sunburned.
(*e*) I am tired out.

Defining and non-defining clauses

Notice these two sentences:

The youngest, who was not in the least ambitious, took no part in their arguments.
An actor who cannot be punctual should not be expected to manage a business.

Each introduces an adjectival clause, but the relationship of this clause to the rest of the sentence is different in each case.

In the second case, the adjectival clause defines the actor, not an actor who is successful, nor an actor who cannot remember his lines, but an actor who cannot be punctual. The clause defines or explains what actor is meant and is therefore a *defining clause*.

In the first case, the adjectival clause merely adds a piece of description: it does not define who the youngest is or which youngest he is as we know who he is already. It is *a non-defining clause.*

A non-defining clause is:

(*a*) separated from the rest of the sentence by *commas.*

(*b*) always introduced by *who, whom, whose* or *which* and these are *never omitted.*

A defining clause is:

(*a*) *not* separated off by *commas.*

(*b*) sometimes introduced by *that* instead of *who, whom* or *which.*
If a preposition immediately precedes the pronoun, *that* cannot be used.

Notice: The *pronoun* may be *omitted* when it is:

(i) the object of the following verb or:

(ii) governed by a preposition.
The brackets below show where a pronoun could be omitted.
With the capital (that)/(which) he had saved, he set up a business.
The student (that)/(whom) I was discussing the problem with...
The student with whom I was discussing the problem ...

Insert the relative pronoun in the following sentences, putting brackets round it if it may be omitted. Put in commas where these are necessary:

(*a*) Here is the medicine......... does you good.

(*b*) Our little puppy.........David adores is always in mischief.

(*c*) The socks.........she was knitting were for the Red Cross.

(*d*) The aged man in a wheel-chair.........is talking to the hospital matron was once a great surgeon.

(*e*) The gate.........you came through must be kept shut.

(*f*) The pen with.........he wrote so many great novels is now carefully preserved.

(*g*) The American ambassador.........you were speaking to a moment ago will be returning home soon.

(*h*) The beauty queen.........was elected in last year's competition is now a rising film star.

(*i*) The news of his death.........has shocked the whole nation has been reported throughout the world.

(*j*) The waiter.........you were enquiring about has been dismissed.

Enough

Notice the use of 'enough' in these two sentences:

He earned enough money to live on.
They made a grant large enough to provide for its upkeep.

'Enough' usually precedes a noun and follows an adjective or adverb.
Insert 'enough' in its correct position in these sentences:

(*a*) Have you blankets on your bed?

(*b*) Is he old?

(*c*) She is not firm with her children.

(*d*) You have not put salt in the stew.

(*e*) Are you looking after that plant carefully?

Various constructions

These are common constructions and quite important, so careful attention should be given to them.

Notice these verbs which are normally followed by an infinitive or a noun clause.

He decided to go.	He decided that she should go.
He determined to go.	He determined that she should go.
He proposed to go.	He proposed that she should go.
He arranged to go.	He arranged that she should go.
	(or, in this case: He arranged for her to go.)

But: He thought he would go. He thought of going.
Not: He thought to go.

He suggested she should go. He suggested her going.
Not: He suggested her to go.

Here are some verbs followed by the infinitive and not the gerund:

He failed to go.	(He missed going.)
He managed to go.	(He succeeded in going.)
He meant to go.	He hoped to go.
He wanted to go.	He wished to go.
He planned to go.	

Remember the construction with 'want'. 'He wanted that I came' is quite impossible. This must be expressed: 'He wanted me to come.'

Use the correct verbal form in these sentences:

(*a*) The firm decided (start) a new advertising campaign.

(*b*) The woman determined (her husband buy himself) a new suit.

(*c*) They managed (rescue) all the sheep stranded in the snow.

(*d*) The explorer succeeded (discover) an unknown tributary of the river.

(*e*) The woman wants her husband (buy) her a new electric cooker.

(*f*) The team failed (score) another goal.

(*g*) The salesman thought (persuade) the housewife to buy a vacuum cleaner.

(*h*) I missed (see) the almond blossom this spring.

(*i*) He hopes (get) a good mark for his essay.

(*j*) He suggested (invest) our money in a building society.

(*k*) The electric cooker firm arranged (present) a cookery demonstration to housewives.

(*l*) They arranged that the demonstration (take place) in their new show-rooms.

Prepositions

Insert the correct preposition in the following sentences:

(*a*) Do you believe......... ghosts?

(*b*) He converted the barn......... a small theatre.

(*c*) He is saving money to provide......... his future.

(*d*) Are you taking part......... the concert they are giving in the Parish Hall next week?

(*e*) He has invested most of his capital......... oil shares.

(*f*) I don't know what has become......... the scarf I was given for my birthday.

(*g*) A spider lives......... (or feeds.........) flies caught in its web.

(*h*) The game resulted......... a draw, two all.

(*i*) He trod......... my toe......... purpose.

(*j*) He is very extravagant and is always......... debt.

(*k*) A circus clown is usually popular......... children.

(*l*) The producer has himself acted......... many outstanding roles.

(*m*) The antique dealer was patronised......... many connoisseurs.

(*n*) If you want to be nimble on your feet, you might profit......... a course in fencing.

(*o*) They were defeated......... their purpose.

(*p*) We are hoping......... a change in the weather.

(one prays for, longs for, asks for, begs for, looks for).

11

Passage for comprehension

Pity for a stranger

The little man came up to me as I was about to enter the telephone box and asked me whether I had a match.

'I'm sorry,' I said. 'I don't smoke, so I haven't any. You had better ask someone else.'

5 He looked rather disappointed, hesitated, and then turned away. I watched him walk slowly down the street before I picked up the telephone directory to look up the number I meant to dial.

I am not used to a public call box so it was not until several seconds after I had been connected that I remembered to insert a coin.

10 When I was at last able to speak, I was told that the person whom I urgently wanted to give a message to had just that minute gone out.

Swearing slightly under my breath, I emerged from the box and came face to face with the little man, who was looking as pathetic as a stray dog. As he raised his hat again, I could see he was quite bald. A thin line, re-
15 sembling a duelling scar, crossed one cheek. He spoke nervously.

'Excuse my troubling you again,' he said. 'May I walk along with you a little way? I must confide in someone. I need help desperately.'

He had an unusually deep voice which suggested a strange combination of shyness and self-confidence. I was conscious of a fairly strong foreign
20 accent and I wondered what country he had actually come from. I said that I had to catch a train in twenty minutes' time, but that he might accompany me to the station.

'I am going to shock you,' he said suddenly, after a moment's silence. 'Can you lend me five pounds? I have no money at all.'

25 I have come across many queer characters during my life and plenty of people have tried to borrow money from me. I have generally managed to avoid lending them any. But, perhaps because of the very directness of his appeal, I somehow had the impression that his need might be desperately urgent.

30 'I'm sorry,' I replied. 'I'm afraid I can't lend you anything, as I'm not in the habit of carrying much money about with me. Don't you think that the police might be the best people to ask for help? They could tell you the address of some hostel or organisation you could go to.'

He hesitated. 'I must not go to the police,' he said quietly. 'If I do go,
35 they will have to send me home. That is what I'm afraid of. I don't know what to do.'

'Why did you come here?' I asked. 'How did you come? And surely you must have some money.'

'I did have a little money,' he replied, 'but it was stolen from my room in the hotel and I dared not complain. As to how I came here, I should 40 rather not say anything about it. I cannot accept the system of government under which I have had to live and life in my own country has become unbearable to me. A friend of mine, to whom I am eternally grateful, agreed to help me to escape.'

Naturally I tend to distrust stories like this, but the little man's quiet firm 45 manner of speaking had impressed me. I felt half inclined to let him have a couple of pounds on the chance that he was telling the truth, but I was rather short of ready cash anyhow, and might have needed what I had with me on the way home.

'I'm sorry,' I said again. 'Why don't you try the police in any case? The 50 authorities usually deal sympathetically with people who have troubles like yours.'

He shook his head rather sadly, raised his hat and left me. I caught my train and soon forgot the incident.

It was three weeks later that I happened to glance at an old evening 55 paper and caught sight of a small paragraph at the bottom of the front page, 'The unidentified body of a short bald man, with a deep scar across one cheek, was recovered from the River Thames yesterday. The police believe he had committed suicide.' I then noticed the date: just two and a half weeks before. 60

I suddenly remembered talking to the little man. It was I who might have been the final cause of this terrible tragedy. For days afterwards the cruelty of my refusal made me suffer continual shame and remorse. I swore that I would never again refuse any appeal for help.

It was some time during the following week that I was coming down 65 another street on my way to an appointment. Two men were in the street, one of whom seemed slightly familiar. The shorter one, whom I seemed to know, was standing by the telephone box, feeling in his pockets. As the other man was about to enter the box, the short man spoke to him, and then lit a cigarette from the lighter he was offered, before strolling away for a short 70 distance, apparently waiting for someone. As I approached on the other side of the road, I noticed a long scar across one cheek.

I need not have reproached myself so bitterly.

Notes on the passage

Vocabulary

line

1 *box (N)—a telephone box*; *a pillar box* (for posting letters—a letter-box is also possible); *a box in a theatre* (at the side of the stage); *a box office* (where one buys theatre and cinema tickets)—(a booking office for travel tickets); *a box number* (used instead of an address in

newspaper small advertisements); *a matchbox* (the container), *a box of matches*. BUT: a *tin* of fruit, meat, fish. *Boxing Day* = the 26th December. *box* (*V*)—fight with the fists; *boxing gloves*; *a boxer*.

2 *match* (*N*): (*a*) a safety match that strikes (*b*) a competitive game (*c*) an equal: *the champion has met his match*; (*d*) something similar or in harmony: *these cushion-covers will be a good match for the chairs*; (*e*) a marriage: *a matchmaker* is someone who enjoys bringing likely marriage partners together. *match* (*V*): (*a*) be similar to or harmonise with: *she had a blue hat and blue gloves and a scarf to match*. Other meanings are less common.

5 *disappointed* (*N disappointment*): unhappy because some pleasant thing has not happened; *deceived* (*N deception*): given a wrong idea. *He was very disappointed by his failure to get the job he wanted. The shop-keeper deceived the customer into thinking he was getting a bargain.*
pretend (*V*) (*N* pretence): try to give the idea of being or knowing something different from reality: *the other guest pretended that he knew all about business but in fact he was only a young office clerk. claim* (*V* and *N*): say that one has the right to something, say that something is true: *He claimed the watch that had been found; he claimed that it belonged to him.*

6 *pick* a flower in the garden/an apple on the tree; *pick up* a flower that has fallen on the ground/a book lying on the table.
Also: pick one's favourite chocolate from those in the box.
fall from above the ground: *an apple falls from a tree*; *fall down*—when already standing on the ground: *he fell down while playing football.*
pick up a language by using it, without methodical study.

6–7 *telephone directory*; a library *catalogue* containing names of books; a furniture catalogue; a *brochure* = a very small book (*booklet*) giving information; a *pamphlet* or a *leaflet* is usually a single sheet giving information.

7 *mean* (*V*): (*a*) What does this word mean? (*b*) I mean what I say, and nothing will make me change my mind. (*c*) I mean to finish this before to-morrow. (*d*) I meant to write to you but I had no time (so I did not). (*Adj*) (*a*) He is so *mean* that he grudges the cost of the polish on his door knocker (OPP generous); (*b*) It was a mean thing to try to get me into trouble like that (*c*) the mean annual rainfall (average). (*N Pl*) (*a*) to have means = to have plenty of money (*b*) the only means of getting there is by boat. He would use any means to get rich. (way)

11 *urgently*—an urgent matter is one that must receive immediate attention.
An envelope may be marked URGENT—the letter must be dealt with at once.
(*N* urgency). *an emergency* is a state of affairs needing urgent attention. An *emergency operation* must be performed at once. Buildings where many people gather together have *emergency exits* in case of fire.

12 *swear* (*a*) use bad language (*b*) give one's solemn word that one will do something: *he swore that he would take revenge.* A *witness* in a *law court* has to *swear* (*take an oath*) to tell only the truth. *vow* (*V* and *N*) has a similar meaning to (*b*): *he vowed never to forget.* Monks, nuns and often people being married take vows. *curse* (*V* and *N*) may mean 'use bad language' or 'wish evil things to happen to one's enemy': *he uttered a curse on those who had destroyed his home and family.*

12 *under my breath*—in a whisper. *out of breath* or *breathless*: having no breath after running (but: breathless with excitement). *panting*—breathing quickly. *gasping*—drawing in air with difficulty.

13 *face to face* (with); *back to back*; *side by side* (four *abreast*); *shoulder to shoulder*; *hand in hand*; *arm in arm.* put on a dress *inside out/back to front.* hang a picture *upside down.*

15 *duel* (*V* and *N*)—an organised fight between two people; *dual* (*Adj*)—double: *dual controls in a car.*

15 *a scar* (from an old wound); *a bruise* (blue-brown); *a bump* on the head; a *spot* on the nose; a *swelling*; a *blister* (from walking); a *corn* (hard skin, often on the foot); a *chilblain* (usually due to poor circulation); a *scratch* (from a cat).
He has a black eye because he bumped into a lamp-post.

17 *confide* (in someone)—tell something secret, hoping for sympathy; say something *in confidence,* trusting it will be kept secret; a *confidential* secretary/document; *confident* (sure) of one's success; *a confidence* (*C, N*)—a secret exchanged; *confidence* (*Unc N*)—sureness: *a mountain-climber must have confidence in his ability*; *self-confidence*; *over-confidence.*

17 *desperate* (*Adj*)—not knowing what to do because no hope is left and so possibly violent; *despair* (*V* and *Unc N*)—lose all hope; *in despair*: *He was so hopeless at housekeeping that, in despair, he decided to get married.*

18 *combination.* An *alliance* between countries. (*allies*). A *union* = a combined group: the Soviet Union; the United States.

19 *shyness*—quietness and reserve with people. *timidity*—fear of people. A girl may be *shy*; a mouse is *timid.*

19 *conscious of* = *aware of. unconsciousness* = unawareness of one's surroundings.

20 a foreign *accent*; a local *dialect*; an *accented* syllable.

20 *actually*—really NOT: at that time

24 *borrow* something from another person (a borrower). *lend* something to another person: a lending library.

27 *very* (*Adj*) is emphatic: *The very idea! I should never dream of it. That was the very thing* (*that*) *I was going to say.*

28 *appeal* (*V* and *N*): an appeal for money and food for famine victims; *call* (*V* and *N*): a loud cry: a drowning man would call for help.

31 a *habit* is personal: smoking is a habit (*Adj habitual*); a *custom* is a practice observed for generations by a group of people (a certain day of the year may have special celebrations): it is similar to a *tradition,*

though the latter has a stronger idea of the past. *Adj customary tradi-tional.*

40 *complain about* the bad food or the noise; *complain of* a headache. A complaint may also be an illness, often one that lasts for a considerable period. bronchitis and rheumatism are common complaints. One can *reclaim* money or demand to have it back but *reclamation* usually refers to bringing back useless land into cultivation.

42–43 *unbearable*—a word of similar meaning: *intolerable. tolerant*: accepting willingly that other people may have opinions different from one's own.

45 *feel (be) inclined to—tend to:* both these suggest that the following action happens naturally, easily or often: *He is inclined to (tends to) exaggerate.*

The very slight difference in meaning can be seen best in the related nouns.

A *tendency* is a general likelihood. It may well express the general or abstract though this is not always the case. An *inclination* suggests a personal feeling of wishing to do something.

to *tend to* may therefore more often be found in connection with more general or abstract cases; to *be inclined to* in more personal and voluntary ones.

Mathematical figures tend to be misleading in the study of human behaviour.
He is inclined to be lazy.

Another less common expression is to be *prone to*: *He is prone to argue. Children are prone to various childish illnesses.*

In very many cases the three expressions can be used interchangeably, *tend to* being probably the most common.

47 *tell the truth* but: *tell a lie.*

48 *short of* money/time = not having enough to spare. *Short of stealing a car, there seemed to be no way of getting home* (apart from, other than by)

49 *on the way* home; your bicycle *is in my way* so you'll have to move it; you can reach the village only by car as it is a very *out-of-the-way* place; he isn't the type of person I admire but *in a way* I like him; oh, *by the way*, I nearly forgot to tell you that Martin asked to be remembered to you. *incidentally* can usually replace *by the way.*

55 I *happened to* glance = I glanced by chance. *I happened to meet him.*

55 *glance* (*V* and *N*) quickly; *gaze* (*V* and *N*) for a long time; *stare* (*V* and *N*) with surprise or curiosity—possibly rudely; *glare* (*V* and *N*) angrily; *peer* (*V*) = look with difficulty; *peep* (*V* and *N*) = take a quick, sometimes furtive look at something; *catch sight of* = see suddenly; *catch a glimpse of* = see suddenly for a very short time.

Which of the above? ...... sadly at a departing ship; ...... ahead through thick fog; a teacher may ...... at a talkative student; ...... at someone wearing extraordinary clothes; ...... a friend travelling in a fast car; the old lady ...... through the closed curtains at her new neighbours; ...... at newspaper headlines when in a hurry; ...... a waiting friend as the train stops.

58 *recovered from*; one also *recovers from an illness* (*N* recovery)

59 *commit* suicide/murder/robbery/theft. A *crime* is *committed.*
commission (*N*) may also be: (*a*) the sum charged by an agent for doing some service such as buying shares: *a ten per cent commission*; (*b*) the special authority given to an officer in the armed forces. A sergeant is a non-commissioned officer.

62 a *tragedy* (*Adj* tragic) a *comedy* (*Adj* comic) A *comedian* is the kind of performer who makes people laugh: he is often not an actor.

63 *continuous* = continuing without a break; *continual* = extending over a long time but with interruptions. Which describes (*Adj* or *Adv*): a railway line? a dog barking? a child asking for sweets? the prairies stretching across Central Canada. *constant* can sometimes have a similar meaning to *continual.*

63 *ashamed of* a bad action; feel *shame* because of it; a *shameful* action is one to be really ashamed of; a *shameless* person is one who does not seem to feel shame.

70 *stroll* and *saunter* (*V* and *N*) both mean 'walk in a leisurely way'. Compare: *march* (as soldiers); *stride*; *pace* (backwards and forwards); *strut* (proudly and often foolishly).
All except the last are nouns and verbs. A *march* can be a musical composition.

Pronunciation

DISTINGUISH BETWEEN: dial [dáɪəl]; duel [djúːəl]; dual [djúəl], mean [mɪːn]; meant [ment]; deal [dɪːl]; dealt [delt]; bold [bould]; bald [bɔːld]; breathe [brɪːð]; breath [breθ].

ə (as in *a*go): urg*e*ntly [ə́ːʤəntlɪ]; emerg*e*ncy [ɪmə́ːʤənsɪ]; f*a*mili*a*r [fəmílјə]; trag*e*dy [trǽʤədɪ]; dist*a*nce [dístəns]; for*eign* [fɔ́rɪn] or [fɔ́rən]; sym-p*a*thetically [sɪmpəθétɪklɪ]; *a*pparently [əpǽrəntlɪ]; consc*ious* [kɔ́nʃəs]; desp*e*rate [désp*ə*rət]; conscient*ious* [kənʃɪénʃəs]; c*o*mmit [kəmít]; syst*e*m [sístəm].

OTHERS: directory [dɪréktərɪ]; or [daɪréktərɪ]; unidentified [ʌnaɪdéntɪfaɪd]; suicide [súɪsaɪd]; accent [ǽksənt]; Thames [temz]; approached [əpróutʃt]; swear [swɛə].

Special grammatical and structural points

(*a*) he *used to get* up early but he no longer does; he *is used to* (*accustomed to*) *getting* up early so he does not mind.
BUT: it is *impossible* to say: he uses to get up early.
This should be: he gets up early or he is in the habit of getting up early.

(*b*) He is *my* father. He is a friend *of mine* = one of my friends. The use of the possessive pronoun after 'of' suggests one of a number. One could not therefore speak of 'a father of mine'.

Other persons: some homework of yours; an idea of his; a ring of hers; a relation of ours; a dream of theirs to live in a country cottage; a mistake of Jock's; a suggestion of the Greys'.

(*c*) The adjective *own* must always be *preceded by* a possessive adjective: *my, his, our etc. or a possessive form of a noun.*
The dog sits on *his* (*its*) *own* chair. Is this *Caroline's own* car?

(*d*) *might have needed* Notice the following constructions and meanings:

you must have seen him (almost certainly)
you might have lost it (this is possible)
you might have told him (but you did not)
you need not have told him (but you did)
you should (ought to) have told him (but probably you did not)

(*e*) someone *else*, everywhere else, nothing else etc.
Do as you are told *or else* you will be in trouble.

(*f*) you *had better* ask first He *would rather* not say.

(*g*) I have to catch a train *in twenty minutes' time* Not: after twenty minutes.

(*h*) *about to do* something—this is the very next thing to happen but it may not happen. *He was about to go out when he had second thoughts and turned back.*

(*i*) the *police are* investigating the crime: this is a *plural* noun.

(*j*) *Verbal Constructions*
Infinitive: manage to avoid; agreed to help me to escape
the best people to ask
made me suffer; had better ask;
should rather (not) say
Gerund: excuse my troubling you.

Prepositions

(*a*) *No preposition:* enter a room; resemble another person

(*b*) conscious/aware *of*; in the habit of talking; afraid of meeting; short of food; the cause of his failure.

(*c*) emerge *from* (come out of); money stolen from her purse.

(*d*) he stood face to face *with* his hated enemy; carry money about with him.

(*e*) I telephoned him *on* the chance that he might be in.

(*f*) confide *in* his best friend

(*g*) muttering *under* his breath

(*h*) grateful *to* him *for* his help

(*i*) *as to* the other two bags, we can carry those ourselves.

Expressions to learn and introduce into written work

(*a*) I was about to speak when I sneezed (*b*) look disappointed

(*c*) insert a coin (*d*) he had just that minute gone out

(*e*) he said something under his breath
(*f*) he came face to face with a bull
(*g*) excuse my troubling you (*h*) I was conscious of a strange silence
(*i*) in twenty minutes' time (*j*) I had the impression that he was afraid
(*k*) as to to-morrow's arrangements, we can discuss them later.
(*l*) he tends to argue (*m*) I felt half inclined to leave at once
(*n*) he stayed on the chance that he might hear something
(*o*) I met her on the way home (*p*) I happened to meet him
(*q*) I caught sight of a stork flying
(*r*) for days afterwards he stayed indoors.

Multiple choice questions

Here are a number of questions or unfinished statements about the passage, each with four suggested ways of answering or finishing it. You must choose the way you consider the most suitable. Write in each case the bracketed number of the question or statement followed by the letters **A**, **B**, **C**, **D**, and then cross through the letter of the answer you choose. Give one answer only to each question. Read the passage right through again before choosing your answers.

1 In asking for a match, the little man clearly wanted to start a conversation. This seems illogical because
A he obviously had no cigarette **B** this was the wrong moment to ask **C** the person he spoke to might not have had a match **D** this is not the way to start a conversation

2 What was the strongest reason why the writer should be swearing when he came out of the telephone box?
A he had just lost his coin **B** he had been both absent-minded and unlucky **C** his friend had not been at home **D** the little man was still there

3 Which of these details about the little man's appearance is not given in the passage?
A he had a scarred face **B** he had no hair **C** he was wearing a hat **D** he looked shabby

4 Which of the following did the little man not say he wanted when he spoke the second time?
A to accompany the writer **B** to be trusted **C** to get assistance **D** to tell the writer his difficulties

5 Why was the writer prepared to listen to the little man's story?
A he had plenty of experience in dealing with this type of man **B** the man's approach suggested that he might really need help **C** the writer had no money with him **D** the writer never carried much money

6 The writer advised him to go to the police because they could give him
A money **B** useful information **C** financial assistance **D** the means to get home again.

7 What was the writer's main reason for not lending him any money?
A he did not want to run out of what he had **B** he seldom gave away money **C** he might not get it back **D** he distrusted the man's honesty

8 According to the newspaper article, the police believed that the man found had
A drowned himself **B** been drowned accidentally **C** died from natural causes **D** met an accidental death

9 Why did the writer feel shame and remorse?
A he had ignored the man **B** he had given no help or advice of any kind **C** he had refused assistance **D** he had been so little concerned that he had soon forgotten the man

10 The writer need not have felt so guilty because
A he had been right to refuse help **B** the man had not suffered by his refusal **C** if he had not read the paper, he would not have known about it **D** the man had got help from other people

Reading comprehension

In this exercise you must choose the word or phrase which best completes each sentence. Write first the number of each sentence followed by the letters **A**, **B**, **C**, **D**, **E**, and then cross through the letter of the correct answer in each case.

1 She felt very .... when her husband forgot her birthday.
A deceived **B** deserted **C** desperate **D** hopeless **E** disappointed

2 After lunch I felt .... enough to ask my boss for a rise.
A strong **B** bold **C** encouraged **D** fearless **E** bald

3 As a result of their .... the three small independent countries felt less afraid of their powerful neighbour.
A combination **B** alliance **C** partnership **D** junction **E** union

4 I .... to my office as it is so near my home.
A use to go **B** go on foot **C** walk **D** wander **E** do not go with my car

5 As a result of the radio .... for help for the earthquake victims, over a million pounds has been raised.
A appeal **B** transmission **C** call **D** programme **E** advertisement

6 An ambulance must have priority as it usually has to deal with some kind of ....
A urgency **B** pressure **C** extremity **D** crisis **E** emergency

7 I have a number of .... to make about this hotel so I wish to see the manager.
A complaints **B** claims **C** reclamations **D** accusations **E** grumbles

8 The road lay ahead of him, a(n) .... grey line stretching to the horizon.
A continual **B** constant **C** eternal **D** continuous **E** prolonged

9 If you are so senseless as to go on long walks in tight-fitting shoes, you must expect to get ....
A scars **B** scratches **C** bruises **D** blisters **E** spots

10 After his prolonged dive in search of the ring he emerged from the water ....
A under his breath **B** breathtaking **C** gasping for breath **D** panting **E** out of breath

Use of English

1 The five phrases below are the answers to five questions that could be asked about the reading passage. Write out the questions.

(i) unusually deep (ii) five pounds

(iii) they will have to send him home

(iv) it had been stolen from his room in the hotel

(v) three weeks later

2 In each group of four words below, three words rhyme but one does not. Write down the number of each group and beside it, the word which does not rhyme with others in its group.

Example: (xi) dare, bear, beer, chair   Answer: (xi) beer

(i)	(ii)	(iii)	(iv)	(v)
wait	pause	short	loose	stirred
height	doors	bought	choose	sword
straight	course	taught	whose	heard
weight	paws	throat	bruise	purred

(vi)	(vii)	(viii)	(ix)	(x)
darn	Swede	warred	ache	please
lawn	guide	guard	steak	geese
warn	skied	scarred	snake	teas
born	speed	yard	beak	cheese

3 For each of the following ten phrases, four suggested explanations are given, from which you must choose the correct one. Write down the numbers

(i) to (x) and against each the letter **A**, **B**, **C**, or **D** according to the explanation you choose.

(i) You had better improve your writing.
A your writing was better earlier **B** it has got to be better **C** you are succeeding in your efforts to do this **D** I advise you to do better writing

(ii) Anne always confides in her sister.
A Anne trusts her in everything **B** Anne feels safe in telling her her secrets **C** Anne feels safe and protected with her sister **D** Anne gives her sister all the advice she needs

(iii) I have come across many unusual people in my travels.
A I have met them **B** I have quarrelled with them **C** I have succeeded in finding them **D** I have known them for a short time only

(iv) He was not inclined to pass over the matter unnoticed.
A he did not intend to do this **B** he did not feel like doing this **C** he did not enjoy doing this **D** he refused to do this

(v) He might have forgotten your request.
A but he has not **B** this could be an explanation **C** he should have done this **D** if only he had forgotten it!

(vi) I shall buy some extra food in case they all come.
A provided they come **B** if in fact they come **C** to provide for this possibility **D** on condition that they come

(vii) He must pull himself together.
A he must take more exercise **B** he must take more share in our work **C** he must improve his figure **D** control himself and start doing something useful

(viii) He says he will continue to use his old car for the time being.
A for at least a short time ahead **B** so long as it lasts **C** at the moment **D** because he already has it

(ix) I dare say the police will do nothing about it.
A I am not afraid to say **B** I think it could happen that **C** I think it likely **D** even though it seems impossible, this is what I think

(x) She enjoys making believe she is a great actress.
A giving this impression **B** imagining that she is one **C** deceiving people by pretending that she is one **D** working to achieve this

4 Mirja and an English lady, who are sitting at the same table in a café, have got into conversation. The English lady's words have been omitted. Write down each of the numbers shown followed by the words that she probably says.

E. How are you getting on in London?
M. I'm really not very happy here.

1 E. ....
M. It's so difficult to get to know people. I often feel lonely.

2 E. ....
M. I'm working as an au pair with a family, looking after two small children.

3 E. ....
M. Yes, they're quite pleasant but I don't see much of them. Both of them work all day and watch television every evening.

4 E. ....
M. No, they seem to have very few. Almost nobody visits them.

5 E. ....
M. I suppose they just don't have time to make friends.

6 E. ....
M. Yes, at a local College. But I'm the only one in my class from my country. And I'm a bit shy and don't like to be the first one to speak.

7 E. ....
M. Well, I've walked in the parks and visited the Tower and Westminster Abbey. But I don't live near the centre and bus and underground fares are rather expensive.

8 E. ....
M. I'm free every afternoon and all day Sunday.

9 E. ....
M. I have a lot of studying to do and I read a good deal.

10 E. ....
M. Oh, I should enjoy that. Which afternoon would that be?

11 E. ....
M. Thursday, yes. What is your address?

12 E. ....
M. Oh, thank you. I'll be outside this café at quarter-past four then.

13 E. ....
M. I shall look forward to that very much.

Composition and summarising

Business letters

The main qualities of a good business letter are *clearness* (which depends partly on the *logical arrangement of ideas*), *exactness* and *concentration on the subject matter to be dealt with.*

Before you start writing the letter, *think over carefully* the ideas you have to convey, and how best to *arrange them* and, when you write, *express these ideas briefly and exactly.*

The *language* of a business letter is necessarily more formal than that of a letter to a friend but it is still *clear, straightforward English.*

Expressions such as 'we beg', 'we tender our thanks', 'your esteemed favour', 'inst', 'ult', and 'prox' are very old-fashioned and should never be used. On the other hand the language is that of formal written English, not that of everyday conversation.

Here is an example of a more formal letter.

A large British travel association has established a centre for British tourists in your town. An advertisement has appeared in one of your local newspapers asking for applications from suitably qualified people to be responsible for the welfare, entertainment and guiding of the visiting tourists. You are interested in this post. Write a letter of application (inventing the name of a Travel Association) in which you state your qualifications and ask for further details. The letter should be headed and ended suitably and, apart from the heading and ending, should be expressed in between 120 and 180 words.

Here is a suggested plan:

1 Expressing your interest in the posts.
2 Qualifications related to these posts
3 Personal qualifications and experience
4 References
5 Request for further information

Here is the letter.

Schloss Bellarosa,
Ruusulinna,
Arkadia.
1st April, 19—.

The Personnel Manager,
The Daydream Tourist Association,
3, Factory Street,
Grimesborough,
Murkshire,
England.

Dear Sir,

I am interested in your advertisement in the 'Arkadia Morning Mail' for hostesses to be responsible for the welfare, entertainment and guiding of British guests in your holiday centre in Ruusulinna.

I am now a third-year student of English and History in the University of Gardenia but am free from early June till late September. I have spent one year in London working in an English family and attending courses in English so I can speak this language fluently.

My father has been a guide and I have often accompanied him and also myself acted as guide to English-speaking groups. My studies and experience have familiarised me with the many interesting places in my country. I am sociable, really interested in people and, I believe, at the same time reliable and sensible.

I enclose the address of the Manager of the local Tourist Information Office who is willing to supply further information about me.

If you are interested in my application, I should welcome further information about these posts, including the salary and general conditions of employment.

Yours faithfully,

Polly Cosmos

(Miss P. Cosmos)

Subjects for Practice

Write a suitable letter of between 120 and 180 words on one or more of the following subjects. The beginning and ending should be that of a business letter but should not be included in the number of words. Where details are not given you can supply your own ideas.

1 You are the secretary of a society. Write a letter to a well-known English-speaking person living in your town asking him/her whether he or she would be willing to lecture to the society. Explain something of the aims and interests of the society and suggest a time, place and a general idea of a possible subject for the lecture.

2 Write a letter to the B.B.C. expressing your dissatisfaction with a radio or television programme dealing with some aspect of life in your country. Explain in what ways you think the programme gives a false impression.

3 Before leaving England you had bought a large box of chocolates for your mother. Shortly after your return, she opened them, only to find that they were stale and uneatable. Write a letter of complaint to the British manufacturers, giving all necessary details.

4 Home circumstances force you to give up an office job you have taken in England. Write a letter of resignation, giving your reasons for leaving, asking for a testimonial and expressing your regret.

5 In an English newspaper you have read an article stating that owing to their school education only young English people are really willing to take an interest in welfare problems throughout the world. Write a letter to this paper in which you set out the attitude of the young people of your own country to these matters. (Remember the suggested word limits.)

6 Explain in between 175 and 200 words why the writer felt guilty about his behaviour towards the little man and why in fact he need not have reproached himself so bitterly.

Spoken English

Exclamations 'Well', 'Oh' and 'Ah'

Probably most languages have their one-word exclamations that can express many different feelings. Those above are the three main ones used by English speakers. They are sometimes similar in use and the same situation could cause different people to use one or another of these.

These are some of the many ideas which can be expressed by *Well*:

(*a*) *Surprise:* Well, I am surprised to see you!

(*b*) *Challenge:* Well, what do you want from me?

(*c*) *Hesitation:* Well, I'm not sure. We'll have to think it over.

(*d*) *Relief:* Well, thank goodness we've arrived safely.

(*e*) *Decision:* Well, I know what I'll do. I'll ask William to give me a lift.

(*f*) *Qualified* (slightly unsure) *approval:* Well, perhaps it will do.

(*g*) *Resignation:* Well, I suppose there's nothing we can do about it.

(*h*) *Sarcasm:* Well, well, look who's come to help—now it's all finished!

Exercise: Explain the meaning suggested by *Well* in each of the following: (i) Well, and what are you going to do about it? (ii) Well, in some ways we enjoyed it. (iii) Well, let me think. Yes, I remember. His name was Alvar. (iv) Well, you are early for breakfast to-day. It's only ten o'clock. (v) Well, that's settled. Now we know what we'll be doing. (vi) Well, I'm glad that's over. (vii) Well, I never thought she'd grow up so beautiful!

Oh can have these uses among others.

Alarm: Oh, you frightened me. *Delight:* Oh, what a wonderful present!

Pain: Oh, that hurts. *Protest:* Oh, that's not fair.

Calling someone's attention: Oh, Miss Smith, can you spare a minute, please?

Ah is a more controlled expression of feeling. It is seldom used by young people.

Ah, so that's what he told you.

Ah, you see. I've known him much longer than you have.

Further question tags

In a few cases affirmative tags follow affirmative statements and negative ones negative statements.

(*a*) *To soften a command:* Open a window, will you? (would you?)

(*b*) *To show interest:* So your brother has directed a film, has he?

(*c*) *To express a challenge:* So you think you can do it better than I can, do you?

(*d*) *To show sarcasm:* Dad, I want to borrow your car.
Oh, you do, do you? And what happened to it last time you had it?

Situations

(*a*) A stranger asks you for money. What is he like? What are you doing at the time? How does he introduce the subject? What reason does he give for asking? What is your reaction?

(*b*) What do you do and say in each of the following cases?

(i) After you have had an expensive meal alone in a restaurant, the bill is presented. You then find you have left your wallet or handbag at home and have no money and also no means of identification. You have never been in the restaurant before.

(ii) You are touring by car a country whose language you do not speak. After a long day's journey, you find you have left your passport in the previous hotel. You had intended to cross the frontier the following day.

(iii) You return after midnight on a Sunday morning to a house where you live alone and find you have no key with you. All doors are locked and windows firmly shut and the neighbours are all in bed.

(iv) After posting a number of letters together, you remember that you have not put a stamp on the most important one, an application for a secretarial post.

(v) A stranger in a train, a pleasant and likeable person, persists in talking to you when you want only to read.

(vi) Somebody knocks at your door and with great sincerity tries to convince you of something you are not in the least interested in. You are too well-mannered to shut the door in the person's face.

Some of the above conversations could be acted between class members.

Subjects for discussion

(*a*) What is your opinion of the habit of swearing? Is it a useful outlet for strong feelings, a form of rebellion, a survival of a forgotten childish desire to shock? Could there be some other reason for it and do reasons vary in different people? Give reasons for your opinion.

(*b*) Nowadays very much is spoken of equality for everyone. Can there be equality resulting from appearance or will there always be a type of person one admires and other types one feels pity for, despises (feels contempt for) or dislikes because of something in his/her appearance?

(*c*) Even to-day some young men think it important to do difficult, possibly painful and dangerous things (such as duelling) as a proof of their strength and courage. Do you consider this a worthwhile form of behaviour in the process of growing-up? What are some of the ways in which a young person can show his or her courage and ability?

(*d*) What is your attitude towards lending and borrowing money?

(*e*) What are some of the ways in which the police can help the individual person?

(*f*) What is your attitude to appeals for financial help (i) from individuals (ii) from charitable organisations?

General guidance and practice

Direct and reported statements

Study these two examples, the first of direct, the second of reported or indirect speech.

'I'm sorry,' said the man. 'I don't smoke, so I haven't any.'
The man said he was sorry. He did not smoke, so he had none.

When converting from direct to reported speech, the following rules usually apply:

(i) *Conversational abbreviations are not used.*

(ii) *Verb tenses normally shift to the past.* The usual changes are:

PRESENT SIMPLE	to PAST SIMPLE
PRESENT CONTINUOUS	to PAST CONTINUOUS
PRESENT PERFECT } PAST SIMPLE	to PAST PERFECT
PRESENT PERFECT CONTINUOUS } PAST CONTINUOUS	to PAST PERFECT CONTINUOUS
FUTURE FORMS	to FUTURE IN THE PAST FORMS

(iii) *Pronouns often change.* First and second person pronouns may shift to the third person; second person pronouns may change to the first person. The same applies to possessive adjectives.

The old man said, 'I can remember the early aeroplanes.'
The old man said he could remember the early aeroplanes.
He shouted, 'You are telling lies.'
He shouted at me, saying that I was telling lies.

(iv) *Certain other appropriate changes are also made.* Here are a few:

to-day	to	the same day; that day.
yesterday	to	the day before; the previous day.
to-morrow	to	the day after; the next day.
this, these	to	that, those.
now	to	then; at once; at that time.
ago	to	before.
the day after to-morrow	to	in two days' time.
last week	to	the week before; the previous week.
next week	to	the week after; the following week
this week	to	the same week.

It is impossible to give all changes, which, in any case, depend on the meaning of the passage, and may usually be decided by common sense.

(v) If only the actual words spoken are given, it is necessary to supply a suitable introductory phrase, e.g. He said; The speaker suggested; The teacher explained. 'That' may sometimes be omitted. The introductory phrase, when supplied in this way, is usually in the past simple tense and has a third person subject:

'The medicine is to be taken every three hours.'
The doctor gave instructions that the medicine was to be taken every three hours.
'I shall arrive to-morrow.'
My sister wrote to say (that) she would arrive the next day.

Change the following examples of direct speech into reported speech.

(*a*) 'I need help desperately,' he said.

(*b*) 'I'm sorry,' he replied. 'I'm afraid I can't lend you anything.'

(*c*) 'I had some money,' he replied, 'but it was stolen from my room.'

(*d*) 'We shall write to you this week,' they promised.

(*e*) 'I am coming now,' he said. 'Perhaps I can give you a lift?'

(*f*) 'My car has been stolen,' he said. 'I shall have to telephone the police.'

(*g*) 'My father came to England fifty years ago, and has been living here ever since.'

(*h*) 'I don't need your help to-day. I shall be busy to-morrow however.'

(*i*) 'You are not to forget what I have told you. You can't go the day after to-morrow.'

Direct and reported questions and commands

The following sentences illustrate the basic changes necessary when converting direct questions and commands into reported speech:

(i) 'Why did you come here?' I asked. 'How did you come?'
I asked him why he had come there and how he had come.

(ii) 'Do you know your way home?' he asked me.
He asked whether I knew my way home.

(iii) 'Go to the police for help,' he said.
He told the man to go to the police for help.

(Negative) 'Don't go to the police for help,' he said.
He told the man not to go to the police for help.

(i) and (ii) A DIRECT QUESTION *is re-arranged* IN STATEMENT FORM *when used in reported speech.*

When it begins with an interrogative verb form, with no interrogative adverb, it is usually introduced by 'whether' or 'if'.

'Whether' must be used when the phrase 'or not' follows.
I didn't know whether he would do it or not.

(iii) An imperative verb form is converted to an infinitive.

Change the following into reported speech. Supply a suitable introductory phrase where this is not given.

(*a*) 'Can you help me?' I asked the porter.

(*b*) 'See me to-morrow afternoon,' he ordered his secretary.

(*c*) 'What shall we do this evening?' the children asked their mother.

(*d*) 'Don't look now,' said my friend, 'but I think the woman who has just come in is the star of that film we saw yesterday.'

(*e*) 'Will you be coming with me?'

(*f*) 'How do you spell your name?'

(*g*) 'Lie down and stop barking.'

(*h*) 'What is the time? Is your watch right?'

(*i*) 'Do you agree or not?'

Be careful with verbs like 'suggest' which are never followed by an infinitive.

'Come next week,' he suggested.
He suggested my coming the following week.
or He suggested that I should come the following week.

Other ways of Expressing the Future

The following ways of expressing the future have already been explained.

(*a*) We shall deal with that to-morrow.
(A plain statement of the future—in certain cases with some suggestion of decision or intention.)

(*b*) We are dealing with that to-morrow.
(It is arranged and settled.)

(*c*) We shall be dealing with that to-morrow.
(The same, but with emphasis that this will happen in the future.)

It is also possible to express the future in other ways:

(*d*) 'TO GO' WITH THE INFINITIVE
This suggests either:

(i) INTENTION OR DETERMINATION;
They are going to let off fireworks to-night.

(ii) (sometimes) TO EXPRESS GREAT PROBABILITY
(often with verbs of thinking or anticipating expressed or understood.)
(I think that) prices are going to rise soon.
(I anticipate that) we are going to have a wonderful day.

Notice that happenings expected in the natural course of events are not expressed with 'go'.

To-morrow will be Sunday. or To-morrow is Sunday.
It will soon be dark.

(*e*) TO MEAN, TO INTEND
He means to build up a large fortune within the next ten years.
I do not intend to put up with any nonsense.

(*f*) TO BE ABOUT TO
This expresses an action which will happen almost immediately.
The race is about to start.
He looked as if he were about to burst into tears.

(*g*) TO BE BOUND TO, TO BE SURE TO
This expresses certainty about the future.
The bus is bound to be late; it always is.
Don't worry! He is sure to remember.

Rewrite the following sentences in as many ways as you can, using the above forms. Give the exact meaning of each form:

(*a*) The Sports Club (hold) a social next Saturday.

(*b*) He (be) ninety on his next birthday.

(*c*) The storm (break).

(*d*) (Make) you any pancakes on Shrove Tuesday?

(*e*) The film (be) popular.

(*f*) He (die), unless help comes quickly.

(*g*) He (find) out what you said.

(*h*) To-morrow's journey (take) five hours.

(*i*) The river (rise) as a result of all this rain.

(*j*) Why (not give) you him a birthday present?

May Might

MAY and MIGHT can have two different meanings:

(i) *Permission*

You may smoke if you wish.
The head teacher said that the children might leave school early.

(ii) *Possibility*

MAY and MIGHT give the idea 'perhaps', 'possibly'.
MAY suggests a stronger possibility than MIGHT, but, in effect, there is little difference in meaning. MIGHT is normally used when the rest of the sentence is in the past.

He is perhaps right = He may be right.
It may rain before morning.
We might catch the train.
The plan might work if we tried it soon enough.

In some cases either meaning may apply. The appropriate one becomes apparent only in speech.

He may come to-mórrow. (Permission)
He máy cóme to-mórrow. (Possibility)

In connection with the second of these uses, 'might' is sometimes used in making a request.

You might help me with this box.

The speaker suggests that the person addressed will perhaps be kind enough to help.

It can also be a reproach:

You might listen while I am speaking.

Here are some verbal constructions with MAY and MIGHT:

You may be lucky in the football pools.
They may be moving soon.
He may have had an accident.
She may have been staying in a hotel.
The house may have been destroyed.
That was a dangerous thing to do; the mixture might have exploded.
He said he might be coming late.
The door might have been locked.

Notice that when MIGHT is followed by a Perfect Infinitive there is in most cases the suggestion that the possibility was unfulfilled.

Rewrite each of the following sentences, introducing some form of MAY or MIGHT. Certain words will have to be left out.

(*a*) You could perhaps have been more careful.

(*b*) Am I allowed to help you?

(*c*) Would I be allowed to open a window?

(*d*) If you had sent your letter yesterday, it could perhaps have been delivered by to-day.

(*e*) The ship will perhaps leave this evening, but I doubt it.

(*f*) Our neighbours are allowed to use our telephone if they ever need to.

(*g*) Unqualified persons are not allowed to practise as doctors.

(*h*) Fancy travelling at that speed! You could possibly have been killed.

(*i*) They are possibly coming to-morrow.

May as well Might as well

Notice the common expressions MAY AS WELL, MIGHT AS WELL.

I may/might as well finish now that I have started.

You might as well be dead as live in such a small place.

The first example suggests, though possibly with no great enthusiasm, that this is or could have been a good idea.

The second gives the impression that one idea is so unpleasant or fruitless that the new suggestion could not be much worse.

Here are two further examples:

You might as well see him now he is here.

I might as well have been speaking to a brick wall. He took no notice at all.

Notice that when 'might as well' is followed by a Perfect Infinitive, the suggestion normally is that the action of the Infinitive did not actually happen.

Rewrite the following sentences, using one or the other of the above phrases. Part of each sentence will be changed considerably. The new subject is in *italics* in sentences (*a*), (*b*), (*c*) and (*d*)

(*a*) It would have been just as satisfactory if *I* had stayed at home. I learned nothing in the class.

(*b*) It will be just as useful for *you* to save your breath. He won't listen to you.

(*c*) It will be a good idea for *you* to get some sleep while you have the chance.

(*d*) I suggest *you* sit down. You have a long time to wait.

(*e*) Why not bring your fishing rod too? We may have some spare time.

(*f*) It could have been a good idea to stay the night there. We gained nothing by returning a day earlier.

Say, Tell

to tell a story
to tell the time
to tell the truth
to tell a lie. (an untruth)
to tell the difference between.

In these and a few more phrases, TELL can be used without an indirect object. Normally, however, *the person told must be indicated* when using this verb. When the person told is not indicated, the verb SAY or some similar verb must be employed.

He told me he was going out.
He said that he was going out.

SAY is used very often with direct speech. It may be accompanied by the person addressed preceded by the preposition 'to'.
TELL is more common with reported speech.

"I have lost my way," he said (to the policeman).
He told the policeman he had lost his way.
He said he had lost his way.

Use the correct form of SAY or TELL in the following sentences:

(*a*) The judge .... the prisoner that he was a menace to society.

(*b*) What did you .... when you found out what he had done?

(*c*) Always .... what you think.

(*d*) Can you .... the difference between a Chippendale and a Hepplewhite chair?

(*e*) "That will be one pound," .... the taxi-driver.

(*f*) They .... that National Insurance contributions are to be raised.

(*g*) The sergeant .... the recruits to stand to attention.

(*h*) I don't often .... lies.

(*i*) "I should leave that alone," he .... to me quietly.

(*j*) "You'll have to be here early to-morrow," he .... me.

Some, Any

The basic rule for the use of SOME and ANY and their compounds is that SOME *is used in an affirmative statement and command,* ANY *in an interrogative form and after a negative.* Verbs such as *to be unable, to fail, to deny, to refuse,* and the conjunction *if* may have a negative force.

I must have put my key somewhere.
The child has bought some sweets.
You should take something to cure that cough.
Do something quickly.
Will you need any of these old magazines?
He had never met anyone like them.

Haven't you anything to do?
He denied that the story had any truth in it.

(i) *Compounds of* SOME *may be used in interrogative sentences when an affirmative answer is expected, and also when the idea is more exact.*

Would you like some fruit?
Have you found somewhere to live?
Have you found anywhere to live?

(ii) ANY *used in an affirmative statement or command can suggest an indefinite idea:*

Ring me up any time you like.
You can ask anyone you know.

Use SOME or ANY or one of their compounds in each of the following sentences:

(*a*) I knew there was .... I forgot to put in the cake.
(*b*) The police have been unable to find .... trace of the criminals.
(*c*) Is there .... that I can find peace?
(*d*) I picked .... mushrooms yesterday morning.
(*e*) They failed to discover .... who could translate the message.
(*f*) The student was looking for .... to sit down.
(*g*) May I have .... more potatoes please? I have used up all those I bought yesterday.
(*h*) She can't find her powder compact ....
(*i*) Take .... one which you think will fit.
(*j*) I am sure there was not .... left over yesterday.
(*k*) Sit .... There is plenty of room.
(*l*) During the winter there is not .... to do in the garden.

Remember that NOT may combine with ANY (adjective NO, pronoun NONE), ANYWHERE (NOWHERE), ANYONE (NO ONE), ANYBODY (NOBODY), ANYTHING (NOTHING), especially when the negative quality is strongly emphasised.

In which of the above sentences could one of these negative forms be used? In which would it be slightly unnatural?

Rather, Fairly

Both of these adverbs are used to modify an adjective or another adverb, indicating the degree to which it applies.

FAIRLY *suggests a reasonable level;* RATHER *a more decided or definite one.*
RATHER *is often used to modify adjectives or adverbs indicating undesirable qualities.*

His drawings are fairly good, but I doubt whether he will ever become a famous artist.
This photograph is rather good. It would be a good idea to enter it for the competition.
I am afraid he is rather dishonest.
She spoke rather sharply.

Notice the difference in meaning here:

The film is fairly long; it lasts about two hours.
The film is rather long: some cutting might have improved it.

Rather usually precedes a comparative form: 'The dress is rather longer than I expected.'

Insert *rather* or *fairly* in each of the following sentences:

(*a*) I'm sorry. I'm .... tired. I think I shall go to bed.

(*b*) It would be as well to bring an overcoat: it is .... cold to-day.

(*c*) She is .... pretty, but not exceptionally so.

(*d*) That remark was .... unkind, wasn't it?

(*e*) I have been .... free from colds this winter.

(*f*) The details are .... accurate but there are a few errors.

(*g*) You had better behave yourself; he is .... strict.

(*h*) The accident was .... serious: in fact it was fortunate nobody was killed.

(*i*) He is .... more intelligent than the average ten-year-old.

In each of the following sentences insert either the phrase *had better* or *should* (or would) *rather* as appropriate:

(*a*) We .... play chess than bridge.

(*b*) You .... hurry up. It is early closing day to-day.

(*c*) There are stinging nettles either side of the path. We .... be careful.

(*d*) .... you .... have rice pudding or cherry tart?

(*e*) He .... not light the geyser until he knows how to use it.

(*f*) Would you prefer to visit Kew Gardens or Hampton Court Palace? I .... see Kew Gardens to-day.

Prepositions

Insert the correct preposition (single word or phrase) in each of the following sentences:

(*a*) You will find the answer .... the bottom of the page.

(*b*) That sharp bend has been the cause .... many accidents.

(*c*) The referee glanced .... his watch.

(*d*) .... the question of refreshments, I should think lemonade and sandwiches will be sufficient.

(*e*) We shall resume the programme .... ten minutes' time.

(*f*) The terrified sheep were conscious .... the presence of the wolf.

(*g*) I shall next deal .... the suggestion to set up a new recreation centre.

(*h*) The Society is appealing .... half a million pounds in aid of the flood victims.

(*i*) I am grateful .... you .... your assistance.

(*j*) The landing-stage is being constructed .... the other side .... the river.

(*k*) He was muttering terrible curses .... his breath.

(*l*) The firm has agreed .... supply the newspaper syndicate with newsprint.

(*m*) Our business rivals have agreed .... our terms.

(*n*) Neither of the hostile groups could agree .... the other and the meeting broke up in disorder.

(*o*) We are running short .... petrol. We must find a filling station.

(*p*) He was so afraid .... being found out that he refused to confide .... anyone.

(*q*) The defeated team challenged its opponents .... a return match.

12

Passage for comprehension

Picnic in the dining-room

'We shall be having a picnic to-morrow afternoon,' said my hostess, Mrs. Brown. 'It will be quite simple and we shan't make any fuss. I think an afternoon in the open air will do us good, don't you? Would you like to come with us?'

I had already made an appointment with the hairdresser but I weakly agreed to cancel it. Mrs. Brown smiled graciously. 5

'I shall be making some cakes this afternoon,' she explained, 'so I shan't have any free time. I wonder whether you would mind doing some shopping for me during your lunch hour, that is, if you can fit it in.'

She handed me a typewritten list made up of twenty-four separate items, 10 from shrimps to sugared almonds, and including an order for a chicken, four sliced loaves, a half-litre of fresh cream and some Camembert, all to be delivered at the house before five o'clock. That still left me with plenty to carry myself, and it seemed that if only I could manage to stagger home with my load, there would be no danger of starving the next afternoon. 15

That evening a violent thunderstorm broke. Rain poured down; the sky was split by terrifying flashes of forked lightning while peals of thunder drowned conversation. But Mrs. Brown was not upset.

'It will have cleared up before morning,' she prophesied. 'When this storm has passed we'll have ideal weather, you'll see. The B.B.C. weather 20 forecast has promised sunshine, and they don't often make mistakes.' She was right. The following morning was glorious. Early in the morning I could hear her moving about in the kitchen. Breakfast was late and consisted of corn flakes and toast.

'I must apologise for neglecting you,' said Mrs. Brown. 'So much to do! 25 You won't mind making your bed this morning, will you? I'm so busy. I'm afraid we shall have to make do with cold meat and potatoes for lunch.'

The whole morning seemed to be spent in loading the car with a variety of bags, baskets and mysterious parcels. After a lunch of cold mutton, 30 boiled potatoes, and limp damp lettuce, we took our mackintoshes and umbrellas and fitted ourselves into the car. I was in the back seat, squeezed uncomfortably in the midst of a mountain of equipment.

We crawled for the next two hours along a main road where a line of traffic was wedged so tightly together that it was almost stationary. Mr. 35 Brown was in charge of the steering wheel but Mrs. Brown controlled the

driving. At last we turned down a narrow lane and started looking for a suitable place for tea. Each one that we saw had its drawbacks: too sunny, too shady, too exposed, too sheltered. 'If we were to picnic there, we should
40 be too hot, cold, conspicuous, shut in,' declared Mrs. Brown as she inspected each in turn.

At last she decided that a certain meadow (in reality no different from any other meadow we had examined) would do. Mr. Brown opened the gate and drove the car inside. We started to unload.

45 I had never in my life realised that so much stuff could be required for a simple picnic. A folding table was produced together with a clean glossy tablecloth, folding chairs (with cushions), enough crockery and cutlery for a banquet and more than enough food for six courses, paper serviettes, a transistor radio, half a dozen illustrated magazines and even soap, a towel,
50 water and a bowl for washing our hands after the meal. I half expected a crimson carpet, possibly footstools for our feet, with red candles as tasteful table decorations. I did discover a tin of fly killer, a bottle of ammonia for the treatment of stings and even some indigestion tablets.

For a whole hour we made our preparations and at last everything that
55 we needed was ready. As we were enjoying our first mouthful of thermos-flask soup, a stout man opened the gate and came towards us.

'Sorry to make a nuisance of myself, but in five minutes we shall have finished milking the cows,' he announced. 'They'll be coming back here directly after.'

60 Mrs. Brown gazed at him speechless for a moment. At last she found words. 'But you can see we've only just started eating,' she protested indignantly. 'Surely you can delay sending them in for an hour or so?'

'Sorry ma'am, we've other jobs to do. We'll give you time to clear up: that's the most that we can allow. Say twenty minutes. You know you're
65 trespassing, of course?'

Mrs. Brown seemed to collapse in her chair. I wished I were fifty miles off. Mr. Brown was the only one that accepted the situation philosophically. 'It seems to be high time we departed,' was his only comment.

Half an hour after we moved off as the cows were wandering down the
70 lane and as the first drops of rain were falling. We joined the traffic jam in the main road. Three hours later we unpacked again and had our picnic in Mrs. Brown's dining-room—with a carpet underfoot but still no candles. We were strangely silent but our deep sense of grievance did not in any way prevent us from eating a great deal.

Notes on the passage

Vocabulary

line

2 *make a fuss* = cause a lot of disturbance and excitement about unimportant things.
fussy (*Adj*) about one's food, clothes, small details in other people's behaviour.

9 *fit*

As a Noun: (*a*) a sudden attack of illness causing unconsciousness or convulsions (as in epilepsy)

(*b*) a fit of coughing

(*c*) a mood, as in a fit of depression or temper

(*d*) a coat or dress should be a good fit.

a fitting—the trying on of a garment that is being made; also: the size of a garment: *we supply overcoats in various fittings.*

As a Verb: (*a*) be the right size: *these shoes don't fit me*

(*b*) occupy a certain place among other things: *Can you fit this into your suitcase? The solicitor is very busy but he can fit you in at two o'clock.*

(*c*) fit out = provide all the necessary equipment for something: *to fit out a climbing expedition*

As an Adjective: (*a*) healthy: *Although he is eighty, he is still quite fit.*

(*b*) suitable: *Is he fit to undertake such a responsible job?*

(*c*) in the right condition: *A drunken man is not fit to drive a car.*

An *outfitter* sells all kinds of men's clothes. A camping *outfit.*

11 Some *shellfish*: shrimps, prawns, crabs, lobsters, oysters.

13 *deliver* letters, parcels, goods to the house (*N* delivery).
A postman *collects* letters from a *pillar box* and takes them to a *sorting office.* People collect stamps. A teacher collects books and examination papers from the class. A rent-collector collects rents and money may be collected for some special purpose. (*N* collection).

14 *stagger* = walk or stand unsteadily so that one nearly falls, often because one is overloaded or ill. *staggered* (*Adj*) may mean 'extremely surprised'. Periods of work may be staggered so that the workers are free at different times: *staggered holidays.*
Sometimes the working-day of twenty-four hours is divided into three periods of work: each of these periods is a *shift.*

16 storms *break.* wars *break out.*

17 forked and sheet *lightning.* peals (more prolonged) and claps of *thunder.*
Thunder may gradually become louder: it mutters, growls, rumbles and crashes.

20 The *B.B.C.* is the British Broadcasting Corporation.

21 *promise* usually suggests pleasant things to come, not extreme cold or fog.
forecast (*V* and *N*) the weather, results of races and matches, success and failure.

30 a *parcel* is usually larger than a packet, which often contains dry food or soap powder bought in a shop. *parcel and letter post.*

31 *limp* as an Adjective usually means the opposite of *stiff* or *crisp.*

limp (V): walk lamely and with difficulty because of a foot or leg injury.
A *lame* person may walk with the help of *crutches.*

31 *lettuce.* Note that a *salad* contains several kinds of vegetables or fruit.

33 *in the midst of* = among—not necessarily in the middle of.

34 *crawl* (usually) in an almost flat position, or: move very slowly: *a snake may crawl.* crawl (*N*)—a stroke used in swimming, with the head low in the water. *creep* most often suggests moving very quietly: *he crept upstairs so as not to disturb the sleeping family. crouch*—remain still, with one's body near the ground and hands and feet close together: *the cat was crouching ready to spring. He crouched behind the low wall, listening.*

34 a *main road* for traffic. a *high street*—the main shopping street of a town.

35 *wedged*—a *wedge* is a small, often triangular-shaped block, used for keeping a window or door in position without movement. The car cannot move in the traffic. It is in a *traffic jam.* A door that will not open may be jammed in some way.

35 SPELLING: *stationary*—without movement. *stationery:* notepaper and envelopes. A stationer sells these in a stationery shop.

36 *Parts of a car:* the steering wheel, the engine (not: the motor); headlights, the bonnet, the windscreen, brakes, gears, the clutch, the accelerator, the boot. A car is powered by (runs on) *petrol.*

40 a *conspicuous* building or other object; an *outstanding* statesman or other well-known person.

42 a *meadow* where cattle may graze or grass is grown; a *field* of corn.

45 *realise*—become aware of an idea: realise that one knows someone one meets; realise that one has lost something.
recognise—know the identity of someone seen: recognise someone one meets from a photograph. These two words are often confused.
understand the meaning of something.

46 *fold* a letter or tablecloth in two or four; a dress or skirt may have *pleats*; a dress taken out of a suitcase may have *creases*; he *crumpled* the letter into a ball and threw it away.
crumple is a verb only; the other three are nouns and verbs.
A *deck chair* is a kind of folding chair.

46 Photograph prints may be *glossy* or *matt.*

47 *cushions* lie on chairs or sofas; *pillows* lie on beds. a cushion-cover; a pillow-case.

47 *crockery:* cups, saucers, plates, dishes and other china tableware.

47 *cutlery:* knives, forks and spoons.
A *cruet* may include salt, pepper, vinegar, mustard. A salt-cellar, a pepper-pot.

48 paper *serviettes*; linen *table-napkins.*

49 A transistor radio is *portable.* A typewriter may also be portable.

49 A *magazine* is a *periodical*, a publication appearing at intervals of a week or more. A *review* is more often a critical article on a book, play,

film or concert though it may be a general account of something: a review of the week's news. A *revue* is a form of often satirical entertainment.

51 a *crimson* rose; *purple* is a mixture of red and blue: *purple heather.*

51 a *carpet* usually covers most of the floor surface of a room; a *rug* is smaller, and often very thick (a hearthrug); a *mat* is usually not so large as a carpet and often fairly thin. A *travelling rug* is like a blanket.

52 *decoration:* making something look bright and pleasant; *a decoration* is anything that does this. An *ornament* is an object such as a vase or brooch that stands in a room or is worn to give a pleasant effect.
Notice: Christmas decorations. They are redecorating the sitting-room, painting all wooden surfaces and hanging fresh wallpaper.

53 A wasp *stings*. Nettles sting. A mosquito *bites*. Thorns and needles *prick*.

55 a *mouthful*; spoonful; cupful; handful; pocketful; roomful (of people).

55 a *thermos flask* is sometimes called a *vacuum flask*. A *vacuum-cleaner* removes dust from a carpet.

57 a *nuisance:* this is a common word in spoken English. It refers to a small thing or a person that causes inconvenience and irritation. Missing a bus can be a nuisance and a person who is often unpunctual is also a nuisance.

61 *protest* (*N* and *V*) In origin the word *Protestant* referred to those people who protested against the Roman Catholic Church. A *Nonconformist* is a person belonging to a religious group that does not accept the doctrines of the Church of England.

65 *Trespassers will be prosecuted* may be written on a board outside private property. Trespassers invade other people's property and they are threatened with some kind of legal punishment.

68 a *comment* is a remark. A *commentary* is a continuous description of something happening at that time: *A football match commentary. A radio commentator.*

73 *grief* is sorrow (*V*) *grieve* over someone's death; a *grievance:* something that causes feelings of resentment at unfair treatment: *the men's grievances include low wages, long hours and badly-cooked food in their canteen.*

Pronunciation

SOUND AND STRESS CHANGES: separate (*Adj*) [sépərɪt]; separate (*V*) [sépəreɪt]; prophecy (*N*) [prɔ́fɪsɪ]; prophesy (*V*) [prɔ́fɪsaɪ]; prepare [prɪpɛ́ə]; preparation [prépəréɪʃən]; philosopher [fɪlɔ́səfə]; philosophic [fɪləsɔ́fɪk].

NOTICE THE STRESS: ideal [aɪdíəl]; magazines [mǽgəzíːnz]; serviettes [sə́ːvɪéts];

ə (as in *a*go): it*e*ms [áɪtəmz]; sug*are*d [ʃúgəd]; alm*o*nd [áːmənd]; vi*o*l*e*nt [váɪələnt]; breakf*a*st [brékfəst]; *a*pol*o*gise [əpɔ́ləʤaɪz]; p*o*tatoes [pətéɪtouz]; mysteri*ous* [mɪstíərɪəs]; station*e*ry [stéɪʃənərɪ]; suitable [sjúːtəbl]; c*o*nspicu*ous* [kənspíkjuəs]; doz*e*n [dʌzn]; crims*o*n [krímzən]; *a*mmoni*a* [əmóunɪə]; nuis*a*nce [njúːsəns]; c*o*llapse [kəlǽps]; griev*a*nce [gríːvəns]; ill*u*strated [íləstréɪtɪd].

ɪ (as in cit*y*): lett*u*ce [létɪs]; banqu*e*t [bǽŋkwɪt]; tabl*e*ts [tǽblɪts]; speechl*e*ss [spíːtʃlɪs]; carpet [káːpɪt].

OTHERS: mackintoshes [mǽkɪntəʃɪz]; towel [tauəl]; indigestion [ɪndɪ-ʤéstjən]; directly [dɪréktlɪ] or [daɪréktlɪ]; ma'am [mǽm] or: [maːm]; situation [sitjuéɪʃən]; comment [kɔ́ment].

Special grammatical and structural points

(i) 'The B.B.C. weather forecast has promised sunshine and they don't often make mistakes.' (11.20–21)

they is often used to indicate some vague authority, group or source of information: *They say that they have already arrested the gang leader.*

Normally, when using a pronoun, be extremely careful that the noun it refers to has been made quite clear.

This is an example of unsatisfactory use of a pronoun: *Long lines of people were waiting at the barriers while worried officials were surrounded by angry passengers. They did not know what to do.*

The impersonal pronoun *one* is less often used in conversation. The pronouns, *we*, *you*, or *they* are used instead:

Nowadays we tend to prefer comfort to adventure.
You seldom see taxis in this part of town.
They have built too many high blocks of flats and not left enough space for children to play in.

(ii) These time expressions contrast with usage in some other languages:

early this morning; early in the morning; late last night; early to-morrow; during the last few days; the other day (a few days ago); the trial will take place in a week's time (after a week—less commonly used—stresses the fact that for some special reason, this length of time must first pass)

(iii) an hour or *so*; a dozen or so;—this phrase, meaning 'about', is most often used with expressions of time or round numbers.

(iv) VERBAL CONSTRUCTIONS

(*a*) *Infinitive:* it is time to go; have time to enjoy life
(*b*) *Gerund:* apologise for neglecting; prevent us from eating (or: prevent our eating); danger of starving.
(*c*) *Clause:* realise that so much stuff could be required

Prepositions

(*a*) *in* the open (fresh) air (indoors; out of doors); in the midst of; each in turn; in reality; in my life.

(*b*) an appointment *with*; this left me with plenty to carry; make do with; load with (loaded with shopping); together with

(*c*) an order *for* a chicken; apologise for; required (needed) for; a bowl for washing; enough for.

(*d*) danger *of*; consist of; make a nuisance of oneself; a sense of loss.

(*e*) twenty-four items, *from* shrimps *to* sugared almonds (these two prepositions suggest a wide range); prevent from.

(*f*) *including* an order.

Useful expressions to learn and introduce into written work

(*a*) a day *in the open* (*fresh*) *air* (*b*) a list *made up of* twenty items

(*c*) there would be *no danger of losing* my way

(*d*) breakfast *consisted of* corn flakes and toast

(*e*) each one *had its drawbacks* (*f*) she inspected *each in turn*

(*g*) I have *never in my life* realised (*h*) I *half expected* a carpet

(*i*) *for a whole hour* (*j*) at last *she found words* (*k*) an hour *or so*

(*l*) it seems to be *high time we departed* (*m*) our deep sense of grievance

Multiple choice questions

Here are a number of questions or unfinished statements about the passage, each with four suggested ways of answering or finishing it. You must choose the way you consider the most suitable. Write in each case the bracketed number of the question or statement followed by the letters **A**, **B**, **C**, **D**, and then cross through the letter of the answer you choose. Give one answer only to each question. Read the passage right through again before choosing your answers.

1 Why did the writer agree to go on the picnic?
A she thought she might enjoy it **B** she thought it would do her good **C** she was a little afraid to refuse **D** she felt really too tired to go to the hairdresser

2 Which of these statements about the writer is true?
A she normally works, though not at week-ends **B** she is on holiday **C** she has retired **D** she is Mrs. Brown's maid

3 What did the writer have to do when she went shopping?
A order all the items and carry some back herself **B** carry back everything for the picnic herself **C** buy some things and order others **D** make her own arrangements about what should be sent and what carried by herself

4 The passage suggests that Mrs. Brown was all but one of the following. The exception is:
A overwhelming **B** bossy **C** fussy **D** suspicious

5 Which of these discomforts did the writer not have to suffer during the car journey?
A too little room **B** a restricted view **C** being shaken up **D** a long period of monotony

6 Which of the following reasons was not one of those which finally caused Mrs. Brown to choose a certain meadow?
A it was just what she wanted **B** she was tired of looking for the right one **C** she could find nothing special wrong with it **D** she realised that what she wanted did not exist

7 Which of these possibilities had Mrs. Brown not provided for?
A bad weather **B** a breakdown **C** minor discomforts **D** boredom

8 Which of these feelings was not experienced by any of the picnickers when they were told to leave?
A anxiety **B** shock **C** resignation **D** embarrassment

9 Which of these statements is true as applied to the farmer's action in telling the group to leave?
A unknowingly he did them a good turn **B** he had no right to behave like this **C** he made things as difficult for them as he could **D** his manner towards them was abrupt and discourteous

10 They were strangely silent while eating in the dining-room because
A they were so hungry **B** they were very tired **C** they were absorbed in bitter thoughts **D** they were intensely disappointed about missing their open-air picnic.

Reading comprehension

In this exercise you must choose the word or phrase which best completes each sentence. Write first the number of each sentence followed by the letters **A, B, C, D, E,** and then cross through the letter of the correct answer in each case.

1 Mrs. Brown was very .... when she broke her beautiful Wedgwood teapot.
A disturbed **B** deranged **C** upset **D** damaged **E** offended

2 He will probably be awarded a Nobel prize on account of his .... achievements in physics.
A exposed **B** outstanding **C** conspicuous **D** high **E** worthwhile

3 Swarms of ants are always invading my kitchen. They are a thorough ....
A nuisance **B** disturbance **C** trouble **D** bother **E** annoyance

4 There is something wrong with his vocal chords and as a result, he has always been ....
A silent **B** dumb **C** speechless **D** quiet **E** deaf

5 As the fat man sat down, the deck chair .... under him, with a loud noise of tearing canvas.
A fell **B** fainted **C** sank **D** dropped **E** collapsed

6 The peasants' many .... resulting from ill-treatment by their landlords led finally to rebellion.
A griefs **B** reclamations **C** grumbles **D** grievances **E** complaints

7 The damage done to my house by the fire has now ....
A done good **B** been made good **C** done me good **D** made me good **E** been for good

8 We have little .... information about developments in this field.
A actual **B** present-day **C** up-to-date **D** modern **E** contemporary

9 You should iron out the .... in that dress.
A creases **B** crumples **C** folds **D** wrinkles **E** pleats

10 Don't annoy that wasp. It will .... you.
A sting **B** prick **C** bite **D** pick **E** stick

Use of English

1 (ii) The five word groups below are the answers to five questions that could be asked about the reading passage. Write out the questions.

(i) an order for a chicken, four sliced loaves, a pint of fresh cream and some Camembert

(ii) corn flakes and toast

(iii) a variety of bags, baskets and mysterious parcels

(iv) the treatment of stings

(v) they had only just started eating (*Reported Speech*)

2 Study the following two examples. Using the same form of expression, explain what each of the objects listed below is for.
Examples: a fork: A fork is for eating with.
a house: A house is for living in.

(i) a knife (ii) soap (iii) a camera (iv) a chair (v) a cup (vi) a purse (vii) a vase (viii) a book

3 Some of the spaces in the sentences A—J need not be filled and some should be filled with THE. Write down the letters of the sentences in which the space should be filled with THE.

A Very much more will have to be done to provide better homes for .... poor.

B He is now on holiday in .... Scottish Highlands.

C You should get into touch with .... Professor White.

D He writes and broadcasts about .... sport.

E He has .... grey hair now.

F At last people are beginning to realise the necessity of preserving .... Nature.

G Scientists are gradually adding to their knowledge of .... space.

H After his serious illness he seemed to lose all interest in .... life.

I She trained as an opera-singer in .... Soviet Union.

J Some people have expressed doubts about .... honesty of the managing director.

4 Write down the numbers (i) to (v) and against each the form appropriate to the sentence of the word given in capitals.
Example: My mother .... the ironing when I got home. DO.
Answer was doing.

(i) The post .... Here are two letters for you. ARRIVE.

(ii) I shall show you my photographs as soon as they .... ready. BE.

(iii) A talkative stranger tried to convince me that we .... before. MEET.

(iv) Someone .... you about an hour ago. TELEPHONE.

(v) He .... for his firm for ten years but now he is looking for another job. WORK.

5 For each of the following six expressions four suggested explanations are given from which you must choose the correct one. Write down the numbers (i) to (vi) and against each the letter **A**, **B**, **C** or **D**, according to the explanation you choose.

(i) You won't mind making your bed this morning, will you.
A this is a very polite request **B** a question is being asked **C** it almost taken for granted that the person asked will agree to this **D** it is uncertain whether the person asked will agree.

(ii) Can you make do with half a litre of milk to-day?
A can you find a use for it? **B** can you let me have it? **C** can you manage with only this amount? **D** can you do without it?

(iii) If we were to picnic there, we should be too hot.
A in this unlikely case **B** if we had to do this **C** if this had been arranged **D** though this is quite impossible

(iv) She decided that a certain meadow would do.
A it would be quite suitable **B** it would be good enough **C** it would be used only as a last hope **D** it would be less unpleasant than the others

(v) I did discover a tin of fly-killer.
A this is not so fantastic as the other two suggestions but extraordinary enough **B** in addition to all the other things **C** this must be emphasised **D** this is a colloquial use of the past tense

(vi) Say twenty minutes. This is:
A a suggestion to be accepted **B** a plain statement **C** a command **D** a polite request

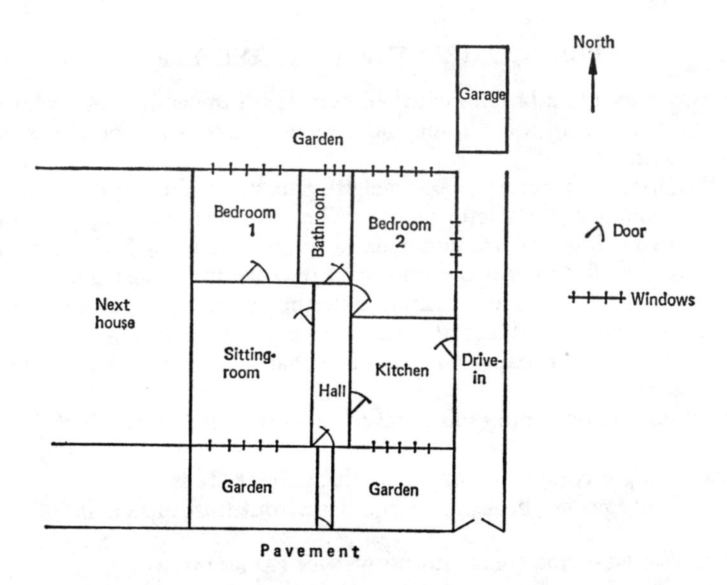

This is the ground-plan of a semi-detached bungalow (it is joined on the left to another similar bungalow). Mr. and Mrs. Bridges, a young married couple, are now living in it.

Study the plan carefully and then answer the following questions about it. Your answers should be written as complete sentences and, unless this is otherwise stated, consist of between 10 and 30 words.

(*a*) Explain the quickest route by which the Bridges could go from the garage to Bedroom 1.

(*b*) Where is the kitchen? Is this an ideal position for it?

(*c*) What are two disadvantages of the hall?

(*d*) The garage might have been built farther forward, at the side of Bedroom 2. Suggest an advantage and disadvantage of this arrangement.

(*e*) What is a possible advantage of having the bedrooms at the back of the house?

(*f*) Why do you think two houses are built side-by-side in this way?

(*g*) What is the main disadvantage of this arrangement?

(*h*) Give your own opinion of this bungalow in between 25 and 40 words.

Composition and summarising

Giving directions

Directions may be written in two different ways:

A. in paragraph form

B. as separate points or instructions, possibly listed with numbers.

A. Give instructions about how to make an omelette.

A PLAIN OMELETTE FOR ONE PERSON

Break two eggs into a basin. Beat them a little till the whites and yolks have mixed properly. Add a little salt and pepper and a tablespoonful of water and mix these in.

Melt a little fresh butter in an omelette pan, remembering that too much butter will make the omelette greasy. When the butter is hot, pour in the eggs, stir twice in the centre and cook the eggs over a low heat. Loosen the edges with a knife to allow the uncooked part to run underneath.

When the under surface is firm, double the omelette over with a knife so that it is crescent-shaped and allow any loose egg to cook. Lift it out on to a hot dish covered with paper with the side that was nearest the pan on top. Serve it at once.

A well-cooked omelette should have a firm surface but be creamy inside.

(148 words)

In this example commands are used throughout. It is possible to use the passive. (The eggs are broken into the basin) but this is less definite.

SUBJECTS FOR PRACTICE (DIRECTIONS GIVEN IN PARAGRAPHS)

You are advised to use between 120 and 180 words in each of the following exercises.

1 Give instructions about how to fry chips OR how to make coffee.

2 Give advice about how to keep healthy and comfortable either during a very cold winter or a very hot oppressive summer.

3 A young friend who lives alone says he feels feverish and thinks he may have influenza. You are sure he should not be at work (or school). Write down the advice you give him about looking after himself at home, including calling a doctor if necessary. Offer to do what you can to help him yourself.

4 Give directions about how to keep a dog in first-class condition.

5 Write down the advice a teacher might give students before they sit for the First Certificate examination.

6 Advise a student how to use a dictionary intelligently when doing a translation.

B. Write the list of instructions that could be placed in each room of a hostel for students and young workers.

NOTICE

1 Meals are served at the following times:

BREAKFAST	7.30–9.00
LUNCH	12.00–14.00
DINNER	18.30–20.00

2 Residents are expected to make their own beds but rooms are cleaned daily by the hostel staff.

3 Please be as quiet as possible after 23.00 as others may already be asleep.

4 Food should not be kept in rooms as this encourages mice.

5 Do not stay in the bathroom for more than twenty minutes as other people may want to use it.

6 Laundry should be taken to the Linen Room before 10.00 on a Monday morning. It can be collected from there on Friday. A list of charges is in the Linen Room.
7 Facilities for washing and drying small items of clothing are available in the Drying Room. An iron is also provided.
8 There is a public telephone in the entrance hall.
9 Payment for accommodation must be made in the Warden's Office every Saturday morning between 9 and 12.
10 A week's notice of departure must be given.

Though polite, these instructions are brief and plain. They include the following kinds of instructions:

(*a*) Commands (3 and 5).

(*b*) The use of 'should', 'must', 'are expected to' (2, 4, 6, 9, 10). Other possibilities are 'may', 'can', 'are advised to', 'may wish to', etc.

(*c*) Statements of fact (1, 7 and 8).

Subjects for practice (listed directions)

The following exercises should be dealt with in the same way as the one above. You are advised to use between 120 and 180 words in each case.

1 A woman calls twice weekly to help in your house. She usually stays two hours each time. You are going to be away for one week so you leave polite instructions about what should be done during the week. One or two details need special attention. Write the list you make. (Remember to be polite and pleasant and not to overwork her.)

2 Mrs. Baker is sending her husband shopping. She wants some meat, bread, cheese and oranges, an electric light bulb and a special magazine. A parcel (not yet stamped) has to be posted. A complaint must be made to the window-cleaner about having failed to come for some time. An appointment with her dressmaker must be cancelled. (Neither of these has a telephone.) Finally she wants the kind of book she enjoys from the Public Library. Write the list she gives him.

3 Mrs. Mason is going on holiday for a month. As she is very forgetful, she makes a list of things she must remember to do before leaving home. Write down eight possible items in her list. (These should not include the actual packing and getting ready.)

4 The instructions normally found in a public telephone box.

Other subjects for composition

(*a*) It is the evening before the picnic. Mrs. Brown is trying to persuade her husband to go on the picnic. He is not at all keen and makes various objections and excuses before being finally persuaded. Write the dialogue that takes place in between 120 and 180 words.

(*b*) It was such a beautiful afternoon that you decided to have tea or some other light meal in the garden. Unfortunately while you were eating, circumstances forced you to go indoors again. Write about your decision to have tea outside, your preparations and what happened, in between 120 and 180 words.

The writer of the comprehension passage had to put up with many inconveniences and disappointments. Explain what these were in two paragraphs, using between 175 and 200 words. The first paragraph should deal with the inconveniences she experienced the day before the picnic, the second those experienced on the day of the picnic.

Spoken English

Exclamations 'Now', 'Why', 'What', 'Here' and 'Look'

Now

Now, what shall we do next? Something has been finished and there is a slight pause for thought.

Be careful now. Warning or advice.

Now what's (has) happened? Impatience.

Now do as I tell you. Introducing an order.

Now then, leave that ladder alone! A sharp challenge.

EXERCISE: Explain the use of *now* in each of the following:

(*a*) Now, what did I tell you? Didn't I warn you? (*b*) Now say that again more carefully. (*c*) Now, how about having a little rest? (*d*) Look before you cross the road now. (*e*) Now then! We're not having that noise here.

Why expresses gentle surprise. *Why, that's just like the one I bought!*

What expresses slightly shocked or horrified surprise. *What, is that all the work you've done in three quarters of an hour?*

Here. Here, give that to me. I can put it right. A way of drawing someone's attention.

Here, this won't do. I want a better one. A challenge.

Look is used to draw someone's attention to something that will be said. (not: 'Hear'—as in some languages.)

Look, we could make do with a snack now and have a meal later.

Look out! is a shouted warning of immediate danger—not: Attention, which is used mainly when drilling soldiers.

A conversation in a shop

Shop Assistant Good morning. Can I help you?

Customer Not at the moment, thank you. I'm just looking round. I'm really looking for a bookcase, glass-fronted and with about three shelves.

SA How about this one? Is this the kind of thing you're looking for?

C Well, it's got a mahogany veneer, hasn't it. I'd prefer walnut.

SA We haven't any walnut ones in stock at the moment. We could order one in this style though, if you like.

C How long would I have to wait for it?

SA Four to six weeks, probably, though I can't guarantee any particular date.

C Would you be able to deliver it to my house when it comes in?

SA Yes, madam, if you live locally. Our vans deliver every day.

C Please order one for me then. And may I have one of these blue rugs. I see the price has been reduced. I can carry that myself.

SA They're a very good bargain, madam. I'll wrap it up for you. There. There's a loop in the string for you to hold it by. Would you be willing to pay a small deposit on the bookcase?

C Yes, I suppose so. How much would you like it to be?

SA Say two pounds. Would that suit you?
Thank you. Here's your receipt for the deposit, your bill for the rug and your change. If you'll leave your name, address and telephone number, I'll get into touch with you as soon as the bookcase comes in.

Situations

(*a*) You're getting ready to go away on holiday and have left most of your preparations till the last minute. On your last day at work you decide to go without lunch and do as many jobs as you can fit in. In fact you do five useful things, all quite different, during the free hour. Suggest what these might be.

(*b*) You have to travel for at least eight hours in a car with two children between the ages of five and eight. What preparations do you make to ensure their good behaviour and comfort and what do you do about this during the journey? (You aren't driving yourself.)

(*c*) What do you do if you cut your hand while working?

(*d*) You hear a noise during the night and bravely go to investigate. You find two burglars in your living-room, searching it and causing considerable damage. What do you do?

Expressing your opinions

(*a*) Describe an ideal place for a picnic.

(*b*) Do you enjoy a thunderstorm or are you slightly afraid of storms? In either case, try to explain your feelings.

(*c*) What effects has the private car had on the countryside?

General guidance and practice

The subjunctive

A few remnants of the subjunctive are still to be found in English. The most obvious affect the verb '*to be*' and though even these are disappearing, they are normally retained in the speech of educated people. *In most cases what is apparently the plural form 'were' is used with a singular subject:*

This occurs mainly in the following three cases:

(*a*) *After 'if' as used in the second type of condition, especially when some doubt is implied*

After 'as if' or 'as though' in comparisons.

If I were cold, I should put a jumper on.

If his pension were to be withdrawn, he would be penniless.

He ran as if / though he were being chased by devils.

Compare: I asked him if he was happy. (Reported Speech)

The mother told the child to call her if he was afraid. (A reasonable possibility)

(*b*) After the introductory verb TO WISH.

I wished I were fifty miles off.

He wishes he were handsome.

The past tense which normally follows this verb is sometimes explained as a form of the subjunctive:

I wish I lived nearer.

(*c*) After the words SUPPOSING and SUPPOSE.

Supposing I were to confess everything.

As in (*b*) above, a past form of any verb may follow 'supposing':

Supposing he came now!

(*d*) Old uses of the subjunctive remain in phrases like 'God save the King!' 'Long live the President!' 'Thy will be done!' 'If it be possible.'

(*e*) *Certain other unexpected past forms* after a few introductory expressions, including some of those above, may be examples of survivals of subjunctive forms:

I think it would be a good idea if we *went* home.

It is high / about time that fence *was mended.*

I'd rather you *did* it. If only I had more time!

Use the correct form of the verb in each of the following sentences:

(*a*) He would be more popular if he (be) less argumentative.

(*b*) He behaves as if he (own) the earth.

(*c*) Our service engineers could come immediately if there (be) a breakdown.

(*d*) I'd rather he (say) nothing about it.

(*e*) I think it would be a good idea if you (get) on with your work.

(*f*) She wishes she (be) a film star.

(*g*) Supposing Father (say) we couldn't go!

(*h*) It is really time we (have) a holiday.

(*i*) We wish you (come) more often.

(*j*) She screamed and laughed wildly as though she (be) mad.

(*k*) If only you (not snore)!

Make, Do

Broadly, TO MAKE implies the creation of something new; TO DO implies the carrying out of some action. One makes a cake, a dress, a sound: one does homework, knitting, a kind action.

But it is often very difficult to decide whether or not a new thing has been created or an action done, and there are an enormous number of exceptions to this statement.

It is therefore advisable to notice and remember each individual case of one or other of these verbs.

Here is a list of a few cases:

Do	*Make*
do work (homework, housework, etc.)	make a dress, a cake, coffee
do a job, an exercise, an examination, a test	make a mistake
do the washing-up	make an appointment
do shopping	make the beds
do lessons	make a fortune
do a translation (or, make a translation)	make money (become rich)
do one's hair	make friends with
do good	make an enemy of
do harm, evil	make a noise
do a good turn	make peace
do one's best	make an agreement
do one's duty	make a will
	make a bargain
	make improvements
	make progress
	make the most of
	make a copy
	make preparations
	make an arrangement
	make a fuss, make a fuss of
	make a nuisance of oneself
	make trouble
	make a fool of
	make fun of
	make up one's mind
	make sure
	make sense
	make time (find time)
	make a difference
	make haste
	make allowances for
	make changes

Notice these expressions:

Yes, those gloves will *do*. I shall take them.

This meat is only *half done*. I don't like underdone food.

It really isn't *done* for you to sit there with your hat on.

Here are some uses of DO and MAKE as phrasal verbs:

DO: It is time you *did away with* that filthy old hat. Why not burn it?
They have bought some paint and intend to *do up* their house.
There is no jam left. You will just have to *do without* it.
I can't *do up* this button. It will just have to stay undone.
I've had little to *do with* him. We seldom meet.
What has dressmaking to *do with* algebra?
Don't trust that waiter. He *did* me *out of* ten pence last week.

MAKE: Nothing in a child's life can ever *make up* for the lack of a good home.
He is *making up* a parcel of small presents.
She is *making up* her face ready for the party.
That story isn't true. You *made* it *up*.
Thank goodness, they have *made up* their quarrel.
I can't *make out* this illegible writing.
What is paper *made of*? It is *made by* machinery.
Flax is *made into* linen. Linen is *made from* flax.
That beach bag was *made out of* an old cotton frock.
If you can't get exactly what you want, try to *make do with* the next best thing.
The thieves *made away* with a thousand pounds' worth of jewellery.

Rewrite the following sentences using some form of DO or MAKE:

(*a*) He has committed an error in this exercise.

(*b*) Try not to be a trouble in the class.

(*c*) Boy Scouts should perform a kindness every day.

(*d*) Can you produce good coffee?

(*e*) He has caused a lot of misfortune to his country.

(*f*) He has gone forward during the last few weeks.

(*g*) Will you please produce another letter like this one?

(*h*) The pirate captain decided to attack the treasure ship.

(*i*) The Transport Board are raising fares to compensate for their recent losses.

(*j*) The fishmonger hadn't any plaice to-day. We'll have to be content with cod.

(*k*) Workmen are redecorating my room.

(*l*) Why doesn't the Corporation get rid of those obsolete trams? (Bodies such as the Transport Board (i) and the Corporation (ii) are treated as singular or plural without any apparent reason.)

(*m*) The imaginative child invented a vivid story about a kindly dwarf.

(*n*) What confusion and trouble you are causing just because you have lost a cheap ballpoint pen.

(*o*) I have forgotten to write my homework.

(*p*) This message is almost impossible to read. Can you understand it?

(*q*) Some people do not wish to have any relationship with their neighbours.

(*r*) You are laughing at me!

(*s*) Hurry up! You'll miss the train!

Reported speech

Here are some more things to remember when you are changing from direct to reported speech.

(*a*) TENSE CHANGES

Certain verbs never change their tense

These are: '*ought*', '*should*' (with the meaning 'ought'), *might* when it suggests possibility.

'You ought to / should rest more.'

The doctor told me I should rest more.

'There might be a storm.'

He was afraid (that) there might be a storm.

Conditions

Study the following examples of the three main conditions:

(*a*) 'If you *are* not quiet, you *will be sent* to bed.'
The mother threatened that if the children *were* not quiet, they *would be* sent to bed.

(*b*) 'If there *were* a revolution, everybody *would get* enough to eat.'
The speaker told his audience that if there *were* a revolution, everybody *would get* enough to eat.

(*c*) 'If the moon *had been shining*, you *would have seen* the old windmill.'
Our host told us that if the moon *had been shining*, we *should have seen* the old windmill.

The *first condition* follows the normal tense change rules.
The verbs in the *second and third conditions* do not change.

Must

The changes affecting this verb depend on the way in which it is used.

(*a*) *A habitual but not eternal action*
'In my job, I *must* speak English every day.'
The secretary said that in her job she *had* to speak English every day.
'We *must* catch a bus whenever we go to the station.'
My cousins complained that they *had to* catch a bus whenever they went to the station.

(*b*) *A future action*
The subject may be just about to do the action but it has not yet happened.

'I must look up his number in the telephone directory.'

The matron said she *would have to* look up his number in the telephone directory.

'You *must* speak more clearly if you want to be understood.'

I told him he *would have to* speak more clearly if he wanted to be understood.

(*c*) *An eternal action*

'Swallows *must* migrate in winter.'

The teacher explained that swallows *must* migrate in winter.

'Every living creature *must* have food.'

He stated that every living creature *must* have food.

(*d*) *Must not*

'You *must not* forget what I have said.'

The old woman warned us that we *must not* forget what she had said.

(*e*) *Need not*

'You need not work so hard.'

My brother told me that I *did not need* to work so hard. (there was no necessity)

My brother told me that I *did not have* to work so hard. (there was no compulsion)

Can Could

(*a*) 'Jeremy *can* now count up to twenty.'

Jeremy's mother said that her son *could* now count up to twenty.

(*b*) 'We *could* not make ourselves understood in that restaurant.'

The tourists said that they *had* not *been able* to make themselves understood in that restaurant.

(*b*) CONFUSION OF MEANING

In converting from direct to reported speech, changes in pronouns may lead to confusion in meaning.

Study this example:

'Mr. Reed, when can I come to your house for my lesson?'

If we change this automatically into reported speech, it may read:

The student asked Mr. Reed when he could come to his house for his lesson.

We are completely confused about who wants to come to whose house for whose lesson. Common sense will adjust this to:

The student asked Mr. Reed when he could come to Mr. Reed's house for his lesson.

(*c*) CHANGE OF INTRODUCTORY VERB

Study this example:

'I'm going to have fish and chips,' announced the stout woman. 'What do you want?'

In this case a direct statement is followed by a direct question. Two different verbs will be needed in the corresponding reported speech.

The stout woman announced that she was going to have fish and chips and asked her companion what she wanted.

(*d*) SOME OTHER POINTS

Certain ideas expressed in direct speech cannot be conveyed exactly in reported speech. Here again common sense is required. Here are some examples:

'Would you give me your name, sir?' said the policeman.
The policeman politely asked the motorist if the latter would give him his name.

'Help!' he shouted.
He shouted for help.

'You idiot,' John yelled, 'you've spoiled everything.'
John yelled that his friend, whom he called an idiot, had spoiled everything.

(*e*) GENERAL USES OF REPORTED SPEECH FORMS

We have been dealing with reported speech as it represents the re-telling of direct speech. Remember however that reported speech forms often appear as we are writing any kind of sentence or passage. Here are only a very few cases:

They knew that they had not a chance.
He wrote about what he had seen.
We had no idea when we would return.
I could not think what his name was.
I hoped the weather would be fine.

(*f*) REPORTED TO DIRECT SPEECH

This is of course a reverse process to the one already described. Remember especially the following points:

(*a*) The rules for the use of inverted commas (Page 112).

(*b*) Certain tenses in reported speech have *two* possible forms in direct speech, depending on their meaning.

The PAST PERFECT SIMPLE may change to the PRESENT PERFECT SIMPLE or PAST SIMPLE.
The PAST PERFECT CONTINUOUS may change to the PRESENT PERFECT CONTINUOUS or PAST CONTINUOUS.
The motorist told me he had left his licence at home.
'I've left my licence at home,' said the motorist.
The motorist told me he had not seen the traffic lights.
'I didn't see the traffic lights,' said the motorist.

(*c*) Direct speech often opens with the words spoken and ends with the main verb and the speaker. The subject and verb here may be reversed in order when the subject is a noun.

(*d*) Colloquial abbreviations are used in direct speech.

(i) Convert the following sentences into reported speech. Suggest a speaker where necessary.

(*a*) 'I am sorry to disturb you, sir,' said the policeman. 'I shall have to ask you a few questions.'

(*b*) 'I must admit that what you say may be true,' said my wife.

(*c*) 'Do you regret coming to live in this small town?' asked my neighbour.

(*d*) 'I protest against your intolerable interference in my affairs,' said the angry tenant to his landlord.

(*e*) 'Lie down!' he told his dog. 'Now be a good dog and don't get up till I tell you.'

(*f*) 'Why didn't you come and see me yesterday? I was expecting you.'

(*g*) 'He will be making a speech here next Friday,' said the election agent. 'Do try to come and hear him.'

(*h*) 'Next time you drop in, you must tell us about your holiday,' my friend suggested.

(*i*) 'If I overslept, I should miss the train.'

(*j*) 'You must speak more politely when you answer your teacher.'

(*k*) 'You must not forget to send us a postcard.'

(ii) Convert the following examples of reported speech into direct speech:

(*l*) The tramp said he had had nothing to eat since the previous Monday.

(*m*) He told me he had been an invalid ever since an accident which had happened three years before but the doctor now had hopes that he would recover.

(*n*) The foreman asked the apprentice whether he had seen the slide rule that the foreman had been using earlier that morning.

(*o*) The sergeant told the soldiers to report for duty the next day. They were not to leave the barracks that evening as there might be trouble in the town.

(*p*) The porter asked me where I wanted him to put my luggage. He wanted to know whether it would be all right in my compartment or whether he should put it in the guard's van.

(*q*) Christopher offered me a cigarette explaining that he had another packet in his pocket.

Various quantities

(i) Remember that MUCH is used for QUANTITY, MANY for NUMBER.

He hasn't *much money*, but he seems to have *many friends*.

The same applies to LITTLE and LEAST (QUANTITY) and FEW, FEWER and FEWEST (NUMBER).

He eats *little chocolate* and *few sweets*.
Write a summary in *fewer than eighty words*.
You have *less patience* than I have.

'Fewest' is not often used. It is usually replaced by 'the smallest number'.

This is *the smallest number* of students that have ever attended.

(ii) MUCH *before a noun or modifying a verb is rarely used in an affirmative statement or command.* It is replaced by 'a lot (of)', 'a good deal (of)', 'plenty(of)'.
NOT: I have spent much money. OR: Bring much cheese. I like it.
(Any of the above alternatives will do here.)
NOT: I enjoyed it much.
I enjoyed it *a lot, a great deal.*

Very much, *too much* and *so much* are, however, more commonly found.
I have spent too much money.
I enjoyed myself very much, *or* I very much enjoyed myself.
There is so much to do.

MUCH is used in a *negative* and less commonly in an interrogative sentence. It can follow verbs of a negative meaning like *deny forbid doubt* even when these are used affirmatively.

You won't find much left.
Have you much to do?
I forbid you to bring much with you.

Use a suitable expression from among those that have just been mentioned in the following sentences. In many cases more than one would be appropriate:

(*a*) He has .... worries or responsibilities. How lucky he is!
(*b*) I can't come now. I have .... to do this morning.
(*c*) We must expect .... people than usual in such bad weather.
(*d*) He doesn't take .... care of his bicycle.
(*e*) He looks half-starved. I'm sure he eats .... food than he ought.
(*f*) I use my vacuum cleaner ....
(*g*) Do you smoke .... cigarettes a day?
(*h*) He buys .... tobacco, and has .... pipes.
(*i*) In our house there are .... rooms but oddly enough, not .... space.
(*j*) He eats .... fruit as he says it doesn't agree with him.

Rearrange list *B* so that the objects correspond with the words in list *A*, e.g. a ball of string.

A a ball, a cake, a tin, a pair, a packet, a bar, a skein (ball), a reel, a bunch (bouquet), a bundle, a pack, a coil.

B cotton, flowers, sardines, wire, wool, toilet soap, chocolate, cards, shoes, firewood, envelopes, string.

Verbal constructions with seeing, hearing and feeling

Verbs of SEEING, HEARING and FEELING can be followed either by the Present Participle or by the Infinitive depending on the meaning expressed.

He saw / noticed the light (i) fade.

He observed / watched the light (ii) fading.

She heard the man (i) whistle twice.
(ii) whistling.

I smelt the potatoes burning.

I could feel the dog (i) shiver.
(ii) shivering.

In each of the cases marked (i) the action happened and was completed: the light faded quickly, he whistled his dog sharply, the dog suddenly shivered.

In each case (ii) the action was continuous and the emphasis is on the doing of the action: the man was whistling a tune, the dog shivered for some time.

Use the correct form of the verb, present participle or infinitive, in each of the following sentences:

(*a*) There is often a crowd standing watching men (dig) up the road.

(*b*) I jumped up when I heard the doorbell (ring).

(*c*) You must have heard the telephone (ring) but you couldn't be bothered to answer it.

(*d*) We saw him (shut) the book and (put) it back on the shelf.

(*e*) He felt the intense cold (creep) into his very bones.

(*f*) Can you smell the dinner (cook)?

(*g*) Did you notice the cat (crouch) just near the mousehole?

(*h*) We felt the ship (give) a violent lurch.

Prepositions

Use a suitable preposition in each of the following sentences:

(*a*) Concrete consists ...... sand, gravel, cement powder and water.

(*b*) If you can improve this .... any way, please do so.

(*c*) Have you enough room in that tiny garage of yours .... your enormous car?

(*d*) We cooked our meal over a fire .... the open air.

(*e*) Sarah came home from the party, loaded .... sweets and toys.

(*f*) A rabbit is different .... a hare.

(*g*) I have made an appointment .... the optician to choose new frames for my glasses.

(*h*) He apologised .... his sarcastic remarks.

(*i*) The coach party had salmon and cucumber salad .... lunch.

(*j*) He gazed in bewilderment .... his own writing.

13

Passage for comprehension

Bitter memories

It is just possible that our village Entertainments Society may dare to present a concert this coming winter. I am doubtful about it. We have not had one for five years, the last having been a catastrophe that some unfortunate victims still brood over to this day, and certainly none of these will risk presenting another yet. 5

It had seemed to have every prospect of success. Most of us had helped to decorate the village Recreational Hall with artificial flowers; the platform had been converted into a stage with thick red velvet curtains and footlights. The performers were all immensely keen on taking part though perhaps not all were brilliantly talented. The Chairman of the Society was going to 10 announce the items and we were pleased to see that, besides our own villagers, the audience was made up of a fair number of people from villages round about.

The early part of the concert went off comparatively satisfactorily. The village blacksmith sang sentimentally, if a little hoarsely, about his passion 15 for the sea, which we knew he had never seen; young Billy Martin recited a poem about a cavalry charge at an appropriate breathless speed; the church choirmaster gave a violin solo and Jimmy Fowler achieved some remarkable conjuring tricks from a book he had been given as a birthday present.

It was Miss Finch's piano solo which was the first of the disasters. Un- 20 fortunately two of the local hooligans, Charlie Brown and Ted Forbes, had somehow been admitted. The former had already been in an approved school, while the latter was on probation. They stood near the exit during the first few items, eyeing Jimmy's tricks contemptuously but silently, merely whistling satirically instead of applauding at the end. As Miss Finch, their 25 former teacher, appeared, they clapped, solemnly and slowly. Nervously and hurriedly she propped her music on the stand and started to play in obvious distress, with more and more mistakes as she became increasingly confused. Suddenly an outer door at the side of the stage blew open with a loud crash. A draught of icy air swept across the stage, lifting Miss Finch's 30 music from the stand and depositing it on the keys with a final impossible chord. As Miss Finch stared, horrified, at the rebellious sheets, Charlie's voice rang out from the back:

'Looks as if even her music book couldn't stand it!'

'Last note wasn't so bad though,' came Ted's comment. 35

While the Secretary's wife went up to console Miss Finch, who had burst into tears (she was having considerable difficulty in comforting her), Frank Bridges, the village constable, was severely reprimanding the two culprits.

'Even you should be ashamed of yourselves,' he growled sternly. 'You 40 thoroughly deserve to be thrown out and if you misbehave yourselves once more, you will be.'

Ted was about to protest insolently, but Charlie knew better. His past experiences with the law had taught him the futility of open defiance so he pretended to be sorry.

45 'Sorry, sir,' he apologised with false humility. 'We just couldn't help laughing.' His eyes were wide and innocent of evil.

Undeceived Constable Bridges returned to his place. Three ladies begged Miss Finch to start again but she refused and escaped from the hall still sniffing audibly.

50 Mrs. Dunn, the butcher's wife, a stout soprano, took her place. Soon she was singing to us about the tall, dark, handsome young man who was breaking her heart, though, as Mr. Dunn was neither tall, dark, handsome nor young, we began to wonder who this could be. It was in the middle of her song that the kitten appeared. Sooty black as a witch's cat, she must 55 have taken advantage of the few moments when the door had been open. She emerged from the side of the stage, momentarily investigated the piano, scampered across and patted the cord attached to the curtain and started playing with the tassel. A few quiet giggles came from a section of the audience; Mrs. Dunn continued singing, ignorant of her rival attraction. 60 Suddenly the kitten noticed this special friend of hers, whose scraps of lamb and liver she had often enjoyed. With a swift leap she scrambled up vigorously on Mrs. Dunn's shoulder and started rubbing the lady's cheek, purring noisily and wagging her tail. Mrs. Dunn's top tragic A became a startled shriek before dying away and Charlie's voice came from the back of 65 the hall:

'Heard one of her pals and wanted to make it a duet.'

By the time Constable Bridges had risen from his chair, both the offenders had cleared out, and had gone to take refuge in their favourite pub. Somewhat flushed and indignant, Mrs. Dunn soon recovered; the kitten was 70 expelled in disgrace, and the lady was persuaded to give an encore, which was loudly applauded.

During the interval, refreshments were served, including sandwiches, sausage rolls, tea and soft drinks. The atmosphere was a little strained but since we had got rid of the unwelcome intruders, everybody was gossiping 75 in a specially friendly way. Surely nothing more could go wrong during the next hour.

For the first half hour everything continued fairly satisfactorily, though there were of course the worrying moments, in particular when little Susan Sykes tripped and fell down during the children's dancing. The final disaster, 80 oddly enough, was apparently the triumph of the whole show.

Little Cecil Timms was the odd-job man of the village. He was short, timid, solemn; he had freckles, thick-lensed spectacles and a pale feeble moustache. Few people ever noticed him, and those that did tended to make game of him and tease him. To the Secretary's amazement he had volun- 85 teered to give some impersonations, and impressed by one or two examples, the Secretary decided that, as no one objected to his taking part, he might be worth seeing.

Blushing, fidgeting nervously with his tie, blinking timidly, he faced us silently for a minute. Then he produced a cigarette which drooped from a corner of his mouth; his hands found his pockets; he sneered insolently. 90
'What, you're offering me a job? Think you'll ever catch me working? What do you take me for?' Cecil Timms had vanished and Ted Forbes lounged arrogantly before us. Before we had time to applaud, back and arms straightened; a frown creased his forehead; his whole body swelled with self-importance. 'Now then, it may be Saturday night, but we're not having that 95
noise': Constable Bridges was keeping order at closing time. Everyone had enjoyed these, but as one by one the well-known villagers were imitated, more and more cleverly and more and more maliciously and cruelly, we realised that Cecil Timms, who had suffered neglect and mockery for too long was having his revenge. We chuckled, then roared with laughter with 100
tears in our eyes—at least all but a few of us, whose enjoyment seemed rather lukewarm. As we came away from the hall we all declared that next year Cecil Timms would be our star performer.

And yet ever since that night there has never been another concert, and Cecil Timms has only to join a group of his associates for an immediate hush 105
to follow. They no longer laugh at him but they remember urgent jobs which call them away within a few minutes. He is treated with respect but is a rather lonely man.

There have been several newcomers to the Society since that date, who urge us to revive our annual concerts. They reproach us for our lack of 110
interest. Now they are insisting on having one just after Christmas. But surprisingly few people have volunteered to perform. And Cecil Timms is not among those that will be asked.

Notes on the passage

Vocabulary

line

Title *bitter:* chocolate, coffee, memories and feelings can be *bitter*
milk or a facial expression may be *sour*
wine is *dry* or *sweet* though it can go sour when opened and unused.

title *memory* (*Unc*)*:* I have a very bad *memory*.
a memory (*C*) = a *recollection:* some remembered experience.
a souvenir: some object that reminds one of an experience such as a holiday.

1 *entertain* friends in one's home = provide hospitality for them.
A conjuror, pianist or comedian entertains people by providing enjoyment.
divert (turn away) people's attention from something.

a diversion: (a) some kind of relaxation (b) an alternative route when a road is being repaired.

4 *brood:* a broody hen is one sitting on eggs, often looking sad and thoughtful.
A person *broods over* (thinks deeply and sadly about) his sorrows.

6 *a prospect:* something that may happen: *his job offers good prospects.*
a prospectus: a booklet explaining the programme of a school or firm.

7 *artificial* flowers, silk, teeth, limbs. *synthetic* rubber.
false documents: a false (forged) passport, identity, beard.
substitute coffee. *counterfeit* money.
imitation jewellery, gold, leather. *fake* pictures (deliberately made to deceive).

8 *footlights* may illuminate a stage. *A spotlight* illuminates one performer. *limelight:* general stage lighting: be in the limelight = *be the centre of public attention.* A building is *floodlit*. A *searchlight* shows an object such as an aeroplane in darkness. Cars have *headlights.*

10 the *Chairman:* the *chairman* of a committee; the *principal* of a college (non-University); the *headteacher* of a school; the *proprietor* of a hotel; the *manager* of a firm; the *landlord* of an inn.

12 an *audience* at a concert; a *congregation* in a church.

14 *comparatively* and *relatively* both mean fairly or moderately.

15 *A blacksmith* hammers on an *anvil* in a *forge.*

19 *A conjuror* performs various tricks, apparently by magic. A *juggler* throws up and catches balls. *An acrobat* balances and leaps. *A clown* amuses.

22 An *approved school* is a place to which young people in serious trouble with the law are sent for training and possible reformation. If the offence is not a very serious one and is their first, they may be *put on probation.* They must report for a certain period to a *probation officer,* who tries to help and advise them.
If goods are bought *on approval,* the customer has the opportunity of examining them thoroughly first before buying them.

24 *contemptuous:* feeling contempt. *contemptible:* deserving contempt: *Cruelty to a helpless animal is contemptible.*

27 *the stand:* the music stand on the piano.

28 *distress:* usually suggests unhappiness but a *ship in distress* needs help.

30 *draught* (dra:ft) has many different meanings.

(*a*) a current of air moving through a room: *catch cold from sitting in a draught.*

(*b*) the amount of liquid drunk at one time: *he finished the beer at one draught.*

(*c*) a rough plan prepared first: *the draft of a treaty, a novel, a scheme.* (this is usually spelt 'draft') (*d*) a *draughtsman* is a person who draws detailed sections of such things as machine parts, vehicles, bridges, buildings.

(*e*) a circular counter used in playing *draughts*, a game similar in some ways to chess and also played on black and white squares.

(*f*) a written order for withdrawing money from a bank (spelling: draft)

(*g*) *draught beer* is beer drawn straight from the cask or barrel without having been bottled.

(*h*) *to draft:* prepare a plan for a document.

31 *a key* (*a*) opens a locked door: a Yale key; a keyhole; a key-ring. *The message was written in a code to which they had no key.*

(*b*) A scale in major key C has no sharps or flats.

(*c*) a piano key; a typewriter key.

32 *a chord:* two or more notes played together. *cord:* thick firm string.
but: *discord*: two or more notes played together without harmony.
also: disagreements and quarrels (*Adj* discordant)

34 Charlie is playing with the two meanings of *stand*—'remain upright' (the music has fallen) and 'endure without complaining' (suggesting that Miss Finch's playing was so bad that even the copy of music could not bear it).
This play on words is known as a PUN.
Ted's 'last note' was the noise made when the music copy fell.

36 *burst into tears:* OPP burst out laughing.

38 *reprimand:* A soldier is reprimanded for not doing his duty.
A wife gently *reproaches* her husband for forgetting her birthday.
Mother *scolds* the children for making too much noise.
A clergyman *rebukes* a young man for drinking too much.

43 Charlie's *experience with the law* included his stay in an approved school.

43 *futility:* He made a *futile* attempt to catch the lizard but his attempts were *unsuccessful/in vain.* (All three of similar meaning.)

43 *defy*/defiance. He *defied* the school rules by refusing to wear uniform. *deny*/denial: The shopkeeper said Gavin had stolen the radio but he *denied* this.

47 He *deceived* me with his lies. He *disappointed* me by breaking his promise to take me to the theatre.

49 *audible* = can be heard. *visible* = can be seen.

55 *take advantage of:* make the most of an opportunity.
By *taking advantage of* my ignorance of local prices he was able to overcharge me.

56 *momentarily:* for a moment. He must have the treatment *hourly, daily, weekly, monthly, yearly.*

57 *scamper:* run excitedly like a small child.
scramble: climb as best one can, using hands and feet.

57 He *patted* the dog and *stroked* the cat.

61 *leap* is similar to *spring* (not to be confused with *run*).
A leap (*Adj*) year has 366 days.
He drank from a cool *spring* (often at the *source* of a river).
Rome has many beautiful *fountains*.

61 *vigour* but vigorous. *humour* but humorous.
Notice however: *honour* but also hon*our*able.

63 A *top A* is a high musical note.

64 He *started* with alarm when the shot was fired. He was *startled* by the shot.

64 Their voices *died away* in the distance. That fashion has quite *died out* now.

66 *pals* is a slang word for 'friends'.
Charlie is suggesting that Mrs. Dunn's singing is like the wailing or screaming of a cat.

68 *clear out* is a colloquial expression meaning 'to go away' 'to leave'.

68 *take refuge* = find a place of safety, some kind of shelter.
A refugee comes from another country to escape danger.
a bus *shelter* is a construction under which *to shelter* when waiting for a bus.

68 *favourite:* my favourite radio programme NOT 'preferred'.

69 A person *flushes* when indignant or offended. He *blushes* when shy or embarrassed.
He probably looks *flushed* when he has a temperature.

69 *recover* from an illness (*N* recovery). He is now *convalescent* and should soon be quite better.

70 *expel* an unsatisfactory pupil from school (expulsion); *send down* a student from University if he is *in disgrace*.
disgraceful = shameful. *admirable* could be an opposite. *graceful/clumsy* (Opp).

73 *soft drinks* include lemonade, orangeade or orange squash, lime juice, ginger beer and milk shakes.

73 *strain* = weaken by overwork. *eyestrain*; *a strained muscle*; *nervous strain.*
strained relations between two countries or people.
A *tea-strainer.*

79 *trip* fall or almost fall while moving: trip over the edge of the carpet; also: move quickly, with light dancing steps; *skip:* jump over a turning rope: *a skipping rope*; this can also have a similar meaning to *trip.*
stumble: fall or nearly fall through putting one's foot down badly.

81 *an odd-job man:* can undertake various small jobs like gardening and repairs without being specially trained for any.

82 *freckles:* brownish spots on the skin caused by the sun; *wrinkles:* folds in the skin, usually that of older people; *dimples:* small hollows in the

cheeks or chin, especially when a person smiles; *spots:* small marks on the skin, possibly caused by an illness such as measles.

82 Telescopes and glasses have *lenses* (*Sing* lens).

85 *impersonations:* imitations of people.

88 People can *fidget* by constantly moving their fingers or other parts of their bodies; they *wriggle* by twisting their whole body, rather like a snake.

90 *blink* by closing two eyes; *wink* by closing one.

92 *insolent; impertinent; impudent; cheeky:* all these adjectives suggest rudeness and offensive behaviour to another person, possibly a teacher or someone in a more important position: *Even when he was only four, he would answer his mother impertinently when she asked him not to do something.* *insolent* (*N insolence*) is the strongest; *impertinent* (*N impertinence*) and *impudent* (*N impudence*) are often interchangeable and *cheekiness* is occasionally considered slightly amusing. *They have picked some of the flowers from our garden. What a cheek!*

93 *What do you take me for?* is a colloquial way of saying: What kind of person do you think I am?

93 *A lounge* is a sitting-room where one can lounge or sit in a relaxed position comfortably.

96 Public houses are forced by law to close at a certain time, and especially on Saturday nights, people who have drunk a good deal may make a lot of noise when they are turned out.

98 *malice* (*N*) *malicious:* spitefulness, the desire to hurt people with what one says.

102 *lukewarm* and *tepid* both suggest a lack of real warmth.

Pronunciation

SPECIAL DIFFICULTIES: conjuring [kʌ́ndʒərɪŋ]; draught [draːft]; chord [kɔːd]; constable [kʌ́nstəbl]; severely [sɪvíəlɪ]; defy [dɪfáɪ]; deny [dɪnáɪ]; butcher [bútʃə]; sooty [sútɪ]; shriek [ʃrɪːk]; encore [ɔ́ŋkɔ́ː]; sandwiches [sǽn(d)-wɪdʒɪz]; sausage [sɔ́sɪdʒ]; welcome [wélkəm]; particular [pətíkjələ]; triumph [tráɪəmf]; fidgeting [fídʒɪtɪŋ].

ə as in *a*go: entertainment [entətéɪnmənt]; success [səksés]; audience [ɔ́ːdɪəns]; comparatively [kəmpǽrətɪvlɪ]; satisfactorily [sǽtisfǽktərɪlɪ]; contemptuously [kəntémptjuəslɪ]; satirically [sətírɪklɪ]; applauding [əplɔ́ː-dɪŋ]; insolently [ínsələntlɪ]; innocent [ínəsənt]; momentarily [móumənt(ə)-rɪlɪ]; tassel [tǽsl]; vigorously [vígərəslɪ]; persuaded [pəswéɪdɪd]; atmosphere [ǽtməsfɪə]; spectacles [spéktəkəlz]; volunteered [vɔ́ləntíəd]; impersonations [ɪmpəːsənéɪʃənz]; arrogantly [ǽrəgəntlɪ]; maliciously [məlíʃəslɪ]; appropriate [əpróuprɪət]; brilliantly [bríljəntlɪ]; artificial [aːtɪfíʃəl].

ɪ as in *city*: remarkable [rɪmáːkəbl]; whistling [wíslɪŋ]; depositing [dɪpɔ́-zɪtɪŋ]; audibly [ɔ́ːdɪblɪ]; revenge [rɪvéndʒ]; recite [rɪsáɪt].

ju as in *use*: contemptuously [kəntémtjuəslɪ]; futility [fjuːtílɪtɪ]; duet [djuːét].

SOUND CHANGES: rebel (*N*) [réb(ə)l]; (*v*) [rɪbél]; rebellious [rɪbéljəs]; able [eɪbl]; ability [əbílɪtɪ].

OTHERS: recreation [rekrɪéɪʃən]; hoarsely [hɔ́ːslɪ]; merely [míəlɪ]; instead [ɪnstéd]; reprimanding [réprɪmáːndɪŋ]; culprits [kʌ́lprɪts]; disgrace [dɪsgréɪs]; lounge [laundʒ]; icy [áɪsɪ].

Special Grammatical and structural points

(i) *Nouns Used as Adjectives* This is a common construction in English.
Examples from the passage: Entertainments Society; village blacksmith; church choirmaster; piano solo.

Other examples: a house door; a dog kennel; a car licence; a clock face; a street lamp; a school playground.

(ii) *the former ...... the latter:*
Mr. and Mrs. Long both have jobs: the former is a builder while the latter is an architect. (Notice: *the former* comes *before the latter.*)
Another use: Miss Finch was their *former teacher*.

(iii) *While* may have the meaning *and* although some slight difference between the two items so joined is often suggested. Notice the example in (ii) above and also: Anne likes to spend her free time out of doors while Graham prefers to stay at home reading.

(iv) Do not mix *no ...... more* and *no ...... longer.*
Compare: I really cannot eat *any more*. He has *no more* money left.
and: I must not stay *any longer*. The old man can *no longer* work. (Time)

(v) *either ...... or; neither ...... nor:* Do not mix these constructions.
We can *either* play cards *or* watch television.
He will *neither* help us *nor* remain quietly out of our way.

(vi) In line 15 *if* means *though*. His writing is clear, if somewhat untidy.

(vii) More *reflexives:* ashamed of yourselves; misbehave yourselves.

(viii) *Verbal Constructions*
Infinitive: deserve to be; beg to start; volunteer to give.
Gerund: risk embarking; can't help laughing; continue singing; catch me working; insist on having; have difficulty in comforting; keen on taking part.
worth seeing.
Clause: We realised that he was having his revenge.

Prepositions

(*a*) ashamed *of*; take advantage of; ignorant of; guilty/innocent of; lack of

(*b*) decorate *with*: with a loud crash; have difficulty with a problem; (but: have difficulty in doing something); oblige with an encore;

fidget with; roar with laughter; with tears in our eyes; treat with respect

(*c*) *in* disgrace

(*d*) burst *into* tears

(*e*) doubtful *about*

(*f*) brood *over*

(*g*) keen *on* (taking); on probation; insist on

(*h*) *at* a certain speed

(*i*) escape *from*; emerge from

(*j*) attached *to*; to his amazement

(*k*) impressed *by*; one by one (one after the other)

(*l*) ability *for* observation (ability to observe); reproach for (forgetting).

Useful expressions to learn and introduce into written work

(*a*) the audience *was made up of* people of all ages (*b*) there may be a fuel shortage *this coming winter* (*c*) *a fair number of* (*d*) he is *reasonably/comparatively* hard-working (*e*) he *achieved* success (*f*) *take advantage of* our low prices (*g*) *by the time* he had finished it was too late to go out (*h*) *refreshments were served* (*i*) he dislikes everybody, his own family *in particular* (*j*) *oddly enough*, we met last in Sydney (*k*) *to my amazement*, the stranger knew my name (*l*) *it might be worth* meeting him (*m*) *one by one* (one after the other) (*n*) he was *having his revenge* (*o*) *surprisingly few* people live in the town centre.

Multiple choice questions

Here are a number of questions or unfinished statements about the passage, each with four suggested ways of answering or finishing it. You must choose the way you consider the most suitable. Write in each case the bracketed number of the question or statement followed by the letters **A**, **B**, **C**, **D**, and then cross through the letter of the answer you choose. Give one answer only to each question. Read the passage right through again before choosing your answers.

1 The performers in the previous concert had been
A professional actors **B** enthusiastic amateurs **C** talented local people **D** people from the village and surrounding areas

2 Which of the following performers did not appear early in the concert?
A an amateur magician **B** a small boy **C** a clergyman **D** a local craftsman

3 In which of the following ways did Charlie Brown and Ted Forbes not make nuisances of themselves?
A applauding at the wrong times **B** making sarcastic comments **C** whistling as a kind of mockery **D** laughing contemptuously

4 Charlie and Ted clapped when Miss Finch appeared because they wanted
A to show their appreciation **B** to mock her **C** to encourage her **D** to prevent her from playing

5 Why did Constable Bridges go up to Charlie and Ted?
A to warn them **B** to punish them **C** to frighten them **D** to make them feel sorry

6 When had the kitten probably come into the hall?
A while Miss Finch was playing **B** just after she had stopped **C** while Mrs. Dunn had been singing **D** before the concert started

7 Why did the kitten jump up on Mrs. Dunn's shoulder?
A she enjoyed the singing **B** she wanted to play **C** she recognised a useful friend **D** she had just had some food

8 Which of these things did not happen after Charlie's remark about the kitten?
A Constable Bridges again dealt with the two boys **B** the kitten was turned out **C** Charlie and Ted left quickly **D** Mrs. Dunn continued her performance

9 Why was the Secretary surprised when Cecil Timms offered to take part in the concert?
A people made fun of Cecil **B** he was shy and inconspicuous **C** he had no regular job **D** he looked unattractive

10 According to the passage Cecil Timm's main reason for giving his performance was that
A He felt bitter and wanted to punish people **B** he enjoyed being the centre of attention **C** he wanted to show how clever he was **D** he wanted people to like him better

Reading comprehension

In this exercise you must choose the word or phrase which best completes the sentence. Write first the number of each sentence followed by the letters **A, B, C, D, E,** and then cross through the letter of the correct answer in each case.

1 Even though he was more than sixty he had very few .... on his face.
A freckles **B** wrinkles **C** spots **D** dimples **E** scars

2 The ball .... two or three times before rolling down the slope.
A bounced **B** sprang **C** leapt **D** hopped **E** skipped

3 When he was questioned about the missing ring, he firmly .... that he had even seen it.
A defied **B** accused **C** refused **D** denied **E** rebelled

4 He often forgets to do what he has been told and is scolded for being ....
A insolent **B** rebellious **C** impertinent **D** malicious
E disobedient

5 If you want to attend a course, you should study the college .... for full particulars of enrolment.
A prospect **B** prospects **C** prospectus **D** syllabus
E programme

6 Spies may have a number of .... names and papers.
A artificial **B** synthetic **C** false **D** imitation
E untrue

7 The actor enjoys giving .... of poems by his favourite poets.
A recitations **B** rehearsals **C** repetitions
D pronouncements **E** performances

8 He has adopted three orphans .... his own six children so that, all together, he has nine children to provide for.
A besides **B** except **C** beside **D** in place of
E instead of

9 He stroked his cat's silky fur and the cat .... contentedly.
A growled **B** snored **C** purred **D** hummed
E roared

10 He had been completely exhausted but felt considerably .... after a meal and a rest.
A renewed **B** renovated **C** refreshed **D** remade
E recreated

11 The cat showed her .... for the stale fish by turning her back on it.
A distress **B** disgust **C** disgrace **D** despair **E** disappointment.

Use of English

1 The five phrases below are answers to five questions that could be asked about the reading passage. Write out the questions.

(i) sooty black as a witch's cat (ii) while the door had been open

(iii) during the children's dancing (iv) she was expelled in disgrace

(v) to revive our annual concerts

2 The blanks in the following eight sentences should be filled by one of the following words or phrases. Write the letter followed by the word or phrase.

already	rarely	with difficulty	still	actually
never	soon	occasionally	hardly	yet

(*a*) The moving men lifted the grand piano and .... carried it on to the stage. Write the letter followed by the word or phrases.

(*b*) Every evening he worked until nine so he .... saw his children after work as they were always in bed by eight.

(*c*) You are not ready to take the examination ....

(*d*) I have .... explained that three times but I suppose I shall have to do so again.

(*e*) He earns .... enough to live on.

(*f*) He had been working in his garden at one o'clock and he was .... there when I passed at eight.

(*g*) He .... offers to help his wife and she accepts his help gratefully.

(*h*) He works very quickly but he is so capable that he .... makes mistakes and he always sees and corrects these.

3 In each of the following sentences the word (or words) which should follow the verb is missing but is included among the five forms listed just underneath. Write the number of each sentence followed by the capital letter which precedes the suitable form.

1 When he heard the bad news, he broke .... completely.
A away **B** in **C** down **D** up **E** out

2 Their walking-tour through Lapland never came ....
A on **B** off **C** out **D** round **E** in

3 He has always gone .... strange hobbies like collecting bottle-tops and inventing secret codes.
A into **B** by **C** in for **D** through **E** for

4 The branch unexpectedly gave .... and the surprised cat found herself suddenly on the ground.
A way **B** in **C** away **D** back **E** up

5 He criticised everything and everybody and even ran .... his few friends.
A up **B** into **C** down **D** over **E** away from

6 I cannot understand how you put .... these depressing surroundings.
A up with **B** out **C** forward **D** by **E** down

7 My eldest brother intends to take .... skating next winter.
A to **B** in **C** away **D** on **E** up

8 Can you possibly make .... what he has written here?
A for **B** up **C** out **D** up for **E** do with

4 Write out the following in dialogue form, making all necessary changes. Begin like this:

Doctor What's your name and address?

I'm Richard Foster and I'm staying just now at the 'Swan Hotel'.

The doctor asked me my name and address. I told him I was Richard Foster and was staying just then at the 'Swan Hotel'. I was a sales representative and had arrived two days before. He asked me what the trouble was and I explained that that day and the previous one I had had a violent headache. The tablets I had taken had made no difference. In reply to his question, I said that I very rarely had headaches. He asked me whether I was accustomed to that very hot and humid weather and brilliant sunshine.

I told him that this was my first experience of the tropics. When he wanted to know how long I would be staying there, I answered that I would be leaving for England the following week. He told me to spend the next day in a darkened room, to wear sunglasses when I went out and to take some tablets which his assistant would give me. These would relieve the headache. If the headaches continued, I was to get into touch with him again. I thanked him and said goodbye.

5 Write down the numbers (i) to (x) and against each the correct form of *do* or *make* as appropriate.

(i) I really can't help .... mistakes in typing.

(ii) He often .... the shopping for his family.

(iii) Malicious gossip may .... a lot of harm to quite innocent people.

(iv) Will you .... me a good turn by posting this letter for me?

(v) She always .... all her housework before going out shopping.

(vi) What arrangements have you .... about your cat while you are on holiday?

(vii) His solicitor .... a copy of the will for him.

(viii) The class are .... their end-of-term examination to-morrow.

(ix) .... your best to be here early this evening.

(x) The noise that the neighbours were .... made him lose his temper.

Composition and summarising

Discussions

This might be a possible subject for a dialogue to be written in between 120 and 180 words:

Two young people, one a member of a small family and the other of a large family, are discussing the advantages and drawbacks of each type of family. Write what they say.

Advice: Before starting to write this dialogue, make a list of the points you intend to introduce. Remember the limit to the number of words you may use. It may happen that you cannot in fact deal with all the arguments you list.

Here are some notes you might make:

Small Family: Advantage: more money for pleasure and education
Drawback: possible loneliness of children and of parents when the children have left home.

Large Family: Advantages: (*a*) companionship (*b*) plenty of things happening (*c*) some of the children will help the parents later

Drawbacks: (*a*) many things missed because of lack of money (*b*) noise and lack of privacy, possibly preventing study (*c*) duty to limit the size of a family because of the future problem of world overpopulation

And here is the dialogue based on these notes:

Nicholas My parents were discussing our holiday plans yesterday. They're taking Jenny and me to France and Switzerland. Where are you going?

Bob Nowhere. We can't afford it. Not with nine of us children.

N I suppose not. But at least you can have a good time together. Jenny's too young to be a companion and I often feel lonely and wish I had someone to share things with.

B I've got too many people to share with. As soon as I'm old enough, I'll have to leave school and get a job to help the family. Anyhow I couldn't study. I share a room with three brothers and there's always a noise.

N But when you're old enough, some of you will still live close enough to keep in touch with your parents. And you must have a lot of fun.

B Yes, that's true. Life is never dull. But when I get married, I won't have more than two children. There are too many people in the world already and we've got a duty not to make matters worse.

(175 words)

Other Subjects for Discussion Dialogues (in 120 to 180 words)

Prepare a list of the ideas you intend to introduce before beginning to write.

(*a*) The advantages and drawbacks of living in a flat compared with those of living in a house.

(*b*) Shopping in a supermarket compared with shopping in a small friendly store.

(*c*) The arguments for and against a woman with a family to look after working outside the home.

(*d*) How far is it true to say that watching television is a complete waste of time?

(*e*) A discussion about whether too much newspaper space and radio time is given to sport.

(*f*) A rich person is likely to be happier than (or not so happy as) a person with just enough to live on.

Other Subjects for Composition

Write between 120 and 180 words on one of these subjects:

(*a*) You are spending a quiet holiday in a village in beautiful surroundings. Write a letter to a friend, describing the place and saying why you are or are not enjoying yourself there. The heading and ending of the letter will not be included in the number of words to be used.

(*b*) Write a short story with the title 'Revenge'.

(*c*) Each of the following people comes to a school to give a short talk to the school-leavers about his job, with the idea of interesting some of the children in it: a farmer; a kindergarten teacher; an actor; a policeman. What does *one* of these people say?

The various minor disasters in the village concert described in the comprehension passage were produced partly by people and partly by other causes. Give an account of these disasters in two paragraphs, the first dealing with the other causes, the second with the unpleasant things caused by people. Use between 175 and 200 words.

Spoken English

Expressing certainty and doubt

Certainty

I'm convinced/(quite) certain/(quite) sure things will improve.
I refuse to/can't believe you're doing your best.

Doubt

I doubt whether I'll understand much of this evening's play.
I wonder whether he'll remember it.

Mixed Certainty and Doubt

I can't help thinking that it'll be a mistake to buy that car.
I suppose you could call her a good cook but she's got no imagination.
I imagine (=I think it likely) he'll have finished by five o'clock.
I dare say (=I think it possible) the play will be successful.
I suspect he'd had something to drink before he arrived at the party.

Other Feelings

I'm pleased to say that my father's quite better now.
I'm thankful we haven't much farther to walk.
I'm surprised how fast my money seems to disappear.
I'm ashamed to say (confess) I've forgotten your name.
I'd like to say how grateful we are to you.
I must say some people seem to have no manners at all. (Indignation)

Making the most of spare time

How do you spend your spare time?
What do you do with your spare time?

A I'm keen on sport, especially football. I play for the local team as a goalkeeper. We usually have a match once a week and we do a fair amount of training during the week.

B I don't play myself but I enjoy watching matches or listening to radio commentaries. I support our local team and sometimes travel with them to watch 'away' matches. ('home' matches)

C I like anything on, in or under water: water-skiing, swimming and under-water photography. Living near the sea gives me plenty of opportunities to enjoy water-sports. I'm saving up to buy a speedboat.

D I spend the week-end climbing whenever the weather's suitable, putting up in mountain huts. I go skiing a lot in winter.

Indoor Entertainment

E I go to the theatre (opera, cinema) as often as I can afford it. I don't much mind what play's on provided the production's of a high standard.

F I'm very keen on dancing and spend a couple of evenings a week in the local discotheque. I also enjoy sitting in cafés talking to my friends.

G I'm usually so tired when I come home that I just watch television—any kind of programme—while I do some knitting. Sometimes I do embroidery. At week-ends I do a lot of reading.

H I collect jazz records and often invite friends to bring theirs for a jazz session.

Situations

1 A visitor to your home town has asked about interesting ways of spending the evening in your own or a nearby large town: theatres, cinemas, cafés, clubs, discotheques. What suggestions do you make?

2 The students in your class have prepared an amateur concert and want you to make the announcements. How do you introduce the concert? Explain that these are amateurs from many countries whose standards may not be professional but whose performances may be interesting.

Subjects for discussion

1 The comprehension passage describes a not altogether successful amateur concert. What are the special attractions of an amateur concert as compared with a professional?

2 Are people of your country interested in taking part in amateur plays and concerts? What opportunities are there of doing so?

3 In what ways do you think that taking part in amateur productions benefits the performers themselves?

4 Do you think theatres in your country should be subsidised?

5 What kind of play do you most enjoy seeing at the theatre?

6 Describe briefly the types of plays written by one playwright of your country.

7 Do you prefer to see a good film or a good play? Why?

8 Are you interested in keeping any kind of domestic pet? Why would you choose this one? Why do people in general keep pets?

General guidance and practice

Revision of the uses of 'Should' and 'Would'

Notice the principal uses:

(*a*) *Reported speech.* (With certain exceptions 'would' is common to all persons.)

(*b*) *In the result clause in the second and third type of conditional sentence.* (Normally 'should' is used in the First and 'would' in the Second and Third Persons.)

Notice also forms like 'I should be pleased to . . .', 'We should like to . . .' which may be described as the first half of a conditional sentence, with an understood ending: 'if I might', or 'if you did not mind'.

(*c*) *Ought to.* ('Should' in all persons.)

(*d*) *As an alternative to 'used to'* when some intention is indicated. 'would' in all persons.)

(*e*) *In requests.* (Would you please . . .) (This is also a form of condition.)

Use a form of the verb incorporating 'would' or 'should' in each of the following sentences. Explain which of the above forms you are making use of:

(*a*) When we were children, we (dawdle) to school.
(*b*) If I were you, I (refuse) to carry out his orders.
(*c*) (Remove) please your shoes from the table.
(*d*) You (persevere) in your ambition: don't get discouraged.
(*e*) He said he did not know whether he (join) the association.
(*f*) The butter (melt) if it had been left near the stove any longer.
(*g*) People who live in glasshouses (not throw) stones.
(*h*) The film star received a letter saying that his son (kidnap) if he did not hand over five thousand pounds. (Passive Voice.)
(*i*) The defeated general announced that his army (surrender).
(*j*) Many years ago country women (spend) much of their time spinning thread and weaving cloth.
(*k*) (Have) you time to knit me a cardigan for next winter?
(*l*) That dog (not keep) outside in his kennel in such bitterly cold weather. (Passive Voice.)
(*m*) He (work) all the afternoon if you had not disturbed him.

Notice the occasional use of the simple past of the verb 'will' followed by the infinitive in the 'if' clause when willingness is indicated. This resembles a conditional form but is not really one.

I should be pleased if you would help your friend with his pronunciation.
It would help me very much if you would all be punctual to meals.
In a first condition, 'should' can suggest even greater improbability.
If you should get lost, you can easily take a taxi.
Take out an insurance in case you should be ill.

(German students—Otherwise, avoid 'would' and 'should' in all conditional clauses.)

Inclusion and omission of the definite and indefinite articles

A noun used in an abstract sense is not accompanied by the definite article unless it is defined in some way.

We all admire courage.
The book describes the courage of a small group of explorers.
The courage that can endure uncomplainingly a long period of suffering is perhaps the noblest.

A noun which is abstract when used in one sense may be common and therefore accompanied by either a definite or indefinite article in some other sense. Examples of some of these nouns are given in Chapter 7, Exercise 5 and they include:

truth, power, light, youth, life, authority, character, virtue.

Is youth the best part of life?
The youth was serving as a building apprentice.
He enjoys life.
He is interested in the life of Cromwell.
He has had an exciting life.

Nature has no definite article when the creative force is referred to.

Weather may be accompanied by 'the' but not by 'a'.

Space—without an article is used as noun and adjective to refer to outer space, and as a noun to space in general. 'The space' refers to the distance between two objects or times.

Gerunds have no article when they refer to the action done, provided they are not limited by a following phrase: 'The writing of books . . .'. A gerund may be accompanied by an article or demonstrative adjective when referring to the product of the action:

I can't read this writing.
We admired the painting.
The singing sounded pleasant.

Remember that an uncountable noun is not in normal circumstances preceded by the indefinite article: bread, money, linen, rain.

Insert definite or indefinite articles *where they are needed* in the following sentences:

(*a*) .... generosity of the old lady was appreciated by all who knew her.

(*b*) .... pride goes before a fall.

(*c*) She has lived .... life of self-sacrifice.

(*d*) .... life is not always what one makes it.

(*e*) Mankind is now exploring .... space.

(*f*) Why not fill .... space between the two houses with a garage?

(*g*) .... riding is a popular form of exercise.

(*h*) He rebels against .... authority.

(*i*) He has been given .... authority over the department.

(*j*) .... local authority controls the public library.

(*k*) Do you believe that statesmen always tell .... truth?

(*l*) I doubt .... truth of his statement.

(*m*) .... truth is not always a comforting virtue.

(*n*) What .... weather! I have never experienced such .... chilly weather in August.

(*o*) .... weather in England is very variable.

(*p*) He is interested in the study of .... nature.

(*q*) .... age often envies .... youth.

(*r*) .... youth touched his cap politely and offered his help with my bag.

(*s*) You have .... power to set matters right.

(*t*) The development of .... nuclear power is one of the major tasks of science to-day.

(*u*) Representatives of .... great powers are meeting in Geneva.

(*v*) .... power does not always corrupt.

(*w*) He had no high opinion of .... singing of the opera but .... acting was superb.

(*x*) .... teaching should be a profession of a high standard.

(*y*) .... teaching we had was not of a high standard.

(*z*) .... drawing shows imagination and skill.

The use of commas

Rules for the use of commas are far less rigid than those in many other languages, and writers vary in the extent to which they employ them. The underlying principle is that the comma indicates a pause of some kind, though it is clear that many pauses are not indicated by commas.

Subordinate noun clauses are not separated off as in Germanic languages:

What you have told me amazes me.
I do not understand what they are saying.
The possession of wealth is what many people desire.

In none of the above cases: noun clause as subject, object and complement respectively, could a comma be used.

Here are a few cases where the comma is normally employed:

(i) To separate phrases in apposition:

Mr. Herbert Smith, the Mayor of Chelmbury, is highly respected in the town.

(ii) Before opening inverted commas within a sentence and when closing them before the end of the sentence:

He whispered, 'Be careful to keep this hidden,' before adding in his normal voice, 'and is your father quite better?'

(iii) To separate off non-defining clauses:

The village of Axton, which dates from Saxon times, will be flooded by the new reservoir.

(iv) To separate the items in a list. A comma is not usual before the final connecting 'and'.

During his life he has collected stamps, butterflies, first editions, antiques, orchids, coins and pepper pots.

(v) When a noun is qualified by two or more adjectives of more than one syllable, the adjectives themselves may be separated by a comma.

He has an abrupt, unpleasant manner of speaking.

(vi) After an opening adverbial clause or, often, after an opening participial phrase. When the main clause comes first, the comma is much less usual.

As he speaks four languages fluently, he hopes to become an interpreter.
He has difficulty in expressing himself as he stammers badly.
Meeting him unexpectedly, I forgot to ask him about his new job.

(vii) After certain introductory phrases which are not essential parts of the sentence, a comma is sometimes used.

e.g. On the other hand, . . .; In brief, . . .;
In any case, . . .; On the contrary, . . .;

A comma may also separate off words like 'however' or 'therefore'. In other cases, rules are very far from rigid, and there are many variations in usage.

Insert commas *where necessary* in the following sentences:

(*a*) The signpost which was leaning sideways seemed to have been there at least a hundred years.

(*b*) He glared suspiciously at the newcomers and then muttered 'I loathe every one of them' adding more threateningly 'clear off before I do you some harm.'

(*c*) The traditional English Sunday dinner consists of roast beef Yorkshire pudding baked potatoes brussels sprouts and gravy.

(*d*) Mr. Aloysius Marbleduck Member of Parliament for Chisley has never been defeated in an election.

(*e*) With certain exceptions all civilians are expected to carry on with their normal duties.

(*f*) If I had a spade I could dig the garden.

(*g*) The statue of Colonel Trot which will be unveiled on Saturday is very impressive.

(*h*) The rumour which is spreading through the village now suggests that a film is to be made in the neighbourhood.

(*i*) I don't understand what you are talking about.

(*j*) He was a tall dark man wearing a ragged untidy ill-fitting raincoat.

Uses of 'Whose'

(i) *Interrogative adjective*

Whose umbrella is this?

Whose camera are you using?
I don't know whose gloves these are.

(ii) *Interrogative pronoun*

Whose is this?
Can you tell me whose this is?

(iii) *Relative pronoun*

SUBJECT: We were talking to the woman whose husband was arrested yesterday.

OBJECT: This is Mr. Atkins, whose book you reviewed last week.
May I introduce you to Mr. Lane, whose cousin you used to live with.
(Notice the word order.)

Where *things* are involved, either 'whose' or 'of which' may be employed:

This is a work of art whose value will be even more highly esteemed by future generations.
(or:—a work of art the value of which—)

Either complete the existing sentence or add another one introducing the word 'whose' in each of the following examples. A suggestion of the sense of the addition is given at the end of each sentence.

(*a*) This valuable sword must have been owned by some great leader. I wonder ...... (be).

(*b*) I have found some gloves. ...... (be)?

(*c*) To-day's sermon was preached by a missionary, ... (life; spend; Africa).

(*d*) At the funeral the chief mourner was the tragic father, ... had killed. (son; the bandits).

(*e*) This is the famous ancient olive-tree, ... (age; unknown).

(*f*) The film star, ..., has given an interview to the press. (new film; show; London).

(*g*) We shall have to select one of these three drawings: John's, Geoffrey's or Mildred's. ......?

(*h*) The director of the company was obviously one of those men ...... (life; devoted to business).

Adverbs

(*a*) The normal rule for forming an adverb is to add -ly to the adjective;

slow slowly
beautiful beautifully

When an adjective already ends in this -l accordingly becomes doubled:

cruel cruelly

(*b*) Spelling changes include the dropping of a final -e when the adjective ends in -le. The same change affects the adjective 'true'.

true truly; whole wholly;
able ably; regrettable regrettably;

but notice: immediate immediately.

(*c*) In certain cases -y changes to -i in polysyllables:

merry merrily

and also in monosyllables ending in -ay: gay, gaily (or gayly) though most monosyllables retain the -y:

dryly, slyly, shyly, coyly.

(*d*) Certain adjectives ending in -ic add an -al before the -ly:

e.g. pathetic pathetically
characteristic characteristically.

Notice: accident (noun) accidental (adjective)
accidentally (adverb)

(*e*) Adverbs cannot be formed in the normal way from adjectives ending in -ly. An adverbial phrase must be used.

friendly in a friendly way }
lively in a lively manner } according to meaning

A similar difficulty applies to certain Past Participles including: tired, bored, frightened, annoyed, worried, offended.

He spoke sharply, as if he were annoyed.
He turned his back on me, as though offended.

There is no adverb from 'difficult'; 'with difficulty' is the usual adverbial phrase.

(*f*) Some adjectives do not change. These include: hourly, weekly, monthly, yearly, fast, hard (compare 'he works hard' with 'he hardly works').
Other adverbial phrases are: every minute, every day (compare with the adjective 'everyday'), once a century, etc.

(*g*) There is the well-known change: good: well.

(*h*) Some adjectives change in meaning when transformed into adverbs. These include:

present	presently	direct	directly ('direct' may be an adverb)
scarce	scarcely	hard	hardly ('hard' may be an adverb)
bare	barely	high	highly ('high' is also an adverb)
mere	merely	short	shortly ('short' may be an adverb: stop short)

---

near	nearly	('near' is also an adverb)
big	large	largely (for the most part)

Notice also the adverbs: *exceedingly*, *extremely*, *immensely*, meaning 'very' in a strong sense and the two adjective forms: *low*, *lowly; kind*, *kindly.*

Give the adverbial form for each of the adjectives in brackets. Do not change the meaning of the sentence:

(*a*) He works (hard).

(*b*) He was (eager) waiting his turn to answer.

(*c*) She greeted me (friendly).

(*d*) Dustmen often empty dustbins (noisy).

(*e*) She paints (good).

(*f*) He climbed the steps (difficult).

(*g*) He is paid (weekly).

(*h*) He is (whole) sincere.

(*i*) He yawned (bored).

(*j*) I dropped it (accidental).

(*k*) We were entertained (royal).

(*l*) She spoke (sympathetic).

(*m*) She smiled (coy).

(*n*) He commented (dry) on the speech.

(*o*) He has promised to come (present). He won't be long.

(*p*) I (mere) asked a question.

(*q*) They giggled (silly).

(*r*) I shall have finished (short).

(*s*) Can I go from Waterloo to Southampton (direct)?

(*t*) He'll be back (direct).

For Since During In

These are all prepositions when used in time phrases.

SINCE can also be a conjunction with a time meaning.

FOR is used to indicate *a length of time*, which passed, has passed, is passing or will pass.

He had travelled *for twenty-four hours*, and he stayed there *for twenty minutes*.
I have already been in England *for three months*.
I am staying in England *for three years*; then I shall go to France.
The acrobats will perform *for a quarter of an hour*.

SINCE as a preposition also indicates a period of time, but *the moment when the period began is indicated*. It is normally used only with perfect tenses, and is rarely used in the future. If the group of words introduced by the conjunction 'since' is a subordinate clause, the Past Simple tense may follow in this clause, though a Perfect Tense will appear in the main clause.

The rain had never stopped *since the time they had* arrived at the holiday resort.

That pipe has been leaking ever *since the plumber installed* a new tank.

DURING *never* indicates length of time.

You cannot say 'I am here during six months.' (Nor can you say, 'I am here since six months.')

During indicates 'in the course of', 'within a certain space of time':

during the interval, during his childhood, during the epidemic.
You must not talk *during his lecture.*
The barrister has dealt with many unusual cases *during his long career.*

IN as a preposition indicating time can be used with three different meanings:

(*a*) Before the end of; in the space of:

If I run, I can get to the station *in five minutes.*

(*b*) at the end of:

The skirt will be ready for you *in a fortnight.*
I shall start work *in a month* (*in a month's time*).

(*c*) To indicate the year, season, month, period of the day in which something happens: *in 1215, in summer, in March, in the afternoon.*

FOR and SINCE may also be used as conjunctions with other meanings.

FOR is a co-ordinating conjunction: that is to say, it can link two clauses of equal importance. When used in this way, it can never begin a sentence. The subordinating conjunctions 'as' or 'because' are far more commonly used.

He knows no one in the town, *for* he has only recently settled down here.

SINCE, a subordinating conjunction, has much the same meaning. It may begin a sentence:

Since you know so much, perhaps you can tell me why you made such a simple mistake.

Insert prepositions 'for', 'since', 'during', 'in' or conjunctions 'for' or 'since' where appropriate in the following sentences:

(*a*) She must have been wearing that hat .... Noah came out of the ark.
(*b*) .... the Great Plague of London .... 1665, hundreds of people were dying every day.
(*c*) I wanted the photographs developed .... not more than five hours.
(*d*) .... he had no ladder, the workman could not erect the television aerial.
(*e*) The strikers have agreed to discuss their grievance with the employers .... two days' time.
(*f*) Nobody knows what became of him .... he never came back.
(*g*) The guarantee lasts .... one year.
(*h*) He has been looking poorly ever .... his serious illness.

(*i*) Many great discoveries were made .... the reign of Queen Elizabeth I.

(*j*) .... you refuse to give me further particulars, I regret that I cannot help you.

(*k*) Having dozed .... half an hour, he was ready to concentrate .... the next four hours.

(*l*) .... he was released from prison, he has managed to keep out of further trouble.

Adverbial expressions with 'At', 'In' or 'On'

AT

at the beginning
at the end (in the end = after all, finally)
at the top
at the bottom
at the side
at the front of the class
at the back of the class
at school
at church

at eight o'clock
at night(fall)
at dawn
at dusk
at Christmas
at the week-end
at present
at home
at sea
at table (eating)

He arrived at the Airport.
Meet me at the far corner of the park.

Notice: The Secretary was sitting *at a table.*
Her typewriter was *on the table.*
The committee sat *round a table.*

IN

in 1837
in February
in winter
in the morning
in the afternoon
in the evening
in daylight
in darkness
(during the day)
in the past
in the future
in time
in the eleventh century
in front of
the fish in the sea
in the sky

in the middle of
in the midst of
in the North
in Japan
in Surrey
in the street
in the road
in the theatre
(or: at the theatre)
in a car
in an armchair
in a deck chair
in my hand
in prison
in the open air
in a loud voice

The bookcase stands in the corner.
He arrived in London.
She has a ribbon in her hair.

On Tuesday (But: He came last Tuesday
He will come next year)

on the 1st April
on his birthday
on the wall
on the blackboard
on a chair
on a bicycle
on one's knees
The shop stands on the corner
a hat on his head
shoes on his feet
(gloves in his hands—carried)
(gloves on his hands—worn)

on the ceiling
on top of the wardrobe
on both sides
on a horse
on foot
on the wireless, on the radio
on television
a smile on his face

Notice: I go home I arrive home I am at home I leave home.

an old man *with a grey beard*
a woman *with a quiet voice*
a man *with slippers on*
a cat *with green eyes*
an actor *with a strong personality*

In some of the above examples other prepositions may be used according to meaning. One leans *against* a wall for example. The ones given above are the most usual forms.

Where necessary replace the blanks in these sentences with a suitable preposition.

(*a*) The child has a balloon .... his hand.

(*b*) There is a big cobweb .... the corner of the attic.

(*c*) She has an emerald ring .... her third finger.

(*d*) The liner arrived .... Liverpool .... six o'clock .... the morning.

(*e*) The beautiful mermaid .... long golden hair and .... a silver comb .... her hand was sitting .... a rock .... the sea, singing happily .... a clear voice.

(*f*) The distinguished visitors were sitting .... chairs .... a platform .... one end of the hall. There was a loudspeaker .... the wall .... the back of the hall.

(*g*) The unhappy recruit, with boots that were too big for him .... his feet and a hat that was too small for him .... his head, was .... his knees .... the floor, a scrubbing brush .... his hand, and a bucket .... front of him, trying to remove the oil and grease from the surface.

(*h*) For your homework do the exercise .... the top of page three, and give it in to me .... Wednesday.

(*i*) He arrived .... home .... half past two .... the afternoon and left .... home .... a quarter to twelve .... night.

Prepositions

Insert suitable prepositions in the following sentences:

(*a*) The prisoner of war escaped .... the fortress.

(*b*) The class treated the teacher's suggestion of extra homework .... silent contempt.

(*c*) She kept fidgeting .... her watch strap and appeared to be in a highly nervous state.

(*d*) He was crouching on a bench in the corner brooding .... his disappointment.

(*e*) One .... one the Members of Parliament filed into the lobbies.

(*f*) Many foreigners in England have considerable difficulty .... making themselves understood.

(*g*) Aren't you ashamed .... your selfish behaviour?

(*h*) The millionaire had a passion .... orchids.

(*i*) At Christmas English homes are often decorated .... holly, mistletoe and paper chains.

(*j*) We must get rid .... that elm tree: it is damaging the foundations of the house.

(*k*) The clergyman reproached the youth .... his thoughtlessness towards his parents.

(*l*) Some people laugh .... the creations of many modern sculptors.

(*m*) A child's life is usually made up .... many small but absorbing experiences.

(*n*) He gave me a gold sovereign .... a present.

(*o*) Science is still largely ignorant .... the causes of many kinds of cancer.

(*p*) The puppy was playing .... a slipper.

(*q*) Most boys are keen .... football.

(*r*) The majority of the club's supporters were doubtful .... the team's chances in the coming match.

(*s*) The clown was so comical that even the circus attendants burst .... laughing.

(*t*) The boy had been up to mischief again and again and at last he was sent to bed .... disgrace.

(*u*) Are you really impressed .... the nonsense he talks?

(*v*) The lorry was travelling .... a considerable speed when the accident happened.

(*w*) The Government has embarked .... a new economy scheme.

(*x*) He bowed low to the aged leader .... a sign of respect.

14

Passage for comprehension

Ghosts for tea

'Ten pence for a view over the bay,' said the old man with the telescope. 'Lovely clear morning. Have a look at the old lighthouse and the remains of the great shipwreck of 1935.'

Ten pence was sheer robbery, but the view was certainly magnificent. 5 Cliffs stretched into the distance, sparkling waves whipped by the wind were unrolling on to the beach, and a few yachts, with creamy-white sails, were curving and dodging gracefully on the sea. Just below, a flock of seagulls were screaming at one another as they twisted and glided over the water. A mile out to sea, the old lighthouse stood on a stone platform on the rocks, 10 which were being greedily licked by the waves. In no way indeed did I grudge my money. As I directed the telescope towards the lighthouse, the man beside me tapped my wrist.

'Have you heard about the terrible tragedy that occurred there in that lighthouse?' he asked in a hushed whisper.

15 'I imagine there may be plenty of legends attached to such a dramatic-looking place,' I suggested.

'It's no legend,' declared the old man. 'My father knew the two men involved. It all took place fifty years ago to-day. Let me tell you.'

His voice seemed to grow deeper and more dramatic.

20 'For a whole week that lighthouse had been isolated by storms,' he began, 'with terrifying seas surging and crashing over the rocks. People on shore were anxious about the two men working there. They'd been on the best of terms until two or three weeks before, when they had quarrelled over cards in the village inn. Martin had accused Blake of cheating. Blake had vowed to 25 avenge the insult to his honour. But thanks to the wise advice of a man they both respected, they apologised to each other, and soon seemed to have got over their disagreement. But some slight resentment and bitterness remained, and it was feared that the strain of continued isolation and rough weather might affect their nerves, though, needless to say, their friends had no idea 30 how serious the consequences would be.

'Fifty years ago to-night, no light appeared in the tower, and only at two o'clock in the morning did the beam suddenly start to flash out its warning again.

'The next morning the light was still visible. The storm had almost blown 35 itself out, so a relief boat set out to investigate. A grim discovery awaited the crew. The men's living-room was in a horrifying state. The table was overturned: a pack of playing cards was scattered everywhere: bloodstains splashed the floor. The relief men climbed the winding stair to the lantern room and there discovered Martin's body, crouched beside the burning lamp. He had been stabbed and was dead. Two days later, Blake's body was 40 washed up, scratched, bruised, and terribly injured.

'Only then could we really start guessing what had happened. This great tragedy could only have been due to a renewal of their quarrel. Bored and depressed as a result of their isolation, Martin and Blake must have started to play cards. Again suspecting cheating, Martin had accused his former 45 friend of dishonesty; a fight had broken out and Blake had seized his knife. In a fit of madness he had attacked his companion, who had fallen mortally wounded. Then, appalled by what he had done, the loneliness, the battering of wind and waves, Blake had rushed to the parapet and flung himself on to the rocks below, where the sea had claimed him. 50

'But Martin was still alive. Hours later, after darkness had fallen, he had recovered consciousness. He remembered his job of lighting the lamp; suffering intense pain, the poor wretch crawled slowly up the winding staircase, dragging himself from step to step till he got to the lantern. At his last gasp he managed to light this before finally collapsing. 55

'For years afterwards it was said that the lighthouse was haunted, and, owing to these stories, they didn't have any applicants for the job of lighthouse-keeper from among the superstitious local inhabitants. And now they say that on every anniversary of that day, especially when the sea is rough, you can stand in the living-room, hear the cards falling and the sound of 60 angry cries, see the flash of a blade, and then glimpse a figure rushing to the parapet. And then you hear the slow dragging of a body from step to step towards the room above.'

The old man paused and I turned to go.

'By the way,' he added, 'have you any free time this afternoon? If so, 65 why don't you have tea in the lighthouse? We are putting on a special boat trip to-day. We're charging a pound. And my brother, who bought the old lighthouse when they built the new one just on the point, can serve very good teas there—included in the price of the boat trip—a bargain, considering the problem of obtaining the food. And if you are at all sensitive to the 70 supernatural, you're likely to have an unusual, perhaps an uncanny experience there.'

I eyed him appreciatively. 'You're wasting your talents,' I said. 'You should have been a fiction writer.'

'You don't believe it?' exclaimed the old man indignantly. 75

'I'd find it a job,' I answered. 'My father, Henry Cox, started as keeper of that lighthouse fifty-two years ago, and he and Jim Dowley, now retired on a pension, were in charge for ten years. Come and see my dad one day with that tale; he'd enjoy it.'

But the old man had already turned his attention to a more likely client. 80

Notes on the passage

Vocabulary

line

1 *a view:* usually a wide area seen from a certain point which may be a high one. An opinion can also be called a view: *one's political views.*
a viewpoint: can be a place from which a view is seen or an opinion.
a point of view: (more commonly used for 'an opinion').
a sight: something seen: *the ceremony was an interesting sight.*
an outlook: (*a*) what can be seen when looking out, possibly from a window. (*b*) what seems likely to happen: *the weather outlook.*
scenery: the general appearance of the countryside to the passer-by.
a landscape: scenery seen as a kind of picture: *a landscape painter.*
a scene: (*a*) a division of an act of a play. (*b*) a view, usually having a definite quality: *the breath-taking scene of the moon rising over the sea.* (*c*) the place where something happened: *the scene of the crime.* (*d*) an unpleasant display of bad temper or emotion: *to make a scene.*
the countryside: the characteristic region away from the town. This is similar in meaning to 'the country'.
Nature: the natural creative force as part of the countryside. NEVER: speak of 'the' Nature: there is no definite article. One cannot speak of admiring Nature: *they admired the beautiful scenery* (*or countryside*). It is possible however to study Nature.

Which? He enjoys wandering in the........; the mountain hotel offered magnificent........; the spoilt actor enjoyed making awkward........; he has no political........; the romantic ....of Norway; the........in the motor industry is depressing; this is the........of the accident; the very........ of food made him feel worse; the........from his room is far from cheerful; I prefer his........pictures to his portraits; ....has adapted these creatures to their surroundings; the Coronation was a brilliant.........

Notice the following expressions: a bird's-eye view; a view-finder (part of a camera);
in view of: *In view of the dangerous condition of the building, the public cannot be admitted until it is repaired.*
the sights of London; come into sight; go out of sight; know someone by sight; fall in love at first sight. sight-read (music); lose sight of.

1 *telescope* telegram telegraph television telepathy: *tele-* in each case meaning 'distant'.
microscope periscope horoscope: *-scope* in each case meaning 'see'.
scope can mean the range of a person's opportunities: *His present job provides little scope for his artistic talents.*

4 *sheer:* (*a*) a sheer drop of eight metres: a quite vertical drop
(*b*) sheer silk: so light and delicate that it is transparent
(*c*) a sheer waste of time: complete, absolute

5 *a whip* is sometimes used when horse-riding.
Other equipment is: *the harness; the saddle; the reins; the bridle.*
At one time *spurs* were used to urge the horse on: *Ambition spurred him on.*
whipped cream has been beaten to make it firm.

6 a *sail* of a ship; the *sale* of a house; spring sales in the shops. a nun wears a *veil.*
Even a steamer can sail: *The 'Queen Elizabeth' will sail at four o'clock.*

7 *curve:* (*N* and *V*): a rounded line. *bend* (*N* and *V*): a line which turns in another direction—also: bend down; bend forward. *fork* (*N* and *V*) a division in a line which goes in two directions.
A road can curve, bend and fork.
An S-bend; a hairpin bend; a roundabout = a large island in the middle of a road junction which traffic must move round; a turning; a cul-de-sac or no thoroughfare.

11 *grudge:* (*N* and *V*—though with a meaning change).
NOUN a feeling of bitterness resulting from the belief that one has been ill-treated: *The men bore a grudge against their employer who refused their claim for higher wages.*
'to have a grievance' suggests the *cause* of the bitterness: a grudge is the bitter feeling itself.

VERB: to give with extreme unwillingness: *The miser grudged his wife even her food. The scientist grudged even time for eating and sleeping.*

ADVERB: grudgingly: *He gave the money grudgingly.*

12 Compare *wrist* = part of the arm and *fist* = the clenched or closed hand.

15 *attached to:* joined to: *A label was attached to the string.* Also: fond of: *She is very attached to her cat.*

23 *term* and *terms* have various meanings:
(*a*) there are usually three terms in a school year or session
(*b*) items agreed to in a contract or treaty (always plural)
(*c*) a price, especially for a service: *hotel terms* (always plural).
(*d*) conditions: *We did not agree to his terms for the release of the hostages.* (always plural)
(*e*) personal relations: *They are on good (bad) terms with each other.* (always plural)

29 *affect* (*V only*) *effect* (*N* and *V*): these are often mixed.
affect: influence: *The dry weather has affected the quality of the fruit.*
effect (*N*)*:* result: *It has had a bad effect on the quality of the fruit.*
effect (*V*): cause a certain result: changes, improvements, are effected.
Notice: to have a good (bad) effect on.

32 a *beam* of light (a sunbeam). He *beamed* (smiled happily) with pleasure.
A beam can also be a strong supporting bar of wood below a ceiling.

35 *relief* (*N*)*:* the taking away of a heavy burden or worry: *There is no danger of my losing my job after all. What a relief!*
The drug provided a temporary relief from pain.

relieved (*Adj*)*:* with the same meaning: *She was relieved to find her children safe.*

relieve (*V*)*:* (*a*) take over someone's job to allow him to rest: *The sentry was at last relieved and could eat and sleep.* (*N*) *a relief* is the person who does this.

(*b*) drive away an army besieging a town: *After a six-month siege, the town was relieved by an allied army.* (*N*) *the relief of the city.*

relief (*Adj*)*:* (*a*) A relief fund for flood, famine or earthquake victims to provide them with food and shelter.

(*b*) a relief bus to take home the extra large crowds.

(*c*) a relief map, showing comparative heights by colours.

35 *grim:* frighteningly serious: *grim reports of starvation in famine areas.* The meaning is not 'cruel'.

gaunt: suggests the thinness following serious illness or hunger when the bone structure is visible.

38 *winding:* wind (*Pron* waind) wool; wind up a clock or a clockwork toy.

Do not confuse: wind wound wound (*Pron* waund) with the other verb: wound (*Pron* wu:nd) wounded wounded: cause injury in war. The Noun *wind* (which blows) is pronounced wind.

40 *stab* Here are a few ways in which the victim in a detective story can be *murdered:*

He may be *stabbed* (with a knife), *poisoned, strangled, suffocated, hanged, gassed* or *pushed over a cliff.* As a result, he *dies* (died died) and when he *is dead* there is an *inquest* presided over by a *coroner.* The doctor who has carried out the *post-mortem* to discover the causes of death will give *evidence.*

41 *scratch:* (*N* and *V*)*:* people scratch with their *nails:* cats with their claws.

This causes a scratch on the skin. Furniture may get scratched.

Potatoes are *scraped* or (like apples) *peeled* later.

Floors are *scrubbed* with a *scrubbing-brush* or washed with some kind of *mop.*

A table is *polished* by *rubbing* polish over it on a cloth.

45 *play cards*, football, chess. *play the piano*, the violin, the trumpet.

play a game. play at Red Indians with small boys.

act on the stage. *act or perform* in a play. *play the part of* Hamlet.

53 *intense* pain, effort, heat, light. an *intensive* study course, lasting only three months.

58 *superstitious* people never walk under ladders: Noun: superstition.

suspicious can describe a feeling: *the dog was suspicious of strangers* and can also describe what causes the feeling: *A suspicious-looking man seemed to be watching the house.*

61 a knife *blade* and also a *blade of grass.*

69 *a bargain:* (a) an agreement in which each person may give up something to get a result that is generally accepted: *We made a bargain that I*

should cook dinner and he would wash up after. After a long discussion, a bargain was made and the carpet was bought for £20.

(b) something of good value that is bought cheaply: *It is sometimes possible to find a good bargain in sales and auctions.*

(c) to bargain: to discuss the price of something: *After a lot of bargaining, he bought the ring at a satisfactory price.*

76 *I'd find it a job:* I should find it difficult.

80 A shopkeeper has a *customer;* a solicitor has a *client;* a doctor has a *patient.*

Pronunciation

ə as in *a*go: *o*ccurred [əkɔ́ːd]; leg*e*nds [lédʒəndz]; is*o*lated [áɪsəleɪtɪd]; *a*pol*o*gise [əpɔ́lədʒaɪz]; par*a*pet [pærəpɪt]; sup*e*rstiti*o*ns [suːpəstíʃəns]; *a*precia*t*ively [əpríʃɪətɪvlɪ]; indign*a*ntly [ɪndígnəntlɪ].

ɪ as in cit*y*: television [télɪvɪʒən]; imagine [ɪmǽdʒɪn]; declare [dɪkléə]; cons*e*quences [kɔ́nsɪkwənsɪz]; barg*ain* [báːgɪn].

OTHER SOUNDS: view [vjuː]; yacht [jɔt]; wretch [retʃ].

Special grammatical and structural points

(*a*) *each other one another*

Earlier *each other* suggested that two people were concerned, *one another* that three or more people were involved.

Nowadays *one another* is often used in the case of two people also. Notice these expressions:

They looked *at* each other/one another in surprise.
They did a lot *for* each other/one another.
They are not speaking *to* each other/one another.
They had to be separated *from* each other/one another.
They have little confidence *in* each other/one another.

(*b*) VERBAL CONSTRUCTIONS

Infinitive: vow to avenge

Infinitive expressing Purpose: a boat set out to investigate

Gerund: accuse someone of doing something

Clause: I imagine (that) there may be many legends. . . .
I had no idea of how late it was.

Prepositions

(*a*) *in* a whisper/in a loud voice. (Notice: say something aloud. Not: in a high voice.)
in a horrifying state.

(*b*) *on* good terms with; on every anniversary of that day.

Multiple choice questions

Here are a number of questions or unfinished statements about the passage, each with four suggested ways of answering or finishing it. You must choose the way you consider the most suitable. Write in each case the bracketed number of the question or statement followed by the letters **A, B, C, D,** and then cross through the letter of the answer you choose. Give one answer only to each question. Read the passage right through again before choosing your answers.

1 The writer thought that the charge was sheer robbery because
A the man was asking too much for what he was offering **B** the view was really not worth much **C** this was a quite large sum of money **D** the man was forcing him to pay against his will

2 What was the weather like?
A calm and sunny **B** windy and grey **C** a strong gale was blowing **D** windy and bright

3 After using the telescope the writer felt
A angry at having paid **B** that he had wasted his money **C** that the view had been worth the money **D** that he would not miss the money paid

4 By speaking of legends, the writer suggested that the old man's story would be
A very old **B** largely imaginary **C** very interesting **D** completely untrue

5 Immediately after Martin's accusation Blake swore that he would
A punish Martin for what he had said **B** prove that what Martin had said was untrue **C** refuse to play again with anyone who could behave in this way **D** challenge Martin to a duel

6 Their friends were slightly worried about the two men because
A the unusually stormy weather could have a bad effect on their relationship **B** the strain on their nerves might interfere with their work **C** they were both irritable and excitable men **D** they had never really liked one another.

7 Why did the relief boat go out to investigate?
A the sea was calm again **B** the storm might have caused damage **C** the light was still on in daylight **D** a warning light had flashed out during the night

8 The main reason for Blake's injuries was
A the knife fight with Martin **B** he had stabbed himself **C** his fall from the lighthouse **D** the force of the sea and storm

9 Why had Blake attacked Martin?
A Martin had cheated at cards **B** Blake had suspected Martin of cheating **C** Blake had been furious about what Martin had said of him **D** Blake himself had cheated

10 Why would no one apply for the job of lighthouse-keeper?
A the loneliness of the lighthouse **B** the building was old and inconvenient **C** people were afraid of ghosts **D** people were afraid of a similar thing happening again.

11 Why did the old man tell this story?
A he enjoyed telling such an exciting tale **B** it made him feel important **C** he wanted to attract customers for the trip **D** he hoped his listeners would persuade other people to use his telescope.

Reading comprehension

(i) In this exercise you must choose the word or phrase which best completes each sentence. Write first the number of each sentence followed by the letters **A, B, C, D, E,** and then cross through the letter of the correct answer in each case.

1 Switzerland is well-known for its impressive mountainous ....
A views **B** scenes **C** scenery **D** sights **E** Nature

2 He has to arrange for the .... of his furniture before he goes abroad.
A sale **B** sole **C** seal **D** veil **E** sail

3 The bank .... planned to escape in a stolen car.
A thieves **B** bandits **C** burglars **D** robbers **E** kidnappers

4 My aunt .... a brightly-coloured thread round her finger so as not to forget her appointment.
A wound **B** curved **C** wounded **D** rang **E** bound

5 As the clouds drifted away an even higher peak became .... to the climbers.
A in sight **B** conspicuous **C** visible **D** obvious **E** apparent

6 We have a .... future ahead with little comfort, food or hope.
A cruel **B** grim **C** pessimistic **D** fierce **E** violent

7 Prices continued to rise while wages remained low .... the Government became increasingly unpopular.
A on condition that **B** with the result that **C** provided that **D** on the chance that **E** in order that

8 An historical novel is a form of .... which may include many facts.
A legend **B** fairy-tale **C** fantasy **D** short story **E** fiction

9 They lay almost flat and .... through the tube-like underground passage.
A crouched **B** crawled **C** glided **D** scrambled **E** slid

10 High in the sky a .... of birds was flying southward.
A pack **B** swarm **C** flock **D** crowd **E** herd

Use of English

1 (ii) The five phrases below are the answers to five questions that could be asked about the reading passage. Write out the questions.

(i) a lovely clear morning (ii) in a hushed whisper (iii) for a whole week (iv) to investigate (v) a pound

2 At each number (i) to (xx) in the following passage there is a blank space to be filled with one or more words. Write down the numbers (i) to (xx), and against each the most suitable word or phrase.

'I'm sorry, sir,' said the bank clerk, 'we can't let you have these travellers' (i) .... until we've entered details in your passport.'

'But I've only got five hours,' said Phillip, anxiously, 'my plane is leaving (ii) .... evening.'

'We remain open (iii) .... three o'clock,' the clerk told him.

So when Phillip was on his way to the airport (iv) .... that afternoon, he asked the driver to wait outside the bank (v) .... he collected the cheques.

The plane was to leave at half-past five and there was still a long (vi) .... to the air terminal. For a time Phillip merely watched his surroundings, but shortly before (vii) .... his destination, he began checking the things he would need for boarding the plane. Tickets, money, the address of his hotel, travellers' cheques. Yes, (viii) .... was there. Just a moment, though. How (ix) .... his passport? Horrified, Phillip went through his pockets. He suddenly (x) .... that he must have (xi) .... his passport at the bank, though he had no memory of doing so.

Whatever could he do? It was now five past four and so there would be (xii) .... little time to return to the bank, which would in (xiii) .... case be closed now. This was the first time he was representing his firm and he had an important appointment with the manager of an insurance firm in Paris at ten o'clock the following morning. Without a passport he (xiv) .... to board the plane.

(xv) .... that moment, the taxi drew up outside the air terminal. Not knowing what to do next, Phillip got (xvi) ...., took his suitcase and paid the (xvii) .... He then became aware of a good deal of confusion in the building. A voice could be heard over the loudspeaker.

'We very much regret that owing to a twenty-four-hour strike of airport staff, all flights for the rest of to-day have had to be (xviii) .... Passengers are advised to get into touch with their travel agents or with this terminal for details of to-morrow's flights.'

The voice continued to give advice and instructions. Phillip gave a deep (xix) .... of relief. He would have to let his firm know about this situation but, thank goodness, he would have the (xx) .... of calling at his bank the following morning to recover his passport.

3 Complete each of the following with an appropriate phrase like the one shown in the examples. Write out the whole sentence.

Examples: He sat down in the armchair he thought of buying *to see how comfortable it was.*

The inspector asked the class a lot of questions *to see how much they knew.*

(i) He took the temperature of the bath water ....

(ii) We asked when the dog had been born ....

(iii) He counted the number of students in the room ....

(iv) When the train arrived at last, I looked at my watch ....

(v) She counted the money in her purse ....

(vi) She checked the distance to London on a map ....

4 Column A lists twelve sentence openings, each of which can be completed by one of the endings in Column B. Write twelve sentences, consisting of each of the sentence openings followed by a suitable ending.

	A	B
	wanted	
	suggested	
	would like	
	thought	to watch television
	did not mind	
He	made us	watch television
	enjoyed	
	spent a lot of time	watching television
	sat	
	saw us	that we would watch television
	let us	
	has stopped	

5 The blanks in each of the following ten sentences can be filled by one of the following six words, changed to the correct form as necessary. In some cases a negative form is needed.

fly flow lie lay need pass

Write only the numbers (i) to (x) and after each the word or words you think correct.

(i) During the past three months, John, who is a salesman, ... to many countries in the world.

(ii) Did you buy any petrol last week-end? No, I had enough so I .... any.

(iii) Thank goodness that restless dog .... down now and is quiet.

(iv) Whenever he .... the statue of Queen Victoria, he raised his hat respectfully.

(v) Whenever the weather was suitable, the twins .... their model aeroplanes in a nearby field.

(vi) He .... a bright pink envelope on the manager's table and then hurried away.

(vii) On the Duke's wedding-day, everybody danced in the streets and wine .... freely from the water-fountains.

(viii) You .... have made so much noise.

(ix) After he ....,.. sleepless for five hours, he got up.

(x) I .... the shop every day this week and have never seen it open.

6 Here are two examples of exclamations that might be made in the cases referred to.

Examples: The audience in a theatre is very small.
What a few people there are in the theatre!
You are surprised that someone has not written to you.
How strange that he hasn't written to me!

Write the exclamation that might be made in each of these cases.

(*a*) You think a room is very warm

(*b*) You are admiring a friend's dress.

(*c*) You are shocked by the number of mistakes a fellow-student has made.

(*d*) You are really tired.

(*e*) You discover it is much later than you had thought.

(*f*) You are expressing your opinion of an acquaintance who always does as little work as possible.

Composition and summarising

1 In a strange town you find an old bridge, an ancient tower or a ruined chapel. The guide book provides a thrilling, romantic or tragic story associated with one of these. Write this story in between 120 and 180 words.

2 The duties of either a secretary, a waiter in an expensive restaurant, an air hostess, a nurse or your class teacher. Your explanation should be between 120 and 180 words in length.

3 If the story of the events in the old lighthouse had been true, a report would have appeared in the local newspaper on the same day as Martin's body was found. This would have started with an account of the sending of the relief boat and the discoveries made in the lighthouse. A second paragraph beginning with the words 'It is reported . . . .' would mention what had happened previously in the village inn and the third make the suggestion that appears in this story of what might have happened in the lighthouse. The whole affair would be reported plainly and without any feeling of sensation or drama. Write this report in between 175 and 200 words.

Spoken English

Watching television or going to the cinema: a discussion

A I'm going to the cinema this evening.
B What's on?
A It's a Western: 'Cowboy Come Home'.
B But there's a Western on television to-night. You're welcome to come in and watch it. Why bother to turn out and pay for a cinema seat?
A There's a wide screen and the colour will be better.
B Here you can have a comfortable armchair, a drink at your elbow and no journey to make. Besides there are three other worthwhile programmes on: a documentary on underwater swimming, half an hour's sports review and an instalment of a mystery serial play.
A I've seen a few instalments of that on Peter's television. You really enjoy that kind of programme, don't you.
B Yes, I do. Last week the hero had kidnapped the gangster boss and was threatening to blow him up if he didn't release his girl-friend—I mean the hero's girl-friend, of course.
A Do you prefer seeing a story as a T.V. film to reading it in a book?
B Oh yes. You can actually see the characters and how they're dressed and watch their expressions. This story takes place in the mountains of Norway and you can enjoy the scenery, the mountains and glaciers and fiords. At one point some of the characters have to ski through a blizzard. It's all so vivid and believable and far more exciting than a book.
A But a film can make everything more exciting and vivid and the darkness cuts out human surroundings completely.
B But you can't choose your programme and it's a waste of money to walk out if you're bored. It's so easy to turn off the T.V.—not that I do turn it off very often.
A That's just it. You're drugged by it: you've given up all your old interests. That's why I won't have a T.V. I still have time to read, invite friends in for a chat or sometimes go to concerts or to the cinema or the theatre.

Situations

1 You are standing in a large crowd with a friend who suddenly feels faint. What do you do?

2 You are coming down a dark and apparently deserted street when you hear someone scream for help. What do you do?

3 You are giving a party and are trying to persuade a special person to come to it. The person does not enjoy noisy wild parties. What various things do you say in trying to persuade him or her to accept your invitation?

4 You are passing a friend's house which is in darkness when you see the light of a torch moving about inside. An unpleasant-looking man is waiting in a car outside. You know your friend is on holiday. What do you do?

5 A sixteen-year-old girl, who is usually reasonably happy at home, has quarrelled with her parents over their insistence that she is home by a certain time each evening. She intends to leave home and also to leave school and take a job for herself. What advice do you give her? This should include your opinion about her plans.

Giving your opinions

1 Do you think there is any possibility of houses being haunted? If not, what do you think is the origin of a belief in ghosts?

2 Describe your ideal seaside holiday place.

3 What types of people are usually superstitious?

4 Suggest the possible origin of one superstition you know of.

5 Is there any superstition that has an influence on you? Can you suggest a reason why?

6 Why do so many people, including very quiet and gentle ones, enjoy detective stories and films involving murders and violence?

7 You are offered a very well-paid job which you would quite enjoy doing but would involve your living in very isolated surroundings with only one or two other people. Why would you accept or turn down this job?

General guidance and practice

Revision of punctuation

Insert whatever punctuation marks or capital letters may be required in the following sentences:

(*a*) blackbirds sparrows and robins busily looking for crumbs were suddenly scared away by a prowling cat.

(*b*) professor gregorys new book which was published earlier this week has the title the unfortunate reign of richard II.

(*c*) why should i have to obey the orders of a boy half my age grumbled the elderly clerk.

(*d*) the bus to liverpool street station goes along oxford street you can catch it at oxford circus.

(*e*) next january he is taking an examination in italian and spanish he is at present studying at the european language college in south middle-sex.

(*f*) we have received messages from mars shouted the small boy isn't it exciting.

(*g*) if they work for forty eight hours a week the workmens wages total £25.

(*h*) students examinations will be set for all intermediate classes before christmas.

(*i*) in less than two months time spring will be here we shall be enjoying all the flowers that make early march so enchanting.

(*j*) shakespeares the merchant of venice one of his comedies which is now being performed at the st jamess theatre contains the well known speech which begins with the words the quality of mercy is not strained.

(*k*) dr smith mr white b a mrs jones and miss e robinson the last of these has already published several books are collaborating in the preparation of a new dictionary.

(*l*) the train leaves at 9 12 a m we should be at the station by nine o'clock.

Due to, owing to, thanks to

Three phrases of somewhat similar meaning which are sometimes confused in usage even by English people are *due to, owing to* and *thanks to*. The phrase '*due to*' consists of an *adjective* followed by a preposition. There should therefore always be present in the sentence a noun or pronoun which the adjective *due* is qualifying. In many cases the phrase follows the verb *to be*:

His irritability was due to ill health.

Here is another possible construction:

A breakdown, due to technical causes, interrupted the play being televised.

Owing to and *thanks to*, being *prepositional phrases*, are probably more common than due to:

Owing to the sudden collapse of the centre half, the football team had to play with only ten men.

Thanks to indicates that one has to be grateful in some way to the person or thing which follows the expression, though the phrase is sometimes used satirically:

Thanks to a prolonged spell of fine weather, they were able to complete the film within the month.
Thanks to your extraordinary clumsiness, I shall have to buy a whole new tea service.

The phrases *as a result of*, or *because of* are often used instead of *owing to, thanks to*.

Use one of the expressions *due to, owing to, thanks to* (*as a result of, because of*) in each of the following sentences:

(*a*) Your dislike for women drivers has no logical foundation: it is...... only...... prejudice.

(*b*) ....an outbreak of measles, the children's party has been postponed.

(*c*) His nickname Lofty is...... ......his height.

(*d*) ....the loyal support of his assistants, the new candidate was returned to Parliament.

(*e*) ....his frank and sincere nature, he is trusted by everyone who meets him.

(*f*) .... a fuse all the lights went out.

(*g*) The late arrival of the aircraft, which was .... fog, delayed the delivery of letters and newspapers.

(*h*) .... his disguise, the explorer was able to mingle with the pilgrims.

(*i*) They have decided to abandon their scheme to establish a research laboratory on the far side of the lake .... the difficulty of finding properly qualified staff.

(*j*) Many doctors believe that lung cancer may to some extent be .... excessive smoking.

Collective nouns

Here are a few of the more common collective nouns:

a staff of teachers (a staff room), of doctors, of nurses, of shop assistants, etc.
a crew of sailors, of oarsmen, of a bus (the driver and conductor)
a crowd of people (streets crowded with people)
a mob of disorderly people (The pop singer was mobbed by fans.)
a procession of people marching
an audience in a theatre, at a concert or at a meeting
a congregation in church (but: People are congregating in the Town Square.)
a pack of cards, of hounds (The Square was packed with people.)
a flock of sheep, of birds (People are flocking to see the new film.)
a herd of cows (the herd instinct)
a gang of criminals (a gangster)
a committee of chosen representatives (an education committee)
a board of directors (who meet in a board room)
a litter of baby animals (litter also refers to rubbish)
a swarm of insects (On warm Sunday afternoons Stonehenge is swarming with tourists.)
a team of players (the team spirit)
a choir of singers (adjective: choral)
a bunch of flowers (a bouquet is given to an actress)
a forest, a wood, a copse, a grove
an orchard, a shrubbery
a suite of rooms, of furniture, of musical compositions.

So far as living things are concerned, a collective noun is normally treated as singular if the rest of the sentence suggests that it may be regarded as a single undivided unit:

The audience is applauding enthusiastically.
The choir sings in church every Sunday.

But if the meaning of the sentence indicates that this is a collection of living things capable of acting separately, or some other word in the sentence suggests a plural idea, the collective noun is treated as a plural:

The mob are now fighting among themselves.

The audience have taken their seats.
The choir have all studied in a College of Music.

A collective noun which applies to things is normally treated as singular as things are incapable of individual behaviour:

The whole bunch of flowers has been scattered over the floor.

Family is often treated as if it were plural even though a singular meaning might be expected:

The Brown family are my employers.

The family I live with is spending a week with relatives.
are spending a week with relatives.

The tendency in speech is to treat most collective nouns as plurals.

Use the correct form of the verb, pronoun, and possessive adjective in the following sentences:

(*a*) The flock of sheep is/are straying in all directions.

(*b*) The Education Committee is/are arguing about the cost of school meals.

(*c*) The procession is/are approaching Trafalgar Square where it/they will be joined by another group of demonstrators.

(*d*) The team has/have scored five goals already and it/they will almost certainly beat its/their opponents.

(*e*) The mob is/are losing its head/their heads and is/are throwing stones at the windows of many houses; the police have been called in to deal with it./them.

(*f*) A swarm of bees has/have invaded my orchard.

(*g*) A suite of rooms has/have been reserved for the millionaire.

The inversion of subject and verb after certain negative expressions

In order to emphasise the idea they convey, certain expressions, many of them adverbial and all having some negative force, may precede the verb they are associated with.

In this case, the subject and verb of the following main clause are inverted, that is to say, the verb precedes the subject as in the normal interrogative form.

The main types of expression involved are:

SINGLE WORDS (these may also introduce phrases or clauses)

Nowhere, Never, Neither, Nor (as conjunctions and also as pronouns or adjectives except when 'neither' is subject of the following verb). The first two often appear as *Nowhere else* and *Never before.*

PHRASES

At no time, by no means, in no case, in no way.
Not even then, not until the end (etc.)
Only then, only after several minutes
(the suggestion is: not before . . .)

CLAUSES

Not until he had finished speaking . . .
Only when he goes to church . . .
etc.

The words *Scarcely, hardly, seldom, rarely* and *little* all have negative force:

Never before *had disaster seemed* so close.
Nowhere else along the coast *is there* such shallow water so far from land.
Not without considerable difficulty and suffering *was the rebellion eventually crushed.*
At no time *did the refugees receive* help from their more fortunate fellow-countrymen.
Seldom *have I seen* such a crowd of people.

Neither, nor

They don't like the cold. Neither *do we.*
Neither of the books is in print. (subject)
In neither room *was there* a wash-basin.
Some people can't swim nor *will they ever learn.*

If the opening expression is a subordinate clause, the verb in that clause is not changed; it is the verb in the following main clause that is affected.

Only when I give special permission, *may you write* in pencil.
Not until he had removed his shoes, *did he enter.*

After such expressions as these, it is quite incorrect to use the subject and verb in the normal order. Yet this inversion occasionally results in what seems a very unnatural form of speech or writing, as for example:

Neither of these books could we obtain.

In such cases, it would be more usual to keep the normal sentence order:

We could obtain neither of these books.

or use either the passive or a verb and adjective.

Neither of these books could be obtained.
Neither of these books was obtainable.

The expressions *so do I; so will they* is a similar construction to those mentioned above.

Rewrite the following sentences so that the adverbial expression in italics comes at the beginning of the sentence. Make any other necessary changes:

(*a*) The critics have *rarely* been so enthusiastic about a Shakespearian production.
(*b*) The college tuition fees will *under no circumstances* be refunded.
(*c*) He will inherit the estate *only if his elder brother has no children.*

(*d*) The tide had *hardly* started to ebb when a damp mist crept over the estuary.

(*e*) I have *never in my life* felt so completely paralysed with terror.

(*f*) You will *not* be allowed to leave the table *until you have eaten your prunes and custard.*

(*g*) You will find such fine and delicate lace *nowhere else in the world.*

(*h*) I have *never* met such a devoted and unselfish couple as our old caretaker and his wife.

(*i*) He appreciated his friend's sacrifice *only when he realised what it had cost him.*

(*j*) The injured man did *not in any way* blame the driver of the van.

(*k*) He realised *little* that he had missed his last chance.

(*l*) She sits out of doors *only when it is exceptionally warm.*

Words beginning with silent letters

Some of the most common of these are:

GN-	H-	KN-	WR-
gnat	heir	knee(l)	wrap
gnaw	honest	knife	wreath
	honour	knight	wreck
	hour	knitting	wrench
		knob	wretch(ed)
		knock	wring
		knot	wrinkle
		know	wrist
		knuckle	write
			wrong
			wriggle

Each of the following definitions refers to one of the above words. Supply the appropriate word in each case:

1 Part of the arm
2 Part of the leg
3 The verb meaning to use No. 2
4 Part of the finger or toe
5 Fold of skin
6 Cover with paper or cloth
7 Eat like a rat
8 Not right
9 A means of joining string
10 Used at meals
11 Sixty minutes
12 Twist one's body restlessly
13 May be trusted, truthful
14 Pull or twist very sharply
15 Eldest son of a rich man
16 Grouping of flowers associated with funerals
17 Stinging insect
18 Medieval noble soldier
19 Record words on paper
20 Something broken or destroyed
21 Tap on a hard surface
22 Special distinction
23 Realise or be sure of mentally
24 Unhappy or bad person
25 An adjective describing No. 24
26 A round handle
27 Form of handwork
28 Squeeze by twisting

Insert the correct prepositions in the following sentences:

(*a*) The apparently tough newspaper editor was surprisingly sensitive ...... criticism.

(*b*) The ambitious draughtsman is applying...... promotion to the post of design engineer.

(*c*) You will find it worth while to keep...... good terms...... the supervisor of your department.

(*d*) She leapt............ a chair and screamed frantically...... me 'Help! Help! There's a mouse over there!'

(*e*) Well-mannered students apologise...... their teacher...... unpunctuality and absence...... class.

(*f*) The whole department was...... a state...... utter disorganisation.

(*g*) ......an embarrassed whisper he asked me if I could lend him five pounds.

(*h*) The retired verger barely exists...... a quite inadequate pension.

(*i*) Please fill...... any further particulars...... the slip attached...... this document.

(*j*) I should like to spend a whole afternoon...... a small boat rocked gently...... a calm sunlit sea.

15

Passage for comprehension

Related talents

I had a curious collection of aunts. They all lived locally and each expected me to visit her at least once a fortnight. I therefore had a frequent opportunity of comparing their individual eccentricities.

Aunt Helen was married to a clergyman, the vicar of an adjoining parish. A conscientious but retiring man, the latter preferred the peace of his library 5 to parish affairs and concerned himself mainly with church duties. It was Aunt Helen who ran the parish. With incredible efficiency, she organised charity bazaars and subscriptions, rebuked the erring, bullied committees and entertained a daily gathering of helpers, voluntary and conscripted, to tea, cake and instructions. It was she who gave me a bicycle for a Christmas 10 present: I was in this way better equipped for her numerous errands. She was an admirable woman, whom I take the greatest pains not to resemble.

Aunt Beatrice, her junior, had divorced her thoroughly unsatisfactory husband several years previously. She opened a snack bar in an area of small workshops; she gave good value, and soon had to extend her premises and 15 employ extra staff. Within two years she could afford to put a manager in charge and give all her time to the care of her four children. She prepared meals substantial enough for a Sahara-bound camel and made me eat up every morsel. She was a shrewd judge of character who expressed her opinions bluntly and frankly, sparing no one's feelings. Nevertheless she was well- 20 liked, and got on well with everybody, largely on account of her honesty, courage and warm-hearted generosity.

Widowed Aunt Dorothy lived alone. Having a comfortable income and no children, she had no need to work. Plump, plain and gifted with a vivid imagination, she devoted most of her time to gossip. Her keen eye missed 25 nothing and she specialised in discovering other people's secrets. She would make some carefully-chosen but apparently innocent remark and then watch the effect it had on each of her companions. She noticed a great deal and skilfully guessed many things she could not actually discover. As a result she could tell her close friends some sensational items of information 30 which only later became generally known. Aunt Dorothy could have been a first-class novelist or adviser to women's magazine readers—as a small-town housewife, she was certainly wasting her unusual abilities.

But it was the shy spinster, Aunt Margaret, who provided the really staggering sensation. For years she had nursed her aged and invalid father, 35 who had died when she was fifty. Faded, inconspicuous, dowdy, she had bought a bungalow, adopted four cats and a parrot, and apparently restricted her ambitions to growing chrysanthemums. It was a year after her father's death that the extraordinary secret of her double life leaked out. 40 For the past ten years she had been supplementing her income by the creation of fiction under a pen name. No fragrant romances or even cosy domestic detective mysteries. Tough Dan O'Ryan, whose heroes had square jaws, handy revolvers and straight punches (together with humorous blue eyes), was in real life a single lady dealing with nothing fiercer than four fluffy 45 tabby cats and a parrot whose knowledge of American slang had always bewildered us.

Notes on the passage

Vocabulary

line

title *related* This is an example of a PUN as the word has two meanings here (*a*) the four aunts were relations (*b*) their talents were related: they had some things in common.

1 *curious* has two meanings (*a*) strange (*b*) inquisitive, interested in finding out more about things and people.
The word can have both meanings in this example: *Cats are curious animals.*
Curiosity (*Unc*)*: Curiosity may lead to interesting discoveries.*
(*C*)*: He has collected many curiosities, including ancient masks, during his explorations of unknown regions.*

2 *a fortnight*—never 'fifteen days'.

2 *an opportunity:* an occasion or chance that one is able to make use of.
a possibility: something that may happen.
Notice: *possibility* rarely follows the verb 'have': *have an opportunity.* There is a *possibility* that before the end of the century there will be regular flights to the moon but few people will have the *opportunity* of going. Which? There was no .... of food supplies running out; he has had no .... of reading your novel; he seized the .... of having a short rest; he was worried by the .... that there might be alcohol in his drink; .... knocks only once; there are plenty of .... to gain promotion in this job; bear in mind the .... of unexpected illness; make the most of your .... (Plural).

3 *eccentricities eccentric* describes behaviour that is unconventional and a little strange and possibly ridiculous but is not really abnormal.
An eccentric is a person of odd behaviour, though probably not a *neurotic* or a psychological or mental case and certainly not a *lunatic.*

4 *a clergyman* is a priest of the Church of England. *A priest* is more usually attached to a Roman Catholic or Greek Orthodox church. In the case of a Nonconformist church or chapel, the word *minister* is often used.

These are Church of England clergymen, arranged in order of importance: *an archbishop, a bishop, a vicar, a curate.*
A *vicar* is under certain conditions called a *rector* (their houses: a *vicarage*; a *rectory*). A *dean* is the clergyman in charge of a cathedral.
A *churchwarden* is a *layman* (not a clergyman) who shares responsibility for church business matters. A *verger* keeps the church tidy and in good order.
The *organist* plays the organ and as *choirmaster* he trains the church choir.
A *parish* is a division of a county, with its own church and vicar.
A *diocese* is controlled by a *bishop.*

4 *adjoining*—next to; *adjacent*—near.

5 *retiring* here means disliking and avoiding social life.

5 *prefer* means 'like better than something else'. Do not use it for 'like'.

5 a *library* in which books are read and from which they are borrowed. a *bookshop* from which books can be bought.

6 *concern* has several meanings. (*a*) anxiety: *there is some concern about his health.* (*b*) something of interest to a person: *that is no concern of mine.* (*c*) a firm: *he has shares in a building concern.* (*d*) have to do with; be of importance to: *this letter concerns you. he is concerned in the discussions.* (*e*) take an interest in: *As Mary's legal guardian, he has always concerned himself in her welfare.* (*f*) *concerned* (*Adj*) *Your friends are very concerned about your safety.*

7 *incredible* = unbelievable.

8 *charity* (*Unc*) giving to those in need. *A charity* (*C*) an organisation doing this.

8 *erring:* to err is to do something wrong or to make a mistake, but it is not often used. *errors* (mistakes) may be made in Arithmetic or Typewriting. An *error of judgment* could be fatal to the driver of a car.
A *fault* can be a bad point in a person's character or in the construction of something. Notice the common accusation: *It's* (*all*) *your fault.*
An *errand* is a short journey made for shopping, taking a message or some similar purpose. An *errand boy* is a boy who takes goods from a shop to customers' homes.

9 *voluntary and conscripted:* a *conscript* is a soldier doing his compulsory military service. A *veteran* is a soldier with long experience. A veteran car. (a very old car)
Notice these apparent but not true opposites:
voluntary service an *involuntary* start at a sudden noise.
different people *indifferent* to criticism (taking no notice of)
valuable pictures he gave *invaluable* advice (very valuable) (*Opp* valueless pictures)
famous writers *infamous* criminals.
sensible ideas lying *insensible* (unconscious) (*Opp* senseless ideas).

12 *take pains* = take trouble: *take pains with one's work*; if one is hurt, one feels *pain*; a wound can be *painful* (*Opp. painless*).

15 Compare: *He did valuable work for the hospital. He bought an expensive car.*

18 The pages of a book are *bound* (bind bound bound) in a cover or binding.
But: The ship is now homeward-*bound* (or: bound for India) = on its way.
A camel bound for the Sahara would have to eat a good deal.

19 *morsel* = *fragment* = small piece.

19 *shrewd:* having a keen judgment of people and business matters.
cunning and *crafty:* both suggest an unpleasant calculating and possibly dishonest cleverness: *a cunning fox*; *a crafty dealer who tries to cheat customers.*
sly: furtive, dishonest, underhanded and mean. People who open and read other people's letters underhandedly and listen at keyholes are sly—and so are people who cheat in examinations.

20 *sparing no one's feelings*—speaking plainly even if it hurts the person addressed.

25 *devoted herself to:* gave all her time to. Compare: a *devoted mother* who loves and gives all her time to her family. *a devoted couple.*
dedicated to an ideal. *affectionate* is not so strong as either of these.

29 *guess* the answer to a *riddle.*

32 a *novelist* writes *novels* which are long stories. *John often reads short stories.* A romantic event or situation is a *romance*: *the romance of the sea and sailing-ships. Non-fiction* is writing about true facts; *fiction* is largely based on the imagination. A novel is written in *prose*, not *poetry* (a *poem*)

33 *ability* is more often used than capability: *He has the ability to do better.*
Compare: *able to: After many weeks' teaching, he is now able to swim.*
and: *capable of: It is so hot. I really don't feel capable of walking far.*

34 *spinster:* the official title of an unmarried woman, who is usually referred to as a single woman. The colloquial 'old maid' suggests that she is plain, narrow-minded, strictly conventional and prim.

35 *staggering: to stagger* is to walk or stand unsteadily so that one nearly falls, often on account of illness or shock. A staggering sensation is therefore a very surprising one.
Periods of work can also be *staggered* so that the workers are free at different times. Sometimes the working day of twenty-four hours is divided into three periods of work: each of these periods is a *shift.*

35 *invalid* An invalid is any sick person who is ill for some time, not a *disabled* soldier.

36 *dowdy:* wearing uninteresting old-fashioned clothes. *shabby* wearing clothes that are no longer in a good condition. *smart* could be the opposite to both these words. Notice also: *fashionable*

39 *The respectable bank clerk is also a safe-breaker. He leads a double life.*

39 A *leak:* a hole through which a liquid can escape. A kettle may leak. Secret information also can *leak out.*

40 *supplement:* some newspapers have extra sections called *colour supplements.*

41 a *pen-name* is another name used by an author. A *stage-name* is used by an actor.
A *nickname* is given to someone, often as a joke ('Shorty' for a very tall man.)
A *pet-name* is given to show special affection—often to small children. A criminal may have an *alias.*

42 *tough* means hard to break or cut: meat may be tough (*Opp* tender). Colloquially it may describe a person, usually someone who can face hardship and danger (sometimes a criminal).

42 A *hero* or a *heroine* is *heroic* and shows *heroism.*
A *villain* is the bad character in a book or play. He may not look *villainous* though his *villainy* soon becomes clear.

42 Adjectives of shape: *square, oblong* (=*rectangular*), *round* (=*circular*), *triangular, oval.*

43 *punch* with a fist; *slap* with the palm of the hand; *kick* with the foot; *poke* with the finger; *scratch* with the nails; *nudge* with the elbow; *shrug* one's shoulders.

44 *deal with* anything that has to be done; *cope with* difficulties and problems.

Phrasal verbs

GET The following are among the most common of the many uses of this verb. *get at* something normally out of reach; *get away*=escape (possibly from daily routine); *get away with*=do something without getting the expected punishment; *get back* (*a*) something lent (*b*) to a point one started a journey from; *get down* from a high place; *get hold of*=grasp or obtain something; *get into/out of* a car, a bus, a train, an aeroplane; *get on/off* a bus, a bicycle; *get into trouble* by doing something that causes punishment or unpleasantness of some kind; *get up to mischief*=do the small naughty things that a child might do; *get on*=make progress; *get on with* (*a*) one's work (continue doing it) (*b*) other people (be on friendly terms with them); *get out* of a room through the window; get out of doing some unpleasant duty (avoid doing it); *get over* an illness or sorrow (recover); *get ready for*=prepare for; *get through* a lot of work OR pass an examination; *get to*=arrive in/at; *get up to* a certain point in a book or in learning; *get one's own way*=do what one wants in spite of opposition.

Which? .... a purse from a handbag; he has never .... the loss of his wife; the cat could not .... from the roof; he always expects to .... as he is thoroughly spoilt; .... apples high on a tree; .... a destination; .... money owed; .... well and hope for promotion; .... the end of Chapter 2; the pilot .... the aeroplane and then .... again; .... for being late for work; our puppy chews slippers and .... in similar ways; how are you ....? .... for a holiday; .... all his homework in an hour; somehow the policeman .... the man's gun; he always .... helping with the washing-up; .... home after midnight; he has .... cheating so far but he will be found out soon; we were locked in and could not ....; .... the wrong bus and then .... again; he does not .... his stepfather.

Pronunciation

THESE NEED CARE: clergyman [klə́ːdʒɪmən]; efficiency [ɪfíʃənsɪ]; bazaar [bəzá]; bullied [búlɪd]; Sahara [səháːrə]; chrysanthemum [krɪzǽnθɪməm]; extraordinary [ɪkstrɔ́ːd(ə)nrɪ]; wild [waɪld] BUT bewildered [bɪwíldəd].

STRESS AND SOUND CHANGES: eccentric [ɪkséntrɪk]; eccentricity [eksentrízɪtɪ]; compare [kəmpέə] comparative [kəmpǽrətɪv]; conscience [kɔ́nʃəns]; conscientious [kɔnʃɪénʃəs]; prefer [prɪfə́]; preferable [préf(ə)rəbl]; preference [préfərəns]; admire [ədmáɪə]; admirable [ǽdmərəbl]; admiration [ǽdməréɪʃən]; courage [kʌ́rɪdʒ]; courageous [kəréɪdʒəs].

ju (as in *u*se): curious [kjúərɪəs]; curiosity [kjuərɪɔ́sɪtɪ]; rebuke [rɪbjúːk]; numerous [njúːmərəs]; inconspicuous [ɪnkənspíkjuəs].

dzu (as in *juice*): individual [ɪndɪvídjuəl]: duties [djúːtɪz]; junior [dʒúːnjə].

ə (as in *a*go): locally [loúkəlɪ]; frequent [fríːkwənt]; vicar [víkə]; library [láɪbrərɪ]; subscriptions [səbskrípʃənz]; committee [kəmítɪ]; voluntary [vɔ́ləntərɪ]; errands [érəndz]; substantial [səbstǽnʃəl]; morsel [mɔ́ːsəl]; character [kǽrɪktə]; opinion [əpínjən]; nevertheless [névəðəlés]; passionately [pǽʃənɪtlɪ]; innocent [ínəsənt]; invalid [ínvəlɪd]; inconspicuous [ɪnkənspíkjuəs]; parrot [pǽrət]; ambitious [ǽmbíʃəs]; fragrant [freígrənt].

ɪ (as in *city*): retiring [rɪtaíərɪŋ]; equipped [ɪkwípt]; resemble [rɪzémbl]; area [έərɪə]; knowledge [nɔ́lɪdʒ]; secret [síːkrɪt]; fiction [fíkʃən]; single [sɪŋgl]; fiercer [fíəsə].

OTHERS: shrewd [ʃruːd]; analysed [ǽnəlaɪzd]; reactions [rɪǽkʃənz]; romance [roumǽns]; tough [tʌf]; square [skwεə].

NAMES: Helen [hélɪn]; Beatrice [bíətrɪs]; Dorothy [dɔ́rəθɪ]; Margaret [máːgərɪt].

Special grammatical and structural points

(i) *therefore* and *then*, being adverbs, *cannot join* word groups.

He is a lawyer (and) therefore (and so) he should have a good income. He finished the letter and signed it, then slipped it into an envelope.

This should have been written: He finished the letter, signed it and then slipped it into an envelope.

Avoid using *also, therefore, especially* to open a sentence.

This area (also) produces excellent fruit.
He is (especially) admired for his brilliant wit.

(ii) Compare the spellings of these nouns and verbs:

NOUNS: advice practice licence device prophecy
VERBS: advise practise license devise prophesy

Which? you need more practi...e in speaking; advi...e to school-leavers; licen...ed for the sale of alcohol; experts prophe...y a growing fuel shortage; an anti-thief devi...e on cars; a driving licen...e; you must practi...e daily; I advi...e you to wait; his prophe...y did not come true; a doctor's practi...e; can you devi...e a method of improving my spelling?

Prepositions

(*a*) concerned with travel arrangements; gifted with musical ability;

(*b*) equipped *for* a long journey

(*c*) specialise *in* eighteenth-century literature

(*d*) adviser *to* school-leavers; benefits restricted to staff members

(*e*) Notice: resemble a relative (NO preposition)

(*f*) Two phrases: *on account of* his illness
all his possessions *together with* his friend's dog

Expressions to learn and introduce into written work

(*a*) my relations all live *locally* (*b*) he organised everything with *incredible efficiency* (*c*) she *gives all her time to* her children (*d*) the judge was *a shrewd judge of character* (*e*) she *expressed her opinions frankly* (*f*) he *spared no one's feelings* in his criticisms (*g*) she *got on well with* everybody (*h*) he was *wasting his ability* (*his talents*) in this job (*i*) the *secret* of his engagement *leaked out* (*j*) *a good command of a* language.

Multiple choice questions

Here are a number of questions or unfinished statements about the passage, each with four suggested ways of finishing it. You must choose the way you consider the most suitable. Write in each case the bracketed number of the question or statement followed by the letters **A, B, C, D,** and then cross through the letter of the answer you choose. Give one answer only to each question. Read the passage right through again before choosing your answers.

1 The four aunts all lived
A together **B** fairly near the writer **C** in small hotels **D** in uncomfortable conditions

2 It is clear from the passage that Aunt Helen's husband was
A elderly **B** strict **C** nervous **D** unsociable

3 Which of these parish duties did Aunt Helen not take charge of?
A conducting services **B** raising money **C** organising parish business **D** seeing that people in the parish behaved themselves

4 Aunt Helen gave the writer a bicycle so that she could
A do Aunt Helen's shopping **B** do many local jobs for her aunt **C** visit her aunt regularly **D** carry things about for her

5 Which of these statements about Aunt Beatrice's snack bar is untrue?
A she had had to make it bigger **B** she cooked the enormous meals there herself **C** she was able to give the responsibility of running it to someone else **D** she had taken on more assistants

6 Which of the following words best describe Aunt Beatrice?
A unpopular **B** malicious **C** extravagant **D** independent

7 One of Aunt Dorothy's methods of gathering information was to
A ask questions **B** collect it from close friends **C** observe people's behaviour in certain situations **D** listen to other people's gossip

8 Besides having the abilities to be a novelist or magazine adviser, she had those of a good
A detective **B** secretary **C** hotel manager **D** teacher

9 Which of the following was not one of Aunt Margaret's characteristics?
A unselfishness **B** modesty **C** respectability **D** frankness

10 Which of the following could have provided a clue to Aunt Margaret's surprising double life?
A her pen-name **B** her parrot **C** her fierce pets **D** her humorous eyes.

Reading comprehension

In this exercise you must choose the word or phrase which best completes each sentence. Write first the number of each sentence followed by the letters **A, B, C, D** and **E** and cross through the letter of the correct answer in each case.

1 He was a highly .... teacher who took his duties seriously but he had neither the personality nor ability to achieve much success.
A conscientious **B** efficient **C** capable **D** hard-working **E** talented

2 Your annual .... to the Social Club is now due.
A investment **B** payment **C** contribution **D** subscription **E** offering

3 With the invention of the train, man could travel overland .... without the need of horses.
A voluntarily **B** freely **C** willingly **D** independently **E** readily

4 His compass proved .... to him when he was lost in unknown country.
A valuable **B** expensive **C** dear **D** precious **E** profitable

5 As one the four .... of the company he often had to attend Board meetings.
A managers **B** directors **C** headmasters **D** proprietors **E** governors

6 His decision to invest in land in the developing holiday resort was a .... one.
A cunning **B** sly **C** crafty **D** underhanded **E** shrewd

7 He does not .... his fellow-workers and there are often disagreements between them.
A go on with **B** take to **C** put up with **D** get on with **E** get into touch with

8 He has impressed his employers considerably and .... he is soon to be promoted.
A nevertheless **B** accordingly **C** however **D** yet **E** eventually

9 During the .... the audience strolled and chatted in the foyer.
A gap **B** pause **C** space **D** interruption **E** interval

10 He is .... a very old man but in fact he is only fifty.
A apparently **B** evidently **C** obviously **D** actually **E** really

11 Polar explorers have to be extremely .... to endure the climate and other hardships.
A hard **B** rough **C** tough **D** brave **E** raw

12 The mother separated the quarrelling children and gave each of them a sharp ....
A punch **B** pinch **C** scratch **D** poke **E** slap

13 Groups of tourists visit the national park to see the many .... animals there.
A fierce **B** wild **C** untamed **D** cruel **E** savage

Use of English

1 (ii) The five expressions below are the answers to five questions that could be asked about the reading passage. Write out the questions.

(i) daily (ii) I was better equipped for her numerous errands
(iii) substantial enough for a Sahara-bound camel
(iv) she had a comfortable income and no children (v) a single lady

2 In each of the following words one letter, which in fact makes no difference to the pronunciation of the word, has been omitted. Write each number and the following word as it should be written in full.

(i) ...neel (ii) han...some (iii) We...nesday (iv) i...land (v) ...onour (vi) s...ene (vii) ...rist (viii) condem... (ix) com...ed (x) i...oning

(xi) r...ythm (xii) Chris...mas (xiii) extr...ordinary (xiv) c...aracter (xv) s...ord (xvi) kno...ledge (xvii) dou...t (xviii) recei...t (xix) ...rap (xx) ...histle (xxi) g...ard (xxii) thre...d (xxiii) w...ether (xxiv) choc...late

3 Each of the following people should know a good deal about the subject most clearly related to his job. Write the name of each person followed by the related subject.

EXAMPLES: a farmer farming a mechanic machines

(*a*) a cook (*b*) a politician (*c*) a soldier (*d*) a jockey (*e*) a scientist (*f*) a thief (*g*) a typist (*h*) a journalist (*i*) a priest (*j*) a poet (*k*) a jeweller (*l*) a photographer (*m*) an athlete (*n*) a librarian (*o*) an aeroplane pilot (*p*) a member of a choir

4 Each of the following conjunctions fits into a different one of the following sentences. Write the letter preceding each sentence followed by the conjunction which could replace the dash in that sentence.
since/although/in case/even if/while/provided that/unless/as soon as

(*a*) Tom often rides without a light .... this is not allowed.

(*b*) You can borrow my tape-recorder .... you return it to me to-morrow.

(*c*) .... he saw me, he shouted that I had cheated him.

(*d*) This room will never be painted .... we do it ourselves.

(*e*) He will make little progress in his studies .... he has little knowledge of the language.

(*f*) .... I had taken a taxi, I should still have missed the train.

(*g*) He has taken out an insurance .... he should be taken ill and be unable to work.

5 Each of the phrases in italic in the following sentences could be replaced by a clause with a subject and verb. The two examples show the kind of word group that should be used. Write the letter of each sentence, followed by the clause which can replace the italic word group.

EXAMPLES: *Living near the sea*, he can often go swimming.
as he lives near the sea

The mechanic was surprised at the poor condition of the car *being serviced.*
which was being serviced

(*a*) Is this coat *lying on the floor* yours?

(*b*) He often falls asleep *watching television in the evening.*

(*c*) *Being an old man now*, he prefers a quiet life.

(*d*) We listened carefully to the record *being played.*

(*e*) *Feeling tired and hungry*, he wanted to play football.

(*f*) I felt sure I knew the woman *walking on the opposite side of the road.*

(*g*) *Having made two telephone calls*, he hurried back to his car.

(*h*) *Explaining the reason for his visit*, he was immediately shown into the manager's room.

6 Mr. and Mrs. Clarke have four children between the ages of three and fifteen. Mr. Clarke has been offered a much better-paid job in New Zealand and has been informed that, though houses are difficult to come by in the town where he would be living, one would be provided for him. He and his wife, however, want to know more about both the house and the town before they decide about the job. Their questions will all seek information about the suitability of the house and town for themselves and their family. Write twelve possible questions the answers to which should provide the most important information they need.

Composition and summarising

1 Write one or more of the following composition exercises. Your answers must follow clearly the instructions and must be between 120 and 180 words each.

(*a*) Alec and Sue have just sat down in their living-room to talk about the unimportant happenings of the day when Sue's brother, Jim, arrives with the bad news that his wife, who has two young children, has suddenly been taken to hospital. The three of them discuss the various things that will have to be done in this emergency.

(*b*) Describe one of the following people, including his appearance, interests and behaviour: a very active and sociable person OR a shy and sensitive person OR a very lazy and untidy person.

(*c*) Write two letters, each of the length recommended above. One is from yourself to a readers' adviser of the magazine 'Challenge' in which you ask for advice about going to England to study against your parents' wishes. The other is the reply you receive. Invent names where necessary.

(*d*) Fred was a quiet middle-aged man who lived alone, worked in the local bank and spent his spare time reading or gardening. One day two thieves with guns came to his house and Fred behaved in a quite unexpected way. Tell the story of what happened.

2 Each of the four aunts was efficient and successful in her own way, though there may be certain characteristics of some of them which people might find unpleasant or annoying.

Taking your information from the reading passage but using your own words as far as possible, write two paragraphs, in 175–200 words together, which deal with these two sides of the various aunts. Explain in one paragraph the ways in which they were efficient and successful and in the second their more unpleasant and annoying characteristics.

Spoken English

Two conversations

(*a*) *In a restaurant*

Head Waiter Good afternoon, madam. Would you like to sit here. I'm afraid there are no other places free at the moment.

Margaret I'd prefer to sit alone but I suppose this will do. Have you a menu, please?

HW Certainly. One of the waiters will bring it at once.

(A waiter brings a menu and waits while Margaret reads it.)

Margaret I'll have the fixed menu at £1. Does that include wine?

Waiter No, madam. Wine is separate.

Margaret I'll have the clear soup, please, followed by roast pork, apple sauce, mashed potatoes and brussels sprouts.

Waiter I'm sorry, madam. The pork's off now. There's only the beef-steak pie still available.

Margaret Anything cold?

Waiter Yes, madam. There's cold chicken and salad and also ham and tongue with salad.

Margaret I'll have the chicken. And I'd be most grateful if you'd serve me as quickly as possible as I've got an appointment at two-fifteen.

Waiter I'll do my best, madam. What would you like to drink with it?

Margaret Oh, a small beer—some kind of lager will do. I shan't have time for dessert but perhaps you could bring a black coffee before I finish the main course.

(*b*) *In a bookshop*

Shopkeeper Can I help you in any way?

Customer Well, I'm trying to find two Christmas presents, both books, one for an elderly aunt and one for my young nephew.

S Could you give me any idea of their tastes in books?

C One of the books could be a crime story, possibly something by Craig Bronx or Rock Cannon. There's a collection of short stories by him that has just come out, I understand, 'Boomerang Bullets'.

S We haven't got that in stock at the moment, but we could order it for you. Do you know the name of the publisher?

C It's a Thriller Society special—a paperback. How long is it likely to take to come in?

S About a week.

C All right. Now the other. Crime wouldn't be approved of, oh no. Perhaps something on wild life or antique furniture. A collection of eighteenth-century essays or I see you've got Henry James's 'Golden Bowl' but that's probably been read before. 'Memoirs of an Ambassador', or no, I'm sure this new edition of 'The Climber's Manual' will be most warmly welcomed.

S But surely your aunt doesn't go climbing, madam?
C My aunt? No, of course not. The crime book's for her.

Situations

1 Imagine you are Aunt Helen. The parents of a young man who has lost his job on account of laziness and drunkenness have asked you to give him some serious advice. What do you say?

2 Aunt Beatrice's neighbour is thoroughly spoiling her two young children and they are almost completely out of hand (uncontrollable). Aunt Beatrice gives blunt, frank but useful advice to this neighbour. What does she say?

Expressing opinions

(*a*) Which of the four sisters do you prefer and why?

(*b*) What is your opinion of efficient independent women who are more interested in a useful career than in running a home?

(*c*) What are some of the reasons why a lot of people enjoy gossip?

(*d*) What is your opinion of detective stories and thrillers.

General guidance and practice

Use the correct form of the verbs bracketed in the following exercises, inserting the adjacent adverbs, nouns or pronouns in the right position.

Immediately I heard the news about Aunt Margaret, I (go) to see her. She (work) in her garden when I (arrive). One of her cats (watch) her. I (go) up to her.

'(Know) you what I just (hear)?' I (say).

'(Be) it about Mrs. Mills's twins?' she (reply). 'I (wonder—Past Simple) whether you (hear). Dorothy already (telephone).'

'It (be) about you,' I (say). 'What (hide) you from us for so long? Why not (tell) you us?'

'I (know) not what you (talk) about,' (say) Aunt Margaret, (look) guilty.

'What (do) you for the past ten years?' I (ask). 'And what (be) the title of the next one when it (appear)?'

'So you (find) out at last,' (say) Aunt Margaret. 'Oh dear, what (think) Aunt Dorothy when she (hear)?'

I (be) suddenly speechless. For once Aunt Dorothy's piercing eye (fail) her. She not (suspect even) the sensation which (be) right under her nose.

Unrelated participle

Be careful when you use a participle adjectivally that the noun or pronoun it qualifies is actually mentioned as subject of the main verb of the sentence. In the following example the participle is unrelated to any other word in the sentence and the effect is therefore ridiculous:

> Walking through the fields, the wild flowers are an interesting subject to study.

This sentence has to be re-written either as:

> Walking through the fields, one can take an interest in the study of wild flowers.

or, better:

> As one walks through the fields, the wild flowers provide an interesting subject to study.

Correct these sentences:

(*a*) Flying at twelve thousand feet, the countryside looks like a green check tablecloth.

(*b*) Settled in a strange country in a completely different society, old habits may soon be forgotten.

(*c*) Being a bachelor, his room was often untidy.

(*d*) Being hungry and thirsty, the food looked uncommonly attractive.

(*e*) Flavoured with curry and some strange kind of sauce, he did not find the food appetising.

Negative and interrogative forms of 'have'

A When the verb 'have' is used with the meaning 'possess', 'own', 'have as part of oneself, or as part of something belonging to oneself' the forms 'have not', 'has not' express the negative and the subject merely follows the verb in the interrogative forms: e.g. Have you a match?

In the simple past, this sometimes applies also, though forms introducing 'did' are more common:

He hadn't two large cars.	He didn't have two large cars.
Had he two large cars?	Did he have two large cars?

B When 'have' is used with any other meaning than 'possess' (e.g. 'eat', 'drink', 'take', 'experience', etc.) forms with 'do' and 'did' are always used in the present and past simple tenses, negative and interrogative:

> They don't have toast for breakfast.
> Does he have a bath every day?
> The baby didn't have a sleep to-day.
> Did you have a good dinner?

C The same rule applies to the verb 'have to' meaning 'must', and the 'have' of 'to have something done.'

> You don't have to curtsey to the headmistress.
> Do we have to stop here?
> He didn't have his photograph taken.

Write (i) the negative and (ii) the interrogative form of each of the following sentences:

(*a*) He has toothache.

(*b*) The journalist had an interview with the inventor of the new plastic.

(*c*) The cabaret singer had a striking personality.

(*d*) The radio factory has to employ at least fifty disabled people.

(*e*) The cyclist has a puncture in the back tyre of his bicycle.

(*f*) The two retired majors often have arguments about past battles.

(*g*) The new church has a beautiful spire.

(*h*) The mother had to coax her son to eat the stew.

(*i*) The workmen have a cup of tea when they get thirsty.

(*j*) The small boy had two dogs, a cat, a tortoise, three rabbits and a guinea pig as pets.

(*k*) The family had a cheap holiday in their caravan.

(*l*) I had these scissors sharpened.

Revision of relative and interrogative pronouns and adjectives

What part of speech and what part of the sentence is each of the words italicised below?

eg The first is an interrogative pronoun and is subject of the verb.

Who is there?

Is there anyone *whom* we can trust?

Whose coat is this?

He asked me *which* one he could have.

Whom have they elected?

Where is the boy *who* looks after the sheep?

Whom can one rely on?

What can I do?

The chops *that* are being fried are for dinner.

Which is best?

WHAT

(*a*) An *interrogative* pronoun or adjective.

(*b*) An *exclamatory* adjective.

What a nuisance!
What stupid people!

(*c*) An adjective meaning *the amount that, that* or *those.*

What money he has is kept in a bank.
I will provide you with what tools you need.

(*d*) A relative pronoun meaning *the thing which, that which.*

What I understand least is the grammar.
What the workers demand is better wages.

Other pronouns and adjectives

WHOEVER (*a*) *anyone who:* Whoever says that is a liar!

(*b*) the *emphatic form* of the interrogative *who?*

Whoever can that be knocking at this time of night?

WHATEVER (*a*) *anything which:* He will do whatever you ask.

(*b*) the *emphatic form* of the interrogative *what?*
Whatever can we do now we have missed the last train?

(*c*) *nothing whatever—nothing at all. none whatever—none at all*

WHICHEVER *the one that*—with slight emphasis.
Choose whichever you prefer.

Adverbs

HOWEVER (*a*) *to whatever degree:* Telephone me, however late it is.

(*b*) *yet all the same:* He protested violently. He obeyed however.

WHENEVER (*a*) *at any time that:* He comes whenever he can.

(*b*) an *emphatic* form of *when.*

WHEREVER (*a*) *at any place that:* Sit wherever you like.

(*b*) an *emphatic* form of *where.*

Relative 'That'

'That' may replace relative 'who', 'whom' or 'which' when the relative introduces a defining clause.

'That' is commonly used as a relative pronoun replacing a noun qualified by 'only' or a superlative adjective, and also to follow the pronouns 'all', 'everyone', 'everybody', 'anyone', 'anybody', 'anything', 'someone', 'somebody', 'no one', 'nobody', 'nothing', 'none'. Here again it may be omitted when it is in the accusative case.

The first that arrives will win.
The only one (that) we saw.
The best thing that . . . The best that . . .
All (that) they can do . . .
Everybody (that) one meets . . .

Use one of the forms dealt with in each of these sentences. The brackets indicate that the pronoun could be omitted altogether.

(*a*) I have no money ......

(*b*) ...... justice can you hope for from those rogues?

(*c*) ...... hair ribbon is this on the floor? Is it Betty's?

(*d*) He adores bananas, ... ripe they are.

(*e*) ...... little Irene tumbles down, she laughs.

(*f*) I could not see ...... it was they were waving to.

(*g*) ...... that plant needs is sufficient soil.

(*h*) The most unusual novelty ...... has appeared this Christmas is ...... one can describe as a musical calendar.

(*i*) ...... obstructs the police will be arrested.

(*j*) All (......) I ask for is peace and quiet.

(*k*) I want something ...... will clean my floor without any effort on my part ......

(*l*) The only opponent ...... can hope to defeat him is Arthur Morgan, ... many people prefer.

(*m*) He groans ...... I try to touch him; ...... he needs is a local anesthetic.

(*n*) His business partner strongly disapproves of ...... he intends to do with the profits; ...... he is doing nothing to stop him.

Another spelling rule

English schoolchildren learn this rule as:

i before *e* except after *c*

This applies only when the sound corresponds to the phonetic ɪ:

brief, chief, belief, grief, thief, piece, niece, priest, hygiene, shriek, re*ce*ive, de*ce*ive, *ce*iling, con*ce*it

There are two exceptions: seize, Sheila (a girl's name).
The sound 'ei' is sometimes expressed by the letters 'ei' or 'eigh':

rein, vein, weigh, eight, reign

The following words are sometimes misspelt:

height, foreign, forfeit, friend.

Remember the rule about the doubling of final consonants (Chapter 7) and the retention of -e after c- and g- when these are followed by the suffix -able. (Page 288, 6(b))
Fill in the missing letters where necessary in the following words:

(*a*) rel...f
(*b*) perc...ve
(*c*) happen(...ed)
(*d*) begin(...ing)
(*e*) matter(...ed)
(*f*) tap(...ing)
(*g*) peac(...able)
(*h*) compar(...able)
(*i*) f...ld
(*j*) heat(...ed)
(*k*) trac(...able)
(*l*) conceal(...ed)
(*m*) s...ge
(*n*) label(...ing)
(*o*) rec...pt
(*p*) challeng(...able)

Words with various meanings—'Treat' and 'Charge'

Suggest the meanings of the words in italics in the following sentences:

TREAT

As a noun: On his small daughter's birthday, he took her to the zoo as a special *treat*.

For their *treat* this summer the Sunday School children will be taken to Brighton.

What a *treat* to see the sun!

As a verb: The doctor is *treating* him for anaemia.

On the whole the lady for whom I am working *treats* me well.

Let me *treat* you to an ice-cream.

In his thesis he intends to *treat* the subject of twelfth-century costume.
They vowed never to *treat* with a victorious enemy.
Try not to *treat* the matter so seriously.

TREATMENT (noun): The judge condemned the parents for their cruel *treatment* of their child.
He is having *treatment* for his rheumatism.

A TREATY (noun): The two countries made a *treaty* of alliance.

CHARGE

As a noun: The sudden cavalry *charge* made the enemy retreat.
The *charge* they made for mending my watch was absurd.
He was arrested on a *charge* of burglary.
A *charge* of electricity. A *charge* of dynamite.
A *charge* of gunpowder.

As a verb: The small boy *charged* down the stairs.
How much do you *charge* for a shampoo and set?
At his trial he was *charged* with forgery.
Is it possible to *recharge* an old battery?

Notice:

(*a*) in charge of—The matron is in charge of the nursing staff of a hospital (responsible for, controlling).

take charge of—'The prefect took charge of the class while the master was away' (take responsibility for).

(*b*) The adjective 'chargeable' as in 'the fees chargeable'.
(When a word ends in -ge, the -e is kept before -able: changeable, manageable.
The same spelling rule applies to words ending in -ce: noticeable, peaceable.)

(*c*) French people should remember that 'chargé de' should normally be translated by 'loaded with' or 'burdened with'.

The woman was loaded with shopping.

There are several other possible meanings of 'charge' but these are less common and not needed at this stage.

Replace each of the groups of words underlined in the following sentences with one of the forms of 'treat' or 'charge'. Certain changes in existing word order and construction may be necessary.

(*a*) After the accident he *received medical attention* for shock.

(*b*) How much did they *make* you *pay* for that blouse?

(*c*) He *burst violently* into the room and demanded an explanation.

(*d*) He protested against their unkind *behaviour towards him.*

(*e*) If I win the first prize I shall *pay for* a bottle of champagne *for* you. (A preposition is needed here and the word order must be changed.)

(*f*) The defendant denied the *accusation* against him.

(*g*) After a day at the sales it's a *pleasant thing* to sit down.

(*h*) Lightning is caused by the passage of a high-powered *amount* of electricity.

(*i*) His article *deals with* the problem of juvenile delinquency.

(*j*) Have you studied the terms of the *signed agreement* between the allies?

Prepositions

Supply the correct prepositions in the following sentences:

(*a*) The tramp prefers a life ...... the open air ...... a settled existence.

(*b*) The nuns devoted their lives ...... helping poor families living ...... the slums.

(*c*) One of our undergraduate guides was specialising ...... science, the other ...... law.

(*d*) A successful spy needs to be gifted ...... an almost photographic memory.

(*e*) That resourceful young officer has been promoted and is now ...... command of a tank regiment.

(*f*) No wonder he is getting fat! He seems to restrict his activities ...... eating and sleeping.

(*g*) The actress has lost the exquisite diamond brooch which she was given ...... a wedding present.

(*h*) No one knows why the ex-king's memoirs were published ...... a pen name.

(*i*) Witches, ghosts and fairies are imaginary creatures that could never exist ...... real life.

(*j*) She often has reason to regret the fact that she is married ...... a test pilot.

(*k*) Wearing high-heeled court shoes, she seemed hardly equipped ...... a day's ramble.

(*l*) The speaker said that he was not concerned ...... people's morals but ...... their education.

(*m*) The shape of Italy on a map has often been compared ...... a long Wellington boot.

16

Passage for comprehension

Frozen paradise

High in a smooth ocean of sky floated a dazzling, majestic sun. Fragments of powdery cloud, like spray flung from a wave crest, sprinkled the radiant, lake-blue heaven.

Relaxed on a bundle of hay in a corner of a meadow bathed in sunlight, 5 Paul lay dreaming. A gentle breeze was stirring the surrounding hedges; bees moved, humming thoughtfully, from scarlet poppy to purple thistle; a distant lark, invisible in blue light, was flooding the vast realm of the sky with glorious song, as the sun was flooding the earth with brilliance. Beyond the hedge a brook tinkled over softly-glowing pebbles. Butterflies hovered 10 above nodding clover. An ant was busily exploring the uncharted territory of Paul's suntanned wrist. A grasshopper skipped briskly over his ankle. And the blazing sun was steadily scorching his fair freckled face to bright lobster red. Neither sun, nor grasshopper, nor ant, however, was able to arouse him.

15 Not even when a fly started crawling over his face did he open his eyes. For Paul was a thousand miles away, in a world of eternal snow and ice. Across the towering mountain range, a bitter gale was screaming furiously as with one hand he gripped a projecting knob of rock while with his axe he hacked out the next narrow foothold in the rock. As their infallible guide, he 20 was leading his gallant party of climbers up a treacherous, vertical wall of rock towards the lofty peak above, hitherto unconquered by man. A single slip, however trivial, would probably result in death for all of them. To his right he could glimpse the furrowed glacier sweeping towards the valley, but he was far too absorbed in his task to appreciate fully the scene around or 25 even to be aware of a view of almost unearthly beauty. A sudden gust of wind nearly tore him from the ledge where he was perched. Gradually he raised his foot, tested the new foothold on the sheer rock wall, transferred his weight, and signalled to the climbers below.

Not until a tractor started working in the next field did he become conscious 30 of his far from icy surroundings. He sat up, wiped his forehead with his handkerchief, glanced at his watch and sighed in resignation. He had a headache through sleeping in the hot sun, a pain in his shoulder from carrying his rucksack; his legs felt stiff and his feet ached. With no enthusiasm whatever he pulled the bulging rucksack over his shoulders and drew a large-35 scale map from his pocket. At the far end of the meadow two slates in the wall, which at this point replaced the hedge, indicated a stile, and beyond he could faintly see a thin thread of path which dwindled and finally disappeared as it climbed the steep slope of the down, quivering in the glare of the sun. The whole of Nature seemed to be luxuriating in warmth, sunshine and peace: wherever he looked, leaves on twigs, grass blades, flower petals, 40 all were sparkling in sunlight.

Fifteen miles off, over the ridge, across a broad valley and then over a higher, even steeper range of hills lay the youth hostel: supper, company, a cool dip in the river. With a momentary intense longing for ice-axe, blizzard, glacier and heroic exploit (none of which was at all familiar to him), Paul 45 strode off unwillingly to less dramatic but equally heroic achievement in the tropical heat of an English sun.

Notes on the passage

Vocabulary

line

1 The following adjectives all have the meaning 'shining' but each is stronger than the one before.

glowing bright brilliant glaring dazzling blinding

One person can *glare* or look at another very angrily.

2 soaked by *spray* from high waves; *froth* on newly-poured beer; a brook breaking into *foam* over pebbles; white *surf* on breaking waves; his face was covered with soapy *lather.*

2 *fling toss cast:* all mean *throw*

fling: toss carelessly: *fling a coat over a chair.*

toss: throw upward: *a ship is tossed on the waves.*

'heads' or 'tails' is called when a coin is tossed to decide something:

'*Let's toss for it*'.

cast: cast a fishing-line into water: a lamp casts light

Other meanings: cast a spell over (influence by magic); cast anchor; cast a vote; cast lots (decide on the choice of certain people by making them select papers, straws etc.); cast on cast off (begin and end a piece of knitting); a castaway (someone abandoned by a ship in a lonely place); the cast of a play (the characters or actors in it). A play is cast when the actors are chosen.

Other meanings of *throw:* throw a stone *at* someone to hit him; throw a ball *to* someone to catch; a fire throws *out* heat; throw *away* a used envelope; throw books *about* carelessly.

Colloquial: throw *out* a man who fights in a public house; throw *up* an unsatisfactory job

BE CAREFUL: THROW *threw* THROWN compare: through

2 *radiant:* shining gloriously. A *radiator* provides heat from central heating.

3 *heaven*—here an alternative to *sky*—has normally a religious meaning. *Good heavens!* is an expression of surprise similar to *good gracious!*

4 *relaxed* (*N relaxation*) is the opposite to *tense* (*N tension*).

4 *hay:* dried grass which is heaped in *haystacks* and stored in *hay-lofts*. *Hay fever*, with sneezing and watering eyes, is an illness caused by *pollen* (dust from plants).

Proverb: Make hay while the sun shines.

straw: the dried stalks of corn. A straw hat; a straw to drink through. *the last straw:* the final difficulty, often quite small, that makes everything quite impossible.

5 a *breeze* *wind* *gale* and *hurricane* are increasingly strong. a *blizzard* is a violent wind bringing heavy snow.

5 *stir* coffee with a spoon; nothing *stirred* in the frozen fields; a *stirring* account of his adventures; he enjoys *stirring up* trouble.

5 a *hedge* is a level row of bushes; a *ditch* is a channel along the roadside, often carrying water; a *moat* is a ditch round a castle; a garden may be surrounded by a wooden or wire *fence*, though *railings*, thin vertical metal rods, may be used instead.

6 A *bee* makes honey, but a *wasp*, also black and yellow, does not. *Butterflies* are more often seen by day and *moths* at night—both may develop from *caterpillars* and later *pupae*. Clothes moths lay eggs in clothes.
A *mosquito* bites or stings and may spread malaria; a *gnat* is less dangerous.
beetles are usually black, with hard wing covers; *crickets* may have an almost continuous high chirp, heard at night; *grasshoppers* jump through the grass; *fleas* jump and bite animals or people; *maggots* are found in fruit or peas; *spiders* spin *webs*, which when dirty are called *cobwebs*.

6 A *thistle* is the Scottish national flower; a *rose* the English; a yellow *daffodil* (with a larger trumpet than a narcissus) the Welsh; a *shamrock*, a form of *clover*, the Irish.

7 Rearrange the second list so that the description fits the bird.

A	B
A lark	talks
A thrush	has a red breast in winter
A blackbird	is yellow and sings in a cage
A starling	is the most celebrated song bird
A nightingale	is a black and white bird with a long tail
A robin	has a magnificent tail
A cuckoo	haunts seas and rivers
A parrot	is small and brown and is often seen in town parks
A canary	builds nests high in trees
A rook	sings high in the sky
A gull	is said to sing each passage twice
A peacock	lays eggs in other birds' nests

A sparrow	is black and has a high clear song
A pigeon	is blackish brown and is often described as greedy
A magpie	certain types can carry messages

10 a *chart* is normally a sea-map, but can also give special information: a temperature chart.

11 *skip* with a skipping-rope. Also: skip (pass over) pages in a book. *hop* on one foot only.

12 *scorch* with dry heat: scorch cloth with an overheated iron. *scald* with boiling water.

12 an amusement *fair* with roundabouts and swings; an industrial fair with a display of new products; a fair-haired girl (*Opp* a dark-haired girl); a fair maiden (poetic use meaning 'beautiful').
fair shares for everyone; fair play; that's not fair (just and honest).
the weather will be fair (there will probably be no rain).
his standard in Mathematics is fair (fairly good) (moderately good).

13 *Shellfish* include: lobsters, prawns, shrimps (smallest): all these are pink (or brown) when boiled; oysters, mussels, cockles, winkles: molluscs with hard shells.

Salt-water fish include: herrings (split in two, dried and smoked for kippers); cod (cod liver oil); plaice (flat, with a brown-spotted grey back).

Fresh-water fish include: salmon (sometimes smoked or tinned); trout (often kept alive in tanks for freshness); eels (long and snake-like).

A fish propels itself with *fins* and breathes through *gills*.
Both animals and fish have *bones*.
Fish is normally both the singular and the plural form.

18 A *ledge* and a *shelf* usually *project* from a wall and *sill* from below a window. A *projector* directs film pictures on to a screen.
A *project* is a plan: a *project to construct a dam.*

18 An *axe* is used for cutting wood. A *chopper* cuts meat. A *hammer* strikes nails.

20 Forms related to *treacherous:*

NOUN	VERB	ADJECTIVE
treachery		treacherous
betrayal	betray	
traitor		

All relate to serious unfaithfulness to a person or country.
If one *betrays* a person, one breaks faith and gives information leading to his capture (*N* betrayal).
A secret can be betrayed: *His face betrayed his alarm.*
Treachery is serious and dangerous unfaithfulness shown by a *traitor.*
Ice, weather, the sea—anything producing unexpected danger—may be *treacherous.*

21 A *peak* is the pointed *summit* of a mountain.
A *ridge* is the extended top of a mountain.
A *range* is a group of mountains.
A road or path crosses a chain of mountains at a *pass*.

22 *slip*

(*N*) (*a*) a small mistake: a slip in calculating; a slip of the tongue.
(*b*) a small piece of paper: *write your name on this slip of paper*.
(*c*) a pillow-slip (or pillow-case); a lady's slip (or petticoat).

(*V*) (*a*) temporarily lose one's balance, sometimes owing to a treacherous surface.
(*b*) put on a garment quickly and easily: *slip on a dressing-gown*.
(*c*) come or go quietly and almost unnoticed: *slip out for a drink*.
(*d*) move suddenly in an unexpected direction: *the knife slipped*.

General meaning: quiet and often quick smooth action.
Adj slippery: *walk carefully on a slippery road*.

23 *furrows* in a field are made by a *plough*.

23 a *glacier* is a river of ice, with deep *crevasses* in it.
an *avalanche:* snow rolling down a mountainside, carrying rocks and trees.
a *crevice:* a small opening or crack in the rock or in a wall.

25 a *gust* of wind: sudden and strong; a light *puff* of air; a powder-puff; puff out smoke; puffing and *panting*: gasping for air when short of breath.

26 a canary usually *perches* on a *perch*.

28 signal (*N*): (*a*) a message given by means of a sign: a signal to stop given by a policeman; a distress signal from a ship.
(*b*) traffic and railway signals: a signalman; a signal-box.
(*V*): give a signal: signal in Morse Code; the train is signalled; the driver signalled that he was turning right.

30 *surroundings* (*N*) has a plural form only: *the surroundings are ugly*.

31 *aches and pains, complaints, illnesses, states of mind.*
In the passage Paul *had a headache*, *a pain in his shoulder*, *legs* that *felt stiff* and *aching feet*. He was also *perspiring* from the heat: he wiped his forehead with his handkerchief. Other complaints are:

To have: a toothache, ear-ache, aching feet, a sore heel (a blister), a sore throat, a temperature, a cold, a cough, hay fever, a pain in one's back, a pain in one's stomach, indigestion, a heart attack, a stroke, a skin disease, a fit, a nervous breakdown, influenza, appendicitis, bronchitis, measles.

To suffer from: rheumatism, arthritis, heart trouble, deafness, high blood pressure—all normally chronic complaints.

To feel: ill, tired, depressed, better.

To be: ill, seriously ill, in poor health, run down, unconscious, convalescent.

To *lose weight* it may be necessary to *go on a diet*; otherwise *weight* may be *gained* (put on weight).

TREATMENT OF A MINOR INJURY

Cleanse the wound thoroughly and apply an *antiseptic* to counteract *germs* (which spread disease. A *disinfectant* is normally for household purposes). Otherwise the wound may *fester*. *Sticking plaster* may be applied or the wound may be *bandaged*—with a bandage. *Ointment* may be smeared over the skin.

A *surgeon sets* a broken bone. He *operates on* a patient only after an *anaesthetic* has been *administered*. The patient *has an operation* (it is machines and schemes that are operated).

Infectious diseases are spread by air-borne germs; *contagious* ones by actual physical contact.

One *registers with* a doctor and is given free treatment as part of the *National Health Service*. When ill, one *consults* (goes and sees or sees) a doctor who *examines* his or her patient. The doctor may write a hospital letter to arrange for *specialist* treatment. The patient may have to go into hospital as an in-patient or attend at intervals as an out-patient. He may go in for observation.

34 horses *draw* carts. Heavy things, like tree-trunks, are *dragged* often with some difficulty along the ground. Time may also drag.

35 *scale* (*N*): (*a*) series of eight musical notes based on an ascending or descending pattern: the scale of C-major (*b*) the hard covering of a fish (*c*) system of measuring: the Centigrade scale (*d*) the measurement according to which a map is drawn: a scale of one inch to the mile, also: large-scale improvements (*e*) a pair of scales is used for weighing objects with appropriate weights.

(*V*): climb to the top of something: *scale a five-hundred-foot high cliff*.

36 Pedestrians can easily scale a wall or fence by means of a *stile*, which may be a series of steps or two or three wooden bars, one above the other.

37 *faint* (*N*) short period of unconsciousness due to weakness or lack of air

(*V*) collapse in this way

(*Adj*) weak, feeble, difficult to see or hear: a faint mark, a faint voice, he feels faint.

37 A needle is *threaded* when *thread* is put through its eye.
Metaphor: I lost the thread of what he was saying.

37 Where there is an existing word, the prefix *dis-* is added to it.
Add dis- to each of these words: appear, satisfied, appoint, inherit, solve, respect, pleasure, regard, miss, similar, infect.

38 A *down* is a grass-covered hill, common in Southern England.
A range of these hills is called *the downs*: the South Downs (near Brighton).

39 After a long cold day out of doors, one *luxuriates in* the heat of a fire, a hot bath, soft sheets and a comfortable bed.
One *indulges in* an extra cream bun, a new unneeded hat, a holiday one cannot really afford—usually with considerable enjoyment but with a slightly guilty conscience.
An *indulgent* parent may spoil a child.

44 A pen is *dipped* in ink. The road *dipped* towards the valley. He went *for a dip* in the sea before breakfast.

Pronunciation

STRESS AND SOUND: majesty [mǽʤɪstɪ]; majestic [məʤéstɪk]; resign [rɪzáɪn].
CHANGES: resignation [rezɪgnéɪʃən]; enthusiasm [ɪnθjúːzɪǽzm]; enthusiastic [ɪnθjuːzɪǽstɪk]; hero [híərou]; heroic [hɪróuɪk]; heroine [hérouɪn].

ə as in *a*go: ocean [óuʃən]; radiant [réɪdɪənt]; heaven [hevŋ]; surrounding [səráundɪŋ]; distant [dístənt]; glorious [glɔ́riəs]; territory [térɪtərɪ]; projecting [prouʤéktɪŋ]; gallant [gǽlənt]; treacherous [tretʃərəs]; trivial [trívɪəl]; glacier [glǽsɪə]; absorbed [əbzɔ́ːbd]; signalled [sígnəld]; petals [pétəlz]; hostel [hɔ́stəl]; momentary [moumənt(ə)rɪ]; blizzard [blízəd]; dramatic [drəmǽtɪk]; tropical [trɔ́pɪkl].
i as in c*i*t*y*: relaxed [rɪlǽkst]; thistle [θɪsl]; beyond [bɪjɔ́nd]; dwindled [dwíndəld]; quivering [kwívərɪŋ].
MEANING CHANGE: (bath) bathed [baːθt] (in a bath); (bathe) bathed [beɪðd] (in the sea); bathe [beɪð] one's eyes in an eye-bath; sunbathed [sʌnbeɪðd].
OTHERS: flooding [flʌ́dɪŋ]; realm [relm]; clover [klóuvə]; guide [gaɪd]; furrowed [fʌ́roud]; handkerchief [hǽnkətʃɪf]; thread [θred]; luxuriating [lʌ́ksjúrɪeɪtɪŋ]; warmth [wɔːmθ]; exploit [éksplɔɪt].
-ough
au: bough [bau]; plough [plou].
ɔf: cough [kɔf]; (trough) [trɔf].
ou: dough [dou]; though [ðou]; although [ɔːlðóu].
ʌ: enough [ɪnʌ́f]; rough [rʌf]; tough [tʌf]; (trough) [trʌf].
u: through [θruː]; thorough [θʌ́rə].

Special grammatical and structural points

(i) These pronouns are all singular: *everybody*, *everyone*, *either*, *neither*, *none*—together with adjectival *every* (every worker):

Everyone (Every passenger) must have a landing-card before he can go ashore.
Neither of the houses is furnished.
None of the shops in the town is closing to-morrow.

In the spoken language these are often used as though they were plural:

Everyone took their places.

(ii) The *present participle* is *active* in meaning and indicates that the noun or pronoun described is doing the action referred to: a dazzling sun; softly-glowing pebbles; nodding clover.
The *past participle* is *passive* in meaning and the action referred to is happening to the noun or pronoun described: a meadow bathed in sunlight; spray flung from a wave-crest; a broken window.

(iii) A *split infinitive* is now accepted by some writers but still disliked by others, who would prefer: '*to appreciate fully* the scene around' to 'to fully appreciate'.

Prepositions

(*a*) bathed *in* sunlight; result in confusion; in resignation; luxuriate in warmth

(*b*) flooding the sky *with* song; with no enthusiasm

(*c*) *beyond* the hedge (on the other side of the hedge)

(*d*) *to* his right; familiar to him; signalled to the climbers.

(*e*) he had a headache *through* sleeping.

(*f*) *at* this point.

(*g*) with a longing *for* home.

Expressions to learn and introduce into written work

(*a*) bathed in sunlight (*b*) hitherto unconquered by man (*c*) however trivial (*d*) he was far too absorbed in his task (*e*) be aware of a view of almost unearthly beauty (*f*) his far from icy surroundings (*g*) sighed in resignation (*h*) with no enthusiasm whatever (*i*) at the far end of (*j*) wherever he looked (*k*) none of it was familiar to him (*l*) less dramatic but equally exciting.

Multiple choice questions

Here are a number of questions or unfinished statements about the passage, each with four suggested ways of answering or finishing it. You must choose the way you consider the most suitable. Write in each case the bracketed number of the question or statement followed by the letters **A**, **B**, **C**, **D**, and then cross through the letter of the answer you choose. Give one answer only to each question. Read the passage through again before choosing your answers.

1 All but one of the following details in the first paragraph suggest water in some way. Which one does not?
A the colour of the sky **B** the position and movement of the sun **C** the size and position of the clouds **D** what the clouds apparently consist of

2 Which one of the following could not been seen moving?
A the bird **B** the bushes **C** the stream **D** the flowers

3 Which of these feelings or ideas was experienced by the ant moving over Paul's wrist, according to the information in the passage?
A this was a new area for discovery **B** this area was very interesting **C** the wrist was large in comparison with its own size **D** this could be a dangerous thing to do

4 The only one of these sounds that could not be heard while Paul was asleep was
A singing **B** buzzing **C** quiet rustling **D** quiet ringing

5 Which of the following difficulties did not apply to Paul in his dream?
A he was moving straight up a precipice **B** he could easily be blown off **C** he had only limited experience **D** he was responsible for other people's lives

6 Which of these statements is true according to the passage?
A the climbing party was already nearly at the top of the mountain
B if successful, they would be the first people to reach the summit
C the rock face was quite smooth **D** they were surrounded by ice

7 One of the ways in which Paul's dream was unlike the journey ahead of him was that
A both involved hardship **B** both could offer worthwhile views
C weather conditions in both were extreme **D** both demanded both skill and courage

8 Which of the following were the aches and pains felt on awaking not due to?
A the weather **B** exhaustion **C** his load **D** the exercise he had already had

9 When Paul woke up
A nobody was anywhere near him **B** at least one person was fairly near him **C** he could just see someone climbing out of sight on the hill ahead **D** his companion had caught up with him and was waiting at the end of the field

10 Which of these qualities shown in his dream would be needed in the rest of the walk?
A toughness **B** judgment **C** concentration **D** skill and experience

Reading comprehension

In this exercise you must choose the word or phrase which best completes the sentence. Write first the number of the sentence followed by the letters **A, B, C, D, E,** and then cross through the letter of the correct answer in each case.

1 Her hair was wet from the .... tossed up by the huge waves.
A foam **B** lather **C** surf **D** froth **E** spray

2 A cool drink .... him after his long hot journey.
A relaxed **B** relieved **C** refreshed **D** recovered **E** rested

3 A horse drives the .... from its body with its tail.
A spiders **B** wasps **C** ants **D** flies **E** butterflies

4 You will .... your hand if you put it into that hot water.
A scorch **B** scald **C** cook **D** bake **E** boil

5 The Alps are one of the best-known mountain .... in Europe
A ranges **B** ridges **C** passes **D** peaks **E** groups

6 With a .... of thankfulness he finished the last of his letters.
A sigh **B** shudder **C** shiver **D** gasp **E** groan

7 The old lady managed to climb the .... which was narrow but not at all steep.
A scale **B** staircase **C** ladder **D** degree **E** escalator

8 The hall seemed .... lit after the bright sunshine outside.
A faintly **B** slightly **C** vaguely **D** obscurely **E** dimly

9 A strong westerly .... flattened the standing corn though it brought no rain.
A gale **B** blizzard **C** hurricane **D** breeze **E** storm

10 The castle was surrounded by a ...., which nowadays contained only occasional rainwater.
A hedge **B** fence **C** dyke **D** wall **E** moat

Use of English

1 (ii) The five word groups below are the answers to five questions that could be asked about the passage. Write out the questions.

(i) on a bundle of hay (ii) he was far too absorbed in his task (iii) he tested the new foothold on the sheer rock wall (iv) Paul became conscious of his far from icy surroundings (v) fifteen miles off

2 Write down the numbers (i) to (xiv) and beside each a suitable form of the verbs *talk*, *speak*, *tell* or *say* as appropriate in each case.

(*a*) During the past three years, he has (i) .... his own language very rarely.

(*b*) Early poems and stories were only (ii) .... as there was no written language.

(*c*) Have you (iii) .... the class where to meet you?

(*d*) He seldom (iv) .... but when he does, he (v) .... sense.

(*e*) He (vi) .... so softly that we could not hear what he (vii) ....

(*f*) 'Be especially careful not to lose your passport,' the guide (viii) .... me.

(*g*) She (ix) .... that she cannot (x) .... the difference between the twins.

(*h*) He always (xi) .... what he thinks about other people.

(*i*) His suggestion of giving up his job is only (xii) ....; he will never do it.

(*j*) Although I (xiii) .... to him in a friendly way, he did not answer.

(*k*) They are (xiv) .... to have spent many years in Alaska.

3 Rewrite each of the following sentences, replacing each of the italicised words or phrases with its opposite.

(*a*) He has *ordered* us to move *quietly*.

(*b*) The food was so *well-cooked* that he ate *a lot*.

(*c*) He was so *hard-working* that he *passed* the examination.

(*d*) He has *a lot of* clothes on because of the *cold*.

(*e*) In some parts where the river was *narrower*, it was very *deep*.

(*f*) He *refused* the *sweet* grapes I offered him.

(*g*) He had *got up* an hour before and now he was *wide awake*.

(*h*) He *refused* to *put down* the two *heavy* cases.

4 Write out the following in dialogue form, making all necessary changes. Begin like this:

Mark Why didn't you telephone yesterday as you promised?
Mark asked Dick why he had not telephoned the previous day as he had promised. Dick apologised for having forgotten to. Some friends of his sister's had arrived unexpectedly from Lapland. Mark told him he did not believe him as nobody lived there. Dick assured him that they had gone to live there three years previously and would be returning the following week. Life there suited them very well. Mark told him not to believe that. Nobody could enjoy the darkness and cold but according to Dick, summers could be really warm and though his friends admitted that winters could be very cold, their home was very warm and comfortable. Dick then started to say something about the children but June interrupted politely and said she would have to leave them at once as she had a dental appointment. She would be meeting Dick's sister the following day so perhaps she would hear more about Lapland then.

5 The following questions relate to the impression of a page of a newspaper shown on page 301. While containing all the information that answers the question, answers should be as brief as possible (maximum fifteen words unless otherwise stated) and except in the case of (g) and (h) should be in a complete sentence.

(*a*) What information that is always at the top of a newspaper is not given here?

(*b*) Suggest a possible cause of the teachers' strike.

(*c*) Explain what a multiple car crash is.

(*d*) What kind of space flight seems to be in preparation?

(*e*) What kind of 'storm' is being referred to in the House? (the House of Commons).

(*f*) Suggest two kinds of happenings that might be dealt with on the Home News page.

(*g*) Suggest the subject of a possible article on the Women's Page.

(*h*) Reviews often deal with books. Suggest two other things which might form the subject of a review.

THE DAILY WORLD 

THREATENED STRIKE OF TEACHERS

fuerte. Null modo
oluptation. Mam
Euae de virtutib
sempitern aut diut
movente propter l
sic amicitian non
fuerte. Null modo
oluptation. Mam e
Euae de virtutib
sempitern aut diut
quis nostrud exer
consequat, vel illu
exceptur sint occq
Nam liber tempor
Temporibud aute
delectus ut aut pr
ante cum memorit
neque pecun mod
and dedocendesse
notiner si effecerit,
null sit caus pecca
ipsinuria detrimen
et carum esse iucu
quod cuis. Cuae a
seque facil, ut mih

DOLORA DELL REMARRIES

plena sit, ratiodips
sic amicitian non r
fuerte. Null modo
oluptation. Mam e
Euae de virtutib
sempitern aut diut
movente propter l
luptas erit praeder
ipsinuria detrimen
et carum esse iucu
quod cuis. Cuae a
seque facil, ut mih
plena sit, ratiodips
consequat, vel illu
exceptur sint occa
Nam liber tempor
Temporibud aute
delectus ut aut pr
ante cum memorit
neque pecun mod
and dedocendesse

PRESTO
PETROL
FOR
POWER
AND
PERFECT
PROGRESS

Lorem ipsum dolor
quis nostrud exerci
consequat, vel illun
exceptur sint occae
Nam liber tempor
Temporibud autem
delectus ut aut pro
ante cum memorite
neque pecun modu
and dedocendesse
notiner si effecerit,
null sit caus peccan
ipsinuria detriment
et carum esse iucun
quod cuis. Cuae ad
seque facil, ut mihi
plena sit, ratiodipsa
sic amicitian non .
fuerte. Null modo
oluptation. Mam et
Euae de virtutib d
sempitern aut diut
movente propter le
luptas erit praeder
movente propter le
luptas erit praeder
bestis, uae putat ess
cronylar at ille pelli
doler, non solud in :
consequat, vel illun
exceptur sint occae
Nam liber tempor
Temporibud autem
delectus ut aut pre
ante cum memorite
neque pecun modu
and dedocendesse v
notiner si effecerit,
null sit caus pecca
ipsinuria detriment
et carum esse iucu
quod cuis. Cuae a
seque facil, ut mihi

MULTIPLE CAR CRASH ON M.1.

notiner si effecerit,
null sit caus pecca
ipsinuria detrimen
et carum esse iucu
quod cuis. Cuae a
seque facil, ut mihi
plena sit, ratiodipsa
sic amicitian non
fuerte. Null modo
oluptation. Mam et
Euae de virtutib d
sempitern aut diut
movente propter le
luptas erit praeder
bestis, uae putat ess
cronylar at ille pell
doler, non solud in
Lorem ipsum dolo
quis nostrud exere
consequat, vel illu

bestis, uae putat esse specula naturae, ut at ille pellit sensar luptas epicur semper in indutial genelation. What gitur conv

MAIDEN VOYAGE OF LINER 'QUEEN MARGARET'

sit amet, consectet
tation ullam corpo
n dolore eu fugiat
nt cupiditat non p
cum soluta nobis
quinuad et aur o
fer endis dolorib a
tum etia ergat. N
t est neque nonor
ideantur. Invitat ig
t opes vel fortunag
d quaet en imige
est quam in his re
d est propter tutic
amicos pertinerer
detur expedium. I
monet amicitian c
odo fautrices fideli
inc amicit firma et
lactam amico con
adipiscing elit, se
uscipit laborios n
illa pariatur. At v
vident, simil sunt
eligend optio cor
se debit aut rerum
priore repellat. Il
amice et nebevol
per ned libiding
tr vera ratio bene
il ingen liberalitat
cupidtat a natura
s emolument pari
vitam et luptat pl
arent esse per se
nim virtutes, de q
parar, quibus pa
m sed etiam effec
rpetuam incandit
neque nostralet

STORM IN COMMONS

nit sit et simul no
jum ailman. Buoni
nit sit et simul no
e specula naturae,
t sensar luptae epi
ndutial genelation.
a dolore eu fugiat
at cupiditat non p
sum soluta nobis
quinued et aur o
fer endis dolorib a
tum etia ergat. N
: est neque nonor
deantur. Invitat ig
t opes vel fortunag
d quaet en imigen
est quam in his re
d est propter tuti
amicos pertinere
detur expedium. I
monet amicitian c
odo fautrices fideli
ine amicit firma et
lactam amico cons
etal guemad mod
ming timer natura
jum ailman. Buoni
odo fautrices fideli
ine amicit firma et
lactam amico cons
etal guemad mod
ming timer natura
ation ullam corpo
a dolore eu fugiat
at cupiditat non p
sum soluta nobis
quinued et aur o
er endis dolorib a
tum etia ergat. N
: est neque nonor
deantur. Invitat ig
t opes vel fortunag
d quaet en imigen
est quam in his re
d est propter tutio
amicos pertineren
detur expedium. It
monet amicitian c
odo fautrices fideli
ine amicit firma et
lactam amico cons
etal guemad mod
ming timer natura
jum ailman. Buoni
nit sit et simul no
est quam in his re
d est propter tutio
amicos pertineren

PREPARATIONS FOR SPACE FLIGHT

WILL MAN GET TO MARS ?

n proficiscit animal illud modo natum
am si dis placet ab picure loqui discim
n proficiscit animal illud modo natum
it diceret abbis duce hanc expetion bihil
cur semper hoc ut provert porultan. F
What gitur convente ab alia dicer natu
nulla pariatur. At vero eos et accusam
rovident, simil sunt in culpa qui officia
est eligend optio comgue nihil impedit
ffice debit aut rerum necessit atib saep
speriore repellat. Hanc ego cum tene
se amice et nebevol molestias access po
imper ned libiding gen epular religuar
itur vera ratio bene sanos ad iustitiam, a
vel ingen liberalitat magis conveniunt,
t cupidtat a natura proficis facile expl
bus emolument pariunt iniur. Itaque n
e vitam et luptat pleniore effit. Tia n
i garent esse per se ans tam expetend q
: enim virtutes, de quib ante dictum est
omparar, quibus part confirmatur anim
ssim sed etiam effectrice sunt luptam a
perpetuam incandit vitae tenere possu
id aeque nostralet parit dolem angorib.
im eae sempan inhaerercent, eadem d
n it salar le grand. Auam multa vitiose
am si dis placet ab picuro loqui discim
ssim sed etiam effectrice sunt luptam a
perpetuam incandit vitae tenere possun
id aeque nostralet parit dolem angorib.
im eae sempan inhaerercent, eadem d
n it salar le grand. Auam multa vitiose
r suscipit laborios nisi ut aliquip ex ea

INDEX

Weather

deantur. Invitat ig
t opes vel fortunag
d quaet en imiger
est quam in his re
d est propter tutio
amicos pertineren
detur expedium. It
monet amicitian c
odo fautrices fideli

Late News

detur expedium. It
monet amicitian c
. dolore eu fugiat
at cupiditat non p
sum soluta nobis
quinued et aur o
er endis dolorib a
tum etia ergat. N
est neque nonor

(*i*) Among the Situations Vacant there is a short advertisement for a suitable person to work as a counter assistant in an official town tourist office giving useful information to visitors to the town. Write this advertisement in not more than 20 words.

(*j*) Study the advertisement for petrol in the bottom left-hand corner. Write a similar advertisement for some kind of tooth-paste in 6–10 words.

Composition and summarising

Write on one of the following subjects, using between 120 and 180 words.

1 You suddenly realise you have forgotten to send birthday greetings to a close friend living at some distance from you. Write a short letter

apologising for and explaining your forgetfulness, giving one item of news and promising to write in more detail in a few days' time. You should make the beginning and ending like those of an ordinary English letter but do not include these in the number of words.

2 The following advertisement appears in a newspaper: 'Beautifully-furnished modern flat to let. Lounge, two large bedrooms, kitchen, bathroom. Central heating. Hot and cold water. Excellent decorative condition. Garage. £14 a week. Telephone 91/827364.' You telephone for further details. Write down the telephone conversation.

3 Explain why a certain district of your country or a certain town attracts tourists and holidaymakers.

4 Explain why you would be contented or bored if you lived in the country.

5 Describe the main shopping street of your town on a very hot day and then on a very windy day.

6 Write the list of instructions which might appear in a room in which you normally work or in a classroom, explaining what should be done if fire breaks out.

7 Give advice to someone who is going to do one of the following things:
  (*a*) go walking and possibly climbing in mountains
  (*b*) buy a second-hand car
  (*c*) go on a camping holiday
  (*d*) start learning a foreign language

8 Describe the room in which you are now sitting.

9 You recently had a meal in a restaurant and came out thoroughly dissatisfied. Write an account of what happened.

10 Write two paragraphs about Paul's experiences, both in reality and in his dream. The first paragraph should deal with the things he might have found enjoyable, the second with the unpleasant things. Use in all between 175 and 200 words.

Spoken English

Daydreams

If I'd had the chance, I'd have been a research chemist who'd have made some great discovery that would have changed the world.
If I'd had the sense to train as a doctor instead of becoming a research chemist, I'd have been able to do something worthwhile and satisfying.
If I had a beautiful figure, I'd be a highly-paid model and perhaps also find a rich husband.
If I hadn't got a husband and family, I'd train as a secretary and get an exciting job abroad.

If I had time, I'd write that novel I've had at the back of my mind for so long.
If I had a car, I'd tour Europe, stopping at all the small interesting places that nobody else has time for.
If I had a long enough holiday, I'd save up for a couple of years and travel round the world.
If I had a house of my own, I'd give up my job as stewardess on a liner and work as a waitress, just to be in one place.
If I weren't so stupid, I'd think of something wonderful that I really could do, though I'm poor, plain, always busy and living in a tenth-floor flat in a suburb of Birmingham.

Situations

(*a*) What do you do (i) when you have a bad headache? (ii) when you feel very stiff after unaccustomed exercise? (iii) when you feel overwhelmingly nervous before an important interview? (iv) when you can't sleep and have a very busy day ahead (you have no sleeping tablets)?

(*b*) You are driving along a lonely country road when you run out of petrol. What do you do?

(*c*) When driving along a road of this kind, where there seem to be no houses, you see a very young child wandering across the road in front of you. What do you do? What do you say later?

(*d*) You are the sole teacher in charge of a group of fourteen children aged ten who have just returned to the station after a day's walk in order to catch the last train of the day. You then find that one child is missing. What do you do?

Subjects for discussion

(*a*) Why do you enjoy (or not enjoy) intense heat?

(*b*) Do you think that climate really influences character to any great extent?

(*c*) What is the appeal of mountaineering to those who practise it?

(*d*) What kinds of pictures have been produced by the great landscape painters of your country? What have been the chief interests of your national painters?

(*e*) Do you believe that as a result of a higher standard of living, many present-day young people are softer, less adventurous and tough than their ancestors?

(*f*) What are the attractions of youth-hostelling?

General guidance and practice

Gerund and infinitive constructions

This is an attempt to put some kind of order into an extremely complicated problem. The list is very far from complete but most of the verbs needed by the Intermediate student are included. The classification is not ideal but may serve as an aid in memorising.

A cross indicates that the form in question is never used, a bracket that it is far less common than the alternative and an asterisk (*) that a note follows the tables.

Like Dislike

VERB	like	should like	love	want	wish
GERUND	reading	(rare)	singing	X	X
INFINITIVE	to read	to come	to sing	to go	to arrange

VERB	long	enjoy	appreciate	prefer
GERUND	X	walking	having	*
INFINITIVE	to travel	X	X	to stay

VERB	dislike	hate	loathe
GERUND	meeting	seeing	being watched
INFINITIVE	(to meet)	to see	X

Start Continue Finish

VERB	begin	start	continue	keep	remain
GERUND	learning	knitting	living	making	standing
INFINITIVE	to learn	to knit	to live	X	X

VERB	spend time	finish	stop*	cease	delay	postpone
GERUND	fishing	ironing	speaking*	trying	having	selling
INFINITIVE	X	X	to speak*	to try	X	X

('I have begun to understand' not 'I have begun understanding.' This construction is typical of verbs which rarely have a continuous tense form. In these cases 'begin' and 'continue' are followed by an infinitive, not a gerund.)

Positive and Negative tendencies

VERB	agree	consent	decide	determine	resolve
GERUND	to starting	to signing	X	X	X
INFINITIVE	to start	to sign	to write	to fight	to climb

VERB	try	attempt	struggle	venture	hope
GERUND	(studying)	X	X	X	X
INFINITIVE	to study	to swim	to reach	to remark	to win

VERB	mean	intend	consider	propose	arrange	plan
GERUND	X	X	building	lending	X	X
INFINITIVE	to give	to stop	X	to lend	to visit	to spend

VERB	prepare	get ready	ask	invite	suggest
GERUND	X	X	X	X	driving
INFINITIVE	to depart	to jump	to fetch	to join	X

VERB	beg	encourage	coax	urge	persuade	inspire
GERUND	X	X	X	X	X	X
INFINITIVE	to allow	to return	to eat	to hurry	to apply	to compose

VERB	advise	tempt	recommend	remind	allow	let
GERUND	X	X	X	X	X	X
INFINITIVE	to invest	to commit	to listen	to shut	to use	help

VERB	make	cause	force	compel	order	teach
GERUND	X	X	X	X	X	X
INFINITIVE	answer	to hesitate	to obey	to retreat	to wear	to observe

VERB	train	help	can't help	can't resist	dare*	need*
GERUND	X	X	coughing	buying	X	mending
INFINITIVE	to carry	to lift	X	X	to try	to mend

VERB	risk	manage	afford	deserve	enable	ought
GERUND	losing	X	X	X	X	X
INFINITIVE	X	to pay	to send	to miss	to attend	to feel

VERB	avoid	omit	neglect	grudge	refuse	deny
GERUND	crossing	stating	cleaning	spending	X	saying
INFINITIVE	X	to state	to clean	X	to change	X

VERB	fail	miss	dread	escape	threaten
GERUND	X	attending	finding	being punished	X
INFINITIVE	to arrive	X	X	X	to report

VERB	regret
GERUND	saying
INFINITIVE	X

Miscellaneous Verbs

VERB	claim	conspire	practise	happen	pretend
GERUND	X	X	entering	X	X
INFINITIVE	to know	to kill	X	to remember	to like

VERB	seem	appear	excuse*	forgive*	mind
GERUND	X	X	my forgetting	my spoiling	waiting
INFINITIVE	to grow	to fall	X	X	X

Positions of the Body: stand looking, sit thinking, lie dreaming, kneel praying.
The Senses: see, notice, watch, observe, hear, smell, feel.

These are accompanied by the *Present Participle* when the action described is *continuous*, otherwise by the infinitive.

WITH A VERY FEW EXCEPTIONS THE GERUND FOLLOWS A PREPOSITION WHETHER IT FORMS PART OF A PHRASAL VERB OR IS USED INDEPENDENTLY.

Here are some examples of *phrasal verbs* and *verbs followed by a preposition*, all of which would require the *gerundial* form of any verb coming after:

confess to, object to, look forward to, submit to.
apologise for, blame for, compensate for, punish for, use for, pay for, reproach for, charge for.
approve of, boast of, despair of, accuse of {think of / think about} Both are used.
complain about, grumble about, talk about
congratulate on, depend on, rely on, insist on, count on, go on, keep on.
profit from, hinder from, prevent from,* save from, protect from.
give up
warn against
succeed in, persevere in, persist in, specialise in
leave off, feel like.

Here are a few other forms to which this rule applies:

used to, accustomed to, afraid of (also: afraid to do), ashamed of (also: ashamed to do), aware of, capable of, conscious of, a method of, the necessity of, the problem of, worth doing, proof of, take pride in, interested in, absorbed in, busy doing.

How about *going*?

Many Adjectives are followed by an infinitive.

difficult to understand, eager to hear, necessary to know, etc.

And Certain Nouns

the courage to risk, the liberty to go, etc.

NOTES ON THE ABOVE TABLE

1 *Prefer* She prefers to stay at home to-day.
She prefers reading to speaking.

2 *Stop* He stopped walking. He stopped to pick up a letter.

3 *Dare* I dare to come. I dare not come. Dare you come?
I don't dare to come. Do you dare to come?
I dare you to jump.

4 *Need* He needs to work. He need not work. Need he work?
He doesn't need to work. Does he need to work?
This shoe needs mending.

5 *Excuse* *Forgive* *Prevent*
Please excuse my coming late.
Please forgive my coming late.
He prevented my studying. *Or:* He prevented me from studying.

6 *Leave* I left her to lock up the house when she was ready.
I left her lying on the divan, half asleep.

7 *Forget* *Remember*
Did you forget to telephone to him?
No, I clearly remember doing it.
(The same rule applies to both verbs.)

8 *Teach*, *Show*, *Explain*, *Demonstrate*, *Learn*, *Know*, *Understand*, etc.

He taught the men to stand to attention when he entered.
He taught the men how to construct bridges.

Apart from 'teach' and 'learn', 'how to' follows all the other verbs listed, not the simple infinitive alone.

9 *Make* His father made him dig the garden.
He was made to dig the garden.

10 An odd construction: You know better than to rush into the road.

11 Used *to* Farm labourers *used to get* up early.
Farm labourers *are used to getting* up early.
(Never: Farm labourers use to get up early.)
It's no use asking him; he doesn't know.

12 THE GERUND AS SUBJECT OR OBJECT OF A SENTENCE

Riding is an enjoyable form of exercise.
Riding a camel is probably not so pleasant.
He teaches riding.

(The gerund follows 'teach' only when a definite subject is taught. One teaches a person *to speak* correctly or *how to speak* correctly see Note 8.)

13 The infinitive is sometimes used as a subject but far less commonly. It usually sounds unnatural though not grammatically wrong. e.g. To ride is . . .

14 THE PERFECT INFINITIVE

You ought to have finished.
He is said to have resigned.
He seems to have fainted.
You must have heard what I said.
You could have written.
They are supposed to have been studying.

15 THE INFINITIVE EXPRESSING PURPOSE

In most cases it is enough to use the infinitive alone.

He stopped to open his umbrella.
She paused to drink some water.
He ran to catch a bus.

There is a slight difference in meaning between the following two sentences, the first suggesting purpose, the second a natural sequence of happenings:

He went out to get a newspaper.
He went out and got a newspaper.

The use of 'and' with a following finite verb is common with such verbs as 'go' and 'come' and sometimes with 'run', 'hurry up', 'sit down' and 'lie down'.
Notice however such expressions as 'to go shopping', 'to go riding'.

Here is an example of the infinitive following an adjective or an adverb modified by 'too'.

It is now *too late to telephone* him.

Here is a slightly different use of the infinitive of purpose:

He was *chosen to, appointed to, bribed to change* the existing regulations.

so as to, in order to—used where the purpose is emphasised; and essential with a negative form of the infinitive

Go to bed early so as to be quite fresh in the morning.
He put his season ticket in his pocket in order not to lose it.

In the following exercise replace the verbal forms in brackets by their correct form, infinitive or gerund. In some cases, the correct preposition or adverb will also have to be supplied.

(*a*) The doctor insisted (give) the patient oxygen immediately.

(*b*) Fascinated, we watched the snake (crawl) silently across the grass.

(*c*) How do you always manage (escape) (help) (do) the washing-up?

(*d*) If you practise (dive) often, you will learn (do) it without (cause) such a splash.

(*e*) Would you like (sit) (watch) television? I should prefer (play) tennis. I prefer (move) about to (sit) still.

(*f*) Do you mean (risk) (catch) pneumonia by (go) out now that it has started (pour) with rain?

(*g*) I cannot forgive her (refuse) (allow) me (use) the telephone. I feel like (write) to the owner of the house (complain).

(*h*) The student hopes (specialise) (photograph) wild life. He is looking forward (spend) his holiday (get) (train) in (use) extremely complex cameras.

(*i*) I blame you (break) that window, and I intend (make) you (pay) (repair) it. That may teach you (be) more careful not (damage) other people's property and (stop) (throw) stones.

(*j*) Your daughter is very anxious (go) to University (study) languages and I should like (suggest) your (encourage) her (do) so. You will not regret (send) her if you can afford (do) it, as she will certainly profit (continue) her education.

(*k*) Would you remind the students (remain) (stand) until the distinguished visitors have left the platform. I ought (remember) (tell) them this morning but I was busy (prepare) a speech and I forgot (do) so.

(*l*) The sick child missed (play) with his friends and never failed (be) at the window (see) them (run) to school.

(*m*) I left her (cook) the dinner while I went (shop) but I cannot rely on her (carry) out anything I ask her (do).

(*n*) Do you remember (warn) me not (be) to quick-tempered and (advise) me (learn) (control) my impatience?

(*o*) Have you succeeded (persuade) your husband that is worth (buy) a washing machine? If he objects (pay) for it, ask him if he would enjoy (stand) (wash) all the morning and promise him (spend) the time you save (attend) classes (improve) your cooking.

(*p*) This room needs (tidy). You need not (tell) me you haven't time (do) it. Get up earlier (have) an extra half hour before (go) to school. Now go (fetch) a duster. You should be ashamed (sit) in such a pigsty. (Put) away your books would improve matters.

(*q*) He was supposed (arrive) by the ten o'clock train and George went (meet) him. It's no use our (wait) any longer; he may come by any train. He is used (find) his way around. He used (be) a travel courier.

Vague use of personal pronouns

Many faults in students' writing arise from carelessness in the use of pronouns.

Always remember that the reason for a pronoun's existence is that it is taking the place of a noun. Except in certain impersonal expressions like 'It is raining' and 'It is impossible', whenever a third person pronoun ('he', 'she' 'it', 'they') is used, the noun to which it refers should be unmistakably clear.

Consider this sentence:

> Small gardens bright with spring flowers surround the neat thatched cottages which cluster together companionably. It is really peaceful and welcoming.

Which noun can 'it' refer to?

Another similar mistake is to use a third person pronoun which may refer to one of a number of nouns.

Here are three examples:

> The tourist asked the policeman the way to the British Museum. He did not know where it was.
> I bought a hat at the shop you often go to. It is an expensive one.
> Parks attract many visitors during the summer months. They are often untidy.

The other common mistake is to mix the pronouns themselves.

Here is a very exaggerated example of this mistake.

> I went into Black's, the grocer's, for some special French cheese—one can only get it there unless you catch a bus to Beechley—but they had nothing but English Cheddar. You know how attached one gets to his favourite kind of cheese. We do get a much better selection nowadays, so one can buy more or less what he prefers.

Remember: he—his; one—one's; you—your; they—their.

Always be sure you are using a personal pronoun logically and exactly, and (in the case of a third person pronoun) correctly related to a noun or another pronoun.

Correct the following sentences:

(*a*) The cake she made won the first prize in the competition. It had plenty of fruit in it.

(*b*) You can never be sure how an English word is stressed. It is usually necessary to have a dictionary showing you the correct stress so that one can be sure that his pronunciation is correct.

(*c*) Owing to the shortage of milk supplies, it must be imported.

(*d*) A few days ago Brian went to catch his bus outside the garage only to discover it was not there.

(*e*) John boarded the bus at the traffic lights and the conductor was very angry with him. He immediately demanded his fare before he had time to get it out for him.

(*f*) The snow gradually settled until it cloaked with white the tree at the end of the garden. It looked incredibly beautiful.

Like as

Many mistakes are made as a result of confusing these two words.

Like

Apart from its use as a verb and a noun ('Have you ever seen his *like*?'—'anyone so unusual as he'), 'like' is an adjective or adverb. Originally it was accompanied by the preposition 'to' which has now been dropped. For this reason, 'like' often seems to behave as a preposition.

He is not in the least like his father.
It looks like leather.
She sings like a bird.
What will the weather be like to-morrow?

Alike is generally used for the adjective with no following noun or pronoun.

The twins are exactly alike.

Notice the idiomatic expressions:

It looks like rain.—It seems as if it is going to rain.
Those hooligans look like causing trouble.
I feel like going for a walk.

As

(*a*) can be an adverb: as good, as much.

(*b*) a relative adverb or pronoun:

As to your salary, that will be settled later.
He is not so clever as you.

(*c*) a conjunction.
As a conjunction, 'as' will join two clauses.
It can have various meanings:

(i) at the moment that

He stopped me as I was passing his gate.

(ii) because

She cannot come as she is busy.

(iii) in the way that

You should speak quietly and slowly as your friend does.

(iv) giving the impression that

He behaves as if he owned the street.

(v) in the position of

He is employed as a clerk (in this one case only a noun follows).
(Speaking as a friend—the following verb 'speaks' is understood.)

A clause which is not expressed but is understood often depends on the 'as':

He is as quick-tempered as his father (is).

In the sentence 'You should write as I do' the second verb is often omitted. In this case it is far more normal to say:

You should write like me.

though this may seem a somewhat odd statement. It is quite wrong, however, to say:

You should write like I do.

When a pronoun follows the relative pronoun 'as', the pronoun should be in the nominative case.

Is he as old as I (am)?

Spoken English normally uses the accusative: 'Is he as old as me?' especially in the case of 'he', 'she', 'we' and 'they'.

The rule (and departure from the rule in Spoken English) applies also in a comparative: 'Is he older than I (am)?'—in colloquial form:

Is he older than me?

Compare: He is acting *as* legal adviser to the company.
He is acting *like* a madman.

It looks like thunder.
It looks as if there will be a thunderstorm.

I feel like nothing on earth. (rather ill)
I feel as if I were going to faint.

Use 'like', 'as', 'as if' or 'as to' (as suitable) to fill the spaces in the following sentences:

(*a*) The Town Council has chosen Thompson .... the next Mayor.

(*b*) Use the margin .... your guide.

(*c*) That tea is .... sweet .... syrup.

(*d*) With a face ...... a pudding she behaves ...... she were a beauty queen.

(*e*) The weather looks ...... improving at last. I feel ...... I were no longer a solid block of ice.

(*f*) He works .... an office boy and spends money .... a duke.

(*g*) The tourist is surrounded by pigeons ...... he walks across Trafalgar Square.

(*h*) The mongrel dog looked .... a bulldog from the front and a greyhound from the rear. People regarded it .... a curiosity.

(*i*) The general insisted on taking hostages .... he did not trust the defeated leaders.

(*j*) If only you could type .... my last secretary!

(*k*) Why not go to evening classes .... she did?

(*l*) Don't dash into the road .... that.

(*m*) The Prince Regent acted .... king when his father was ill.

(*n*) I should like your advice .... whether I should sell the property at the price offered.

There is, It is

Basically it is easy enough to distinguish between these two expressions.

It is/they are normally introduces something already known or that has at least been mentioned or suggested.

There is/there are introduces something new.

What is that? It is a baby tortoise.
There is a canary in the garden.

In practice 'it is' may introduce ideas not previously referred to.

These include expressions dealing with (*a*) the weather. It was a hot day.
(*b*) with time: It is six o'clock (possibly answering the question, What is the time?) It is a long time to wait till supper.
(*c*) with a journey: It is a long way to London.

Many other expressions are introduced by 'it is' such as:

It is a pity that . . . It is essential that . . ., It is easy to . . ..

Perhaps the two following examples best show the difficulty of distinguishing between these two introductory expressions:

It is a long journey from London to Edinburgh.
There is a long journey ahead of you.

Students normally pick up the correct usage by reading or listening.
Replace the spaces in the following sentences by 'there is', 'there are' or 'it is':

(*a*) .... far too much spice in this cake. .... not necessary to use so much.

(*b*) .... a year since we met.

(*c*) Please try this chocolate. .... a free sample from the makers. .... three different flavours available.

(*d*) .... time to go now. No, it isn't. .... still time to have a cigarette.

(*e*) Don't eat that. .... a poisonous berry. .... many of them in these parts.

(*f*) .... a frog on the edge of that pool. .... one of those creatures that do not appeal to me.

(*g*) .... a train leaving at nine o'clock. .... a fast one.

(*h*) .... often a difficult job to trace the owner of lost property.

(*i*) .... a shame that even to-day .... so many homeless people.

(*j*) .... no time to stop and talk. .... a bus to catch. .... a fair distance to the terminus.

(*k*) .... (Future tense) an hour to wait at the station and .... a twenty minute walk to the station.

(*l*) .... (Present Perfect tense) a big fire in the warehouse. .... (Past Simple tense) a great pile of timber stored there.

(*m*) .... (Past Perfect tense) a tiring day and .... (Past Simple tense) still a lot to do.

(*n*) .... (Conditional Perfect tense) thousands more visitors to the exhibition if .... (Past Perfect tense) more widely advertised.

Illnesses

Answer the following questions:

(*a*) When do you have to use your handkerchief very often? What do you use your handkerchief for?

(*b*) What is almost certainly true of a person with a flushed face and a hot forehead? What does a doctor use a thermometer for when examining a patient?

(*c*) What might be the cause of a sore heel?

(*d*) What painful complaint do people risk getting by sleeping in damp sheets?

(*e*) What has to happen in hospital to a person suffering from acute appendicitis? What does one call the doctor qualified to do this job?

(*f*) What does the ordinary person often use an antiseptic for?

(*g*) What may happen to a person who works and worries too much?

(*h*) What may happen to a person who eats too much (i) at one meal? (ii) over a long period? What can a person do to lose weight?

(*i*) What are some of the symptoms of being run down?

(*j*) What conditions may cause one's feet to ache?

Prepositions

Fill the spaces in the following sentences with suitable prepositions, single words or phrases.

(*a*) The shepherd signalled .... his dog to drive the sheep into the fold.

(*b*) In all his songs the composer expresses a longing .... his own country.

(*c*) He was already familiar .... the gloomy room. Its dreary furniture was only too familiar .... him.

(*d*) He obtained his release from jail .... the successful efforts of his friends to prove his innocence.

(*e*) The teacher's insistence .... high standards resulted .... excellent work.

(*f*) At the far side of the farmyard there was a kitchen garden, and .... that was the orchard.

(*g*) After washing up, the youth hostellers scrubbed the kitchen table ...... a large scrubbing brush and then wiped it down .... a cloth.

(*h*) Our ginger cat loves to lie on the hearthrug luxuriating .... the cosy warmth of the fire.

(*i*) The dark pavement was suddenly flooded .... light from the headlights of a car.

(*j*) He was too absorbed .... pedalling his bicycle through the driving sleet to notice me.

Subjects for debate

A debate is a formal discussion. A motion (a certain statement) is presented; one speaker proposes (or supports) the motion by making a speech in its favour; another speaker opposes the motion. Each of these speakers may have a seconder, who also speaks. The Chairman, who is in charge of the meeting, then throws the motion open to discussion by the whole group, who speak in favour of or against the motion, each addressing his remarks to 'Mr. Chairman'. The latter has the duty of seeing that only one person speaks at a time. Starting with the opposer, the two chief speakers sum up the opinions expressed in the discussion and a vote is then taken, for or against the motion.

Here are some suggestions of motions for debate:

That mass-production has destroyed the values of craftsmanship.

That mankind would be better off without the private car.

That the large-scale invasion of a country by tourists is regrettable.

That living abroad spoils one for living at home.

That standards of behaviour are lower to-day than they were a century ago.

That the citizen has the duty of being completely honest in his everyday life.

That the Government should be responsible for the care of the nation's health.

That a woman's world should be the kitchen and the nursery.

That man is actually the weaker sex.

That the strict observance of fashion is a sign of a weak character.

That education should increasingly be carried out by machines.

That money is indeed the root of all evil.

That a little too much discipline is better for a child than too little control.

That at least half the leaders of a nation should be under thirty-five.

That younger people make the best leaders.

That society makes the criminal.

That high standards of living produce weak character.

That all our actions are ultimately selfish.

That chance and circumstance produce the great man.

That the more popular newspapers are of service to the community.

That the dreamer is happier than the realist.

That all women want a husband.

That we could do without examinations.

That it is better to be able to do many things fairly well than one thing superbly.

That men enjoy talking more than women do.

Appendix

Words and expressions which need special attention

This is a summary of some of the words and expressions that are often confused or which may be used wrongly in English. A space is left below each group for the student or teacher to add any others that he has found need careful attention.

It may be useful to study these carefully, especially those known to cause individual difficulty, a few days before doing the examination.

Elementary points

Any mistakes made with these are serious ones. Written work should be checked carefully to make sure that no such mistakes have been made.

1 *Common words confused because of their sound and spelling*

were/where; their/there; no/know; new/knew; to/too; of/off; being/been; than/then; by/buy; quite/quiet; blue/blew; through/threw; red/read; full/careful(ly); till/until; leave/live; beat/bit; seat/sit; feel/fill; thing/think; who's/whose; it's/its; dinner/dining; writing/writer/written; four/fourteen/forty; left/felt; passed/past; weather/whether; cloths/clothes; lose/loose; at last/at least.

2 *Common words sometimes spelt wrongly (other than those above)*

with; which; goes; tries; another; cannot; except; goodbye; homework; all right.

3 *Common verb forms sometimes used wrongly*

run ran run; choose chose chosen; hide hid hidden;
fall fell fallen; feel felt felt; send sent sent;
lay laid/say said/pay paid BUT: play played/stay stayed.

4 *Other words or phrases confused*

interesting/interested (and other -ing and -ed forms);
become/get; high/tall/long; wide/large; thick/fat;

while/because; when/if; at first/first; at last/last;
look for/look after; bring/take; put on/wear; put off/take off;
can/can speak; turn on/open; turn off/close; sea/lake.

5 *Singular and plural forms and use of articles*

SINGULAR ONLY: information furniture luggage money hair (of the head) news weather shopping

(Singular Verb—Pronoun IT—Possessive Adjective ITS—no A)

PLURAL ONLY: people (Singular: a person) the police

COMPARE: travel/a journey; work/a job;
trousers scissors are/a pair of trousers a pair of scissors is

ARTICLE: He is *a* doctor/*a* teacher.
Doctor Morgan Captain Harris
most houses both brothers
go to school/to church/to bed.

6 *Adjectives*

(*a*) It is a very bad mistake to confuse HIS and HER: his wife her brother. (In some languages HE and SHE are the same and it is even worse to confuse these)

(*b*) Another very bad mistake is to add -e or -s to an adjective.
The only adjectives with a plural form are THIS/THESE THAT/THOSE

(*c*) a lot of/a great deal of/plenty of work (Singular)
many/plenty of/a lot of friends (Plural)

(*d*) a little work/a few friends (some); little work/few friends (not enough)
only a little/only a few

(*e*) he is very tired/he is too tired to work

(*f*) as hard as/not so (as) hard as

(*g*) work hard (a lot)/hardly work (very little)

7 *Adverbs* speak loudly run quickly (fast)

8 *Verbs*

SOME VERY BAD MISTAKES

(*a*) Wrong forms: he go (es) he did not walk~~ed~~ I ~~did not be~~ (I was not).

(*b*) Wrong question form: ~~Go you~~? (Do you go?) Where ~~he went~~? (Where did he go?)
When ~~you come~~ to-morrow? (When are you coming to-morrow?)

(*c*) Omission of the subject: (It) Is a cold day.
When he came to the house, (he) knocked at the door.

(*d*) Two objects: He is looking for a paper which he has seen (it) recently.
THE ABOVE MISTAKES SHOULD BE IMPOSSIBLE AND ARE USUALLY CAUSED BY CARELESSNESS

(*e*) TENSES: (i) Do not start in the past and then change to the present so as to make your writing more exciting. Mixing past and present tenses when there is no reason for this is also a bad mistake.

(ii) Try not to confuse:
Present Simple/Present Continuous
He *comes* from Italy. The house *stands* in a park.

Past Simple/Present Perfect
You *made* a cup of tea *an hour ago.*/She *has just made* a cup of tea so it is still hot.

Present in Adverbial Time Clauses
I shall go home as soon as/when/before it *gets* dark.
Notice: He *was* born

(*f*) USE OF VERBS: He *is* hungry, thirsty, hot, cold, right, wrong, sleepy
He *is* twenty OR He *is* twenty years old.
He gave his bag to a porter (Not: to the train—give to a person but not to a thing)

(*g*) REFLEXIVES: She has washed her hands. He has broken his leg.
He feels ill/tired/cold.
He enjoyed himself (at the party). He enjoyed the party.

(*h*) CONSTRUCTIONS: before/after/by/for (Prepositions) *doing*
enjoy doing; stop working.
make him go away; let him help.
he *wants his son to be* a doctor.
he *thinks he is* right/he *is thinking of buying* a car.
know how to address an envelope
see him *fall*/*see* him *reading*
he used my pen to write his name with (Purpose).
he is *too* ill *to come*/he is not old *enough to read.*

9 *Prepositions*

ON: on the wall; on the blackboard; on the first floor; on Wednesday; on the first of July; on my birthday; be on holiday.

IN: in a picture; in the sky; in the street; in January; in autumn; in two hours' time; interested in.

TO: go to London; talk/speak to friends; say goodbye to a friend.

CONTRASTS: IN the morning/AT night; arrive IN London/AT a station.
come OUT OF/wait OUTSIDE.
I stayed FOR a week/I met him a week AGO.
SINCE last Saturday/FOR five days.

10 *Word order*

These are two bad mistakes: (*a*) Then ~~went he~~ (he went) home.
When I have time, ~~can I~~ (I can) finish it.
(*b*) I have ~~it sold~~ (sold it). If I ~~him see~~ (see him).

Other mistakes: (*c*) I enjoyed/liked ~~very much~~ that book.
This can be: I very much enjoyed/liked that book.
or: I enjoyed/liked that book very much.
He read ~~slowly~~ the letter.
should be: He read the letter slowly.

(*d*) ~~In the garden~~ there are flowers.
Better: There are flowers in the garden.

11 *Punctuation*

COMMAS: I know where it is. What I need is a holiday. (No comma.)

APOSTROPHE: the man's leg (a person). the leg of the table (a thing).

CAPITAL LETTERS: speak Greek; an Italian city (nouns and adjectives of nationality).
Cambridge Street Waterloo Station the River Severn.
Uncle George Aunt Elizabeth.

Points which may cause difficulty at an intermediate level

These need careful study and revision. In some cases students may have to refer back to the course book to make sure which form is correct. Most mistakes in using these words and expressions probably result from carelessness however, so written work should be checked carefully with these points in mind.

1 *Words whose meanings are sometimes confused*

opportunity/possibility meaning/opinion/intention library/bookshop
novel/short story teacher/professor client/customer
announcement/advertisement prospect/prospectus
receipt/recipe/prescription will/testament
(an) allowance/permission/leave (for a soldier) repetition/rehearsal
invalid/disabled person vicar/curate factory/fabric
warehouse/department store oven/stove cooking/kitchen.

understand/realise realise/recognise ignore/not know know/get to know
look at/watch notice/remark
say (to someone—direct speech)/tell (someone—reported speech) rent/hire
save/spare lend/borrow drive/ride go/walk (not: go on foot)
go with/follow run/spring bring/take forget (to bring)/leave (something at home) wait for/assist/attend like/prefer criticise/blame
claim/pretend deny/defy inspect/control overwork/do overtime
must not/need not lose/loose (Adjective)/loosen pick/pick up
grow/grow up fall/fall down
take place/take one's place/take a seat/take part/take someone's part
agree to do/agree with an opinion/accept an offer or gift (NEVER: accept to do)
persuade to do/convince someone that something is true he died/he is dead

enter for/take/pass an examination go to a dance/go dancing
act (in) a play/play a game affect (Verb)/effect (Noun and Verb: effect a change).

worn/worn out hard-working/busy careless/carefree bored/annoyed advanced/superior punctual/exact older/elder deceived/disappointed late/too late favourite (not: preferred) middle-aged/medieval (Nouns: middle age/the Middle Ages).

3 *Verb forms sometimes confused*

find found found/found founded founded buy bought bought/ bring brought brought fly flew flown/flow flowed flowed/flee fled fled wind wound wound/wound wounded wounded rise rose risen/raise raised raised lie lay lain/lay laid laid get got got/forget forgot forgotten beat beat beaten hurt hurt hurt.

4 *Uncountables, plurals and the use of articles*

UNCOUNTABLES: knowledge advice progress employment traffic shopping sightseeing dancing aircraft spacecraft machinery (a machine).

PLURAL: contents cattle surroundings.

ARTICLES: No article with abstract nouns that are not defined:
quietness/the quietness of the night/a strange quietness.
No article: man (=mankind) Nature space (in the universe) youth (the period) life (in general) Page two.
Articles: the Mediterranean (a sea) the twentieth century the River Trent the 5th September the North the United States the Alps.
Compare: have a cold, a headache, a pain, a cough. have toothache, earache, indigestion, influenza. play the piano, the violin. play football, cards.

5 *Adjectives:* last (next) week/the last (the next) week; latest/last later/latter next/nearest.
Possessive adjective always before 'own': my/his/our own house; the actual pen he used/present-day events; so small/many such a small house/such small houses; everybody (Pronoun) (not: all people); a stone wall a silk dress; paint something green.

6 *Adverbs:* no more (quantity)/no longer (time) in a friendly (leisurely) way this afternoon (not: to-day afternoon or: to-day in the afternoon)

ADJECTIVE:	everyday	indoor	outdoor
ADVERB:	every day	indoors	out-of-doors

yet/still/always; ago (Direct Speech)/before (Reported Speech).
a fortnight (not: fifteen days).

7 *Verbs:*

(*a*) CONSTRUCTIONS WITH THE GERUND

suggest/avoid/risk/mind/spend time/keep/finish doing.
busy/worth doing used to/accustomed to doing.
prevent from/succeed in/look forward to doing.

CONSTRUCTIONS WITH THE INFINITIVE

It is impossible for him to do it.
You had better ask. He would rather stay.

(*b*) have something done: he has had his watch repaired

(*c*) look like an invalid look, as if he is very ill

(*d*) NEVER: ~~use to do.~~ He gets up very early (Never: ~~he uses to get up~~).

(*e*) You do not/did not have to stay.

(*f*) I hope so I want to I know (in answer to a question).

(*g*) Not: ~~there happened~~ ~~there came~~. An accident happened A man came.

(*h*) CONDITION (Second Type) He would help you if you asked him. (Not: ~~would ask~~)

(*i*) REPORTED SPEECH:

He told me he had first met her a week before (Tense Changes)
He asked me where I was living. (Word Order in a Reported Question)

(*j*) *make* a mistake *do* homework, an examination, a test, shopping, a course, exercises.
have a picnic have a dream go for a walk/a drive take a photograph ask a question give a lecture pay a visit.
Notice: a lot to do (Not: to work)

8 *Prepositions*

beside/besides as far as/until go towards/fight (lean) against.
at the same time at that moment at university at (a speed of) ten kilometres an hour at my friends' (house) at the fishmonger's.
on holiday on business on fire on a journey on the way to on the sea.
in my opinion in this way in the north of in German in a field the highest mountain in the world.
at Christmas/*on* my birthday/a present *for* Christmas.
at the age of sixty/a man *of* sixty climb (*up*) *to* the top
pleased/satisfied/angry/disappointed *with* stay with proud/sure/afraid *of* enter a room leave a house sorry for a person sorry about an action surprised *by* a play by Shakespeare *with* grey hair/a long beard/blue eyes run *past* the house *pass* the house succeed *in* insist *on*

depend/rely on talk/speak to someone about something remind of apologise for provide a person with something/provide something for a person marry someone married/engaged to someone divorce someone divorced from someone he is divorced

9 *Conjunctions*

(*a*) I shall not go *if* it rains.
I shall go *even if* it rains.
I shall take an umbrella *in case* it rains.

(*b*) *while* he was walking/*during* his walk (Preposition).

(*c*) He took a map *so as to find* his way.
He took a map *so that he could find* his way.

10 *Expressions*

I don't know what he looks like (Not: how he looks).
What was the film like? (Not: How was the film?)

Index

Acknowledgement

We would like to thank the following for permission to reproduce copyright photographs on the cover of this book.
J. Allan Cash, the Danish Tourist Board, the Italian State Tourist Office, the German Embassy, the Cyprus Tourist Office, the National Tourist Organisation of Greece, the Finnish Travel Association, the Japan National Tourist Organisation, the Swiss National Tourist Office, Iranian National Tourist Office, and Documentation Française.